DIGITAL GEOGRAPHIES

Sara Miller McCune founded SAGE Publishing in 1965 to support the dissemination of usable knowledge and educate a global community. SAGE publishes more than 1000 journals and over 800 new books each year, spanning a wide range of subject areas. Our growing selection of library products includes archives, data, case studies and video. SAGE remains majority owned by our founder and after her lifetime will become owned by a charitable trust that secures the company's continued independence.

Los Angeles | London | New Delhi | Singapore | Washington DC | Melbourne

DIGITAL GEOGRAPHIES

EDITED BY
JAMES ASH | ROB KITCHIN | AGNIESZKA LESZCZYNSKI

$SAGE

Los Angeles | London | New Delhi
Singapore | Washington DC | Melbourne

SAGE

Los Angeles | London | New Delhi
Singapore | Washington DC | Melbourne

SAGE Publications Ltd
1 Oliver's Yard
55 City Road
London EC1Y 1SP

SAGE Publications Inc.
2455 Teller Road
Thousand Oaks, California 91320

SAGE Publications India Pvt Ltd
B 1/I 1 Mohan Cooperative Industrial Area
Mathura Road
New Delhi 110 044

SAGE Publications Asia-Pacific Pte Ltd
3 Church Street
#10-04 Samsung Hub
Singapore 049483

Editor: Robert Rojek
Assistant editor: John Nightingale
Production editor: Katherine Haw
Copyeditor: Richard Leigh
Proofreader: Sharon Cawood
Indexer: Judith Lavender
Marketing manager: Susheel Gokarakonda
Cover design: Francis Kenney
Typeset by: C&M Digitals (P) Ltd, Chennai, India
Printed in the UK

Chapter 1 © James Ash, Rob Kitchin and Agnieszka Leszczynski 2019
Chapter 2 © Agnieszka Leszczynski 2019
Chapter 3 © Andrés Luque-Ayala 2019
Chapter 4 © Martin Dodge 2019
Chapter 5 © Matthew W. Wilson 2019
Chapter 6 © Tim Schwanen 2019
Chapter 7 © Jim Thatcher 2019
Chapter 8 © Rob Kitchin and Tracey Lauriault 2019
Chapter 9 © Meghan Cope 2019
Chapter 10 © Hilary Geoghegan 2019
Chapter 11 © David O'Sullivan 2019
Chapter 12 © Daniel Arribas-Bel 2019
Chapter 13 © James Ash 2019
Chapter 14 © Sam Kinsley 2019
Chapter 15 © Gillian Rose 2019
Chapter 16 © Mark Graham and Mohammed Amir Anwar 2019
Chapter 17 © Matthew Zook 2019
Chapter 18 © Lizzie Richardson 2019
Chapter 19 © Bruno Moriset 2019
Chapter 20 © Dorothea Kleine 2019
Chapter 21 © Rob Kitchin 2019
Chapter 22 © Taylor Shelton 2019
Chapter 23 © Linnet Taylor 2019
Chapter 24 © Jason C. Young 2019
Chapter 25 © Jeremy Crampton 2019

First published 2019

Apart from any fair dealing for the purposes of research or private study, or criticism or review, as permitted under the Copyright, Designs and Patents Act, 1988, this publication may be reproduced, stored or transmitted in any form, or by any means, only with the prior permission in writing of the publishers, or in the case of reprographic reproduction, in accordance with the terms of licences issued by the Copyright Licensing Agency. Enquiries concerning reproduction outside those terms should be sent to the publishers.

Library of Congress Control Number: 2018940535

British Library Cataloguing in Publication data

A catalogue record for this book is available from the British Library

ISBN 978-1-5264-4728-9
ISBN 978-1-5264-4729-6 (pbk)

At SAGE we take sustainability seriously. Most of our products are printed in the UK using responsibly sourced papers and boards. When we print overseas we ensure sustainable papers are used as measured by the PREPS grading system. We undertake an annual audit to monitor our sustainability.

CONTENTS

Contributor Biographies — vii

1 Introducing Digital Geographies — 1
   James Ash, Rob Kitchin, and Agnieszka Leszczynski

I DIGITAL SPACES — 11

2 Spatialities — 13
   Agnieszka Leszczynski

3 Urban — 24
   Andrés Luque-Ayala

4 Rural — 36
   Martin Dodge

5 Mapping — 49
   Matthew W. Wilson

6 Mobilities — 60
   Tim Schwanen

II DIGITAL METHODS — 71

7 Epistemologies — 73
   Jim Thatcher

8 Data and Data Infrastructures — 83
   Rob Kitchin and Tracey Lauriault

9 Qualitative Methods and Geohumanities — 95
   Meghan Cope

10 Participatory Methods and Citizen Science — 106
   Hilary Geoghegan

11 Cartography and Geographic Information Systems — 118
   David O'Sullivan

12 Statistics, Modelling, and Data Science — 129
   Dani Arribas-Bel

III DIGITAL CULTURES — 141

13 Media and Popular Culture — 143
James Ash

14 Subject/ivities — 153
Sam Kinsley

15 Representation and Mediation — 164
Gillian Rose

IV DIGITAL ECONOMIES — 175

16 Labour — 177
Mark Graham and Mohammad Amir Anwar

17 Industries — 188
Matthew Zook

18 Sharing Economy — 200
Lizzie Richardson

19 Traditional Industries — 210
Bruno Moriset

V DIGITAL POLITICS — 223

20 Development — 225
Dorothea Kleine

21 Governance — 238
Rob Kitchin

22 Civics — 250
Taylor Shelton

23 Ethics — 260
Linnet Taylor

24 Knowledge Politics — 270
Jason C. Young

25 Geopolitics — 281
Jeremy W. Crampton

Index — 291

CONTRIBUTOR BIOGRAPHIES

Mohammad Amir Anwar is a researcher at the Oxford Internet Institute. Amir's research focus is on the political economy of neoliberal globalization in the global South, mainly in India and Africa, with a particular interest in the growth of the knowledge economy in sub-Saharan Africa and its developmental impacts.

Dani Arribas-Bel is Lecturer in Geographic Data Science and member of the Geographic Data Science Lab at the University of Liverpool. Dani is interested in computers, cities, and data. His work focuses on the spatial dimension of cities, computational methods, and new forms of data.

James Ash is a geographer and Senior Lecturer in Media Studies at Newcastle University. His work investigates the cultures, economies, and politics of digital interfaces. He is author of *The Interface Envelope: Gaming, Technology, Power* and *Phase Media: Space, Time and the Politics of Smart Objects*.

Meghan Cope is a Professor in the Geography Department at the University of Vermont. Her areas of interest include urban geography, geographies of children and youth, race geographies, qualitative research methods, and qualitative GIS. She is currently working on a digital project in historical geographies of childhood called 'Mapping American Childhoods'.

Jeremy W. Crampton is a Professor at the University of Kentucky. His interests consist of critical approaches to mapping, geosurveillance, and security. His work emphasizes how and why the geoweb, spatial big data, and algorithmic governance produce urban and everyday subjectivities and well-being. He is currently working on a new book entitled *The Map and the Spyglass: Automation, Algorithms and Anxiety*.

Martin Dodge is a Senior Lecturer in Geography at the University of Manchester. His intellectual interests focus on the social and spatial enrolment of digital technologies as well as research on urban historical geography and the politics of maps. He has co-authored three books on digital technologies: *Mapping Cyberspace*, *Atlas of Cyberspace*, and *Code/Space*.

Hilary Geoghegan is Associate Professor of Human Geography at the University of Reading. Hilary's research explores enthusiasm and more-than-rational ways of knowing the world. Most recently, she has pursued this interest through interrogating the motivations of volunteers, scientists, policy-makers, and practitioners involved in citizen science, as well as via a study of more-than-human tree health management.

Mark Graham is Professor of Internet Geography at the Oxford Internet Institute, a Senior Research Fellow at Green Templeton College, and a Faculty Fellow at the Alan Turing Institute. He is interested in who benefits most and least from the world's increasing connectivity.

Sam Kinsley is a Lecturer in Geography at the University of Exeter. His teaching, research, and associated writing explore geographies of technology by unpicking what 'technologies' are and how they are involved in our understandings and experiences of space. He has presented and published his research in various disciplinary contexts.

Rob Kitchin is a professor and ERC Advanced Investigator at the National University of Ireland, Maynooth. He has been researching digital geographies for two decades. His books include *Cyberspace*, *Mapping Cyberspace*, *Atlas of Cyberspace*, *Code/Space: Software and Everyday Life*, *The Data Revolution*, and *Code and the City*. He is presently (co)principal investigator of the Programmable City project and the Building City Dashboards project.

Dorothea Kleine is Professorial Research Fellow at the University of Sheffield where she leads the Digital Technologies, Data and Innovation group at the Sheffield Institute for International Development. She is the Chair of the Digital Geographies Working Group of the UK Royal Geographical Society (with IBG). Her research investigates sustainable human development, global justice, and the role of digital technologies in making progress towards these aims.

Tracey Lauriault is an Assistant Professor of Critical Media and Big Data in the School of Journalism and Communication, Communication Studies, at Carleton University in Ottawa. Her research focus is part of a new field entitled critical data studies.

Agnieszka Leszczynski is an Assistant Professor in the Department of Geography at Western University in London, Ontario. Her work engages the social, economic, and technological shifts associated with the commercialization of digital location through studying a number of phenomena, including map-based apps, location-based services, sensors, and geocoded content.

CONTRIBUTOR BIOGRAPHIES

Andrés Luque-Ayala is an Assistant Professor in the Department of Geography at Durham University. His research focuses on the politics of urban infrastructures in the global South. Currently he is working on the coupling of digital and material infrastructures as a new security apparatus in the city.

Bruno Moriset is Associate Professor in the Department of Geography and Planning at Jean Moulin University Lyon 3, France. His research focuses on the geography of information technology and the digital economy. He is co-author, with Edward J. Malecki, of *The Digital Economy: Business Organization, Production Processes and Regional Developments*.

David O'Sullivan is Professor of Geography and Geospatial Science at Victoria University of Wellington, New Zealand with research interests in simulation models and geographic complexity, urban neighbourhood change, and the social implications of geospatial technology. He is author of numerous peer-reviewed papers, and co-author of *Geographic Information Analysis* and of *Spatial Simulation*.

Lizzie Richardson is Leverhulme Early Career Fellow in the Department of Geography, Durham University. Much of her current research examines the relationships between technology, culture, and work.

Gillian Rose is a cultural geographer. She is Professor of Human Geography at the University of Oxford. She has a long-standing interest in how images mediate relations with places, spaces, and landscapes, and in visual methods. Her current research focuses on digital visualizations, and in particular how they are shifting our experiences of cities.

Tim Schwanen is Associate Professor in Transport Studies and Director of the Transport Studies Unit, a research institute in the School of Geography and the Environment of the University of Oxford. His research is concerned with the geographies of mobility and addresses broader theoretical and empirical questions about inequality, well-being, socio-technical transitions, and processes of technological innovation.

Taylor Shelton is an Assistant Professor in the Department of Geosciences at Mississippi State University. His research interests lie at the intersection of digital geographies, critical GIS and urban geography. In particular, his work focuses on how new sources of data can be used to rethink urban socio-spatial inequalities.

Linnet Taylor is Assistant Professor of Data Ethics, Law and Policy at the Tilburg Institute for Law, Technology, and Society (TILT), where she leads the ERC-funded DATAJUSTICE project. Her research focuses on global data justice – the development of a framework for the ethical and beneficial governance of data technologies across different regions and perspectives.

Jim Thatcher is an Assistant Professor at the University of Washington Tacoma. His research examines the recursive relations among extremely large geospatial datasets, the creation and analysis of those datasets, and society. This work often falls into critical data studies or digital political ecology.

Matthew W. Wilson is Associate Professor of Geography at the University of Kentucky, Visiting Scholar at the Center for Geographic Analysis at Harvard University, and the Distinguished Larry Bell Visiting Associate Professor at The University of British Columbia. His is the author of *New Lines*.

Jason C. Young is a Senior Research Scientist with the Information School at the University of Washington. His research interests include digital geographies, indigenous knowledge systems, knowledge politics, and participatory research design. He has worked on digital projects with indigenous communities in the Peruvian Amazon and the Canadian Arctic.

Matthew Zook is Professor of Information and Economic Geography in the Department of Geography at the University of Kentucky. His research focuses on the production, practices and uses of big geodata and how code, algorithms, and mobile digital technologies help shape everyday, lived geographies.

1

INTRODUCING DIGITAL GEOGRAPHIES

James Ash, Rob Kitchin, and Agnieszka Leszczynski

DIGITAL GEOGRAPHIES

It is now somewhat obvious to state that digital phenomena have radically transformed almost every aspect of human life. From economies to cultures to politics, there is almost no area that remains untouched by digital techniques, logics, or devices. For instance, economies are now based upon the production of digital goods and services, and the global stock market is managed via high-speed algorithmic trading and digital networks that communicate at speeds faster than humans can directly perceive. Many aspects of cultural life, including how we identify and socialize with others, express ourselves, and consume popular content and entertainment, are now highly mediated through social media platforms such as Facebook, Twitter, and Instagram. Governments fear cyberattacks, develop digital strategies for international development, and utilize digital technologies to enable new logics of governance based on highly dynamic and individualized modes of spatial segregation and control. These shifts across political, economic, and cultural spheres of everyday life are tied to a whole range of objects, processes, practices, and materialities. From consumer PCs to commercial server farms, and from smartphones to apps, the ubiquity and pervasiveness of digital technologies and their effects are of immediate concern to geographers, underwriting transformations of the space economy and economic relations; modes of management and governance of cities and regions; the production of space, spatiality, and mobilities; the processes, practices, and forms of mapping; the contours of spatial knowledge and imaginaries; and the formation and enactment of spatial knowledge politics (Elwood and Leszczynski, 2011; Graham and Marvin, 2001; Kitchin and Dodge, 2011; Rose et al., 2014; Wilson, 2012). Digital presences, practices, and effects are characterized by uneven geographies of underlying infrastructures, component resources, and sites of creation and disposal (Lepawsky, 2015; Pickren, 2018; Zook, 2005). Similarly, there are distinct geographies of digital media such as the internet, games, and social, locative, and spatial media (Ash, 2015; Leszczynski, 2015; Kitchin et al., 2017).

At the same time, digital technologies also alter how we, as geographers, go about engaging with and researching the digital world. Digital devices (computers, satellites, GPS, digital cameras, audio and video recorders, smartphones) and software packages (statistics programs, spreadsheets, databases, geographic information systems (GIS), qualitative analysis packages, word processing) have become indispensable to geographic practice and scholarship across sub-disciplines, regardless of conceptual approach. Current modes of generating, processing, storing, analysing and sharing data; creating and circulating texts, visualizations, maps, analytics, ideas, videos, podcasts, and presentation slides; and sharing information and engaging in public debate via mailing lists and social and mainstream media are thoroughly dependent on computational technologies (Kitchin, 2013). Digital platforms are changing what constitutes 'the field'; the rise of digital content comprises new forms of evidence with which to approach long-standing geographical concerns; and digital presences and praxes are provoking new questions and opening up new lines of geographical inquiry (Leszczynski, 2017).

In the context of these profound shifts, this collection charts a diverse range of digital geographies, identifying the conceptual, theoretical, and empirical axes along which geographers are engaging with the digital, addressing how and why digitality matters to geography, and highlighting the insights that geography can offer to the study of digital phenomena. This short introductory chapter provides some important definitions and maxims that frame 'digital geographies' and situate the contributions which follow. We begin by discussing and defining the key term 'digital'. We suggest that rather than a sub-discipline unto itself, digital geographies are best understood through the lenses of extant as well as emerging fields of geographic inquiry. It is along these axes of inquiry that we have organized this collection, and the contributions brought together herein trace how digital phenomena, practices, and presences inflect and reconfigure geographical thinking about and approaches to questions of epistemology and knowledge production, space and spatiality, methods and methodologies, culture, the economy, and politics.

DEFINING THE DIGITAL

The term 'digital' has a variety of meanings across a range of literatures, from geography (Ash et al., 2018) to media and cultural studies (Manovich, 2013) and software studies (Fuller, 2008). As such, we espouse a broad definitional position that incorporates a range of engagements with the digital, which we suggest may be understood variously as ontics, aesthetics, logics, and/or discourses (Ash et al., 2018). Digital in the sense of ontics designates the ways that digital systems 'translate all inputs and outputs into binary structures of 0s and 1s, which can be stored, transferred, or manipulated at the level of numbers, or "digits"' (Lunenfeld, 2000: xv). Thought of as the universe of physical literals (Coyne, 1994), ontics simultaneously emphasizes an understanding of digitality as comprised of material digital objects: the hardware, software, devices, content, code, and algorithms that underwrite access to digital phenomena and mediations, which comprise the artefacts of our digital praxes, and which structure our experience of digitality. These digital technologies have recoded – or remediated (Bolter and Grusin, 1999) – multiple other technologies, media, art forms, and spatialities in ways coincident with the binary nature of computing architectures. Digitality, then, is also an aesthetics, capturing the pervasiveness of digital technologies and shaping how we understand and experience space and spatiality as always-already 'marked by circuits of digitality' that are themselves irreducible to digital systems (Murray, 2008: 40). As we adopt and seamlessly embed networked digital technologies throughout the fabrics of our landscapes, they come to enact progressively routine orderings of quotidian rhythms, interactions, opportunities, spatial configurations, and flows (Franklin, 2015). Alongside these ontics, aesthetics, and logics, a whole set of digital discourses have arisen which actively promote, enable, secure, and materially sustain the increasing reach of digital technologies in the spaces and practices of our daily lives.

This multi-faceted definition is not, however, intended as an overarching rubric under which anything may be characterized or engaged with in terms of the 'digital'. We seek to avoid this key pitfall of academic discussions of digital technology, which is related to generality. The term 'digital' can easily be deployed vaguely, as a kind of discursive label or blanket that is thrown over a series of quite different things. In doing so, this label can obfuscate more than it reveals about what are highly heterogeneous sets of objects, practices, and processes. Avoiding this generality requires that the term 'digital' always be qualified in relation to specific objects, techniques, logics, processes, practices, and affects. These qualifications are important because they force us to focus on the empirical specificities of the phenomena of study. The first of these specificities is that while 'digital' designates a genre of social, cultural, technological, and economic productions historically associated with the advent of digital computing, digital computing technologies are necessary to, yet insufficient for, 'the digital'. Following Horst and Miller (2013), 'digital' designates objects and artefacts that are ultimately compatible with or which arise from binary code and architectures, yet which produce further 'proliferations' that exceed the binary logics and materialities of digital systems. For instance, digital maps on smartphones encourage new forms of navigational practice and spatial movement, but these practices exceed the software itself, creating new cultures of movement that cannot be anticipated in advance (Verhoeff, 2012).

Second, these proliferations arise from the empirical ability of digital systems to differentiate and mark at speed, which produces new capacities to act. For instance, a light detection and ranging (LIDAR) sensor on an autonomous vehicle shines light and measures the time it takes the light to return, in order to differentiate between objects and empty space. This information is then differentiated according to machine learning algorithms to determine whether an object is moving or still, human or non-human. In this case, such differentiations allow the machine learning algorithms to navigate around obstacles and so enable the vehicle to travel safely without a human driver. From this position, the emphasis becomes examining how digital code, algorithms, and binary architectures construct the thresholds between these differentiations through a whole variety of factors. In the case of autonomous vehicles, these could include the industrial design and manufacture of LIDAR sensors, the broader market forces and governmental rationales and techniques that dictate where and how autonomous vehicles can be tested, and public fears around whether such vehicles can mark and differentiate between human and non-humans quickly and accurately enough (Ash, 2017). In turn, one might understand how the differentiations digital technologies enact feed into and alter human sensory capacities (Ash, 2015), cognition (Hayles, 2017), and decision-making more broadly.

This begets a third empirical specificity, which is that there is no monolithic 'the digital', only a variety of differently materialized objects, subjects, spatialities, effects, and affects that arise from varied practices and processes of digital production, circulation, use, and mediation. In making reference to 'the digital', then, we are accordingly invoking 'digital' in its myriad and non-mutually exclusive senses of the term. This is commensurate with the impetus for this collection, which is to name, empirically and conceptually frame, and theorize digital geographies. In the same way that we maintain that there is no singular 'digital', there is no singular or monolithic digital geography. As the contributions in this collection attest, engagements with the digital in geography inform and are informed by a range of intellectual positions, philosophical commitments, epistemologies, subjects and objects of study, and methodological practices across the breadth of human geography's sub-disciplinary foci and research communities.

THE DIGITAL TURN

In understanding the digital as a set of ontics, aesthetics, logics, and discourses that mark and differentiate by way of the designator 'digital geographies' we, as editors of this collection, are not suggesting that a new subfield of digital geography be established to study these processes. Such attempts have been under way in anthropology (Horst and Miller, 2013) and sociology (Lupton, 2014) for a number of years. In both cases the focus is broad, encompassing the anthropology and sociology of, produced by, and produced through the digital. The consequence, we believe, is to recast nearly all of anthropology and sociology as 'digital anthropology' and 'digital sociology' to some degree, especially given the pervasive reliance on digital technologies in all aspects of scholarly knowledge production. The result is that there is no sociology or anthropology that is not 'digital'. We adopt a different track. Rather than subsuming all of (human) geography to 'digital geography' or proclaiming digital geography a new distinct sub-discipline, we instead advance 'digital geographies' to signal a fundamental disciplinary turn that has inflected epistemological and scholarly communities of geographic praxis (Ash et al., 2018). Referring to digital geographies in this way avoids issues of generality that come with recasting all of disciplinary practice as 'digital'. While we do maintain that there is a need to think critically about the relationship between geography and the digital, thinking of 'digital geographies' as a turn *towards* the digital as object and subject of inquiry in geography, and as a simultaneous inflection of geographical scholarship *by* digital phenomena, is more meaningful in that it allows us to think about how the digital reshapes many geographies, mediates the production of geographic knowledge, reconfigures research relationships, and itself has many geographies.

By framing the digital in this way, we avoid the decontextualization of digital approaches, methodologies, and research studies from their sub-disciplinary domains such as urban geography or geographies of development. Instead, the emphasis remains on how an engagement with the digital develops our collective understandings of cities and development, as well as health, politics, economy, society, culture, and the environment, among others. It also allows for 'the digital' to function as a site and mode for intersectional research that cuts across research foci and leverages methodologies from multiple geographical sub-disciplines, intellectual traditions, and epistemological communities. Attending to the geography of rare metals used in the production of digital technologies, for instance, raises questions in the fields of resource and development geographies, postcolonial studies, as well as geopolitics. This enables the differences the digital makes to research, epistemology, and knowledge production to be contextualized within a broader knowledge base and history of theory, concepts, models, and empirical findings within and across geographic sub-domains. For example, we feel it makes sense to frame smart city developments within debates around the long history of urbanization and urbanism, rather than to set them apart within a separate field of digital geography. Building on this commitment to geographical intradisciplinarity, this collection is organized around five themes that capture the key axes of inquiry along which the digital has been taken up most directly in geography: the theorization of space and spatiality, geographical methods and methodologies, and cultural, economic, and political geographies. This allows us to capture the diverse ways – epistemological, theoretical, and methodological – in which the digital has been explicitly engaged in geography, and areas of scholarly praxis where digital objects, subjects, and mediations are anticipated to continue to inflect geographical theory, praxis, and method.

THIS BOOK

The chapters in each of the five parts of this book – spaces, methods, cultures, economies, and politics – attend to the myriad ways in which digital technologies feed into, alter, and are altered by a range of activities, practices, objects, and aesthetics. While the contributions to each part are unified by their engagement with 'the digital' in its myriad senses, they are diverse in their methodological orientations, subjects/objects of concern, the intellectual traditions on which they draw, as well as their ontological and epistemological positionings. The title of each chapter signals a key concept that constitutes a lens through which to begin to distil the relationship between the digital and space, methods and methodologies, culture, the economy, and politics. In each instance, this key concept could be prefaced by 'digital' – for instance, (digital) labour, (digital) mapping, and (digital) governance. In keeping with our commitment to geographical intradisciplinarity and to avoiding recasting all geographies as always-already 'digital' geographies, however, we omit the 'digital' prefix. In so doing, the individual contributions organized around the five themes speak to the ways in which geographical inquiry has *turned to* and been pervasively inflected by the digital across human geography's sub-disciplines and axes of inquiry.

As geographers, we are affiliated with one another by our concern and engagement with spaces, places, and spatialities. As such, we lead this collection with five contributions devoted to digital spaces. In Chapter 2, Agnieszka Leszczynski outlines a range of theories and approaches to understanding the relationship between spatiality and digital technologies. While these positions are diverse, all provide different ways of attending to the processes by which different digital technologies produce, co-constitute, and generate the appearance of socio-spatial relations that alter how space is perceived, known, used, and experienced. Moving beyond theories of digital space in general, Chapter 3 discusses the specific spatialities of the digitally-mediated urban environment. Here, Andrés Luque-Ayala points to the transformations in cities such as Rio de Janeiro brought about by the introduction of a range of digital technologies such as screens in control rooms and smart sensors in the environment, illuminating how these digital technologies enable distinct forms of real-time governance. Chapter 4 turns to rural spaces, which have generally been understudied in relation to digital technologies. Martin Dodge usefully points out that digital technologies, from sensor-enabled combine harvesters to automated milking machines, have transformed rural space at least as much as, or perhaps more than, urban spaces. Mapping is a key technology that has always been central to the production and knowledge of space, and in Chapter 5 Matthew Wilson demonstrates the importance of the shift associated with the digitization of mapping for professional geographers as well as movement through space in everyday life. Closing Part I, Tim Schwanen provides an important reminder that access to digitally mediated transport technologies is unequal and unevenly affects mobilities.

How we know and make sense of digital spaces raises questions about geographical methods and methodologies while simultaneously provoking new methodological developments. Beginning Part II on methods, Jim Thatcher's chapter on epistemologies suggests that utilizing digital technologies in geography – specifically GIS – is part of a longer history of knowledge in which the visual is prioritized. In turn, digital methods should be critiqued with this occularcentrism in mind, while recognizing the new possibilities brought with these technologies. In Chapter 8, Rob Kitchin and Tracey Lauriault point to the changing nature of data underwritten by the emergence of digital techniques, and how this allows new forms of analysis utilizing data infrastructures. The following chapter expands debates around data and digitality, with Meghan Cope demonstrating how digital technologies can be used in the generation of new qualitative methods that can attend to the complexity of human experience. Hilary Geoghegan continues a focus on ground-level digital data collection in Chapter 10, detailing that digital technologies provide an important opportunity for the development of participatory methods, while cautioning against the idea that digital technologies are themselves the solution for the generation of a properly citizen-led science. Following this, David O'Sullivan provides an account of cartographic practice in relation to geographic information science (GIScience) and suggests that critique of this field must be more than theoretical and instead work with these technologies to generate critically engaged GIScientific practice. In the final chapter of Part II, Dani Arribas-Bel focuses on the use of spatial statistics, emphasizing how digital techniques and developments in data science are transforming this important field.

Part III shifts the focus onto digital cultures. James Ash's contribution leads this part by suggesting that popular culture is now fundamentally mediated by digital platforms, which shape the type of content that is produced and how it is experienced, and which amplify the circulation of affects and emotions associated with this content. Next, Sam Kinsley demonstrates how a range of digital technologies, from Twitter to the US VISIT visa programme, mediate and produce different modes of subjectivity. Finally, in Chapter 15, Gillian Rose interrogates the concept of representation in relation to digital media and suggests that the term mediation may be more useful to get at the complexity and specificity of digital content as it is translated across multiple interfaces, servers, websites, and platforms.

Part IV moves from cultural engagements to examine digital economies. In the opening chapter, Mark Graham and Mohammad Anwar argue that digital labour complicates the relationship between labour and place, enabling new forms of exploitation but also the potential for digital workers to generate their own modes, conditions, and sites of working. Chapter 17 provides an account of digital industries. Here, Matt Zook suggests that it is important to locate these industries physically while also understanding how they produce their own forms of digital spatiality. Lizzie Richardson then focuses attention on the sharing economy, which has elsewhere also been termed the 'on-demand', 'gig', and more recently 'platform' economy. She demonstrates how ride-hailing services such as Uber are based on problematic discourses of sharing and the fundamental role that digital platforms and interfaces play in the existence and power relations of this economy. Closing out Part IV, Bruno Moriset usefully outlines the way that so-called non-digital or traditional industries, such as banking and retail, have been altered by digital technologies, driving the globalization of value and blurring the boundaries between different sectors of the economy.

The final part of the book turns to digital politics and the political geographies of the digital. Chapter 20 by Dorothea Kleine provides a helpful summary of the role that digital technologies are playing in global development and how issues such as gender inequality and environmental sustainability are reflected in digital technologies and attendant policies, while also being potentially transformed by these technologies, at times with unintended – and not necessarily positive – outcomes. Next, Rob Kitchin demonstrates how digital technologies have led to new modes of governance. Through a discussion of closed-circuit television, smartphone tracking, and a range of other technologies, Kitchin points to a shift from disciplinary governance to a society of control. Taylor Shelton then discusses digital civics, using examples from smart cities such as Atlanta to discuss how digital civics are both spatialized and corporatized. In Chapter 23, Linnet Taylor discusses the relationship between data and ethics and uses the example of the commercialization of public space to understand how ethics are changed under regimes of datafication. Jason Young then examines the knowledge politics of geospatial media, focusing on issues of access, bias, and the material effects of this inequality in relation to indigenous knowledges. Closing out the collection,

Jeremy Crampton's chapter charts digital geopolitics, specifically in relation to military and surveillance practices, with a focus on technologies such as Google Earth. He highlights the ways in which academic, commercial, and military practices may be more closely tied than many would be comfortable with.

While covering a huge range of empirical objects, situations, events, and approaches, and bringing together scholarship from across a range of intellectual traditions, this collection offers a starting point and guide to studying digital geographies. Exploring the chapters, we hope readers gain insight into a variety of phenomena while also being inspired to interrogate how digital technologies are altering their own areas of study.

Acknowledgement

Rob's contribution to this chapter and the collection as a whole was undertaken as part of The Programmable City project funded by the European Research Council (ERC-2012-AdG 323636-SOFTCITY).

REFERENCES

Ash J. (2015) *The Interface Envelope: Gaming, Technology, Power*. New York: Bloomsbury.
Ash, J. (2017) *Phase Media: Space, Time and the Politics of Smart Objects*. New York: Bloomsbury.
Ash, J., Kitchin, R. and Leszczynski, A. (2018) 'Digital turn, digital geographies?', *Progress in Human Geography*, 42(1): 25–43.
Bolter, J.D. and Grusin, R.A. (1999) *Remediation: Understanding New Media*. Cambridge, MA: MIT Press.
Coyne, R. (1994) 'Heidegger and virtual reality: The implications of Heidegger's thinking for computer representations', *Leonardo*, 27: 65–73.
Elwood, S. and Leszczynski, A. (2011) 'Privacy, reconsidered: New representations, data practices, and the geoweb', *Geoforum*, 42: 6–15.
Franklin, S. (2015) *Control: Digitality as Cultural Logic*. Cambridge, MA: MIT Press.
Fuller, M. (2008) *Software Studies: A Lexicon*. Cambridge, MA: MIT Press.
Graham, S. and Marvin, S. (2001) *Splintering Urbanism: Networked Infrastructures, Technological Mobilities and the Urban Condition*. London: Routledge.
Hayles, K. (2017) *Unthought: The Power of the Cognitive Nonconscious*. Chicago: University of Chicago Press.
Horst, H.A. and Miller, D. (2013) *Digital Anthropology*. London: Bloomsbury.
Kitchin, R. (2013) 'Big data and human geography: Opportunities, challenges and risks', *Dialogues in Human Geography*, 3: 262–267.
Kitchin, R. and Dodge, M. (2011) *Code/Space: Software and Everyday Life*. Cambridge, MA: MIT Press.

Kitchin, R., Lauriault, T.P. and Wilson, M. (eds) (2017) *Understanding Spatial Media*. London: Sage.

Lepawsky, J. (2015) 'The changing geography of global trade in electronic discards: Time to rethink the e-waste problem', *Geographical Journal*, 181: 147–159.

Leszczynski, A. (2015) 'Spatial media/tion', *Progress in Human Geography*, 39(6): 729–751.

Leszczynski, A. (2017) 'Digital methods I: Wicked tensions', *Progress in Human Geography*. DOI: 10.1177/0309132517711779.

Lunenfeld, P. (2000) *The Digital Dialectic: New Essays on New Media*. Cambridge, MA: MIT Press.

Lupton, D. (2014) *Digital Sociology*. London, New York: Routledge.

Manovich, L. (2013) *Software Takes Command*. New York: Bloomsbury.

Murray, S. (2008) 'Cybernated aesthetics: Lee Bull and the body transfigured', *Performing Arts Journal*, 30: 38–65.

Pickren, G. (2018) '"The global assemblage of digital flow": Critical data studies and the infrastructures of computing', *Progress in Human Geography*, 42: 225–243.

Rose, G., Degen, M. and Melhuish, C. (2014) 'Networks, interfaces, and computer-generated images: Learning from digital visualisations of urban redevelopment projects', *Environment and Planning D: Society & Space*, 32: 386–403.

Verhoeff, N. (2012) *Mobile Screens: The Visual Regime of Navigation*. Amsterdam: Amsterdam University Press.

Wilson, M.W. (2012) 'Location-based services, conspicuous mobility, and the location-aware future', *Geoforum*, 43: 1266–1275.

Zook, M. (2005) *The Geography of the Internet Industry: Venture Capital, Dot-coms, and Local Knowledge*. Malden, MA: Blackwell.

PART I
DIGITAL SPACES

2

SPATIALITIES

Agnieszka Leszczynski

INTRODUCTION

Geographers have recognized technology to be central to the production of space and socio-spatial relations (spatiality). Historically, engagements of the co-articulation of technology and spatiality have emphasized 'the map' and related spatial technologies such as survey instruments and cartographic techniques. They have examined the ways these technologies have been deployed within the remit of calculative strategies for defining and legitimating claims to geopolitical notions of territory, for example. The rise of digital computing since the 1960s and the more recent decade-plus-long boom in commercial geolocation technologies have catalysed the development of new conceptual frameworks for grappling with natively *digital* technologies, digital content productions, and space and spatiality.

In this chapter, I identify and provide an overview of the theoretical and conceptual frameworks that have been advanced for unpacking the relationship between spatiality and technology – and now more recently spatiality and digitality – in Western geographical thought. I set the stage by discussing *map–territory* relations in the critical cartographic tradition. I then move on to profiling contemporary frameworks for engaging the role of the digital in technology–society–space relations. These include *hybrid spaces, digital shadows* and *augmented realities, code/space, mediated spatialities* and *diffractive technospaces*, and *atmospheres*.

MAP–TERRITORY RELATIONS

Critical cartographers have demonstrated that rather than mirroring spatial reality, maps precede – that is, produce – the territories they represent (Pickles, 2004). The map in this sense designates the use of spatial technologies (survey instruments, projections, etc.) to generate a scientific visual product that serves to delineate, name, legitimate, secure, and maintain access to and control over bounded expanses of territory: a land, its resources, and people. Leveraged as instruments of territory, maps were central strategies of state, empire, and colonialism. For instance, the earliest maps of the Americas represented the New World as great swathes of empty land devoid of the presence of indigenous peoples, rendering them ripe for 'conquest, appropriation, subdivision, [and] commodification' (Harley, 1992: 524).

Maps not only legitimized the dispossession of peoples from their lands, but also further solidified colonial control over territory by enabling rule at a distance through the quantification of lands, their resources, and inhabitants. The success of the British occupation of Egypt (1882–1952), for example, was underwritten by the cadastral mapping of the entire country, an initiative that produced the *Great Land Map of Egypt* (see Mitchell, 2002). The *Great Land Map* both consolidated spatial knowledge into a cohesive cartographic product (the *Map*), and also centralized this knowledge exclusively in the hands of British colonial power. This solidified imperial control over Egypt by allowing Britain to leverage the geographic knowledge bound up in the *Great Land Map* towards various kinds of spatial interventions (taxation, infrastructure projects, insertion of military presence, etc.). Moreover, it allowed for the business and administration of empire to be conducted from a distance via remote practices of spatial calculation, quantification, and regulation.

In these historical accounts, spatial technologies are understood as strategies of calculation that, when applied to space, render space as territory: a cartographically demarcated geopolitical entity that is naturalized and made transparent by the very map used to produce it (Crampton, 2010; Elden, 2007). For Pickles (2004), the subsequent development of digital spatial infrastructures such as geographic information systems (GIS) beginning in the 1960s has served to further obfuscate the role of technology in the production of space. GIS engendered a 'new scopic regime of transparency' wherein space is rendered not only mappable in two dimensions, but can also be interrogated and reshaped using digital technologies (Pickles, 2004: 162). Pickles's concern is with the unequal power relations of the technological production of space/territory. This concern likewise resonates in many engagements of technology–space–society relations in the critical GIS tradition. Participatory or public participation GIS (P/PGIS) scholarship in particular demonstrated that digital mapping technologies are not only the preserve of the state, but are also enrolled by communities, indigenous peoples, and civil society organizations to actively resist and counter narratives of the legitimacy of state claims to land and resources, and to advance and negotiate their own geopolitical and economic claims (see, for example, Elwood, 2006).

These concerns with knowledge politics bound up in the technological production of space and spatiality continue to be a focus of contemporary geographic scholarship (e.g., Elwood and Leszczynski, 2013). However, the more recent proliferation, diversification, and commercialization of digital spatial technologies and data productions beyond the unique assemblages of GIS architectures – including, but not limited to, interactive web maps, geofence technology, native geotagging functionalities, map APIs, and location-based services – have diversified the focus of attention beyond the emphasis on state–civil society relations enacted through the kinds of spatial technologies described above. Geographers and other scholars have become interested in examining and theorizing the spatialities produced with, through, and by digital devices, services, and content productions that have become expected and entirely ordinary presences in the spaces and practices of everyday life (Ash et al., 2018).

HYBRID SPACES

The understanding of technology as productive of space and spatiality advanced by critical cartographers continues to be axiomatic to present-day efforts to grapple with and theorize the co-articulation of the digital and the spatial. An initial approach to thinking about the relationship between space and digital media is the notion of *hybrid spaces*. Hybrid spaces are theorized to be constituted by the enmeshing of two distinct realms of space and spatiality: digital (or virtual) spaces, and real (physical, material, and/or actual) spaces. Hybridity theses hold that the digital and real worlds are (or at one point were) ontologically and materially distinct, and have only more recently been brought into intersection with one another by the pervasiveness of digital technologies. At the height of its popularity in the mid-late 2000s, the virtual social environment *Second Life* was championed in popular discourse as an exemplar of the digital as a separate sphere of intimacy, dis/embodiment, and sociality to which users could escape by animating a virtual avatar and leaving the trappings of the material world behind (Johnson, 2007). However, as scholars such as de Souza e Silva (2006) have more recently pointed out, this disconnection between physical and digital spaces has effectively been eroded by the rise of location-aware mobile devices. The quotidian enrolment of mobile digital technologies has functioned to effectively 'hybridize' virtual and real spaces (de Souza e Silva, 2013; de Souza e Silva and Frith, 2012), producing mobile spaces that emerge as by-products of people moving around cities with location-enabled mobile devices (de Souza e Silva, 2006). The actual (physical) sites where the material and digital 'hybridize' by way of the digital being brought into physical spaces have been termed *net localities* (de Souza e Silva and Frith, 2012). In this conceptualization, digital technologies both engender the hybridization of space and serve as interfaces through which to access hybrid spaces and spatialities.

Hybrid spaces are seen to 'enable new forms of interaction with computing, including location-based service' and geocoded content (Wilson, 2014: 538). Focusing on content productions, Zook and Graham (2007b) have examined algorithms for sorting geocoded content, such as Google's PageRank algorithm, which determines the cardinality (order) of places in the results chain of a Google Maps query. For Zook and Graham (2007b), algorithms are generative of a spatial hybridity, wherein users come to see themselves as inhabiting the interstices of 'two worlds' in a virtual–physical spatial amalgam that results from the 'use of information ranked and mapped in cyberspace to navigate and understand physical space' (Zook and Graham, 2007b: 468, 466). Geocoded content and the algorithms that structure its delivery shape spatial mobilities and behaviours. For instance, the order in which results appear in response to a Google Maps query for 'pizza' shapes consumption patterns by directing people to establishments that appear nearer the top of the results chain (Zook and Graham, 2007a).

The limitation of hybridity for theorizing space and spatiality *vis-à-vis* digital media is that it suggests that virtual spaces are, or at least initially were, ontologically distinct from each other, and have only recently been 'hybridized' by contemporary digital media. The implication of this suggestion is that by virtue of being originally distinct from 'real' or 'actual' spaces, digital spaces are immaterial in essence. This fails to acknowledge the ways in which digital spaces are necessarily always-already physical-material, comprised of vast networks of physical infrastructures such as data centres, internet exchanges, deep-sea fibre-optic cables, continental broadband, and routers (see, for example, Blum, 2012).

DIGITAL SHADOWS AND AUGMENTED REALITIES

Adding nuance beyond hybridity theses, Graham (2013) has argued that cities in particular are now constituted as much by their digital shadows as by bricks and mortar. *Digital shadows* are the layers of digital content generated *about* city spaces *from* city spaces. These shadows emanate from quotidian uses of social media as plumes of data propagated and transmitted by the connected devices of the internet of things, and data trails generated through sensor–network interactions in the smart city. These layers are particularly dense over cities. Not only is there a greater density of both denizens and devices in urban as compared to rural areas, even when accounting for differences in population density, geocoded content production is a distinctly urban phenomenon (Hecht and Stephens, 2014). Yet beyond the distinct urban–rural divide, data shadows also (re)produce long-standing urban inequalities. The spatial distributions of geocoded content, the languages in which they are generated, and the sorting of these data productions by proprietary algorithms produce uneven urban geographies by promoting certain places to prominence while obfuscating others. Looking at geocoded content for Tel Aviv, Graham and Zook (2013) identify that a Google Maps query for 'restaurant' conducted from the same location in Arabic and Hebrew returns radically different results, with different establishments appearing at the top of the results chain for a query conducted in either language in ways that entrench the linguistic-spatial segregation of the city.

As urban landscapes are increasingly translated into data, we simultaneously come to experience cities in terms of their digital shadows. We can digitally tap into these data streams to gain insight into the cultural, social, and political 'pulses' of cities, enrolling content about city spaces while we are *in* those spaces *experiencing* those spaces. In other words, digital shadows *augment* or enhance our everyday spaces and spatialities. Graham et al. (2013) characterize these experiences of digital shadows as *augmented realities*. Augmented realities are constituted by the 'material/virtual nexus mediated through technology, information and code, and enacted in specific and individualized space/time configurations' (Graham et al., 2013: 465).

Rather than focusing on the distinctiveness of the virtual and the real and privileging technology as a digital intermediary which brokers a hybridized spatiality that is simultaneously both virtual and real, 'augmented realities' emphasize the interstitial moments at which digital platforms, hardware, and geocoded content come together to produce spaces that we experience *in situ* as 'augmented' by layers of digital information. In this way, augmented realities implicitly acknowledge the *ontogenesis of space*, which is the notion that the technological production of space is always incomplete. Space is always in the process of becoming, and this becoming is performative by virtue of being highly subjective and contingent on the technologies present and available to differentially embodied subjects. In the case of augmented realities, any individual's experience of digitally supplemented space is contingent on the geocoded content available, network availability, the devices being used, and even the time of day. Realities are thereby 'augmented' in moments in time and place rather than pre-existing, and are also highly individualized while simultaneously being delimited by the availability and corporate shaping of content flows (e.g., what kinds of information about places casts the strongest digital shadow).

CODED SPACES AND CODE/SPACE

Graham et al.'s (2013) ontogenetic conceptualization of digitally supplemented spatialities or 'augmented realities' builds directly on Kitchin and Dodge's (2011) groundbreaking theorization of the nature of the spatialities produced through the pervasive presence of code and software in everyday spaces. They advance two concepts to capture the increasing centrality of code and software to the production of space: coded spaces and code/space. *Coded spaces* are spaces in which code and digital software maintain a strong presence, but where their failure may be replaced by an analog transaction. An example is a retail space wherein the sudden non-functioning of electronic payment devices may be compensated for by a cash transaction. Here, the social relation of exchange is facilitated by, but not contingent upon, digital technologies in the retail space.

Coded spaces may be contrasted with *code/space*, or spaces to which the functioning of code/software is essential, and where the failure of digital technologies results in the failure of the space and spatiality (socio-spatial relations). The spaces of air travel are quintessential code/spaces. A failure of digital technologies – biometrics, passport verification, body and luggage scanners – would result in the failure of the space. An airport would cease to function as such; the sociality of the space – people moving between places – would similarly fail. No analog alternative exists for the code/spaces of air travel. Code/space captures the capacities for the *transduction* of space by code – or the potential for previously non-coded spaces to become recast as code/space. This occurs 'when software and the spatiality of everyday life become mutually constituted, [i.e.], produced through one another' (Kitchin and Dodge, 2011: 16). The ascendance of code and software in a space changes the nature of that space, how it is utilized, as well as the spatiality of that place. Take, for example, an urban café that begins offering free WiFi access. This may transform the space from one of primarily social interaction (casual face-to-face encounters) to a hot-desk workspace. The emergent spatiality of the space (from interaction-centred to work-centred) in turn solidifies the centrality of the presence of code and software to that space. Code/space is inherently ontogenetic. Both the nature of the space and its spatiality are re-created in moments of the utilization and occupation of the space in particular ways, be it as a workspace, or a primarily social space.

MEDIATED SPATIALITIES

While the ontogenetic theory of the technological production of space captures the ways in which the role of technology in the production of space is dependent on the individual, the nature of the technology, and the time/spaces of its deployment, the concept is not unique to digital technologies. For example, it also captures the contingencies of analog map use. Leszczynski (2015) has recently expanded on the ontogenetic theorization of code/space in the context of natively digital media by proposing *mediation* as a conceptual framework for understanding the multiple yet contingent comings-together of technology, people, and place and space that are productive of our quotidian lived realities. Mediation speaks to the contemporary condition of how we experience being with both human and non-human digital others in the spaces and practices of everyday life, in which we come to understand spaces, experiences, and interactions as the *effects* of the myriad comings-together of technology, society, and space relations. As with augmented realities, mediation is largely unconcerned with how content, technology, space, and the social are brought together, but rather with the fact *that* they are brought together. However, rather than understanding digital technologies as interfaces to spaces augmented by digital content, here the interface is itself understood as an effect of these intersections (Galloway, 2012). Alternatively stated, our lived reality is the result of the mutual co-constitutions of technology, sociality, and spatiality.

In this formulation, the production of space remains inherently ontogenetic. A theory of spatial mediation, however, destabilizes the ontological privileging of technology over space and/or sociality. Digital technology, for example, is not positioned as an active agent in the form of an intermediary or broker of social relations across space. Similarly, space is not rendered as a passive entity amenable to transduction. Technology, social relations, and space – as well as natures – are all active in effecting our lived spatialities. To say that spatiality is mediated is to assert that physical spaces are always-already information spaces (Jurgenson in Madrigal, 2012) *beyond* – and independently of – their capacity to be transduced (shaped, produced) by code and software. It importantly asserts that space is as much of an active participant in comprising and shaping 'the digital' as digital technologies are themselves productive and generative of spatiality.

Given a theory of mediation, technologies do not mediate *per se*. This is to say that they are not conjunctive intermediaries; rather, they capture, enrol, and put information into circulation in new and unprecedented ways that are generative of emergent forms of sociality and spatiality that we experience and understand as mediated. Federica Timeto (2015: 1) provides some more specificity to the mediated spatiality via the concept of *diffractive technospaces*, which are 'sociotechnical environments in which humans and machines relate and intersect'. As 'dynamic and contingent formations', the 'emergence [of technospaces] cannot be disjoined from the generativity of the mediations that traverse them' (Timeto, 2015: 1).

The sharing of images via the social platform Instagram is an example of precisely such a mediating/mediated performative experience in which humans, digital platforms, and spatiality implicate each other. Instagramming is an exercise of bringing spaces into being via both actively shaping and reflecting back the ways in which different places/spaces/locations rise in cultural and social significance at particular moments only to subside from importance at others. Hochman and Manovich (2013), for example, identified distinct 'signatures' in Instagram activity across a period of time of national events of sombre commemoration followed almost immediately after by events of joyous reverie. The geography of Tel Aviv Instagram activity was characterized by a swing in terms of areas of the city being Instagrammed during moments of national mourning and remembrance followed almost immediately by events of festive celebration. Yet the spatiality of this Instagram activity during these distinct periods was simultaneously also concentrated in a handful of locations across the city. This reflects what Boy and Uitermark (2017: 612–3) characterize as an 'aestheticisation of everyday life' that effectively '[reassembles] the city' in Instagram's own image by mobilizing and circulating specific places as preferred sites of consumption in ways that actively divert and concentrate flows of bodies and resources at those sites. This only reinforces the Instagram-worthiness of these places in ways that prime them for gentrification. Here, the city is brought into being through social media activity, but Instagram activity is no mere mirror. These piecemeal digital urban performances are implicated in both spatially reorienting and deepening uneven urban geographies which are then reflected back through digital channels. Mediation and reality, in other words, are co-implicated (Timeto, 2015) – digitality and spatiality cannot be experientially or materially disentangled from one another.

MORE-THAN-HUMAN SPATIALITIES

Breaking away from the human-centric framing of spatiality that underwrites the approaches to technology–society–space relations profiled above, scholars have begun advancing a theorization of digital spatialities beyond the preserve of the exclusively human. For Ash (2013, 2017), digital technologies have a unique sociality outside of human interactions with them. Ash positions digital technologies as relating to each other outside of human consciousness through series of 'perturbations', or capacities of digital objects to shape the conduct of other digital objects. Similar to Leszczynski (2015), Ash (2013: 22) does not see technologies as 'shap[ing] pre-existing space[s] or creating a hybrid form of reality'. Rather, perturbations generate *atmospheres*, or space-times 'local to the [digital] objects in question' (Ash, 2013: 22). Atmospheres not only present themselves to other objects (via their perturbations), but also organize space-times for human subjects.

Ash (2013) illustrates the ways in which atmospheres shape the capacities and conduct of both humans and non-humans with reference to smartphones. Mobile digital devices communicate with WiFi network access points (NAPs) through the transmission and reception of radio waves, which are imperceptible to humans. Every time a WiFi-enabled device comes within range of a NAP, the network presents itself as available to the device, perturbing it to register its time-stamped, geolocated presence against the access point, even where the NAP is a WiFi mast emulator that does not enable actual network connectivity (see Leszczynski, 2017). Oftentimes, a device will be within range of multiple NAPs, with an indeterminate cardinality of networks (the order in which networks are to be joined; usually organized by signal strength). Elsewhere, the spatial extents of network range are themselves subject to perturbation by elemental factors such as winds.

These ambiguities of connectivity emerge from how the objects in question structure relations between themselves (which access points present themselves to devices; which networks are joined).

At the same time, digital objects also shape the conduct of human subjects by organizing space-times for the human. One way is through feedback loops (Ash, 2013). Dead zones (areas of no connectivity) or poor network connectivity (sporadic connectivity, low data transfer speeds) may become obvious to humans, compelling them to engage with their devices in ways that exacerbate rather than resolve connectivity issues. For example, attempting to manually force connection to a network may prolong the time it takes to establish a reliable connection compared to allowing the device to automatically connect to the best (most reliable, strongest signal strength) available network.

Elsewhere, where network connectivity is functional, perturbations between digital objects can influence human capacities by shaping subjects' spatial trajectories. For example, applications running in the background of a mobile device may sporadically 'push' digital recommendations for consumption (eating, drinking, entertainment, and shopping) as notifications to individuals' devices. These spontaneous pings appear as simple notifications, but they are actually the results of myriad factors, including a user's real-time location and the historical consumptive behaviours of members of their social graph (if, for example, a restaurant was recently patronized by individuals in a person's social network, it may be suggested to them as they come within proximity of the establishment). These affective incitements towards consumption through the suggestive shaping of human mobilities are only possible given the successful perturbations of digital objects outside of immediate human consciousness of them. In the instance of push notifications, this includes functional connectivity and applications successfully refreshing 'in the background' (i.e., even when the application is not actively open on-screen).

Going forward, engagements with the non-human promise to open up exciting avenues for thinking about the nature of digital productions and reconfigurations of space and spatiality. One avenue is continued explorations of the spatialities and space-times of the non-human *à la* the work of Ash briefly profiled above. Another prong of related emergent research emphasizes the digital non-human reconfigurations of the spaces and spatialities of what have heretofore been understood as uniquely human relations, such as sexuality and intimate encounter (e.g., Cockayne et al., 2017). A third direction ripe for conceptual exploration involves non-human spaces and spatialities in the context of socio-technical natures. To date, little attention has been given in geography to how *nature* as an assemblage of both human and non-human organic life intersects with or fits into what is often presented as a triad of technology–society–space relations. This promises to be an exciting avenue for research going forward.

REFERENCES

Ash, J. (2013) 'Rethinking affective atmospheres: Technology, perturbation and space times of the non-human', *Geoforum*, 29: 20–29.

Ash, J. (2017) *Phase Media: Space, Time and the Politics of Smart Objects*. New York: Bloomsbury.

Ash, J., Kitchin, R. and Leszczynski, A. (2018) 'Digital turn, digital geographies?', *Progress in Human Geography*, 42(1): 25–43.

Blum, A. (2012) *Tubes: A Journey to the Center of the Internet*. New York: HarperCollins.

Boy, J.D. and Uitermark, J. (2017) 'Reassembling the city through Instagram', *Transactions of the Institute of British Geographers*, 42: 612–624.

Cockayne, D., Leszczynski, A. and Zook, M. (2017) '#HotForBots: Sex, the non-human, and digitally-mediated spaces of intimate encounter', *Environment and Planning D: Society and Space*, 35(6): 1115–1133.

Crampton, J.W. (2010) 'Cartographic calculations of territory', *Progress in Human Geography*, 35(1): 92–103.

de Souza e Silva, A. (2006) 'From cyber to hybrid: Mobile technologies as interfaces of hybrid spaces', *Space and Culture*, 9(3): 261–278.

de Souza e Silva, A. (2013) 'Location-aware mobile technologies: Historical, social and spatial approaches', *Mobile Media & Communication*, 1(1): 116–121.

de Souza e Silva, A. and Frith, J. (2012) *Mobile Interfaces in Public Spaces: Locational Privacy, Control, and Urban Sociability*. New York: Routledge.

Elden, S. (2007) 'Governmentality, calculation, territory', *Environment and Planning D: Society and Space*, 25(3): 562–580.

Elwood, S. (2006) 'Negotiating knowledge production: The everyday inclusions, exclusions, and contradictions of participatory GIS research', *Professional Geographer*, 58(2): 197–208.

Elwood, S. and Leszczynski, A. (2013) 'New spatial media, new knowledge politics', *Transactions of the Institute of British Geographers*, 38(4): 544–559.

Galloway, A.R. (2012) *The Interface Effect*. Cambridge: Polity Press.

Graham, M. (2013) 'The virtual dimension', in M. Acuto and W. Steele (eds), *Global City Challenges: Debating a Concept, Improving the Practice*. London: Palgrave. pp. 117-139.

Graham, M. and Zook, M. (2013) 'Augmented realities and uneven geographies: Exploring the geo-linguistic contours of the web', *Environment and Planning A*, 45(1): 77–99.

Graham, M., Zook, M. and Boulton, A. (2013) 'Augmented reality in urban places: Contested content and the duplicity of code', *Transactions of the Institute of British Geographers*, 38(3): 464–479.

Harley, J.B. (1992) 'Rereading the maps of the Columbian encounter', *Annals of the Association of American Geographers*, 82(3): 522–542.

Hecht, B. and Stephens, M. (2014) 'A tale of cities: Urban biases in volunteered geographic information', in E. Adar and P. Resnick (eds), *Proceedings of the Eighth International AAAI Conference on Weblogs and Social Media*. Palo Alto, CA: AAAI Press. pp. 197–205.

Hochman, N. and Manovich, L. (2013) 'Zooming into an Instagram city: Reading the local through social media', *First Monday*, 18(7). Available at: http://firstmonday.org/article/view/4711/3698 (accessed 1 February 2018).

Johnson, C. (2007) 'Living a virtual life on the internet', *CBS*, 8 February. Available at: www.cbsnews.com/news/living-a-virtual-life-on-the-internet (accessed 1 February 2018).

Kitchin, R. and Dodge, M. (2011) *Code/Space: Software and Everyday Life*. Cambridge, MA: MIT Press.

Leszczynski, A. (2015) 'Spatial media/tion', *Progress in Human Geography*, 39(6): 729–751.

Leszczynski, A. (2017) 'Geoprivacy', in R. Kitchin, T.P. Lauriault and M.W. Wilson (eds), *Understanding Spatial Media*. London: Sage. pp. 239–248.

Madrigal, A.C. (2012) 'How Google builds its maps – and what it means for the future of everything', *The Atlantic*, 6 September. Available at: www.theatlantic.com/technology/archive/2012/09/how-google-builds-its-maps-and-what-it-means-for-the-future-of-everything/261913 (accessed 1 February 2018).

Mitchell, T. (2002) *Rule of Experts: Egypt, Techno-Politics, Modernity*. Berkeley: University of California Press.

Pickles, J. (2004) *A History of Spaces: Cartographic Reason, Mapping and the Geo-coded World*. New York: Routledge.

Timeto, F. (2015) *Diffractive Technospaces: A Feminist Approach to the Mediations of Space and Representation*. Farnham: Ashgate.

Wilson, M.W. (2014) 'Continuous connectivity, handheld computers, and mobile spatial knowledge', *Environment and Planning D: Society and Space*, 32(3): 535–555.

Zook, M.A. and Graham, M. (2007a) 'The creative reconstruction of the Internet: Google and the privatization of cyberspace and DigiPlace', *Geoforum*, 38(6): 1322–1343.

Zook, M.A. and Graham, M. (2007b) 'Mapping DigiPlace: Geocoded Internet data and the representation of place', *Environment and Planning B: Planning and Design*, 34(3): 466–482.

3

URBAN

Andrés Luque-Ayala

INTRODUCTION

Over the past decades, digital technologies have had a profound impact on how human geography understands the urban. To a large extent, this is the outcome of an ongoing transformation of the city and its spaces, resulting from the vast and ubiquitous use of computers, information and communications technology (ICT) and digital systems. It is also the result of broader changes in processes of global urbanization markedly influenced by the rapid growth of ICT worldwide and by the spatial agglomerations generated in the production and consumption of computing technologies. Taking this context into account, this chapter introduces the multiple ways in which digital spaces and urban spaces are intertwined and co-constituted. The emphasis is on how the city, materially, culturally and politically, has been and continues to be rapidly transformed by a range of computational and digital logics and devices. The chapter focuses on how digital technologies in the city, underpinned by techno-utopian narratives around efficiency, productivity, and transparency, alter the functioning of power in cities while reshaping many aspects of urban governing and control.

COMPUTING THE CITY: A BRIEF HISTORY

From the late 1950s, drawing on the principles of cybernetics developed by Norbert Wiener, the city increasingly came to be seen as a communication system (Meier, 1962; Webber, 1964; Light, 2003). Embracing cybernetics, alongside a set of information technologies developed by scientists working within the American defence industry, urban planners reconceptualized the city both as a machine and a living organism. This enabled a new type of urban planning: one that took advantage of advances in mathematics, systems analysis, and computing technologies for decision-making. In the early 1960s American cities such as Pittsburg, New York City, and Los Angeles started experimenting with computers in their urban renewal programmes. Through a combination of computing, cybernetics, and military expertise, urban planning took a problem-oriented approach to local administration. The urban problem started to be framed from a militaristic/defence perspective, its solution increasingly seen as a function of managing processes. The city became a 'battleground', 'fighting a war on poverty', while urban problems were reinterpreted as processes to be solved via feedback loops and continual self-adjustment (Light, 2003). At the time, the *Journal of the American Institute of Planners*, hailed computers as the drivers of a revolution in urban planning (Harris, 1966). Along with their databases and simulations, computers were seen as capable of enhancing existing planning tools such as maps and three-dimensional models; they were capable of handling large datasets; they would enable the visualization of problems in novel ways; but most importantly, they appeared to turn planning into a scientific endeavour (Light, 2003). Information systems became a form of urban response arguably capable of depoliticizing the planning process while forcing scientifically verifiable outcomes.

Beyond the specific domain of urban planning, there was a belief between the 1960s and 1990s that the growth in computer use and a resulting dematerialization of society would undermine processes of urbanization, threatening the very existence of the city. The 'theology' of *cyberspace* (Bolter and Grusin, 2000) – a belief in the ability of computers, digital systems and new media to create a dematerialized world of information that we can inhabit – underpinned a futuristic and euphoric technological utopianism where reality was to be replaced, bit by bit, by information. Scholars and technologists such as Marshal McLuhan (1994 [1964]), Alvin Toffler (1980), Nicholas Negroponte (1995), and Bill Gates (1995) commented on the extent to which digital communications would overcome the need for spatial proximity, and through this, a catastrophic collapse for cities. Such predictions never turned out to be true. The fallacy of this post-urban fantasy lies in failing to understand the complex relationship and interdependencies between ICTs and the city. Rather than replacing the urban, the world of ICT and computers has played an important role in facilitating global urbanization (Graham, 2004). Throughout the second part of the twentieth century, a growth in global telecommunications and the urban transformations characteristic of advanced industrial societies occurred in parallel; the very configuration of the post-industrial city became a matter of the relationship between the city and telecommunications (Graham and Marvin, 1996). No longer were cities simply dense physical nodes of buildings, transport networks, economic activity and cultural life; they also became electronic hubs, the centres of demand for telecommunications and the powerhouses of global digital communications.

The ubiquitous nature of computing established an urban world governed more by interconnectivity than by boundaries. In the emerging *networked city*, the urban was no longer defined by physical enclosure (i.e., the city walls), but by digital connectivity. Here, '[c]ontrol of territory means little unless you also control the channel capacity and access points that service it' (Mitchell, 2004: 10). The internet itself has an urban geography, as selected cities play an important role in its production through clustering (Townsend, 2001; Zook, 2005). From the physical networks that allow digital connectivity – optic fibres, cooper cables, communication towers, antennas – to the patterns of employment and political-economic landscapes associated with the digital economy, information technologies materially co-constitute the city.

EARLY PERSPECTIVES: THE GEOGRAPHY OF THE CYBERCITY

In 1992 Christine Boyer developed one of the first critical analyses of the by then popular dematerialized accounts of cyberspace – a notion that ironically was often conceived, in urban terms, as a huge megalopolis without a centre (Boyer, 1992). Advancing the idea of the *cybercity*, Boyer highlighted the hybrid material and socio-technical nature of the growing informational network. Urban geography's engagements with the cybercity foreground both space and materiality in the digital world, arguing that technology does not substitute the city or body, but rather mediates social, physical, economic, and cultural relations (Graham, 2004). In turn, digital technology transforms the cultural geography of the city and everyday life in a myriad of ways (Crang, 2010). Wakeford, for example, draws on feminist approaches to examine the hybridity of internet cafés and the embodied gender identities of users forged through digital mediation. The city, as part of a landscape of computing, consists of a multiplicity of hybrid spaces – a set of 'material and imaginary geographies which include, but are not restricted to, on-line experiences' (Wakeford, 1999: 180). Following a similar approach, Forlano (2009) examines the ways in which WiFi technologies produce socio-cultural and economic reconfigurations of the city, generating a set of new *codescapes*.

Perhaps some of the most discussed hybrid spaces in the coming together of digital technology and the city are the spaces of surveillance. Digital technologies facilitate and enable urban surveillance not simply through data collection and recombination but also through techniques of visualization and simulation (Graham, 1998). Taking Foucault's notion of panopticism to new heights, and drawing on the ability of computers to store and recombine large quantities of information in near real-time, Graham and Wood (2003) suggest the emergence of a 'super-panopticon': 'a system of surveillance without walls, windows, towers or guards' (Poster, 1990: 93, cited in Graham and Wood, 2003: 230), pointing to a quantitative change in the state's ability to govern via direct surveillance. The implications of this process, they suggest, go significantly beyond issues of privacy and/or disciplinary control. From closed-circuit television (CCTV) and smart utility metering to social targeting and marketing facilitated by data collection, surveillance fuels the growing information economy of the city while supporting a particular political-economic configuration. This continuous and real-time tracking of bodies and behaviours supports a segmentation of service provision (differentiating users between levels of ability to pay, risk or eligibility) and fosters a neoliberal logic that prioritizes the privatization of public services, the commodification of the city and the development of urban markets (Graham and Wood, 2003: 229).

An examination of potential inequalities embedded in the urban operations of code led to the formulation of *software-sorted geographies*, the digitally mediated sorting techniques 'applied in efforts to try to separate privileged and marginalized groups and places across a wide range of sectors and domains' (Graham, 2005: 562). Software-sorting, exemplified by face-recognition CCTV and electronic mobility systems, illustrates the role that code and programming play as mediators of urban practices, shaping both the city and its politics (Thrift and French, 2002; Kitchin and Dodge, 2011). Such a digitally-mediated city is a *sentient city*, an ubiquitous computing environment that 'is not a passive backdrop but an active agent in organising daily lives … It is a world where we not only think of cities but cities think of us' (Crang and Graham, 2007: 789). This ubiquitous computing characteristic of the contemporary urban condition, described by Greenfield (2006) as *everyware*, 'seeks to embed computers into our everyday lives in such ways as to render them invisible and allow them to be taken for granted' (Galloway, 2004: 384).

SMART URBANISM

A recent and popular configuration of digital urbanism is the idea of the *smart city*, that extends and actualizes the digital promise of urban problem-solving. Promoted by the corporate sector, international organizations, national and local governments alike, the dominant vision of the smart city is one of a digitally enhanced urbanity that combines intelligent infrastructure, high-tech urban development, the digital economy, and e-citizens. Narratives around smart cities are deeply rooted in seductive and normative visions of the future, where technology stands as the primary driver for change (Luque-Ayala et al., 2016). The idea has gained global recognition through the publicity associated with the IBM-owned trademark Smarter Cities®. It also inherits elements from academic ideas developed in the 2000s on *intelligent cities* – which emphasize a problem-solving approach through partnerships between academia, business, and government, where ICT operates as a key input towards regional innovation, competitiveness, and economic development (Komninos, 2002; Caragliu et al., 2011).

Since its inception, the smart city has been a vague and nebulous concept. It comes charged with aspirations for a better future, alongside expectations of green growth, infrastructure flexibility, new urban services, transparency, demand responsiveness, social inclusion and urban sustainability. Smart city interventions take a broad range of forms, in most cases (but not always) foregrounding the role of urban computing and digital technologies. Examples include Barcelona's *Sentilo*, a municipally owned open source platform aimed at collecting data from and operating urban sensors, and Chicago's *SmartData*, an experimental predictive analytics platform. Smart city initiatives are often an amalgam of loosely connected projects of various sizes, under the leadership of both public and private stakeholders – as in the case of the *Amsterdam Smart City* initiative, which is a collection of about 200 projects involving digital technologies.

Rio de Janeiro provides an example of the transformations that digital technologies are spearheading in contemporary urban governance. In 2010, following an extreme rain event that resulted in widespread flooding and landslides, Rio's mayor commissioned IBM to design and implement a digitally-enabled municipal-scale control centre. Rio's Operations Centre (COR; see http://cor.rio) facilitates the integration of urban services, including transport, energy, emergency response, waste management, and social assistance. The COR, ubiquitously showcased as an exemplar 'smart city' initiative, 'operates 24 hours a day and 7 days a week, interconnecting the information of several municipal systems for visualization, monitoring, analysis and response in real-time' (Prefeitura Rio de Janeiro, 2011: 14). With over 80 customizable computer monitors forming a gigantic screen, the COR resembles a 1960s NASA control room. From here, city officials take decisions to manage the city's everyday flows and circulations and, when needed, respond to emergencies. Through radio and TV broadcasts as well as a vigorous presence on Facebook, Twitter, Waze, YouTube, and Instagram, the COR actively engages the citizen in the everyday functioning (and breakdown) of urban infrastructures – fostering a mediatic atmosphere of emergency. A new way of governing the city stems from this 'collapse in relations of control (of the everyday and the emergency) and the transformation of forms of engagement with the public (where the public does no longer operate as the final receiving end-point of the infrastructure network but as an essential functional or operational element)' (Luque-Ayala and Marvin, 2016: 204). Luque-Ayala and Marvin argue that these digitally-enabled logics of transparency and visibility, mobilizing the emergency as part of the everyday, do not question established orders but rather ensure their maintenance: 'in being offered the viewpoint of the control room, the citizen, rather than a political subject, becomes an operational component of the infrastructure' (Luque-Ayala and Marvin, 2016: 206).

Over the past decade, scholars within geography and urban studies have started to ask critical questions of the smart city (Hollands, 2008; Luque-Ayala and Marvin, 2015). How are these new forms of digital technology transforming urban flows and reshaping urban politics and governance? What are the dominant logics and pathways at play, and to what extent can 'smart' embrace progressive agendas? How do different forms of urbanity and citizen imaginaries take shape and become contested through the smart city? (Luque-Ayala and Marvin, 2015). Kitchin et al. (2016: 17-22) have identified a set of common critiques of the smart city. First, the smart city advances a reductionist form of technocratic governance that presumes that all aspects of a city can be measured or monitored; urban problems are treated as technical problems, and, accordingly, smart cities prioritize technological solutions. Second, the smart city is buggy, brittle, and hackable: it is 'prone to viruses, glitches and crashes' and 'vulnerable to being maliciously hacked'. Third, in line with the critique of digital surveillance identified in the previous paragraphs, the smart city's mobilization of big data puts in place forms of panoptic surveillance, predictive profiling, and social sorting. Finally, smart city interventions and their mobilization of data create the illusion of neutrality, overlooking both urban politics and the politics of big data. Yet, data collection and code development always involve value judgements, and through this, they represent a political intervention.

These critiques start unpacking the power/knowledge dimensions of smart urbanism, pointing to the ways in which the smart city, as a techno-utopian discourse, promotes neoliberal rationalities and specific private interests. A growing critique of the smart city highlights its role in the corporatization of urban governance. Both smart urbanism and urban big data can be seen as agendas mobilized by ICT corporates to 'capture' government functions and develop new market opportunities – a corporate endeavour advancing entrepreneurial goals (Greenfield, 2013; Townsend, 2013; Vanolo, 2013; Söderström et al., 2014; Barns, 2016). Transmuting all sorts of urban flows into data, the emerging flow that enables urban computational logics plays an important role in reconfiguring the city as a business-led, entrepreneurial, and corporate entity (Marvin and Luque-Ayala, 2017).

The experience of New York City (NYC) illustrates the growing role of entrepreneurial logics in the digital city, specifically through the idea of the 'data-driven city' constituting urban data as an infrastructural utility, this also points to the emergence of data as a novel infrastructural form. For New York, 'a data-driven city is a city that intelligently uses data to better deliver critical services, while increasing accountability through transparency' (New York City, 2013: 7). Under the leadership of mayor Bloomberg, the City Council approved the Open Data Law, requiring all city agencies to open their data by 2018. The law is expected not only to generate economic opportunities, but also to 'permit the public to assist in identifying efficient solutions for government' (NYC Local Law 11 of 2012). This led to the development of NYC OpenData, the city's open data platform (see https://opendata.cityofnewyork.us). As of July 2014 the city had made available to the public nearly 1300 datasets through the portal. Open data platforms aim to standardize forms of data collection and make it available in machine-readable formats. Unlike with digital urban dashboards (Kitchin et al., 2015; Mattern, 2015), the emphasis is not so much on data visualization as on opening up the possibility for calculation via the provision of raw data – which, in turn, is usually accessed by civic hackers, code developers, and entrepreneurs in an attempt to reimagine urban processes. Barns (2016) argues that these platforms support the municipal adoption of entrepreneurial goals, prioritizing competitive positioning and attracting investment. This marks 'a recent shift in the rhetorical aspirations of the open data movement away from the values of openness and transparency and towards a more confined focus on value generation', where local government is reinterpreted as a platform or the provider of a marketplace for a new urban flow (Barns, 2016: 554).

DIGITAL URBANISM BEYOND THE SMART CITY

In trying to avoid black and white critiques of the smart city, scholars have pointed to the need to question the ontological and epistemological underpinnings and implications of the now pervasive computational urbanism. The argument is that an understanding of how digital technologies transform and shape the city cannot simply be limited to an analysis of how, where, and on behalf of whom such technologies are used. Drawing on philosophy and media studies, urban computation is framed as a 'metaphor, method and organizing frame' (Golumbia, 2009: 1) for the city, an abstract machine that 'constructs a real that is to come, a new type of reality' (Deleuze and Guattari, 1987: 142; see Marvin and Luque-Ayala, 2017). As such, the smart city is not simply a 'top-down attempt to discipline citizens', neither 'could it be challenged by a simple inversion of this relation, via a bottom-up liberation of technologies in the name of people' (Krivý, 2018: 14). Likewise, the implications of the corporate smart city cannot simply be counterbalanced through embedding digital technologies with the 'liberal humanist values of inclusion, empowerment, sustainability and digital privacy' (Krivý, 2018: 14). Scholars seeking to transcend simplistic top-down or bottom-up analyses of the smart city argue that the emerging wave of digital urbanism, regardless of who it is enacted by and for, puts in place a distinctive regime of urban governance – one that, in instilling a new way of mapping and shaping relationships between forces, 'inscribes particular ways of seeing the city, representing relationships and anticipating a changed material future through connections and disconnections' (Marvin and Luque-Ayala, 2017: 86).

So, while the future shape of the digital city is largely unknown, increasingly the coming together of the digital and the urban is recognized as a project of futuring, a speculative endeavour that, in mobilizing algorithmic prediction, defies traditional scientific logics of causality. The coming together of big data and forms of 'algorithmic speculation' is likely, both materially and discursively, to 'anticipate particular kinds of cities to come' (Leszczynski, 2016: 1692). As the digital algorithm imagines a particular urban future, it also performs it. This calls for a better understanding of the role of algorithms in the making of the city. Yet, it is clear that in imagining an urban future, urban big data and its analytics can only reproduce existing urban fragmentations and socio-economic inequalities; the tangible materiality of the latter persists beyond the digital intervention, and the only certainty projected into the future is the characteristic unevenness of the contemporary city (Leszczynski, 2016).

To conclude, it is important to highlight the need to further examine the stereotyped and hybrid bodies, agents, and agencies at play in the making of digital urbanism. First, this means asking questions about how difference and multiplicity, gender and race, are incorporated and/or mobilized. Gillian Rose (2016), pointing to the absence of women's voices in smart city events, calls for a research agenda around 'how different social categories are constituted' in the digital city – acknowledging that digital data and devices both create and solidify social stereotypes but also allow people to navigate between and against them. An emerging queer and feminist critique of digital space seeks to uncover the 'colonizing, racializing and universalizing processes' at play (Cupples, 2015), pointing to the different ways in which different bodies experience relationships across code (both as norms and algorithmic instructions) and space (Cockayne and Richardson, 2017). Second, it means asking questions about the types of bodies engaged in making the digital city. It is well known that, when it comes to the city, the most effective technologies are those that are adopted as infrastructures (Thrift, 2014).

This requires attentiveness to the various digital systems and processes that, embedded in the background, become urban infrastructural flows in their own right. Thrift has suggested, for example, that data is likely to become embedded in urban surfaces (walls, screens, and so on), so that every surface of the city could speak back to us, every urban moment and encounter mediated through digital processes. Yet, in the view of Rose (2017), while digital agencies (the agencies of the technological non-human) have been the subject of detailed analyses, digitally-mediated human agency still demands further attention. She refers to a posthuman agency 'always already co-constituted with technologies' (Rose, 2017: 779) – an agency that is technologically mediated, diverse, and inventive; a radically expanded human that plays a role in co-producing and re-creating the city. This is a call for reintegrating the now technologically-mediated human into our understanding of urban digital spaces, and, most importantly, to reconsider its capacity to reinvent urban futures.

REFERENCES

Barns, S. (2016) 'Mine your data: Open data, digital strategies and entrepreneurial governance by code', *Urban Geography*, 37: 554–571.

Bolter, J.D. and Grusin, R. (2000) *Remediation: Understanding New Media*. Cambridge, MA: MIT Press.

Boyer, M.C. (1992) 'The imaginary real world of cybercities', *Assemblage*, 18: 115–127.

Caragliu, A., Del Bo, C. and Nijkamp, P. (2011) 'Smart cities in Europe', *Journal of Urban Technology*, 18: 65–82.

Cockayne, D.G. and Richardson, L. (2017) 'Queering code/space: The co-production of socio-sexual codes and digital technologies', *Gender, Place & Culture*, 24(11): 1642–1658.

Crang, M. (2010) 'Cyberspace as the new public domain', in C. Wanjiku Kihato, M. Massoumi, B.A. Ruble and A.M. Garland (eds), *Urban Diversity: Space, Culture and Inclusive Pluralism in Cities Worldwide*. Baltimore, MD: Johns Hopkins University Press. pp 99–122.

Crang, M. and Graham, S. (2007) 'Sentient cities: Ambient intelligence and the politics of urban space', *Information, Communication & Society*, 10: 789–817.

Cupples, J. (2015) 'Coloniality, masculinity and big data economies', *Julie Cupples: Geography/Development/Culture/Media*. Available at: https://juliecupples.wordpress.com/2015/05/11/coloniality-masculinity-and-big-data-economies (accessed 1 February 2018).

Deleuze, G. and Guattari, F. (1987) *A Thousand Plateaus*. Minneapolis: University of Minnesota Press.

Forlano, L. (2009) 'WiFi geographies: When code meets place', *The Information Society*, 25: 344–352.

Galloway, A. (2004) 'Intimations of everyday life: Ubiquitous computing and the city', *Cultural Studies*, 18: 384–408.

Gates, B. (1995) *The Road Ahead*. London: Hodder and Stoughton.

Golumbia, D. (2009) *The Cultural Logic of Computation*. Cambridge, MA: Harvard University Press.

Graham, S. (1998) 'Spaces of surveillant simulation: New technologies, digital representations, and material geographies', *Environment and Planning D: Society and Space*, 16: 483–504.

Graham, S. (2004) 'Introduction', in S. Graham (ed.), *The Cybercities Reader*. London: Routledge. pp. 1–29.

Graham, S. (2005) 'Software-sorted geographies', *Progress in Human Geography*, 29: 562–580.

Graham, S. and Marvin, S. (1996) *Telecommunications and the City: Electronic Spaces, Urban Places*. London: Routledge.

Graham, S. and Wood, D. (2003) 'Digitizing surveillance: Categorization, space, inequality', *Critical Social Policy*, 23: 227–248.

Greenfield, A. (2006) *Everyware: The Dawning Age of Ubiquitous Computing*. Berkeley, CA: New Riders.

Greenfield, A. (2013) *Against the Smart City*. New York: Do projects.

Harris, B. (1966) 'The uses of theory in the simulation of urban phenomena', *Journal of the American Institute of Planners*, 32: 258–273.

Hollands, R.G. (2008) 'Will the real smart city please stand up? Intelligent, progressive or entrepreneurial?', *City*, 12: 303–320.

Kitchin, R. and Dodge, M. (2011) *Code/Space: Software and Everyday Life*. Cambridge, MA: MIT Press.

Kitchin, R., Lauriault, T.P. and McArdle, G. (2015) 'Knowing and governing cities through urban indicators, city benchmarking, and real-time dashboards', *Regional Studies, Regional Science*, 2: 6–28.

Kitchin, R., Lauriault, T.P. and McArdle, G. (2016) 'Smart cities and the politics of urban data', in S. Marvin, A. Luque-Ayala and C. McFarlane (eds), *Smart Urbanism: Utopian Vision or False Dawn*. London: Routledge. pp. 16–33.

Komninos, N. (2002) *Intelligent Cities: Innovation, Knowledge Systems, and Digital Spaces*. London: Taylor & Francis.

Krivý, M. (2018) 'Towards a critique of cybernetic urbanism: The smart city and the society of control', *Planning Theory*, 17(1): 8–30.

Leszczynski, A. (2016) 'Speculative futures: Cities, data, and governance beyond smart urbanism', *Environment and Planning A*, 48: 1691–1708.

Light, J.S. (2003) *From Warfare to Welfare: Defense Intellectuals and Urban Problems in Cold War America*. Baltimore, MD: Johns Hopkins University Press.

Luque-Ayala, A. and Marvin, S. (2015) 'Developing a critical understanding of smart urbanism?', *Urban Studies*, 52: 2105–2116.

Luque-Ayala, A. and Marvin, S. (2016) 'The maintenance of urban circulation: An operational logic of infrastructural control', *Environment and Planning D: Society and Space*, 34: 191–208.

Luque-Ayala, A., McFarlane, C. and Marvin, S. (2016) 'Introduction', in S. Marvin, A. Luque-Ayala and C. McFarlane (eds), *Smart Urbanism: Utopian Vision or False Dawn*. London: Routledge. pp. 1–15.

Marvin, S. and Luque-Ayala, A. (2017) 'Urban operating systems: Diagramming the city', *International Journal of Urban and Regional Research*, 41(1): 84–103.

Mattern, S. (2015) 'Mission control: A history of the urban dashboard', *Places Journal*, March. Available at: https://doi.org/10.22269/150309 (accessed 1 February 2018).

McLuhan, M. (1994 [1964]) *Understanding Media: The Extensions of Man*. Cambridge, MA: MIT Press.

Meier, R.L. (1962) *A Communications Theory of Urban Growth*. Cambridge, MA: MIT Press.

Mitchell, W.J. (2004) *Me++: The Cyborg Self and the Networked City*. Cambridge, MA: MIT Press.

Negroponte, N. (1995) *Being Digital*. London: Hodder and Stoughton.

New York City (2013) *Chief Information & Innovation Officer Progress Report – December 2013*. New York: NYC Department of Information Technology and Telecommunications (DoITT). Available at: www1.nyc.gov/site/doitt/about/reports-presentations.page (accessed 17 May 2018).

Prefeitura Rio de Janeiro (2011) *Plano de Emergência para Chuvas Fortes da Cidade do Rio de Janeiro*. Rio de Janeiro: Defesa Civil/Prefeitura Rio de Janeiro. Available at: www.rio.rj.gov.br/dlstatic/10112/4402327/4109121/RIODEJANEIRO RESILIENTE_2013.pdf (accessed 17 May 2018).

Rose, G. (2016) 'So what would a smart city designed for women be like? (and why that's not the only question to ask)', *Visual/Method/Culture*. Available at: https://visualmethodculture.wordpress.com/2016/04/22/so-what-would-a-smart-city-designed-for-women-be-like-and-why-thats-not-the-only-question-to-ask (accessed 1 February 2018).

Rose, G. (2017) 'Posthuman agency in the digitally mediated city: Exteriorization, individuation, reinvention', *Annals of the American Association of Geographers*, 107: 779–793.

Söderström, O., Paasche, T. and Klauser, F. (2014) 'Smart cities as corporate storytelling', *City*, 18: 307–320.

Thrift, N. (2014) 'The promise of urban informatics: Some speculations', *Environment and Planning A*, 46: 1263–1266.

Thrift, N. and French, S. (2002) 'The automatic production of space', *Transactions of the Institute of British Geographers*, 27: 309–335.

Toffler, A. (1980) *The Third Way*. New York: William Morrow.

Townsend, A. (2013) *Smart Cities: Big Data, Civic Hackers, and the Quest for a New Utopia*. New York: W. W. Norton.

Townsend, A.M. (2001) 'Network cities and the global structure of the Internet', *American Behavioral Scientist*, 44: 1697–1716.

Vanolo, A. (2013) 'Smartmentality: The smart city as disciplinary strategy', *Urban Studies*, 51: 883–898.

Wakeford, N. (1999) 'Gender and the landscapes of computing in an Internet café', in M. Crang, P. Crang and J. May (eds), *Virtual Geographies: Bodies, Space and Relations*. London: Routledge. pp. 178–200.

Webber, M. (1964) *Explorations into Urban Structure*. Philadelphia: University of Pennsylvania Press.

Zook, M. (2005) *The Geography of the Internet Industry: Venture Capital, Dot-coms, and Local Knowledge*. Malden, MA: Blackwell.

4

RURAL

Martin Dodge

RURAL TECHNOLOGY

Rural space is distinctive because of its low population density and its territorial extensiveness. Settlements are small in size and people, and economic activity are widely dispersed geographically. The resulting condition of remoteness in terms of physical distance and transport inaccessibility correlates with higher costs of delivering public services and the provision of infrastructures in rural areas. Indeed, it is a symptomatic characteristic of true rurality to live 'off the grid' in terms of access to services like electricity, telephony, mains drinking water and sewage systems that are ubiquitous and taken-for-granted in cities (Vannini and Taggart, 2014).

Rural places are typically also politically and culturally peripheral from new ideas and political power. In many places, rural residents are economically poorer and less educated than comparable people in cities. Given these conditions, peripheral rural regions have traditionally been backwaters for technology and slower adopters of new digital developments (cf. Salemink et al., 2017). This chapter is focused on the rural space in a broadly Western developed economy context, with empirical examples drawn from contemporary farming practice in Britain.

It is well known that telecoms and internet services available to residents and businesses in rural areas are often of poorer quality, lower capacity, less sophisticated and without choice, more unreliable than in urban areas, and yet ironically they can also be more expensive. The high cost of physical cabling to connect widely dispersed households has held back high-speed broadband (Skerratt, 2010). The difficulty and cost of siting antennas to service scattered populations, which can often be in challenging terrain, have meant mobile telephony and 3G/4G provision can be patchy at best and completely unavailable in more remote places.

These 'not-spots' in broadband internet connectivity and mobile phone coverage persist in parts of rural Britain, for example, despite several years of significant capital investment and government subsidies to commercial providers (Philip et al., 2017). As part of wider 'digital divide' debates, the relatively poor provision of internet infrastructure and lower-level enrolment of digital technologies are seen as significant impediments to the socio-economic development of rural areas (Malecki, 2003). It is therefore somewhat paradoxical that for decades information and communication technologies (ICTs) have been championed as a possible way to overcome the disadvantages of rurality in development projects, particularly the sense of remoteness (cf. Kleine, 2013).

AGRICULTURE, INDUSTRIALISM AND THE RURAL IDYLL

In economically developed nations, the majority of the population live in cities and tend to overlook and underappreciate what happens beyond the urban hinterland. In part, this is because the notion of the rural as a tranquil backwater, the antonym to busy urban modernity, remains potent, even while being patently untrue. The idyllic countryside is a fantasy but with real effects on how society in general relates to rural space and, in particular, understands agriculture. It can also be argued that these deep misperceptions contribute to the absence of the rural from most mainstream reporting and contemporary scholarly analysis of digital technologies. Most academic researchers, technology journalists and major philosophers of 'the digital' – who are almost all urbanites – have a blind spot with regard to consideration of the particular 'impacts' of computerization in rural contexts. The countryside is usually completely missing in descriptions of the organizational effects of software systems, in consideration of the social implications of the internet of things, and in analysis of the possibilities of the sharing economy and so-called 'big data'.

Yet rural spaces are a heterogeneous set of productive landscapes, most of them owned and actively managed by conventional information systems and economic activities planned by software algorithms, with results stored in spreadsheets and databases. So, while overlooked in scholarly analysis, it is self-evident that software increasingly makes a material difference to how the rural is brought into being. While the physical prevalence of computer hardware equipment and other visible ICT infrastructure is considerably less, in part, as the population densities of rural areas are low and the activities are spatially dispersed, the algorithmic processes of code are no less intensive or significant.

This is demonstrated by changes in agricultural systems – the most significant use of rural space and its most distinctive economic feature – and the everyday practices of farmers. To most outside observers living in cities, the superficial appearance and social perception of agriculture, for example in lowland Britain, is that of a 'green and pleasant' landscape as it lacks most of the overt signs of technological dependency: the human-made infrastructures and the hard materiality of steel and concrete associated with industrial production and consumption. People see fields of crops, familiar farm animals grazing on grass and green trees. While there are signs of orderly cultivation and elements of management, such as gates and fences, nevertheless farming space is perceived as being essentially rooted in 'natural' processes (unlike cities).

Agriculture is also widely perceived as being less technologically advanced, yet it is often an intensive and industrial-scale activity. Most farming landscapes have been thoroughly technologically dependent since the start of the twentieth century and progress in mechanization and the replacement of horse power by cheaper and more capable diesel engines and electrical motors. During and immediately after the Second War World, in the UK, there was a major push to increase individual farm outputs, raise crop yields per hectare, and improve overall productivity while also reducing the labour force. Government subsidies and price guarantees encouraged the consolidation of farms, specialization, and intensification in production. Wholesale modernization across agricultural practice meant the enrolment of more and larger machinery, new types of buildings, improved livestock breeds, and the application of biochemical breakthroughs in the form of pesticides and herbicides.

While the push for ever more intensive industrialized agricultural production may have diminished somewhat in the UK in recent decades – in part due to concerns about food quality, animal welfare, biodiversity and sustainability – the application of ICTs and more digital technology for automation has become more evident throughout farming. Code now makes a difference to daily farming practice and more widely in the operation and governance of agro-industrial food systems – with some parts coming to *depend* on software and distributed information systems to function.

HOW CODE IS CHANGING AGRICULTURAL PRODUCTION – THREE CASE STUDIES

Industrial-scale farms are complex spatial and economic entities that are 'made (and constantly remade) through the entanglement and interaction of the social and the natural, the human and the non-human, the rural and the non-rural, and the local and the global' (Woods, 2007: 495). The entanglements that bring contemporary farms into being now include multiple instantiation of ICTs and increasing layers of 'pervasive computing', environmental sensors, automated identification systems, distributed databases, software algorithms and simulation models.

To illustrate how digital technologies, particularly software, are making a real difference to agricultural practices and changing the farming landscape, we present three brief case studies in a British context: (i) precision-agricultural techniques in arable production; (ii) bio-digital livestock production and food traceability systems; and (iii) dairy production and robotic milking.

Precision-agricultural techniques in arable production

One area of agriculture where digital code has had most impact in terms of changing practice to enhance yields and improve profitability is in arable farming, particularly for large-scale cereal production. During the twentieth century, increasing mechanization had already transformed cereal farming into an efficient industrial activity. To further raise productivity, digital technology has been enrolled to overcome the lack of information about how crop yields vary within fields and where best to apply inputs like fertilizers and pesticides to have maximum impact (in the past, farmers had to apply inputs uniformly across large fields, which was ecologically inefficient and economically wasteful). Computerization of key farm machinery to record spatial position through on-board GPS and monitor crop and environmental conditions through sensors, in combination with external data (such as high resolution, multi-spectral satellite imagery and meteorological data; Yang, 2009), is facilitating the informatization of farmers' working practices in what has been termed 'precision agriculture'.

Mobile digital technologies and analytical software packages have transformed the tacit and embodied knowledge of the farmer (their 'feeling' for land, one might say) into quantified automated procedures, using digital data that is captured largely autonomously and processed algorithmically to give actionable spatial knowledge (Tsouvalis et al., 2000; see also Figure 4.1). In large-scale cereal production, where a single farm might have several thousand hectares growing one crop, even relatively small gains in yields per hectare and reductions in chemical inputs, enabled by the algorithms in precision agriculture software, represent significant financial returns. Derived information from precision farming on crop yields, land quality and varying soil capabilities, coupled with details on prices, subsidy payments, environmental grants, etc. are then fed into long-term forecasting models for food supplies.

The combine harvester, initially developed in the 1930s to bring together several key stages in the harvesting of cereal crops into a single mobile machine, is one of the iconic symbols of industrial-scale farming. Today it is the central mechanical component in precision agriculture and is packed with digital technology. Integrated software systems and a raft of sensors continuously monitor and control many aspects of the harvesting process; this includes being capable of running semi-autonomously with steering via laser guidance and positioning the

Grower:
Farm:
Field: WDR25SE12
Area: 68.61 ac

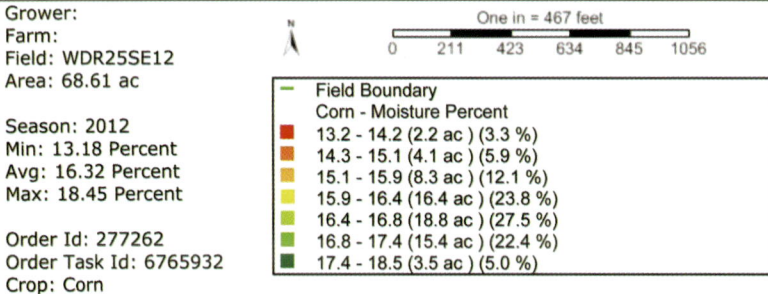

Season: 2012
Min: 13.18 Percent
Avg: 16.32 Percent
Max: 18.45 Percent

Order Id: 277262
Order Task Id: 6765932
Crop: Corn

One in = 467 feet
0   211   423   634   845   1056

- Field Boundary
Corn - Moisture Percent
- 13.2 - 14.2 (2.2 ac) (3.3 %)
- 14.3 - 15.1 (4.1 ac) (5.9 %)
- 15.1 - 15.9 (8.3 ac) (12.1 %)
- 15.9 - 16.4 (16.4 ac) (23.8 %)
- 16.4 - 16.8 (18.8 ac) (27.5 %)
- 16.8 - 17.4 (15.4 ac) (22.4 %)
- 17.4 - 18.5 (3.5 ac) (5.0 %)

Figure 4.1 Detailed yield mapping of productivity enables input resources to be spatially targeted for best effect. Here in-field variability is visualised as a continuous surface by software algorithms from a grid of sampled data. Courtesy of Viafield/AgriCharts, a Barchart.com, Inc. company.

reel and cutting bar using cameras and image-recognition algorithms. As well as handling the complex tasks around crop harvesting, they operate as mobile data collection platforms, with detailed measurements of yield volumes, quality, and moisture content being gathered continuously and georeferenced by GPS. The driver's cab, traditionally a noisy and dusty place, is now fully sealed, soundproofed and air-conditioned, and is as much a software monitoring centre as a site to physically manoeuvre the machine. Code has transduced farmers into screen-workers, spending as much time monitoring sensor outputs as looking at the crop in the field (Figure 4.2).

Figure 4.2 Operator control panels in a combine harvester. Courtesy of CLAAS UK. http://www.claas.co.uk/fascination-claas/media/download-center

The code underpinning precision agriculture and the algorithms in expensive machinery like combine harvesters have developed to a point where there are viable attempts at a fully automated arable production system using smart technologies, big data and machine-learning algorithms (Wolfert et al., 2017). Given the scale and capital intensity in the arable sector, it is here that autonomous farm robots could feasibly replace humans completely for open-field operations. As such the future combine harvester, working all day and all night to gather in the wheat, will not need an air-conditioned cab at all because there will be no person on-board.

Bio-digital livestock production and food traceability systems

Information systems and complex software databases are now a crucial aspect of livestock farming. Agro-food manufacturers and major retail corporations have implemented systems of hazard analysis and complete life-cycle traceability for meat products, and changed their sourcing and standards of production to enable auditing and accountability (Freidberg, 2007).

The goal is 'farm-to-fork' traceability, which is only achievable in a financially and logistically efficient fashion through the enrolment of sensors and digital identification systems. These systems automatically record material flows and changes in status, which are controlled through software algorithms, with the results being stored in distributed databases that feed into different actors in the supply chain. Analysis by Buhr (2003) details multiple different track-and-trace systems relating to meat supply and demonstrates that in each case, individual animals, and subsequently post-slaughter component parts of the carcass, are abstracted and monitored through various mechanisms. This requires a lot of abstraction and identification, much of which is invisible to the various parties involved. One mode of identification is the use of mandatory ID coding of animals, such as wing tags on birds, barcode ear tags on livestock, and cattle passports (Figure 4.3), which make farm animals into easily machine-readable commodities. Database records build up around the livestock over its life, including the details of breeding, farm location(s), feeding regimes, and space-time points of interaction or transformation (such as vet check-ups, vaccinations, slaughter and the packaging, processing, and distribution of the animal as separate meat products). These audit trails can also collect the names of the human operators involved to provide a chain of responsibility/liability for any failure or contamination. Much of this data outlives the animal and is folded into livestock breeding databases to deepen knowledge about the productivity of genetic lineages and then worked upon by software algorithms to predict and determine the next generation of cattle, pigs, and poultry through genetic selection and artificial breeding.

One driver of computerized traceability, which seeks to fully regulate the rearing, movement, and approved slaughter of livestock in Britain, is past failures in audit systems, which exasperated the impact of diseases in the 1990s and 2000s, including scrapie in sheep, BSE in cattle, and avian-flu risks in poultry (Barker, 2015).

Some elements of these traceability databases have also been opened up to consumer-facing inquiry, enabling shoppers with the inclination to be able to 'look up' details on the source of food, which typically reveals the name of the farm and its geographical location (Figure 4.4).

Figure 4.3 The printed manifestation of the 'passport' required to rear cattle for human meat consumption in the UK. The ID codes are linked into digital records relating to the individual animal. Courtesy of Crabbs Bluntshay Farm, Bridport, UK.

In spite of extensive computerized audit systems and the sophistication of resulting traceability databases, they are not infallible and there is ample evidence that meat hygiene and quality are still being compromised by mistakes, accidents and cases of deliberate fraud (Manning, 2016). This is, in part, because of how the code operates in actuality, being active across many thousands of different farms, abattoirs, food production facilities and packing factories and distribution warehouses. There are many points where something can go wrong or where tampering can occur. For instance, illegal horse meat contamination was uncovered in many European countries in 2013 and millions of eggs entered the human food chain despite being potentially contaminated by illegal insecticide use in 2017. Of course, food fraud and deliberate adulteration by producers for profit is a centuries-old problem and it is therefore unsurprising that software systems cannot eradicate such criminality.

Despite continued failures in traceability systems, there is no doubt that digital technology and the agency of software are significantly changing the short lives of animals bred for food. The cattle grazing in the field or the pigs raised intensively indoors are in a very real sense dependent on code to live – if their correct registration and logging in audit systems fail then in practical terms the animal is dead.

While it would be biologically and cognitively functional, it would become economically unviable because it could not be legally slaughtered and sold into the food chain. Farmers would be compelled to dispose of the animal as waste. So the livestock we see in fields and millions that are reared in farm sheds now comprise bio-digital animals, brought into being according to production plans on spreadsheets, selected from breed stock according to predictive outputs from genotype databases and choices made on interactive pedigree charts on computer screens (cf. Holloway et al., 2009).

Figure 4.4 The web interface that allows consumers to enter the production ID code, laser-etched on the shell, to find out some details on the origin of their eggs. It is unclear how widely queried such public links to traceability databases are, or the degree to which the information provided helps reassure customers.

Dairy production and robotic milking

Daily farm practices relating to livestock rearing and the management of unpredictable animals and their changing welfare needs have been much harder to remake with automation compared to cereal production. However, there are significant efforts under way in the agro-industry to take code and apply it much more directly to animal husbandry, particularly through altering practices around milk production.

While significant mechanization of farm milking parlours has occurred over the last century to raise productivity and ensure greater hygiene of the milk, it remained a labour-intensive practice. This has changed with the advent of automatic milking systems (AMS), and companies selling the systems make significant claims that they offer the farmer greater control as well as labour savings (Holloway, 2007). In material form AMS are large robotic machines that literally envelop the cow and can conduct the whole milking process without human intervention or direct oversight (Figure 4.5). Their operation is dependent on code, particularly in positioning the electro-mechanical component smoothly upon the body of the cow, using inputs from its sensors. Code must also continuously monitor and respond appropriately to unpredictable events (such as 'kick-offs' when an animal's foot detaches the suction cups from its udders). Software algorithms controlling the machine are able to recognize the cow as an individual in the database, utilizing the sensed ID number in the radio collar tag, registering her current visit and

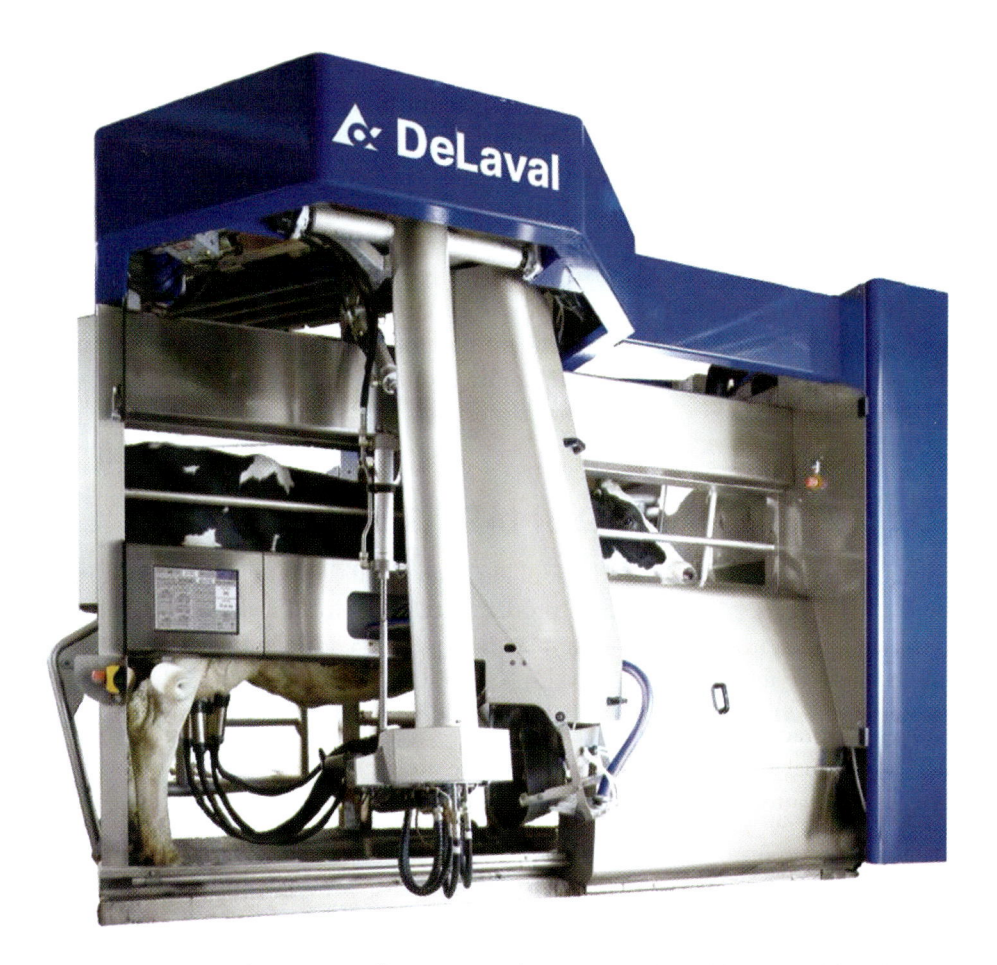

Figure 4.5 A typical automatic milking system. The cow is barely visible inside, although most animals are easily trained to accept the machine and the robotic processes. Courtesy of DeLaval A/S.

dispensing a calculated amount of concentrated cattle feed into the hopper to keep her contented during the ensuing milking. Her flow of milk is continuously monitored for quality, and the overall yield per milking is logged as part of the ongoing record of productivity. In other words, to be milked the cow itself becomes a very real code/space (Kitchin and Dodge, 2011). In doing so, the cow's space-times of activity are also altered as she gains a new degree of autonomy. The cow is no longer considered part of a herd, but an individual that is able to milk on-demand, being able to choose when to walk into the robotic unit, rather than driven *en masse* into the milking parlour at fixed times. In doing so, the individual logging of the cow's activity enables algorithms to flag atypical patterns that might indicate a health problem with that cow and alert the farmer to investigate.

AMS represent a substantial capital investment for individual dairy farming businesses. The marketing rhetoric from the manufacturers of AMS focuses in large part on the beneficial changes in the labour practices of the farmer, promising to free them from a twice-daily manual chore and allow them to devote more time to other aspects of the farm. Furthermore, the manufacturers also claim that AMS potentially improve animal welfare, providing a less stressful milking environment for the cow. However, it is unclear how reliably these AMS work in real contexts on different farms and to what degree dairy farmers must maintain a 'hands-on' role for mechanical breakdowns or faults in the complex software. It is also not clear to what degree farmers are comfortable in handing over so much control of their animals to code and simply monitoring activity through statistics on screens and updates sent to smartphones.

FUTURE FARMS AND SMART RURAL SPACES

The human population has nearly doubled from 4 billion to over 7 billion during the last forty years, and agricultural productivity, on a global scale, has kept abreast of these population changes in large part through the enrolment of more technology to intensify activity and raise yields (Godfray et al., 2010). Will farming be able to keep pace with the population in the next decades as the number of people on the planet is projected to pass 9 billion before 2050 (Tomlinson, 2013)?

It seems likely that software will take over more aspects of governance of rural space and play an ever larger role in primary food production. Aspects of 'smart' agriculture are coming (Wolfert et al., 2017), and there are serious schemes for developing fully automated farms that operate 24/7 without human intervention. Is this trend inevitable? It might not be a desirable trajectory to some, but it might be necessary, particularly in respect of the overwhelming pressure to feed the millions living in the global megacities and the major threats to agricultural land from climate change. There have been calls for 'sustainable intensification' in agriculture

(Godfray et al., 2010) with the aim of maximizing global productivity and reducing the carbon footprint of farming. Taking account of diverse ecological landscapes of production and the varying environmental and social justice outcomes will only be achievable by the greater use of smart techniques, digital sensors and data science; in many respects, arable agriculture is better suited to fully autonomous vehicles and mobile robots compared to driverless taxis on crowded city streets.

However, the use of digital and smart technologies also brings a risk to the fundamental ecological sustainability of agriculture, and critics like Michael Pollan point out that enrolment of this technology is premised on trying to keep 'business as usual', which is a high-energy, hugely wasteful and grossly inequitable food system. It is also evident that much smart farming rhetoric is laden with techno-science hype and naïve utopian belief in technical fixes. For critics of intensive industrialized agriculture, there is an alternative farming future, and arguably the only viable and sustainable solution to feeding the world requires socio-political change in terms of fairer distribution of resources, waste reduction, ending subsidy regimes, and providing better support for organic systems and localized supply chains. This would be combined with a radical rethink of Westernised dietary behaviour (from excessive meat consumption to vegetable-based diets) and checking human population growth. Of course, one might question whether, in this alternative future, there would be much less need for digital technology or perhaps a reimagining of the use of software in progressive ways in order to help the wider food system rather than to boost the profits of a few self-interested parties. In this alternative future, digital geographers might examine how software is used to better connect local producers and to help share out resources, reduce food waste, and reconnect urban consumers to rural producers.

REFERENCES

Barker, K. (2015) 'Biosecurity: Securing circulations from the microbe to the macrocosm', *Geographical Journal*, 181(4): 357–365.

Buhr, B.L. (2003) 'Traceability and information technology in the meat supply chain: Implications for firm organization and market structure', *Journal of Food Distribution Research*, 34(3): 13–26.

Freidberg, S. (2007) 'Supermarkets and imperial knowledge', *Cultural Geographies*, 14(3): 321–342.

Godfray, H.C.J., Beddington, J.R., Crute, I.R., Haddad, L., Lawrence, D., Muir, J.F., Pretty, J., Robinson, S., Thomas, S.M. and Toulmin, C. (2010) 'Food security: The challenge of feeding 9 billion people', *Science*, 327(5967): 812–818.

Holloway, L. (2007) 'Subjecting cows to robots: Farming technologies and the making of animal subjects', *Environment and Planning D: Society and Space*, 25(6): 1041–1060.

Holloway, L., Morris, C., Gilna, B. and Gibbs, D. (2009) 'Biopower, genetics and livestock breeding: (Re)constituting animal populations and heterogeneous biosocial collectivities', *Transactions of the Institute of British Geographers*, 34(3): 394–407.

Kitchin, R. and Dodge, M. (2011) *Code/Space: Software and Everyday Life*. Cambridge, MA: MIT Press.

Kleine, D. (2013) *Technologies of Choice? ICTs, Development, and the Capabilities Approach*. Cambridge, MA: MIT Press.

Malecki, E.J. (2003) 'Digital development in rural areas: Potentials and pitfalls', *Journal of Rural Studies*, 19(2): 201–214.

Manning, L. (2016) 'Food fraud: Policy and food chain', *Current Opinion in Food Science*, 10: 16–21.

Philip, L., Cottrill, C., Farrington, J., Williams, F. and Ashmore, F. (2017) 'The digital divide: Patterns, policy and scenarios for connecting the "final few" in rural communities across Great Britain', *Journal of Rural Studies*, 54: 386–398.

Salemink, K., Strijker, D. and Bosworth, G. (2017) 'Rural development in the digital age: A systematic literature review on unequal ICT availability, adoption, and use in rural areas', *Journal of Rural Studies*, 54: 360–371.

Skerratt, S. (2010) 'Hot spots and not spots: Addressing infrastructure and service provision through combined approaches in rural Scotland', *Sustainability*, 2: 1719–1741.

Tomlinson, I. (2013) 'Doubling food production to feed the 9 billion', *Journal of Rural Studies*, 29: 81–90.

Tsouvalis, J., Seymour, S. and Watkins, C. (2000) 'Exploring knowledge-culture: Precision farming, yield mapping, and the expert-farmer interface', *Environment and Planning A*, 32: 909–924.

Vannini, P. and Taggart, J. (2014) *Off the Grid: Re-assembling Domestic Life*. London: Routledge.

Wolfert, S., Verdouwa, C. and Bogaardt, M.J. (2017) 'Big data in smart farming – a review', *Agricultural Systems*, 153: 69–80.

Woods, M. (2007) 'Engaging the global countryside: Globalization, hybridity and the reconstitution of rural place', *Progress in Human Geography*, 31(4): 485–507.

Yang, C. (2009) 'Airborne hyperspectral imagery for mapping crop yield variability', *Geography Compass*, 3(5): 1717–1731.

5

MAPPING

Matthew W. Wilson

The relationship between the discipline of geography and mapmaking is made more complicated under the weight of a location-aware digital culture. There is a range of popularly experienced digital geographic technologies, including satnav, global positioning systems, Google Maps, and location-based services that underlie our use of digital media applications. However, the general population might not appreciate how these technologies relate to the discipline of geography, how the work of geographers relates to the development of these technologies and the study of their implications. Perhaps surprisingly, these geotechnologies rely on mapping interfaces but have been developed with little input from geographers or cartographers. To reconsider mapping from the perspective of digital geographies is to engage in these moments, where practices of mapping (as spatial orderings and orientations) and mapmaking (as expressions and representations of these orderings) seemingly expand, alongside the emergence of new forms of spatial media which both produce the spatiality of everyday life and support its analysis and representation (Kitchin et al., 2017).

How, then, do we sort mapping from mapmaking in this pervasive digital culture? What might a digital geographies perspective bring to mapping? How might the practices of digital mapmaking contribute to the conceptual force of digital geographies? We find ourselves in a discipline amplified and altered by the map, but what does this mean for geographic thought and practice? The growing interest in digital geographies encounters *philosophies* of mapping and *techniques* of mapmaking that have shifted and multiplied. Non-representational perspectives on mapping proliferate (Kitchin and Dodge, 2007; Kwan, 2007). Radical and participatory mapmaking emphasizes processes over products (Bhagat and Mogel,

2008; Preston and Wilson, 2014). In what follows, I discuss the intersections of mapping, mapmaking and digital geographies, providing an introduction to the histories, debates, and futures of mapping.

INTRODUCTIONS

I am a human geographer, so I do not really deal with maps. When responding to the question of why they call themselves geographers, some human geographers engaged in social theory may hold the *making* of maps at arm's length, as beyond or outside their expertise and training, while also expressing a love of maps. Some may even insist further that geographers don't just make maps or memorize the facts on them: *We are serious scholars who study space and society!* At times, I am guilty of this sentiment. However, the concept of digital geographies is an opportunity to renew our relationship to mapping and mapmaking, to flip the script and insist on our responsive and responsible study of mapping. As such, I provide three introductions.

First, one must clarify the relationship between mapping and geographic information systems (GIS). I treat the latter as a more specific expression of the former (GIS is examined in Chapter 11). To speak of mapping is to assemble a range of heterogeneous practices and concepts, to intervene in spatial order in some way. Mapping may or may not involve graphic representation. It may or may not involve representation, period. For instance, Denis Wood (1993) would argue that mapping is a cognitive process of ordering the world. Indeed, its powers of ordering may be subtle or grand, individual or collective, cognitive or precognitive. The point is not to elide GIS as irreducible to mapping, but to think how GIS operates as but one type of mapping, allowing for the multiple ways in which mapping occurs, proliferates, and makes a difference. This might mean thinking of mapping as a cognitive process (McCleary, 1987; Wood, 1993), as a specific communicative relationship subject to objective evaluation (Robinson, 1952; MacEachren, 1995; Roth, 2013), as a domain of speculative experimentation (Cosgrove, 2005; Debord, 2008 [1955]), or as 'maps 2.0', where the conventional distinctions between the making and reading of maps become blurry (Crampton, 2009; Caquard, 2014). The edited collection *Rethinking Maps* performs much of this reintroduction to the object of the map and the mapping practices that are assembled by such objects (Dodge et al., 2009).

Second, while mapping and mapmaking are often thought of as distinct (as the difference between spatial ordering and the representation of that ordering), Wood (1993, 2010) reminds us that there is an opportunity to disentangle these practices, to both examine their capacities and amplify their intervening possibilities. He draws a comparison between two maps, one the product of hand gestures in an explanation of some happenings and the other a sketch upon a placemat at the dining room table. He writes, 'It's a thin line …, but it *is* the difference between mapping and mapmaking. In the latter the map is always … *inscribed*. It cannot be shaken off, it adheres, it sticks to the surface. No matter where you take it, it holds fast, it clings' (Wood, 1993: 51).

Here, Wood illustrates the crucial difference between the inscribed and material manifestation of mapping (as mapmaking) and the potentially immaterial gestures and thoughts that cohere as mapping. However, under the sign of 'the digital', these distinctions become more complicated and blurry. No longer printed maps, folded neatly in our glovebox, nor only digital interactive interfaces in our pockets. The digital map nudges us, proposes our range of movements, and directs our attention (Curry, 1998; Thatcher et al., 2016). It is productive of specific geographies. And while critical cartography has long grappled with the way in which the map *produces* the territory (Harley, 1989), the digital map calls for a renewed study of the attendant discourses, materialities, and affective registers.

Third, and finally, mapping mediates and operates as media (Sui and Goodchild, 2011; Leszczynski, 2015). The emergence of location-based services, digital check-ins and traces, and digital fumes underlines new political and attentional economies that exceed tidy stories around the development of digital mapmaking methods (Kelley, 2013; Lin, 2013; Thatcher, 2014). The adding to space by digital technologies – its augmentation – provides yet more evidence of the need to reconsider the relationship between the discipline of geography and mapping (Graham and Zook, 2013). An opportunity exists to resituate the digital practices associated with mapping, such that they may be practised more responsibly and responsively. This of course requires that digital mapping, as a method and a phenomenon, be opened for study and experimentation beyond the narrower concerns of geographic information science (GIScience) and cartography – not unlike the development of the digital spatial humanities. But there are other histories, other challenges to situate digital mapping.

HISTORIES

The tendency for practitioners of mapmaking is to brush aside the importance of the social and historical conditions of geographical techniques. Of course, this is a dangerous position, as various historians of mapmaking from Arthur Robinson (1967) to Brian Harley (1989) and Judith Tyner (1999) have warned. Indeed, for more established mapmakers like Robinson, the finer techniques of cartography were made more resonant by the study of historical precedent – an often ignored aspect of Robinson's scholarship. Too often, historians of cartography are thought to not *do*, just as mapmakers are thought to not *study* such histories.

Again, the opportunity of digital geographies is to make a mess of such distinctions around digital mapping.

Those interested in the histories associated with the digital map may want to start with the recently published Volume 6 of *The History of Cartography* (initiated in 1987 by Harley and David Woodward), edited by Mark Monmonier (2015). Whether national pride, or genealogical connection, or corporate mission, or simply the convenience of stories that come most immediately to mind, we discuss origins because these stories illuminate our contemporary fixation on the digital map. We look toward those early programmers and the technical solutions to techno-social problems, as they provide us with fantastic stories of progress amid happenstance. In short, the history of digital mapping is contested (inheriting, of course, the contested histories of cartography as well; see Fabrikant, 2003).

Indeed, there is a sense of a 'choose your own adventure' when it comes to situating the origins of digital mapping. Some, myself included, gravitate towards the drama surrounding the Harvard Laboratory for Computer Graphics and its emergence following Harvard's dismissal of their geography programme at mid-century (McHaffie, 2000; Chrisman, 2006; Wilson, 2017). Others point to origins with Roger Tomlinson's (1968) Canada Geographic Information System (CGIS), or to a first-published reference to GIS by Dacey and Marble (1965). Still others might note the degree of experimentation with digital mapping techniques in Britain (Gaits, 1969). I remain curious about these more easily rehearsed stories, such as the ways in which corporations like Esri (2012) point to foundations in Tomlinson while much of Esri's earliest software (now a global standard) began as computer punch cards at Harvard in the mid-1960s. Even these stories need more elaboration, as this work at Harvard began earlier with Betty Benson and Howard Fisher in 1964, and earlier still with Ed Horwood in 1962 and with graduate students like Waldo Tobler (1959; see also Berry et al., 1964) at the University of Washington. More origins can be found in forms of automation developed at the US Geological Survey and in social physics perspectives on spatial analysis in the 1950s (McHaffie, 2002; Barnes and Wilson, 2014). We could (and should!) go on (in particular, to recover the role of women in these digital experiments with mapping; see Pavlovskaya and St. Martin, 2007). We should tell these histories of digital mapping, to assemble many threads, even reaching into the earliest attempts to create standards and conventions in hand-drawn mapmaking.

For instance, that mapping exceeds the graphic representation of spatial relationships is often thought to be a particularly postmodern understanding of 'the map' and the processes that assemble such an object. Certainly, at the heart of mapmaking has been a question of correspondence – of how to best represent reality through graphic expression. Erwin Raisz wrote *General Cartography* in 1938, considered by Arthur Robinson (1970) to be the first book for cartographic instruction written in English. Raisz (1938) outlined a pedagogy that showcased a mapmaker's signature craft – a creation born of muscular capacity, bodily comportment, and specific style. While many of these cartographic ideals would persist, digital interventions into mapmaking would accelerate both making and reading. Most importantly, the flourishes that made hand-drawn maps specific to the mapmaker's craft would be made absent and digital maps would emerge with different indicators of authorship.

The point is that the histories of digital mapping are productive. They produce associations and legitimacies, just as they sidestep complicities, inconvenient implications, structural inequities, and biases of language. And while the stories told about location-based services, which perhaps connect our SnapChat maps to enhanced 911 regulations and earlier military innovations in global positioning, appear distinct from our desktop and browser-based mapmaking software, these various developmental histories mingle and provide a rich agar for new techniques and associated technocultures. These histories interact. Only their selective telling will trace unique threads and produce reactive potentialities.

DEBATES

The hardening of disciplinary boundaries is an irresistible target of reterritorialization. As new forms of computation and automation altered both the production of cartographic representations and the performance of spatial analysis during the 1980s, the relationship with traditional (even if systematic) subfields of human geography (such as urban, economic, political, as well as feminist and Marxist) became more crystallized. Critical GIS has been one such resistive line of flight, emerging from the so-called 'GIS wars' in the 1990s and the debates around automated geography by the late 1980s (see Schuurman, 2000, for a review). Indeed, Nadine Schuurman's (1999) dissertation, published as 'Critical GIS: Theorizing an Emerging Science' in its entirety as a monograph in the journal *Cartographica*, demonstrated a remixing of the discipline. Schuurman waged an argument that was *both* social and technical, discussing the technical issues in interoperability and models of representation while analysing the production of theory, ethics, and the social within GIScience. This intervention was necessary, and would require different thinking about geographic pedagogy. As Pickles (2006: 765) would later argue about the 1990s, '[s]tudents and training suffered on both sides', as critical human geographers tended to ignore the role of the rising GISciences in the discipline, just as GIScientists considered their work more relevant than the work of their colleagues in critical human geography. (Those new to these 'debates' might revisit Schuurman, 2000, and Pickles, 1995.)

However, perhaps these tensions are irreconcilable, as we witness redefinitions of the discipline, yet again (as big data science, critical data studies, and digital spatial humanities). The residue of the debates around mapping in the 1990s have left the discipline largely unprepared for studying the increasing importance of digital geographies today (although this volume is meant to focus our preparations for these debates on ethics, civics, representation, politics, labour, inequalities, etc.). There are emerging technocultural conditions that unsettle any easy bounding of mapping and mapmaking. The opportunity of digital geographies is to re-examine these conditions, in order to register the reverberations of the technologies of spatial ordering (as mapping and mapmaking). For instance, I have previously suggested that big data, neogeography, and the quantified self are but 'reconfigurations … for the rapid reorganization of everyday life', wherein 'big data operates as infrastructure, neogeography enables new labor relations, and quantified self enables methods of self and collective governance' (Wilson, 2017: 34). Indeed, digital mapping now entails location-based services, geofencing and geosocial networking, and the many forms of augmentation that are built on top of these platforms. And while not engaged in the direct drawing and reading of maps *per se*, these new digital technologies amplify the long-standing questions of representation, legibility, and legitimacy.

In other words, mapping and mapmaking are no longer only circumscribed by debates around generalization, scale, cartographic conventions, and spatial modelling (witness the steady, if slow, expansion of topical coverage within the *International Journal of Geographic Information Science*). Instead, mapping and mapmaking are impacted by broader debates around digital culture, around questions of access, privacy, surveillance, attentional demands, demographic profiling, new global divisions of labour, structural inequities, militarization, and commodification (Elwood and Leszczynski, 2011; Lin, 2013; Stephens, 2013; Graham et al., 2015; Kitchin et al., 2017; Wilson, 2017). And while GIScience is beginning to incorporate these concerns within the field, there is much to be considered and fresh perspectives are necessary. To engage in a digital geographic study *of* mapping is to draw upon discussions, long under way, about the relationships between technology, technical practices, and society.

However, what about digital geographic study *with* mapping? New forms of mapmaking have tilted toward intervention, toward the projection of futures not yet realized. Consider the contemporary role of radical cartography, which attempts to alter the coming present by countering dominant representations of the recent past (see, for instance, Bhagat and Mogel, 2008). These efforts have important roots in Guy Debord (2008 [1955]) and Bill Bunge, Gwendolyn Warren, and their collaborators in Detroit in the production of *Fitzgerald* in 1971 (see Bunge, 1971). More than a record of spatiality, mapping was a means of altering present conditions, of bringing radical attention to issues of inequity.

However, this passion to intervene is also shared by recent developments in geospatial design, or geodesign – seeking to project, through processes of decision-making, new visions for future spaces of our cities, new relations of humans to landscapes, and new solutions to social and environmental catastrophes (Steinitz, 2012; Wilson, 2015). These intervening, projectionist practices of mapping destabilize any simple notion of the relationship between the map and the territory, between the actual and the virtual, even between long-held assumptions about the domains of space and time.

FUTURES

We have already mapped the world – *why bother studying geography?* To this sentiment, geographers often retort with the dynamisms of the planet, the changing relations between humans and the environment, and looming crises that stretch the globe as evidence of the urgency for geographic thought. *A large chunk of ice just broke free of Antarctica. To the maproom!* And as the discipline tilts towards new formulations of the urgency – as digital spatial humanities, as geodesign, as digital geographies – I am reminded of the similar claims of yesteryear. Warren Strain (1938: 26) in an article titled 'The "New" Geography', writes:

> In an attempt to develop something new, to recast our knowledge of the earth and its inhabitants to conform to modern ideas, many have become hopelessly muddled, created a dislike for geography both for themselves and their students, and fallen into practices which do not justify the expenditure of time or money on the subject.

Now, as 80 years ago, geographers seek out new urgencies, just as we worry about the ways in which these chaotic forces cause some reorganization of the conventions and traditions of our discipline. For Strain in 1938, 'automobiles, radios, airplanes, and sound pictures' were reorganizing society, and therefore, the study of geography. His point was to reconsider the pedagogical underpinnings of the field, to better prepare a new generation of students to engage in geographic thought. How might the discipline of geography adjust accordingly? I suggest two starting points, from a digital geographies perspective on mapping.

First, digital geographers must acknowledge that they have much to say about the ubiquity of mapping, beyond the narrow scope of the GISciences. We should be uniquely qualified to understand the discourses and materialities of a location-aware society, as these manifest in personal activity monitors, smart cities, drone warfare, geodemographic algorithms, social networking, etc. The point is that mapping, from a digital geographies perspective, incorporates a variety of software and hardware, cultural appropriations and scientific innovations, as well as resistances and disruptions. To abandon these developments and the study of their implications to other fields would be to admit the irrelevance of the discipline.

Second, digital geographers must understand the significance of digital technology expertise to the study of digital geographies. In doing so, this perspective might heed the lessons of the GIS wars of the 1990s: by waging critique in the terms of the technology, critique might actually shape technical practices (Schuurman and Pratt, 2002). In other words, it is not sufficient (nor perhaps fair) to insist that technologists understand and incorporate the concerns of social theorists. Instead, collaborations with developers and incorporation of their terminologies and design constraints might help cohere approaches to mapping technologies that address long-standing concerns around access, privacy, surveillance, representation, dispossession, etc. Learn to write in JavaScript. Work with spatial data in GeoJSON. Collaborate with community partners and engineers. Tinker, fail, and try again.

REFERENCES

Barnes, T.J. and Wilson, M.W. (2014) 'Big Data, social physics, and spatial analysis: The early years', *Big Data & Society*, 1(1). DOI: 10.1177/2053951714535365.

Berry, B.J.L., Morrill, R.L. and Tobler, W.R. (1964) 'Geographic ordering of information: New opportunities', *Professional Geographer*, 16(4): 39–44.

Bhagat, A. and Mogel, L. (eds) (2008) *An Atlas of Radical Cartography*. Journal of Aesthetics and Protest Press.

Bunge, W. (1971) *Fitzgerald: Geography of a Revolution*. Cambridge, MA: Schenkman Pub. Co.

Caquard, S. (2014) 'Cartography II: Collective cartographies in the social media era', *Progress in Human Geography*, 38(1): 141–150.

Chrisman, N.R. (2006) *Charting the Unknown: How Computer Mapping at Harvard became GIS*. Redlands, CA: Esri Press.

Cosgrove, D.E. (2005) 'Maps, mapping, modernity: Art and cartography in the twentieth century', *Imago Mundi*, 57(1): 35–54.

Crampton, J.W. (2009) 'Cartography: Maps 2.0', *Progress in Human Geography*, 33(1): 91–100.

Curry, M.R. (1998) *Digital Places: Living with Geographic Information Technologies*. London: Routledge.

Dacey, M. and Marble, D. (1965) 'Some comments on certain technical aspects of geographic information systems', *Technical Report No. 2, ONR Task 1, No. 389-142, Contract NONR 1288 (35)*. Evanston, IL: Northwestern University.

Debord, G. (2008) [1955] 'Introduction to a critique of urban geography', in H. Bauder and S. Engel-Di Mauro (eds), *Critical Geographies: A Collection of Readings*. Kelowna, BC: Praxis. pp. 23–27.

Dodge, M., Kitchin, R. and Perkins, C. (eds) (2009) *Rethinking Maps: New Frontiers in Cartographic Theory*. Abingdon: Routledge.

Elwood, S. and Leszczynski, A. (2011) 'Privacy, reconsidered: New representations, data practices, and the geoweb', *Geoforum*, 42(1): 6–15.

Esri (2012) 'The 50th anniversary of GIS', *ArcNews*, Fall. Available at: www.esri.com/news/arcnews/fall12articles/the-fiftieth-anniversary-of-gis.html (accessed 1 February 2018).

Fabrikant, S.I. (2003) 'Commentary on "A History of Twentieth-Century American Academic Cartography" by Robert McMaster and Susanna McMaster', *Cartography and Geographic Information Science*, 30(1): 81–84.

Gaits, G.M. (1969) 'Thematic mapping by computer', *Cartographic Journal*, 6(1): 50–68.

Graham, M. and Zook, M. (2013) 'Augmented realities and uneven geographies: Exploring the geolinguistic contours of the web', *Environment and Planning A*, 45: 77–99.

Graham, M., Straumann, R.K. and Hogan, B. (2015) 'Digital divisions of labor and informational magnetism: Mapping participation in Wikipedia', *Annals of the Association of American Geographers*, 105(6): 1158–1178.

Harley, J.B. (1989) 'Deconstructing the map', *Cartographica*, 26: 1–20.

Kelley, M.J. (2013) 'The emergent urban imaginaries of geosocial media', *GeoJournal*, 78(1): 181–203.

Kitchin, R. and Dodge, M. (2007) 'Rethinking maps', *Progress in Human Geography*, 31(3): 331–344.

Kitchin, R., Lauriault, T. and Wilson, M.W. (eds) (2017) *Understanding Spatial Media*. Thousand Oaks, CA: Sage.

Kwan, M.P. (2007) 'Affecting geospatial technologies: Toward a feminist politics of emotion', *Professional Geographer*, 59(1): 27–34.

Leszczynski, A. (2015) 'Spatial media/tion', *Progress in Human Geography*, 39(6): 729–751.

Lin, W. (2013) 'Situating performative neogeography: Tracing, mapping, and performing "Everyone's East Lake"', *Environment and Planning A*, 45(1): 37–54.

MacEachren, A.M. (1995) *How Maps Work: Representation, Visualization, and Design*. New York: Guilford Press.

McCleary, G.F. (1987) 'Discovering cartography as a behavioral science', *Journal of Environmental Psychology*, 7: 347–355.

McHaffie, P.H. (2000) 'Surfaces: Tacit knowledge, formal language, and metaphor at the Harvard Lab for Computer Graphics and Spatial Analysis', *International Journal of Geographical Information Science*, 14(8): 755–773.

McHaffie, P.H. (2002) 'Towards the automated map factory: Early automation at the U.S. Geological Survey', *Cartography and Geographic Information Science*, 29(3): 193–206.

Monmonier, M.S. (ed.) (2015) *Cartography in the Twentieth Century*. Chicago: University of Chicago Press.

Pavlovskaya, M. and St. Martin, K. (2007) 'Feminism and geographic information systems: From a missing object to a mapping subject', *Geography Compass*, 1(3): 583–606.

Pickles, J. (ed.) (1995) *Ground Truth: The Social Implications of Geographic Information Systems*. New York: Guilford.

Pickles, J. (2006) 'Ground truth 1995-2005', *Transactions in GIS*, 10(5): 763–772.

Preston, B. and Wilson, M.W. (2014) 'Practicing GIS as mixed-method: Affordances and limitations in an urban gardening study', *Annals of the Association of American Geographers*, 104(3): 510–529.

Raisz, E. (1938) *General Cartography*. New York: McGraw-Hill.

Robinson, A.H. (1952) *The Look of Maps: An Examination of Cartographic Design*. Madison: University of Wisconsin Press.

Robinson, A.H. (1967) 'The thematic maps of Charles Joseph Minard', *Imago Mundi*, 21: 95–108.

Robinson, A.H. (1970) 'Erwin Josephus Raisz, 1893-1968', *Annals of the Association of American Geographers*, 60(1): 189–193.

Roth, R.E. (2013) 'Cartographic interaction: What we know and what we need to know', *Journal of Spatial Information Science*, 6: 59–115.

Schuurman, N. (1999) 'Critical GIS: Theorizing an emerging science', *Cartographica*, 36(4): 7–108.

Schuurman, N. (2000) 'Trouble in the heartland: GIS and its critics in the 1990s', *Progress in Human Geography*, 24(4): 569–590.

Schuurman, N. and Pratt, G. (2002) 'Care of the subject: Feminism and critiques of GIS', *Gender, Place and Culture*, 9(3): 291–299.

Steinitz, C. (2012) *A Framework for Geodesign: Changing Geography by Design*. Redlands, CA: Esri Press.

Stephens, M. (2013) 'Gender and the GeoWeb: Divisions in the production of user-generated cartographic information', *GeoJournal*, 78(6): 981–996.

Strain, W. (1938) 'The "new" geography', *Peabody Journal of Education*, 16(1): 26–30.

Sui, D.Z. and Goodchild, M.F. (2011) 'The convergence of GIS and social media: Challenges for GIScience', *International Journal of Geographical Information Science*, 25(11): 1737–1748.

Thatcher, J. (2014) 'Living on fumes: Digital footprints, data fumes, and the limits of spatial big data', *International Journal of Communication*, 8: 1765–1783.

Thatcher, J., O'Sullivan, D. and Mahmoudi, D. (2016) 'Data colonialism through accumulation by dispossession: New metaphors for daily data', *Environment and Planning D: Society and Space*, 34(6): 990–1006.

Tobler, W.R. (1959) 'Automation and cartography', *Geographical Review*, 49(4): 526–534.

Tomlinson, R.F. (1968) 'A geographic information system for regional planning', in G.A. Stewart (ed.), *Land Evaluation: Papers of a CSIRO Symposium*. South Melbourne: Macmillan of Australia. pp. 200–210. Available at: https://gisandscience.files.word press.com/2012/08/1-a-gis-for-regional-planning_ed.pdf (accessed 28 May 2018).

Tyner, J. (1999) 'Millie the mapper and beyond: The role of women in cartography since World War II', *Meridian*, 15: 23–28.

Wilson, M.W. (2015) 'On the criticality of mapping practices: Geodesign as critical GIS?', *Landscape and Urban Planning*, 142: 226–234.

Wilson, M.W. (2017) *New Lines: Critical GIS and the Trouble of the Map*. Minneapolis: University of Minnesota Press.

Wood, D. (1993) 'The fine line between mapping and mapmaking', *Cartographica*, 30(4): 50–60.

Wood, D. (2010) *Everything Sings: Maps for a Narrative Atlas*. Los Angeles: Siglio.

6

MOBILITIES

Tim Schwanen

INTRODUCTION

The digital has, for some time now, been constitutive of the physical mobility of people, goods, and information across the globe. This is most obvious for information, where the internet and mobile phone have changed the amount, diversity, speed, and geographical scale of communication beyond recognition over the past 40 years. But profound changes have also occurred in relation to the mobility of people and freight. For instance, aviation and container shipping systems are textbook examples of code/space – the mutual constitution of code and the spaces of everyday life (Kitchin and Dodge, 2011) – and the vast majority of cars currently on the roads will stop driving in the event of a major software problem. Even walking and (conventional) cycling are increasingly mediated by ubiquitous computing, software, digital interfaces, and environmental sensors, as indicated by the proliferation of targeted smartphone apps.

This chapter provides an overview of the debates in geography and cognate research fields about how the digital mediates and co-constitutes physical mobility. It concentrates on the mobility of people rather than goods, and it adopts the tenet of the mobilities turn that mobility is more than movement from A to B (Sheller and Urry, 2006). As Cresswell (2010) and others have suggested, mobility is the entanglement of movement, representation, and practice. Movement here refers to displacement from A to B; representation to the meanings and social codings of movement; and practice to the embodied experience and conduct of movement. The chapter surveys a range of often disparate literatures over three sections loosely configured around three modalities of interaction between digital technologies and personal mobility. Attention is first directed to constellations of technology performing a specific function, for instance communication at-a-distance with one's employer. This is followed by a focus on interconnected networks of digital technologies performing a wider range of functions simultaneously, as with smart mobility. The chapter ends with a discussion of automation as the latest surge of digital technology that will only deepen the entanglement of physical and digital mobilities in everyday life.

While broadly following the recent evolution of debates around digital technology and mobility, the literature reviewed is not presented chronologically. This is because older debates continue today. Geographical scholarship on mobility and the digital is characterized by the addition and diversification of themes rather than waves succeeding each other. There are also important continuities over time in the conclusions drawn by geographers. For instance, the incorporation of the digital has not eviscerated the importance of space and place to the constitution of mobility systems, practices, and experiences and it has probably increased rather than reduced socio-spatial inequalities of mobility. It is also clear that the overall logic of embedding digital information and communication technologies (ICTs) into mobility systems – often through corporate actors – has long been and continues to be based on speed, efficiency, convenience, safety, security, and/or environmental sustainability. However, the effects co-produced by digital technologies are often more complex and ambiguous than prevailing discourses suggest.

DIGITAL TECHNOLOGIES WITH SPECIFIC FUNCTIONS

Substitution and beyond

Transport and economic geographers have been interested in the intersection of mobility and digital ICTs fulfilling functions such as communication at-a-distance, telecommuting or e-commerce since at least the 1980s (e.g., Salomon, 1986). A key concern has long been the question of to what extent the physical movements of people and goods could be replaced by interaction at-a-distance by wired computers and wireless devices. Such substitution has long been touted as desirable because of perceived benefits such as reduced congestion; improved productivity; decreased environmental burden; and better accessibility for people for whom physical movement poses all sorts of barriers, such as many disabled and older people. Salomon (1986) criticized a narrow focus on substitution, arguing that a wider range of interrelations between physical and digital mobility needed to be considered. He distinguished substitution from generation (when use of ICTs increases physical movement and vice versa), modification (when ICT use changes certain aspects of movement, such as the transport mode used), and neutrality (no effect of ICTs on physical movement). Salomon also noted that ICTs can be used to improve the operational efficiency of mobility systems, for instance through real-time information provision and computerized systems for traffic or parking management, and have indirect impacts on mobility via the changes in land use they induce.

Salomon's (1986) framework has been used in many studies by transport geographers, engineers and other to analyse how people's physical movement is affected by telecommuting and e-shopping (Cohen-Blankshtain and Rotem-Mindali, 2016, offer a recent review). Results across empirical studies are diverse but seem to suggest that substitution of physical movement by ICT has been the overall net effect. While useful, much empirical research building on Salomon's framework has conceived of physical mobility and the digital realm in a binary and dualistic manner as separated spheres. It is also common to equate mobility to movement without due consideration for representation and practice (Cresswell, 2010). The same points hold for research that has drawn on other analytical frameworks to better understand the effect of ICTs on physical movement, including time geography and sociology's time-displacement hypothesis, according to which internet and digital media use displaces social and other out-of-home leisure activities requiring mobility (Kwan, 2002).

Representation and practice, as well as the entanglement of physical and digital mobilities, play a much larger role in mobilities research in geography and the wider social sciences. For instance, recent studies on the effects of video-conferencing on business travel have shown how social norms and the need for embodied experience and face-to-face interaction create complex amalgams of interdependent physical and digital mobility between business partners and colleagues (Haynes, 2010; Storme et al., 2017). Other research has shown how wireless technologies have become embedded into physical movements, reconfiguring practices, meanings, and experiences in complex and sometimes ambiguous ways. Studies of the everyday logistics of family life have shown that, especially for employed mothers, mobile phones enable on-the-fly rescheduling of work commitments and child pick-ups. Other consequences can be 'driving at the edge of time' (Line et al., 2011: 1493), with parents leaving minimal margins for contingency, and (slight) reductions in guilt and anxiety about arriving late or one's children having to wait (Schwanen, 2008). Yet in other family situations on the move, digital technologies may deliberately be kept at bay. Waitt and Harada (2016) discuss how some parents in their ethnographic study in New South Wales let children use digital media in the family car to avoid tantrums, whereas others forbid such technologies so that shared trips can be moments of shared fun, intimacy, and care.

Social differentiation

Mobilities scholars have also drawn attention to various ways in which the mediation of digital technologies in mobility practices has accentuated existing social inequalities and created novel stratifications. The best-known example is the work of John

Urry and others on 'mobile lives' and 'network capital' (Elliott and Urry, 2010). Mobile lives, for Urry, consist of everyday practices and identities organized around fast transport and communication systems and are characterized by individuality, flexibility, adaptability, and reflexivity. They are enabled by network capital – a new form of capital alongside economic, cultural, and social capital that highlights the capacity of individuals to enter into and maintain beneficial social relations at-a-distance through physical and digital mobilities. Computing, software and digital interfaces are here implicated in the production of new social hierarchies alongside gender, class, and so on. Central to these hierarchies is, on the one hand, the valorization of particular ways of enacting and organizing mobility (e.g., the use of multiple modes of transport accessed and paid for with radio frequency identification (RFID) technologies, real-time rescheduling, access to luxury lounges in airports and train stations) and, on the other hand, the immobilization in particular places of usually precarious workers such as baggage handlers who make the mobility of others possible. Urry's ideas have been developed subsequently, for instance in Sheller's (2016) research in post-earthquake Haiti. She shows not only how international aid unintentionally reinscribed unequal network capital into local communities during reconstruction, but also how those communities sometimes reappropriated provided equipment, such as water filtration installations, into technologies to fulfil their needs for recharging mobile phones and laptops.

Another way in which mobilities scholars have shown that digital technologies with specific functions contribute to social stratification is through research on the securitization of mobility. Here the focus is on digital technologies such as digital passports, biometrics, behavioural profiling techniques, facial recognition software, and even mobile phones which are used to pre-empt or obstruct mobilities considered risky and undesired. The argument is that those technologies do more than monitor, detect, deter, and enact or symbolize power, for the computer code they rely on reflects and enacts ideas about which bodily comportments, types of dress, facial expressions, eye movements, and so on are appropriate or normal (Graham, 2005; Adey, 2009). Nowhere is this more obvious than in airports – the site *par excellence* where digital security technologies reconfigure mobilities (Adey, 2009).

Yet, digital surveillance of mobilities is enacted in myriad ways in the present era, most of which are technologically less sophisticated than the examples discussed above. Consider, for instance, how in the context of moral panics over crime victimization, children's everyday mobilities have been reshaped by parental attempts at monitoring at-a-distance using mobile phones, and some children's subsequent attempts to resist such surveillance (Pain et al., 2005). Consider also the ways in which RFID and other digital technologies are used to monitor products in the logistics industry as well as the people and machines that move them (Kanngieser, 2013). In all cases, digital technologies are implicated in the creation of norms about appropriate and desirable ways of being and moving for human subjects.

INTERCONNECTED DIGITAL TECHNOLOGIES

Segregation of the physical transportation of people and goods from communication by radio, TV, and telephone defined the twentieth century, but technologies such as mobile phones, miniaturized computers, satellites, and ubiquitous computing have rapidly come to interconnect moving objects, infrastructures, and wider environments since the 1990s (Sheller, 2007). The logistics systems mentioned at the bottom of page 63 provide one example of this, the modern car another (Sheller, 2007). This section focuses on two further sets of interconnected digital technologies with diverse functionalities that are significantly reconfiguring people's everyday mobility as part of what Gabrys (2014), after Michel Foucault, calls 'computational dispositifs' – constellations of digital technologies, discourses, knowledges, materialities, business models, and practices that are organized around a specific problem.

Continuous connectivity

The first dispositif is that of continuous connectivity (Wilson, 2014). It revolves at first sight around handheld devices such as the smartphone, but actually involves a host of connected technologies (e.g., GPS, wireless networks), techniques (e.g. synchronization protocols, ergonomics), practices (e.g., information search, social media), expectations and mentalities (e.g., 'always-on' mentality, near-synchronous response), fantasies (e.g., cyborg visions of chips implanted in human bodies), and languages as used, for instance, by virtual assistants and chatbots. For Wilson (2014: 539), 'handheld computing did not emerge from within a problem to be solved, a science to be practiced (and a nation to be "saved") but as an idea born of Silicon Valley venture capitalism and competitive entrepreneurialism'. Nonetheless, handheld computing quickly became appropriated for commercial ends by a wide range of firms and corporations. They relied on continuous connectivity to sell specific services and/or offer advertisements and sponsored information to people. At a more abstract level, therefore, the continuous connectivity dispositif addresses the problems of profit-seeking and need for new markets – with due consequences for people's everyday mobility.

One set of consequences revolves around location-based services (LBSs). As Wilson explains elsewhere, LBSs not only make users aware of where they are and what the surroundings have to offer in terms of goods and services, but also 'restructure urban experiences as transactions' (Wilson, 2012: 1270). Apps offering LBSs urge people to check in, upload pictures, make comments and so add greater richness to GPS traces already captured by IT companies. The result is the production of what Watson calls 'conspicuous mobility', a narrative crafted by individual users of which places they visited, activities they undertook, and services they consumed. As part of this, mobility habits and practices may be altered in subtle ways.

Another set of consequences of continuous connectivity arises from the numerous apps and devices that now exist for self-monitoring physical activity, mental health, greenhouse gas emissions, and so on. Relying on gamification, quantification of bodies and selves, and a neoliberal ethos of constant self-improvement, these digital technologies mediate and reconfigure individuals' mobility (Schwanen, 2015; Barratt, 2017). For instance, in the case of the cycling-tracking fitness app Strava, its gamification, visualization, and community-building qualities increase cycling levels among users (Barratt, 2017).

Smart mobility

As a key constituent of the smart city, smart mobility refers to the provision of mobility options and services that are purportedly efficient, green, and inclusive and that usually rely on the operation of digital technologies. The term is easily used, but at best loosely defined: '[t]here is precious little explicit consideration, let alone critique, of what is meant by smart (urban) mobility in academic and wider literature' (Lyons, 2018: 6).

Smart mobility is another computational dispositif seeking to solve concurrent problems of congestion, air pollution, noise, greenhouse gas emissions, traffic accidents, social exclusion, urban decline, and physical inactivity. The central aims are to save time and resources across operators, end users and other actors, and to contribute to economic growth. Interconnected environmental sensors, digital interfaces, and software are embedded into mobility systems and practices in order to reduce the friction of distance and open up business opportunities for incumbents (e.g., bus/taxi operators, car manufacturing/hiring firms) and new actors (e.g., car/bike/ride sharing operators, IT firms). Enacting a shift from individual ownership to mobility-as-a-service – increasingly known by its acronym, MaaS – is widely seen as key to smart mobility.

The role of digital technologies is here not only to reconfigure mobility systems but also to enable modes of participation in which '[t]he citizen is a data point, both a generator of data and a responsive node in a system of feedback' (Gabrys, 2014: 38). Knowledge is integral to the smart mobility dispositif and is assembled from registering movement along mobile phone towers, entrance to rail/buses, bike docking stations and other sensors in fixed locations (Eulerian data) and from sequences of time-stamped spatial positions obtained from tracking technologies (Lagrangian data). The point of data monitoring and analysis is not so much to discipline mobile subjects through the creation and circulation of certain norms and ideals (e.g., the green motorist, the healthy cyclist) but to establish the environmental conditions that allow people to self-regulate their mobility practices (e.g., by making more shared cars or bikes available at sites of high demand at specific times). Logics of anticipation and pre-emption as well as machine learning and real-time forecasting techniques are key to this mode of operation.

Comprehensive investigations of smart mobility dispositifs in particular places remain to be undertaken. Nonetheless, geographers have contributed to a rapidly expanding multidisciplinary evidence base about who partakes in smart mobility practices and what the quantifiable effects are in terms of trips taken, reduced congestion and emissions, and extra physical activity (for bike-sharing, see Corcoran and Li, 2014). Results vary across locality and specifics of the mobility service considered, but young/millennial, middle-class, white men in high-density settings are overrepresented among shared mobility users (Prieto et al., 2017). Perhaps more so than enabling social inclusion, smart mobility seems to disproportionally benefit already advantaged groups in Western cities, reinforcing ongoing processes of gentrification and displacement of poorer populations.

Research deploying qualitative methods has developed deeper insights in mobility rather than movement. Kent et al. (2017) show how, among a sample of Sydney residents, life events such as moving house or international migration catalyse a shift towards car sharing if skills, dispositions and beliefs supporting this practice have been developed earlier during the life-course and digital-cum-physical infrastructure can be accessed. As part of an urban experiment with smart e-bikes in Brighton, UK, Behrendt (2016) has explored the lived experience of smart velomobility. She shows how exposure to Lagrangian tracking of e-cycling induced various responses in participants, including reflexivity, for instance about which route was quickest; affect/emotion as in pride and anxiety about privacy; and community building through sharing of one's data. Behrendt's results are in line with the argument above that smart (velo)mobility dispositifs evoke novel practices and experiences through self-regulation rather than through disciplinary mechanisms premised on externally determined norms and ideals.

Studies of the effects that smart mobility dispositifs generate on the development and use of cars tend to be speculative and optimistic in the sense that ubiquitous computing, software, digital interfaces, and environmental sensors are anticipated to diminish the dominance of privately owned vehicles. For Canzler and Knie (2016: 65), '[t]here is no going back': the traditional automobile as key enabler of prosperity, individualization, and well-being is being overtaken by digital platforms as the new facilitators of these social goods. Others are more cautious, suggesting that smart mobility developments around cars reflect automobility's capacity to endure through adaptation – as with car manufacturers moving into car sharing to make private ownership more attractive to millennials – and may perpetuate existing socio-spatial inequalities (Schwanen, 2016).

AUTOMATION

While currently existing smart mobility dispositifs may expand and evolve, they can also change beyond recognition if automated vehicles (AVs), such as driverless cars and drones, diffuse as rapidly as many commentators believe. Compared to existing smart mobility technologies, road vehicles at autonomy level 4 (fully autonomous within 'operational design domains') or level 5 (fully autonomous in every driving situation) offer unseen levels of technicity – the capacity of technologies, in this case particularly machine learning, to generate and transform mobility systems, practices, and experiences (Kitchin and Dodge, 2011). However, as the widespread embedding of cruise control and automatic parking in cars suggests, automation of road transport 'proceed[s] through slow upheaval [rather] than some kind of ecstatic change' (Thrift, 2014; see also Sheller, 2007).

As with previous digital technologies, AVs are touted to be the inevitable solution to road mobility's problems: transport will be safer, less congested, cleaner, and cheaper, and there will be more car sharing and greater social inclusion for those groups who are marginalized by conventional automobility, such as the disabled and elderly. Visions of how AVs will radically reconfigure mobility systems abound. Some of the anticipated benefits may indeed be realized, but the overall effects are likely to be complex and ambiguous. Geographers are well placed to dispel some of the myths around AVs. For instance, analysis of YouTube clips of people using assisted or autonomous driving systems (Brown and Laurier, 2017) and ethnographies of truck driving (Gregson, 2017) have already suggested that human drivers will not disappear as easily as some public commentators suggest.

Whatever AVs may bring, geographers interested in mobility should experiment with new conceptualizations of mobility, embodiment, and the digital. Approaches from transport geography can generate useful representations of potential improvements in accessibility (Meyer et al., 2017), but other questions – already raised by currently existing smart mobility dispositifs – will only become more pressing: what sort of mobile subjectivities will be enacted? What does a car become and how is it experienced when it is no longer driven by a human? What place-specific effects will be generated by the risk of software failure? How will cities and notions of the good life be reconfigured in different geographical settings? Will AVs reinforce coloniality – the enduring legacy of colonialism – when they diffuse across the non-Western world? Recent conceptualizations of digital objects and their effects (e.g., Ash, 2015; Schwanen, 2015) and of post-human agency as always-already co-constituted with technologies (Rose, 2017) offer useful starting points to investigate these questions, and future research could utilize these approaches to understand the particularities of digital mobility in more detail.

REFERENCES

Adey, P. (2009) 'Facing airport security: Affect, biopolitics, and the preemptive securitisation of the mobile body', *Environment and Planning D: Society and Space*, 27: 274–295.

Ash, J. (2015) 'Technology and affect: Towards a theory of inorganically organised objects', *Emotion, Space and Society*, 14: 84–90.

Barratt, P. (2017) 'Healthy competition: A qualitative study investigating persuasive technologies and the gamification of cycling', *Health & Place*, 46: 328–336.

Behrendt, F. (2016) 'Why cycling matters for smart cities: Internet of bicycles for intelligent transport', *Journal of Transport Geography*, 56: 157–164.

Brown, B. and Laurier, E. (2017) 'The trouble with autopilots: Assisted and autonomous driving on the social road', in *CHI '17: Proceedings of the 2017 ACM SIGCHI Conference on Human Factors in Computing Systems*. New York: Association for Computing Machinery. DOI: 10.1145/30255453.3025462.

Canzler, W. and Knie, A. (2016) 'Mobility in the age of digital modernity: Why the private car is losing its significance, intermodal transport is winning and why digitalisation is the key', *Applied Mobilities*, 1: 56–67.

Cohen-Blankshtain, G. and Rotem-Mindali, O. (2016) 'Key research themes on ICT and sustainable urban mobility', *International Journal of Sustainable Transportation*, 10: 9–17.

Corcoran, J. and Li, T. (eds) (2014) 'Special section on spatial analytical approaches in public bike sharing programs', *Journal of Transport Geography*, 41: 268–345.

Cresswell, T. (2010) 'Towards a politics of mobility', *Environment and Planning D: Society and Space*, 28: 17–31.

Elliott, A. and Urry, J. (2010) *Mobile Lives*. London: Routledge.

Gabrys, J. (2014) 'Programming environments: Environmentality and citizen sensing in the smart city', *Environment and Planning D: Society and Space*, 32: 30–48.

Graham, S.N.D. (2005) 'Software-sorted geographies', *Progress in Human Geography*, 29: 562–580.

Gregson, N. (2017) 'Mobilities, mobile work and habitation: Truck drivers and the crisis in occupational auto-mobility in the UK', *Mobilities*, DOI: 10.1080/14450 101.2017.1343987.

Haynes, P. (2010) 'Information and communication technologies and international business travel: Mobility allies?', *Mobilities*, 5: 547–564.

Kanngieser, A. (2013) 'Tracking and tracing geographies of logistical governance and labouring bodies', *Environment and Planning D: Society and Space*, 31: 594–610.

Kent, J., Dowling, R. and Maalsen, S. (2017) 'Catalysts for transport transitions: Bridging the gap between disruptions and change', *Journal of Transport Geography*, 60: 200–207.

Kitchin, R. and Dodge, M. (2011) *Code/Space: Software and Everyday Life*. Cambridge, MA: MIT Press.

Kwan, M.P. (2002) 'Time, information technologies and the geographies of everyday life', *Urban Geography*, 23: 471–482.

Line, T., Jain, J. and Lyons, G. (2011) 'The role of ICTs in everyday mobile lives', *Journal of Transport Geography*, 19: 1490–1499.

Lyons, G. (2018) 'Getting smart about urban mobility – aligning the paradigms of smart and sustainable', *Transportation Research, Part A*, 115: 4–14.

Meyer, J., Becker, H., Bösch, P.M. and Axhausen, K.W. (2017) 'Autonomous vehicles: The next jump in accessibilities?' *Research in Transportation Economics*, 62: 80–91.

Pain, R., Grundy, S., Gill, S., Towner, E. Sparks, G. and Hughes, K. (2005) '"So long as I take my mobile": Mobile phones, urban life and geographies of young people's safety', *International Journal of Urban and Regional Research*, 29: 814–830.

Prieto, M., Baltas, G. and Stan, V. (2017) 'Car sharing adoption intention in urban areas: What are the key sociodemographic drivers?', *Transportation Research, Part A*, 101: 218–227.

Rose, G. (2017) 'Posthuman agency in the digitally mediated city: Exteriorization, individuation, reinvention', *Annals of the American Association of Geographers*, 107: 779–793.

Salomon, I. (1986) 'Telecommunications and travel relationships: A review', *Transportation Research, Part A*, 20: 223–238.

Schwanen, T. (2008) 'Managing uncertain arrival times through sociomaterial associations', *Environment and Planning B: Planning and Design*, 35: 997–1011.

Schwanen, T. (2015) 'Beyond instrument: Smartphone app and sustainable mobility', *European Journal of Transport and Infrastructure Research*, 15: 675–690.

Schwanen, T. (2016) 'Rethinking resilience as capacity to endure: Automobility and the city', *City*, 20: 52–160.

Sheller, M. (2007) 'Bodies, cybercars and the mundane incorporation of automated mobilities', *Social & Cultural Geography*, 8: 175–197.

Sheller, M. (2016) 'Connected mobility in a disconnected world', *Annals of the Association of American Geographers*, 106: 330–339.

Sheller, M. and Urry, J. (2006) 'The new mobilities paradigm', *Environment and Planning A*, 38: 207–226.

Storme, T., Faulconbridge, J.R., Beaverstock, J.V., Derudder, B. and Witlox, F. (2017) 'Mobility and professional networks in academia: An exploration of the obligations of presence', *Mobilities*, 12: 405–424.

Thrift, N. (2014) 'The promise of urban informatics: Some speculations', *Environment and Planning A*, 46: 1263–1266.

Waitt, G. and Harada, T. (2016) 'Parenting, care and the family car', *Social & Cultural Geography*, 17: 1079–1100.

Wilson, M.W. (2012) 'Location-based services, conspicuous mobility, and the location-aware future', *Geoforum*, 43: 1266–1275.

Wilson, M.W. (2014) 'Continuous connectivity, handheld computers, and mobile spatial knowledge', *Environment and Planning D: Society and Space*, 32: 535–555.

PART II
DIGITAL METHODS

7

EPISTEMOLOGIES

Jim Thatcher

INTRODUCTION

The editors of this collection have argued that geography 'is in the midst of a digital turn' (Ash et al., 2018: 25). Over the course of 2016 and 2017, the Association of American Geographers and the Royal Geographical Society similarly recognized this transition with the official formation of a specialty group and a working group in digital geographies, respectively. In these moves, as well as a growing number of publications centred around digital methodologies, objects, and aesthetics (e.g., Bergmann, 2016; Leszczynski, 2017; Moran and Etchegoyen, 2017; Thatcher et al., 2016a), we find a recognition of the countless ways that 'the digital' has become an intrinsic and pervasive element of the practice of geography. This chapter introduces and examines both the epistemologies and epistemological critiques that are bound up within the production of new geographic knowledges.

To do so, the chapter proceeds in three parts. First, it gives a brief history of some of the epistemologies found within geography's ongoing engagement with the digital. It begins with the rise of the use of digital objects in geography via the computational methods of early spatial science, moves through resulting critiques of GIS and its related epistemologies, and concludes with more recent work that might be considered as having a processual epistemological orientation. Second, the chapter highlights two further epistemological critiques of the digital in geography – an over-privileging of scopic regimes and visual representations and the bounded nature of knowledge production with capitalist systems. Finally, the chapter outlines some potential future approaches to epistemological work within digital geographies, emphasizing the inherently partial nature of any epistemological frame.

Before proceeding further, it is necessary to briefly define the term 'epistemology' as it is understood within this chapter and to contrast it with its often paired term from metaphysics, 'ontology'. In computer and information science, ontology refers to a formalized structure or naming of the types of objects or things within a domain, their properties, and the relations between said types that exist within the domain; however, in metaphysics, the term refers more broadly to what can be said to be real, to exist. Geographers have explored the tensions and intersections between these definitions with respect to spatial objects, spatial information, and spatial data. For example, Smith and Mark (1998: 308) attempted to bridge the divide through a recognition that geographic objects are 'not merely located in space' but are rather 'tied intrinsically to space'. In their argument, an ontology of geographic kinds would bridge between the nature of being and the requirements of communication and data structure necessary for human–computer interactions. Another approach, by Schuurman and Leszczynski (2006: 709), used the informatics definition of ontology – 'the possible range of meaning offered by an encoded field'. They proposed the expansion of possible meanings within metadata to include 'qualitative, ethnographic data about data' to better capture the 'deep context' elided from current database constructions (Schuurman and Leszczynski, 2006: 717). Thatcher et al. (2011) similarly used ethnographic methods, such as interviews and participant observation, to capture and render legible the politics behind the construction of data ontologies. Work such as Pavlovskaya (2009) has more generally exposed the ontological power intrinsically called forth in the act of mapping.

While work within geography on the nature of epistemology and ontology with respect to human geography and GIS has an uneven and incomplete history (O'Sullivan et al., 2018), in the context of this chapter, the philosophical definition of ontology will be the focus. Ontology can be thought of as what can be said to exist. In contrast, epistemology is the branch of metaphysics concerned with what can be known and how we can know it. It is thus a foundational element of theoretical critique and knowledge production.

HISTORY, GEOGRAPHY, AND THE DIGITAL

The significance of digital technologies in the practice of geography is hard to overstate (Sui and Morrill, 2004). From geographic information systems analysing remotely sensed data from satellites to the recording of interviews on mobile phones, digital devices suffuse and mediate geography across its subdisciplines (Ash et al., 2018; Rose, 2015); and while the roles that quantification and abstraction have played in the production of knowledge and practice of science are entwined with the formation and functions of the modern state (Foucault, 2008; Rose-Redwood, 2012; Scott, 1998), looking historically within the field of geography, digital objects first become foundational in the practice of geography during the quantitative revolution and the accompanying emergence of spatial science.

Early members of the quantitative revolution within geography epistemologically aligned themselves with empiricism and positivism. Empiricism is the school of thought in which facts are believed to speak for themselves and require little theoretical explanation, while positivism accepts that it is possible to objectively measure social phenomena and determine natural laws which predict and explain human behaviour. Taken together, early quantitative revolution members saw an 'isomorphic correspondence' between knowledge and the real world (Sheppard, 2015), one in which the world could be known through quantification, analysis, and the scientific method as applied in the physical sciences. In other words, objective truth could be produced through a continuous, iterative process of hypothesis generation, testing, observation, and analysis of real-world phenomena. Through this a 'new geography' emerged that emphasized 'discerning predictable empirical patterns by applying relatively simple mathematical formulae to increasingly large data sets', a situation that Barnes (2014: 51) has noted is being replicated with respect to 'big data'. Historically, it was from this strand of nomothetic spatial science that early GIS emerged and around which GIScience organized.

While some practitioners of spatial science were interested in relational and non-Euclidean theories of space (e.g., Couclelis, 1999), as GIS instantiated itself as a sub-discipline it brought with it an ontology of space as absolute, discrete, empty, and regular and, with this, an epistemological orientation that accepted knowledges built from this ontology (Dixon and Jones, 1998). By the 1990s, the underlying epistemologies of GIS as both technological system and science were under critique for their oft-unconsidered acceptance of the essentialist nature of space and knowledge. With digital mapping projects largely well established and even associated with the state security apparatus (Clarke and Cloud, 2000), critical GIS scholars now 'deconstructed' the map to reveal the ways in which it reified a 'rationalistic logic – a universal calculus' (Harley, 1989; Pickles, 1995: 231).

With the rise of critical GIS in the 1990s, practitioners began to question the ways in which the objects they produced (often digitally created maps) reified and enforced the 'god trick' of a 'view from nowhere' through which representation was impartial and, above all, 'true' (Haraway, 1988; Leszczynski, 2009; Schuurman, 2000). Epistemologically, feminist and other critiques (such as Marxist; see Smith, 1992) highlighted that the world could not be 'colonized by a single system of spatiotemporalities' (Harvey and Haraway, 1995: 516). Standpoint theory (Harding, 1986), situated knowledges (Haraway, 1988), the concept of limited epistemic culture (Knorr-Cetina, 1999), as well as other critiques of the social and cultural production of scientific knowledge (e.g., Latour, 1988) suggested the need for a more nuanced epistemology of the digital within geography, one aware of its own assumptions, but still invested in the subject of its enquiry (Schuurman and Pratt, 2002: 291).

One example of such work can be found in ongoing efforts to 'queer' the map. Brown and Knopp (2008), working with the Northwest Lesbian and Gay History Museum Project, sought to bring the epistemologies of queer theory into tension with the representational frame demanded by GIS as a technology. Through deeply engaged ethnographic work, they 'opened the process of map production and consumption to multiple forms of representation, multiple ways of knowing, and multiple interpretations' (Brown and Knopp, 2008: 55). Gieseking (2018: 151) has extended this work to examine the inclusion, exclusion, and representation of queer subjects in 'big data' archives, finding that in society's recent obsession with big data, the marginalized are further oppressed through the creation of 'a false norm to which they are never able to measure up'.

More recently, alongside and influenced by feminist epistemologies, those practising digital geographies have focused their gaze on the processes through which objects and knowledges are brought into the world. These approaches question the ontological security of objects and ideas, such as maps (Dodge et al., 2009), to instead interrogate the constantly repeated, contingent practices that must constantly (re)create and interpret said objects and ideas. In the context of the digital, these processural epistemologies often consider technicity – the 'coconstitutive milieu of relations between human and their technical supports' (Crogan and Kennedy, 2009: 109). For example, Dodge and Kitchin (2005) define the technicity of code as its ability to 'make things happen in conjunction with people'; and for other definitions, see Ash (2012). Digital geographies are never simply digital, but are rather assemblages constituted of, among other things, embodied practices, technical infrastructure, databases, and visualizations.

SCOPOPHILIA AND CAPITAL: TWO FURTHER EPISTEMOLOGICAL CRITIQUES

Maps may 'make' geography (for a recent discussion, see Aalbers, 2014a, 2014b, 2014c; Wilson, 2014) and they may remain its 'preeminent form of representation' (Harvey, 2000: 557), or they may not; however, the above history is not meant to suggest that maps and mapmaking have always or continue to be the principle means by which digital geographies are practised or understood. The first widespread use of digital objects may have emerged within geography through the broadly positivist, empirical work of spatial science, but, currently, a geographer would be hard pressed to produce a single work of scholarship without enrolling some form of digital mediation and practice – be it a GIS or a word processor. As such, the underlying epistemologies of digital practices must be understood. Where the previous section charted a history from spatial science, through feminist epistemological critiques, and into recent work on processural epistemologies, this section highlights two related means of further understanding and critiq epistemologies of digital geography.

Melissa Gregg (2014: 37) coined the term 'data spectacle' to refer to how th 'aesthetic pleasure and visual allure of witnessing large data sets at scale' draws upon the modernist tendency to privilege the visual and state fantasies of command and control to produce new epistemologies (see also Halpern, 2014, for ties to earlier cybernetic movements). Referring specifically to GIS and mapping, but presaging Gregg's 'data spectacle', Pickles (2004) criticizes an epistemology of the digital which holds the world as fully knowable, quantifiable, and representable. Rejecting the idea that data is 'never ontologically prior to its interpretation' (Thatcher et al., 2016b: 993), this epistemological myth forms the basis of how 'big data' seeks to make, not simply interpret, the world, and reflects a re-emergent positivism (boyd and Crawford, 2012; Kitchin et al., 2015; Wyly, 2014). The influence and already existing power of an epistemology that seeks to encode and understand the world as digital information can be seen in many realms of life, among them the growing self-tracking movement (Neff and Nafus, 2016), the power of search engines to shape knowledge (Pasquale, 2015), calculative border security apparatuses (Amoore and Hall, 2009), and new assemblages of land for investment (Li, 2014).

Theorizations of 'the spectacle' are prone to mistake a move towards a social totality for its existence as such; and, similarly, despite the burgeoning realm of data analytics and visualizations, its accompanying epistemology is not universal. First, as a top-down theorization of representation and visualization, it overlooks the embodied, quotidian practices that produce much of this data (Leszczynski, 2015; Wilmott, 2016). Second, such critiques may fetishize or reify certain aspects of the digital (e.g., large-scale distributed computation) at the expense of more reflexive critiques of the digital as a whole. All forms of knowledge production represent, and critiques which insist upon top-down framings ignore, the wealth of participatory practices which have emerged and continue to emerge through digital practices.

Another, related, means of critiquing the digital and its epistemologies has been to situate its existing production within larger systems of capitalist imperatives. Recognizing that digital firms are largely 'all here to make as much fucking money as possible' (Ameriquest manager quoted in Pasquale, 2015: 208), these critiques highlight how the imperatives of capitalist accumulation shape what is and can be known of the world. For example, the data which are produced, dispossessed, accumulated, and analysed from users of mobile devices are those data which technology firms have decided capture excess value (Thatcher et al., 2016b). Further, and akin to the data spectacle, the digital identities which emerge to represent individuals need not be wholly accurate, they need only be accurate enough to produce profit in a competitive sector (Dalton and Thatcher, 2015). For digital geographers, care must be taken to question what knowledges cannot be produced through such data, both in terms of what is not captured and in terms of to which data researchers do and do not have access (Thatcher, 2014). This is the epistemological critique underlying much work in critical data studies (Dalton and Thatcher, 2014; Dalton et al., 2016), but like other critiques it is not without its limits. In its focus on data, CDS approaches sometimes reify the very object which they seek to question, inadvertently marking off data as somehow apart from the socio-technical assemblage through which it emerges and from which it is never ontologically prior.

CONCLUSION: AGAINST UNIVERSAL EPISTEMOLOGIES

This brief chapter has covered some of the major epistemological orientations found within the practice and critique of digital geographies. Beginning with the rise to prominence of the digital as a privileged object and method of study within geography during the quantitative revolution, the chapter examined the move from those broadly positivist, empiricist epistemological orientations to more partial, situated knowledges via work done in critical GIS by feminist and other scholars. Finally, highlighting epistemologies that focus on process and the ontogenetic nature of the digital, the chapter offered two further, current critiques: first, the privileging of scopic regimes and representational epistemologies; and second, the delimiting of knowledge production within capitalist enframings of the world.

Any piece or practice of digital geographies will inevitably involve an epistemological frame, whether explicitly expressed or found only through close examination, and those covered in this chapter are not meant to be exhaustive. Rather, each is meant to demonstrate the partiality of a given epistemological framework. The ubiquity of digital devices and mediation, of data, computation, and infrastructure, increasingly means that geography is digital geography or, as the editors of this volume have put it, that geography is 'in the midst of a digital turn' (Ash et al., 2018: 25). What this chapter argues in light of that is that we must take care to choose the epistemological underpinnings of our work. None of the epistemological approaches described above are without their limitations and, conversely, none have failed to contribute to the production of knowledge.

As the interest in and practice of digital geographies continue, we must, on the one hand, constantly recall that technology will never be neutral (Heidegger, 1977). From gender and racially biased artificial intelligences (Hudson, 2017) to databases which elide all indigenous land claims in favour of speculative investment (McCarthy and Thatcher, 2017), digital objects and practices, through their technicity, always and inevitably make claims upon, mediate, and structure what we can know of and do in the world. On the other hand, we cannot deny the epistemological and ontological power of the digital. By choosing an epistemology for our work that makes knowable our object of study, digital geographers are able to grant some degree of ontological security to said objects (Pavlovskaya, 2009). But, we must also recall, as Brown and Knopp (2008) demonstrated drawing on queer theory, that some objects, ideas, and subjects may remain unrepresentable or unknowable in any epistemological framework. Moving forward, we must 'stay with the trouble' of the digital and its effects on the world (Haraway, 2016), recognizing how the epistemological underpinnings that go into its creation, its practice, and its study always both enable and constrain knowledges.

For some, this may mean speculative feminist epistemologies that seek out alternative potential worlds of liberation through digital praxis. For others, it will mean a harsh critique of capitalism's structural effects on the epistemologies and ontologies of the present. The same object of study may be approached productively from differing epistemological positions and, in fact, much future work will necessarily blend and mesh theoretical and epistemological approaches in order to produce more nuanced work. Avoiding polemics and recognizing the limitations of any epistemological frame will be necessary to engage the digital in a critical and robust manner. This, however, is not a call for the end of critique, rather for its continuation. For a recognition of where epistemological blind spots exist, a calling to attention of the limitations of approaches – whether reflexively or from the outside – is the path forward.

REFERENCES

Aalbers, M.B. (2014a) 'Do maps make geography? Part 1: Redlining, planned schrinkage, and the places of decline', *ACME*, 13(4): 525–556.

Aalbers, M.B. (2014b) 'Do maps make geography? Part 2: Post-Katrina New Orleans, post-foreclosure Cleveland and neoliberal urbanism', *ACME*, 13(4): 557–582.

Aalbers, M.B. (2014c) 'Do maps make geography? Part 3: Reconnecting the trace', *ACME*, 13(4): 586–588.

Amoore, L. and Hall, A. (2009) 'Taking people apart: Digitized dissection and the body at the border', *Environment and Planning D: Society and Space*, 27: 444–464.

Ash, J. (2012) 'Technology, technicity, and emerging practices of temporal sensitivity in videogames', *Environment and Planning A*, 44: 187–203.

Ash, J., Kitchin, R. and Leszczynski, A. (2018) 'Digital turn, digital geographies?', *Progress in Human Geography*, 42(1): 25–43.

Barnes, T.J. (2014) 'What's old is new, and new is old: History and geography's quantitative revolutions', *Dialogues in Human Geography*, 4(1): 50–53.

Bergmann, L. (2016) 'Toward speculative data: "Geographic information" for situated knowledges, vibrant matter, and relational spaces', *Environment and Planning D: Society and Space*, 34(6): 971–989.

boyd, d. and Crawford, K. (2012) 'Critical questions for Big Data. Information', *Communication & Society*, 15(5): 662–679.

Brown, M. and Knopp, L. (2008) 'Queering the map: The productive tensions of colliding epistemologies', *Annals of the Association of American Geographers*, 98(1): 40–58.

Clarke, K.C. and Cloud, J.G. (2000) 'On the origins of analytical cartography', *Cartography and Geographic Information Science*, 27(3): 195–204.

Couclelis, H. (1999) 'Space, time, geography', in P. Longley, M.F. Goodchild, D. Maguire and D.W. Rhind (eds), *Geographical Information Systems: Principles, Techniques, Management, and Applications*. New York: Wiley. pp. 29–38.

Crogan, P. and Kennedy, H. (2009) 'Technologies between games and culture', *Games and Culture*, 4(2): 107–114.

Dalton, C.M. and Thatcher, J. (2014) 'What does a critical data studies look like, and why do we care?'. *Society and Space*, 12 May. Available at: http://societyandspace.org/2014/05/12/what-does-a-critical-data-studies-look-like-and-why-do-we-care-craig-dalton-and-jim-thatcher (accessed 1 February 2018).

Dalton, C.M. and Thatcher, J. (2015) 'Inflated granularity: Spatial "Big Data" and geodemographics', *Big Data & Society*, 2(2). DOI: 10.1177/2053951715601144 .

Dalton, C.M., Taylor, L. and Thatcher, J. (2016) 'Critical data studies – a dialog on space', *Big Data & Society*, 3(1). DOI: 10.1177/2053951716648346.

Dixon, D.P. and Jones, J.P. III. (1998) 'My dinner with Derrida, *or* Spatial analysis and poststructuralism do lunch', *Environment and Planning A*, 30: 247–260.

Dodge, M. and Kitchin, R. (2005) 'Code and the transduction of space', *Annals of the Association of American Geographers*, 95(1): 162–180.

Dodge, M., Perkins, C. and Kitchin, R. (2009) 'Mapping modes, methods and moments: A manifesto for map studies', in M. Dodge, R. Kitchin and C. Perkins (eds), *Rethinking Maps: New Frontiers in Cartographic Theory*. Abingdon: Routledge. pp. 220–243.

Foucault, M. (2008) *Security, Territory, Population: Lectures at the College de France 1977–1978*. New York: Palgrave.

Gieseking, J. (2018) 'Size matters to lesbians, too: Queer feminist interventions into the scale of big data', *Professional Geographer*, 70(1): 150–156.

Gregg, M. (2014) 'Inside the data spectacle', *Television & New Media*, 16(1): 37–51.

Halpern, O. (2014) *Beautiful Data: A History of Vision and Reason since 1945*. Durham, NC: Duke University Press.

Haraway, D. (1988) 'Situated knowledges: The science question in feminism and the privileges of partial perspective', *Feminist Studies*, 14(3): 575–599.

Haraway, D. (2016) *Staying with the Trouble: Making Kin in the Chthulucene*. Durham, NC: Duke University Press.

Harding, S. (1986) *The Science Question in Feminism?* Ithaca, NY: Cornell University Press.

Harley, J.B. (1989) 'Deconstructing the map', *Cartographica*, 26(2): 1–20.

Harvey, D. (2000) 'Cosmopolitanism and the banality of geographical evils', *Public Culture*, 12(2): 529–564.

Harvey, D. and Haraway, D. (1995) 'Nature, politics, and possibilities: A debate and discussion with David Harvey and Donna Haraway', *Environment and Planning D: Society and Space*, 13(5): 507–527.

Heidegger, M. (1977) *The Question Concerning Technology and Other Essays*. New York: HarperCollins.

Hudson, L. (2017) 'Technology is biased too. How do we fix it?', *FiveThirtyEight.com*, Available at: https://fivethirtyeight.com/features/technology-is-biased-too-how-do-we-fix-it (accessed 1 February 2018).

Kitchin, R., Lauriault, T. and McArdle, G. (2015) 'Knowing and governing cities through urban indicators, city benchmarking, and real-time dashboards', *Regional Studies, Regional Science*, 2(1): 729–751.

Knorr-Cetina, K. (1999) *Epistemic Cultures*. Cambridge, MA: Harvard University Press.

Latour, B. (1988) *Science in Action*. Cambridge, MA: Harvard University Press.

Leszczynski, A. (2009) 'Quantitative limits to qualitative engagements: GIS, its critics, and the philosophical divide', *Professional Geographer*, 61: 350–365.

Leszczynski, A. (2015) 'Spatial media/tion', *Progress in Human Geography*, 39(6): 729–751.

Leszczynski, A. (2017) 'Digital methods I: Wicked tensions', *Progress in Human Geography*, DOI: 10.1177/0309132517711779.

Li, T.M. (2014) 'What is land? Assembling a resource for global investment', *Transactions of the Institute of British Geographers*, 39: 589–602.

McCarthy, J. and Thatcher, J. (2017) 'Visualizing new political ecologies: A critical data studies analysis of the World Bank's renewable energy resource mapping initiative', *Geoforum*, DOI: 10.1016/j.geoforum.2017.03.025.

Moran, D. and Etchegoyen, L. (2017) 'The virtual prison as a digital cultural object: Digital mediation of political opinion in simulation gaming', *Environment and Planning A*, 49(2): 448–466.

Neff, G. and Nafus, D. (2016) *Self-Tracking*. Cambridge, MA: MIT Press.

O'Sullivan, D., Bergmann, L. and Thatcher, J.E. (2018) 'Spatiality, maps, and mathematics in critical human geography: Toward a repetition with difference', *Professional Geographer*, 70(1): 129–139.

Pasquale, F. (2015) *The Black Box Society*. Cambridge, MA: Harvard University Press.

Pavlovskaya, M. (2009) 'Feminist visualization', in R. Kitchin and N. Thrift (eds), *International Encyclopaedia of Human Geography*. Amsterdam: Elsevier. pp. 157–164.

Pickles, J. (ed.) (1995) *Ground Truth*. New York: Guilford Press.

Pickles, J. (2004) *A History of Spaces*. New York: Routledge.

Rose, G. (2015) 'Rethinking the geographies of cultural "objects" through digital technologies: Interface, network and friction', *Progress in Human Geography*, 40(3): 334–351.

Rose-Redwood, R. (2012) 'With numbers in place: Security, territory, and the production of calculable space', *Annals of the Association of American Geographers*, 102(2): 295–319.

Schuurman, N. (2000) 'Trouble in the heartland: GIS and its critics in the 1990s', *Progress in Human Geography*, 24: 569–590.

Schuurman, N. and Leszczynski, A. (2006) 'Ontology-based metadata', *Transactions in GIS*, 10(5): 709–726.

Schuurman, N. and Pratt, G. (2002) 'Care of the subject: Feminism and critiques of GIS', *Gender, Place and Culture*, 9(3): 291–299.

Scott, J.C. (1998) *Seeing Like a State: How Certain Schemes to Improve the Human Condition Have Failed*. New Haven, CT: Yale University Press.

Sheppard, E. (2015) 'Thinking geographically: Globalizing capitalism and beyond', *Annals of the Association of American Geographers*, 105(6): 1113–1134.

Smith, B. and Mark, D.M. (1998) 'Ontology and geographic kinds', in T.K. Poiker and N.R. Chrisman (eds), *Proceedings of the Eighth International Symposium on Spatial Data Handling* (SDH '98), Vancouver, Canada. Burnaby, BC: International Geographical Union. pp. 308–320.

Smith, N. (1992) 'History and philosophy of geography: Real wars, theory wars', *Progress in Human Geography*, 16(2): 257–271.

Sui, D. and Morrill, R. (2004) 'Computers and geography: From automated geography to digital earth', in S.D. Brunn, S.L. Cutter and J.W. Harrington (eds), *Geography and Technology*. New York: Springer. pp. 81–108.

Thatcher, J. (2014) 'Living on fumes: Digital footprints, data fumes, and the limits of spatial big data', *International Journal of Communication*, 8: 1765–1783.

Thatcher, J., Bergmann, L., Ricker, B., Rose-Redwood, R., O'Sullivan, D., Barnes, T.J., et al. (2016a) 'Revisiting critical GIS: Reflections from Friday Harbor', *Environment and Planning A*, 48: 815–824.

Thatcher, J., Mülligann, C., Luo, W., Xu, S., Guidero, E. and Janowicz, K. (2011) 'Hidden ontologies – how mobile computing affects the conceptualization of geographic space', in K. Janowich, M. Raubal, A. Krüger and C. Keßler (eds), *Proceedings of the Workshop on Cognitive Engineering for Mobile GIS* (CEMob2011), In conjunction with the Conference on Spatial Information Theory (COSIT'11), Belfast, Maine. Available at: http://ceur-ws.org/Vol-780 (accessed 18 May 2018).

Thatcher, J., O'Sullivan, D. and Mahmoudi, D. (2016b) 'Data colonialism through accumulation by dispossession: New metaphors for daily data', *Environment and Planning D: Society and Space*, 34(6): 990–1006.

Wilmott, C. (2016) 'Small moments in Spatial Big Data: Calculability, authority and interoperability in everyday mobile mapping', *Big Data & Society*, 3(2). DOI: 10.1177/2053951716661364.

Wilson, M.W. (2014) 'Map the trace', *ACME*, 13(4): 583–585.

Wyly, E. (2014) 'The new quantitative revolution', *Dialogues in Human Geography*, 4(1): 26–38.

8

DATA AND DATA INFRASTRUCTURES

Rob Kitchin and Tracey Lauriault

INTRODUCTION

This chapter is centrally concerned with the production of and access to digital data that are reshaping how geographical research is undertaken. The chapter starts by outlining the changing nature of data, and the relatively recent wide-scale digitization of non-digital data sources and the production of big data. It then discusses cyber-infrastructures and data infrastructures – archives and repositories – that facilitate the sharing of data for research. It concludes with a brief discussion of the emerging field of critical data studies and its relevance for geographical epistemology.

DIGITAL DATA AND GEOGRAPHICAL RESEARCH

Data are often understood as the building blocks for information and knowledge. They are the raw material produced by capturing and abstracting the world into measures and other representational forms (numbers, characters, symbols, images, sounds, electromagnetic waves, bits, etc.). Data are typically representative, wherein measures explicitly seek to denote the characteristics of a phenomenon (e.g., a person's age, height, weight, opiniWon, habits, location). They can also be derived (e.g., produced from other data) or implied (e.g., through an absence rather than a presence). In broad terms, data vary by:

- *form*, being quantitative (e.g., numeric, categories) or qualitative (e.g., words, images);
- *structure*, being structured (a defined data model with consistent measures/categories), semi-structured (no predefined data model/schema), or unstructured (no defined data model and highly variable data);
- *source*, being captured (deliberately sourced) or exhaust (inherently produced as a by-product of another process);
- *producer*, being primary (generated by a person, organization, or community for a specific purpose), secondary (made available by a third party), or tertiary (third party derived or aggregated data);
- *type*, being indexical (uniquely identified, enabling linkage), attribute (representative but not indexical), or metadata (data about data that facilitate their use, such as data definitions, provenance, and lineage) (Kitchin, 2014).

Data have long been generated by societies for the purposes of administration, business and science, though the term 'data' was only used for the first time in the English language in the seventeenth century (Rosenberg, 2013). From this time on, the generation, storage, and analysis of data grew enormously due to the utility and value of the insights and processes they facilitated, being used to create new knowledge, policies, innovations, and products, and to manage and regulate populations and run businesses (Poovey, 1998).

While large quantities of analog data were produced in the nineteenth and twentieth centuries, the amount generated was very modest compared to the present digital deluge. Traditionally, data were time-consuming and costly to produce, analyse and interpret because they involved a lot of labour – all the data had to be collected and analysed by hand (Grier, 2007). Even with the first computers, data generally had to be digitized by hand and the computational analysis was relatively slow by today's standards (taking hours or days to do what would now take milliseconds – and coding errors would mean starting again). As a consequence, data generation was narrowly focused to answer specific questions and produced using well-tested techniques in tightly controlled ways. And outside of public administration they tended to be generated periodically (e.g., annually) or on a one-off basis using sampling techniques to produce data that were hopefully representative of whole populations and had limited levels of error, bias, and uncertainty (Miller, 2010). Beyond some exceptions, such as population censuses or meteorological data collections, individual social science and physical geography datasets tended to be quite small in size, especially those that were not produced by institutions, such as those generated using surveys or interviews or fieldwork. Datasets generated in traditional ways were thus typically characterized by limited volume, sampled collection, small geographic extent, and narrow variety and framing. In the case of meteorological data, even though their global collection constituted a 'vast machine' (Edwards, 2010), they were not collected in an integrated, standardized manner or in real-time.

In contrast, new forms of big data have quite different qualities. While there has been much discussion in recent years as to what constitutes big data, Kitchin (2014) details that they have the following characteristics:

- huge in *volume*, consisting of millions or billions of records, or terabytes or petabytes in storage;
- high in *velocity*, being created continuously and in or near real-time;
- diverse in *variety*, being structured and unstructured in nature;
- *exhaustive* in scope, striving to capture entire populations or systems (n = all);
- fine-grained in *resolution* and uniquely *indexical* in identification;
- *relational* in nature, containing common fields that enable the conjoining of different datasets; and
- *flexible*, holding the traits of *extensionality* (new fields can easily be added to the method of generation) and *scalability* (datasets can expand in size rapidly).

In an examination of 26 datasets widely thought to constitute big data, Kitchin and McArdle (2016) contend that the two most important distinguishing characteristics are velocity and exhaustivity. Big data are produced continuously and are n = all samples within a domain or a platform. For example, automatic number plate recognition cameras continuously scan and capture the license plate of *every* vehicle that passes the camera, rather than being a sample at a particular time (as with a traditional traffic survey). And with a network of cameras one can both track the routes of individual vehicles and calculate city-wide patterns of traffic on a 24-hour, 365-days-a-year basis. Instead of producing static, often coarse, snapshots of traffic conditions, there is a quantum shift in the resolution and coverage of the data available for traffic analysis, including real-time monitoring.

High velocity and exhaustive data have been part of the physical sciences for quite some time with respect to oceanography, meteorology, and earth sciences, where sensors have been deployed to measure waves, temperature, or earthquakes. Such data are now becoming more widespread, with big data being generated across a whole range of domains of interest to geographers, being used to monitor and sense the environment, and to mediate and deliver services and products. Much of the big data produced are inherently spatial data, given that the technologies that generate them automatically add georeferenced attributes (e.g., coordinates calculated using GPS or other forms of addressing). Sources of georeferenced big data include mobile phones, smartphone apps, smart meters and utilities, logistics systems, environmental monitoring, sensor networks, navigation systems, autonomous cars and heavy machinery, social media sites, travel and accommodation websites, online and offline financial transactions, surveillance and security systems, and emergency services. In many cases, the data are exhaust in nature – a by-product of systems – which can then be used to examine a variety of issues. For example, georeferenced social media data, such as Twitter, were not produced for the purposes of modelling mobility or sentiment patterns, but they are now often used in this way.

In addition to big data, there is improved access to traditional datasets as they become increasingly digitised and shared. For example, millions of documents, books, statistical surveys, public administration records, photographs, analog sound recordings and films are being transferred to digital media. In addition, local and traditional knowledge that was normally transmitted aurally by indigenous peoples is also now being digitized and mapped (Taylor and Lauriault, 2014). These media can be combined to scale the scope of analysis, are searchable in new ways, and are open to the application of big data analytics such as data mining, pattern recognition, data visualization, statistics, and modelling. As such, data analysis that was once difficult or time-consuming to perform by hand and/or required using analog technologies becomes possible in just a few microseconds, enabling more complex analysis to be undertaken. Consider, for example, the computational power now found in most smartphones. Moreover, these data are more and more being made available through new data infrastructures and cloud storage platforms and thus are open to be used in geographical research.

DATA INFRASTRUCTURES, OPEN DATA, AND APIS

Given the effort and cost of producing good quality data, traditional datasets were considered a valuable commodity, often either jealously guarded or expensively traded. Most social science data generated by academics were not archived or shared. Public administration and state data, and data generated by statistical agencies, could largely only be accessed through visiting archives and often only with special permission. Access to data to undertake geographical research was therefore problematic. The internet, new archiving technologies, a massive expansion in digital data storage, data standards, and open science and open data movements have transformed data access.

The collection and storage of data have been, and continue to be, both informal and formal in nature. The informal approach consists simply of gathering data and storing them, and might best be described as data holdings or backups. Many academics have informal collections of data from their research stored on their computers and backed up on external media such as a datastick or personal cloud. These data generally lack curation and metadata, and are usually difficult to make sense of by anyone other than the person who produced them. The formal approach is much more professional in orientation, consisting of a set of curatorial practices and institutional structures that creates and manages an archive (Lauriault et al., 2007). Digital data archives or trusted digital repositories explicitly seek to be long-term endeavours, preserving the full record set – data, metadata, and associated documentation – for future reuse. Increasingly, academics are being encouraged, or compelled by funding agencies, to adopt data management plans and are lodging the digital data from their research in archives.

A data infrastructure is a digital means for storing, sharing, linking together, and consuming data holdings and archives across the internet. Over the past two decades, considerable effort has been expended on creating a variety of related science and research data infrastructures: catalogues, directories, portals, clearinghouses, and repositories (Lauriault et al., 2007). These terms are often used interchangeably, though they are slightly different types of entities. Catalogues, directories, and portals are centralized resources that may detail and link to individual data archives (e.g., the Earth Observation Data Management Service of the Canada Centre for Remote Sensing), or data collections held by individual institutions (e.g., the Australian National Data Service), or are federated infrastructures which provide the means to access the collections held by many institutions (e.g., the US National Sea Ice Data Center). They might provide fairly detailed inventories of the datasets held, and may act as metadata aggregators, but do not necessarily host the data (e.g., the GeoConnections Discovery Portal). Single-site repositories host all the datasets in a single site, accessible through a web interface, though they may maintain back-up or mirror sites in multiple locations (e.g., the UK Data Archive). A federated data repository or clearinghouse can be a shared place for storing and accessing data (e.g., NASA's Global Change Master Directory). It might provide some data services in terms of search and retrieval, and data management and processing, but each holding or archive has been produced independently and may not share data formats, standards, metadata, and policies. Nevertheless, the repository seeks to ensure that each archive meets a set of requirement specifications and uses audit and certification to ensure data integrity and trust among users (Dasish, 2012).

A cyber-infrastructure is more than a collection of digital archives and repositories. It consists of a suite of dedicated networked technologies, shared services (relating to data management and processing), analysis tools such as data visualizations (e.g., graphing and mapping apps), metadata and sharing standards (e.g., ISO19115, web map services (WMS), web feature services (WFS), semantic interoperability and structured vocabularies, and shared policies (concerning access, use, intellectual property rights, etc.) which enable data to be distributed, linked together, and analysed (Cyberinfrastructure Council, 2007). Such cyber-infrastructures include those implemented by national statistical agencies and national or international spatial data infrastructures (SDIs) that require all data stored and shared to comply with defined parameters in order to maximize data interoperability and ensure data quality, fidelity, and integrity that promote trust. The objectives of SDIs are to ensure that users from multiple sectors and jurisdictions can seamlessly reuse these data and link them into their systems. The Arctic Spatial Data Infrastructure, for example, aligns with global, regional, and national geospatial data contexts such as the Infrastructure for Spatial Information in Europe, the United Nations Committee of Experts on Global Geospatial Information Management, Global Earth Observation System of Systems and the Canadian Geospatial Data Infrastructure; is open data; is International Standards Organization and Open Geospatial Consortium standards based; and is an official spatial data collaboration between Canada, Denmark, Finland, Iceland, Norway, Russia, Sweden, and the USA.

The benefits of creating data infrastructures include the following: ready access to more data; the data have improved quality and integrity through the adoption of standards, protocols, and policies; combining datasets can produce new insights; there are scales of economy through sharing resources and avoiding replication; and there is improved return on investment for research funders by enabling data reuse. Indeed, data infrastructures have become a significant source of secondary and tertiary data for geography scholars, significantly increasing the ease and speed of access to useful data.

Nonetheless, there are still access issues with respect to both traditional and big data. Traditional data produced by academia, public institutions, non-governmental organizations, and private entities can be restricted in use to defined personnel or be available only for a fee or under license. In recent years there has been an attempt to change this situation by making data produced using funding from the public purse open in nature. Pollock (2006) contends that 'data is open if anyone is free to use, reuse, and redistribute it – subject only, at most, to the requirement to attribute and/or share-alike'. There are, however, different understandings as to what openness means, with some open data archives having some restrictions with respect to use and reuse, reworking, and redistribution. Many jurisdictions now have open data repositories that make some of their administrative and operational data freely available for analysis and reuse, thus fostering transparency and accountability in public services and enabling the creating of an open data economy. However, there is a wide variation in how extensive these repositories are, and many are little more than data dumps, more like data holdings than archives in their organization and operation (Lauriault and Francoli, 2017). Similarly, there has been a strong drive to promote open science in which the data generated from publicly funded research is made available for reuse, sharing the data via institutional repositories or dedicated disciplinary data infrastructures (Borgman, 2015).

The situation with respect to private companies is somewhat different. Data produced by companies are valuable assets that produce products for profit and provide competitive advantage. Consequently, companies are often reluctant to openly share their data with others. Since big data are predominately produced by the private sector, access to them is usually restricted, available for a fee, and/or subject to proprietary licensing. In some cases, a limited amount of the data might be made available to researchers or the public through application programming interfaces (APIs). For example, Twitter allows a few companies to access its firehose (stream of data) for a fee for commercial purposes, but researchers are restricted to a 'gardenhose' (about 10 percent of public tweets), a 'spritzer' (about 1 percent of public tweets), or different subsets of content ('white-listed' accounts) (boyd and Crawford, 2012). One consequence of limited access to big data in geography and academia more broadly is that some datasets, such as Twitter, Flickr, and Instagram, receive disproportionate attention, sometimes being repurposed to examine issues for which they are ill-suited (Kitchin et al., 2017).

It should also be noted that, while data infrastructures can improve the quality and usability of a dataset, data quality – how clean (error- and gap-free), objective (bias-free), and consistent (few discrepancies) the data are – and veracity – the extent to which they accurately (precision) and faithfully (fidelity, reliability) represent what they are meant to – remain significant issues. And while some have argued that big data do not need to meet the same standards of data quality and veracity as traditional data because their exhaustive nature removes sampling biases and compensates for any errors, gaps, or inconsistencies in the data or weakness in fidelity (Mayer-Schönberger and Cukier, 2013), the maxim 'garbage in, garbage out' still holds. Indeed, big data can be full of dirty (through instrument bias), fake (through false accounts), or biased (due to the non-representative nature of the demographic being measured) data, or be data with poor fidelity and constitute weak proxies (the data are often exhaust and are being repurposed) (Crampton et al., 2013). A number of experiments conducted by national statistical agencies to assess the suitability of a number of big data sources for official reporting purposes (e.g., debit cards and credit cards for household spending) have demonstrated that while some big data sources can augment knowledge, these data cannot replace existing approaches because of data quality issues, standards, completeness, privacy issues, costs, proprietary ownership, and sustainability (Vale, 2015). When using digital data for geographic analysis, therefore, it is important to consider the integrity and fitness for purpose of the data (Miller and Goodchild, 2015). The data deluge might lead to enormous quantities of data with which to make sense of the world, but that does not mean that they will automatically lead to greater insights. Sometimes it is more profitable to work a narrow seam of high quality data than to open-pit mine a dirty deposit.

CRITICAL DATA STUDIES AND GEOGRAPHIC SCHOLARSHIP

Corresponding to what has been termed the 'data revolution' or 'data deluge' has been a more sustained analytical and critical focus on data, databases, data infrastructures, and how they are produced and employed. While there has long been some critical attention applied to data, in the main this has been concerned with technical issues such as quality, interoperability, and representativeness, rather than the politics and praxes of data generation, processing, analysis, and application. Instead, the theoretical and analytical focus has been targeted at the production and use of information and knowledge. Data were largely cast as pre-analytic and pre-factual in nature, that which exists prior to interpretation and argument – that is, they are benign, neutral, objective, and non-ideological in essence, capturing the world as it is subject to technical constraints (Gitelman and Jackson, 2013). In other words, it is only the uses of data that are political, not the data themselves.

Critical data studies takes the politics and praxes of data as its central concern. Drawing on critical social theory, it posits that data are never simply neutral, objective, independent, raw representations of the world, but rather are situated, contingent, relational, contextual, and do active work in the world. Data are constitutive of the ideas, techniques, technologies, people, systems, and contexts that conceive, produce, process, manage, and analyse them (Bowker, 2005). In other words, data do not pre-exist their generation; they do not arise from nowhere and their generation is not inevitable. Their generation, processing, and analysis are shaped by protocols, standards, measurement processes, design decisions, disciplinary norms, and institutional politics, and their use is framed contextually to try and achieve certain aims and goals. As Gitelman and Jackson (2013: 2) put it, 'raw data is an oxymoron' as 'data are always already cooked'.

Similarly, databases and repositories are not simply neutral, technical means of assembling and sharing data. Rather, they are complex socio-technical systems that are embedded within a larger institutional and political landscape, shaped by institutional and organizational cultures and practices, systems of thought, financial regimes, and legal and regulatory requirements (Ruppert, 2012; Kitchin, 2014). As we can attest from personal experience, creating and running a repository involves a lot of institutional, political, and personnel work – negotiating, debating, cajoling, lobbying, and wheeling-and-dealing – with a number of stakeholders. Moreover, databases and repositories are expressions of knowledge/power, shaping what questions can be asked, how they are asked, how they are answered, how the answers are deployed, and who can ask them (Ruppert, 2012).

Critical data studies seeks to unpack how data are always already cooked, and how they are constitutive of power/knowledge. As the field has emerged, it has sought to examine a range of related processes and issues. For example, there are now a number of studies that have sought to: document the data practices utilized to handle and store data; chart the politics of open data and of sharing and accessing data repositories; detail the genealogies, temporalities, and spatialities of datasets and archives; uncover the workings and economies of data markets and the commercial trading of data; plot the governmentalities that shape the generation and use of data; and examine and debate the ethics of producing, sharing, and extracting value and utility from data (see the journal *Big Data & Society*). In addition to critical data scholars, some First Nations groups are advancing the concept of 'data sovereignty' (Phillips, 2017), whereby First Nations and Inuit are demanding that data about them be returned, are questioning data indicators models that claim to measure their health and well-being (which, in fact, measure ills rather than resiliency, indigenous knowledge assets, and community health), and are revisiting the power/knowledge of researcher and research subject when it comes to data collected about them and their local and traditional knowledge. In Canada, the First Nations Information Governance Council's principles of ownership, control, access and possession and the collective licensing of local and traditional knowledge (Canadian Internet Policy and Public Interest Clinic, 2016) are two examples of this fledgling movement.

Geographers have been at the forefront of developing the field of critical data studies. For example, in an influential position paper, Dalton and Thatcher (2014) set out seven provocations needed to provide a comprehensive critique of the new regimes of data:

1. Situate data regimes in time and space.
2. Expose data as inherently political and whose interests they serve.
3. Unpack the complex, non-deterministic relationship between data and society.
4. Illustrate the ways in which data are never raw.
5. Expose the fallacies that data can speak for themselves and that big data will replace small data.
6. Explore how new data regimes can be used in socially progressive ways.
7. Examine how academia engages with new data regimes and the opportunities of such engagement.

In terms of operationalizing these provocations, Kitchin (2014) has suggested unpacking what he terms 'data assemblages', while Kitchin and Lauriault (2018) discuss Michel Foucault's idea of the 'dispositif' and Ian Hacking's 'dynamic nominalism' to make sense of the politics and praxes of data production and use. Crampton et al. (2013) outline the shortcomings of spatial big data and associated data analytics and forward an alternative epistemology. Leszczynski and Crampton (2016) outline what they term 'data anxieties'; that is, a paradoxical concern that spatial big data are simultaneously insufficient for tasks at hand, while also being excessive and over-sufficient. Shelton (2017) details the politics and ethics of big data in underpinning urban science and new urban imaginaries. GIScience scholars, such as Harvey Miller and Michael Goodchild (2015), have been critically and empirically examining data-driven geography. And there are numerous other contributions.

These accounts draw to a large degree on critical GIS scholarship that has sought to expose the politics of GIS and their deployment, and to formulate and practise a more situated and reflexive form of GIScience (which itself is rooted in feminist critiques of science) (Schuurman, 2000). The latter behoves GIS practitioners to explicitly recognize and account for their positionality (with respect to their knowledge, experience, beliefs, and aspirations), how their research and practices are framed within disciplinary debates and institutional politics and ambitions, how their data are cooked and hold certain characteristics (relating to cleanliness, completeness, consistency, veracity, and fidelity), and how their analytical methods have opportunities and pitfalls that affect methods, models, findings, and interpretations. We believe all geographical scholarship should be mindful of such epistemological considerations. In other words, in practising digital geography – generating or sourcing digital data from data infrastructures and using digital methods – one should critically reflect on and account for their politics and praxes. This is not to say that all digital geography should be undertaking critical data studies, but rather that it takes heed of its ontological, epistemological, and ethical observations.

Acknowledgements

The research for this chapter was enabled by a European Research Council Advanced Investigator Award, 'The Programmable City' (ERC-2012-AdG-323636). The chapter draws on two previously published papers: Kitchin, R. and Lauriault, T. 2015 and 2018.

REFERENCES

Borgman, C. (2015) *Big Data, Little Data, No Data: Scholarship in the Networked World.* Cambridge, MA: MIT Press.
Bowker, G. (2005) *Memory Practices in the Sciences.* Cambridge, MA: MIT Press.
boyd, d. and Crawford, K. (2012) 'Critical questions for big data', *Information, Communication and Society*, 15(5): 662–679.
Canadian Internet Policy and Public Interest Clinic (2016) 'A proposal: An open licensing scheme for traditional knowledge'. Available online: https://cippic.ca/en/TK_Open_Licensing_Proposal (accessed 1 February 2018).
Crampton, J., Graham, M., Poorthuis, A., Shelton, T., Stephens, M., Wilson, M.W. and Zook, M. (2013) 'Beyond the geotag: Situating "big data" and leveraging the potential of the geoweb', *Cartography and Geographic Information Science*, 40(2): 130–139.
Cyberinfrastructure Council (2007) Cyberinfrastructure vision for 21st century discovery. Available online: www.nsf.gov/pubs/2007/nsf0728/index.jsp?org=EEC%20National%20Science%20Foundation (accessed 1 February 2018).

Dalton, C. and Thatcher, J. (2014) 'What does a critical data studies look like, and why do we care?'. *Society and Space*, 12 May. Available online: http://societyandspace.org/2014/05/12/what-does-a-critical-data-studies-look-like-and-why-do-we-care-craig-dalton-and-jim-thatcher (accessed 1 February 2018).

Dasish (2012) 'Roadmap for preservation and curation in the social sciences and humanities'. Available online: http://dasish.eu/publications/projectreports/D4.1_-_Roadmap_for_Preservation_and_Curation_in_the_SSH.pdf (accessed 1 February 2018).

Edwards, P. (2010) *A Vast Machine: Computer Models, Climate Data, and the Politics of Global Warming*. Cambridge, MA: MIT Press.

Gitelman, L. and Jackson, V. (2013) 'Introduction', in L. Gitelman (ed.), *'Raw Data' is an Oxymoron*. Cambridge, MA: MIT Press. pp. 1–14.

Grier, D.A. (2007) *When Computers Were Human*. Princeton, NJ: Princeton University Press.

Kitchin, R. (2014) *The Data Revolution: Big Data, Open Data, Data Infrastructures and their Consequences*. London: Sage.

Kitchin, R. and Lauriault, T. (2015) 'Small data in the era of big data', *GeoJournal*, 80(4): 463–475.

Kitchin, R. and Lauriault, T.P. (2018) 'Towards critical data studies: Charting and unpacking data assemblages and their work', in J. Eckert, A. Shears and J. Thatcher (eds), *Geoweb and Big Data*. Lincoln: University of Nebraska Press. pp. 3–20.

Kitchin, R. and McArdle, G. (2016) 'What makes big data, big data? Exploring the ontological characteristics of 26 datasets', *Big Data & Society*, 3(1). DOI: 10.1177/2053951716631130.

Kitchin, R., Lauriault, T.P. and Wilson, M. (eds) (2017) *Understanding Spatial Media*. London: Sage.

Lauriault, T.P. and Francoli, M. (2017) 'Openness, transparency, participation', in R. Kitchin, T.P. Lauriault and M.W. Wilson (eds), *Understanding Spatial Media*. London: Sage. pp. 188–203.

Lauriault, T.P., Craig, B.L., Taylor, D.R.F. and Pulsifier, P.L. (2007) 'Today's data are part of tomorrow's research: Archival issues in the sciences', *Archivaria*, 64: 123–179.

Leszczynski, A. and Crampton, J. (2016) 'Introduction: Spatial Big Data and everyday life', *Big Data & Society*, 3(2). DOI: 10.1177/2053951716661366.

Mayer-Schönberger, V. and Cukier, K. (2013) *Big Data: A Revolution that will Change How We Live, Work and Think*. London: John Murray.

Miller, H.J. (2010) 'The data avalanche is here: Shouldn't we be digging?', *Journal of Regional Science*, 50(1): 181–201.

Miller, H.J. and Goodchild, M.F. (2015) 'Data-driven geography', *GeoJournal*, 80: 449–461.

Phillips, G.W. (2017) 'Indigenous data sovereignty and reconciliation', opening keynote address, Data Power Conference, Ottawa, Canada.

Pollock, R. (2006) 'The value of the public domain'. Institute of Public Policy Research, London. Available online: www.ippr.org/files/images/media/files/publication/2011/05/value_of_public_domain_1526.pdf (accessed 1 February 2018).

Poovey, M. (1998) *A History of the Modern Fact: Problems of Knowledge in the Sciences of Wealth and Society*. Chicago: University of Chicago Press.

Rosenberg, D. (2013) 'Data before the fact', in L. Gitelman (ed.), *'Raw Data' is an Oxymoron*. Cambridge, MA: MIT Press. pp 15–40.

Ruppert, E. (2012) 'The governmental topologies of database devices', *Theory, Culture & Society*, 29: 116–136.

Schuurman, N. (2000) Critical GIS: Theorizing an emerging science. PhD dissertation, University of British Columbia. Available online: https://open.library.ubc.ca/cIRcle/collections/ubctheses/831/items/1.0089782 (accessed 1 February 2018).

Shelton, T. (2017) 'The urban geographical imagination in the age of Big Data', *Big Data & Society*, 4(1). DOI: 10.1177/2053951716665129.

Taylor, D.R.F. and Lauriault, T.P. (2014) *Developments in the Theory and Practice of Cybercartography*. Amsterdam: Elsevier Science.

Vale, S. (2015) 'International collaboration to understand the relevance of Big Data for official statistics', *Statistical Journal of the IAOS*, 31: 158–163. Available online: https://statswiki.unece.org/display/bigdata/International+collaboration+to+understand+the+relevance+of+Big+Data+for+Official+Statistics+2015 (accessed 1 February 2018).

9

QUALITATIVE METHODS AND GEOHUMANITIES

Meghan Cope

INTRODUCTION: ON BEING COINCIDENT

The development of cheaper, faster, and more powerful digital tools, and the way they have fed the 'digital turn', has been largely contemporaneous with the (re)activation of qualitative research in geography. While qualitative research has always been important in the discipline, the period since the late 1990s has seen a deepening and diversification of the use of, and critical reflection upon, qualitative methods; this lines up coincidentally with the evolution of the internet, smartphones, and instantaneous global connectivity, making for a productive convergence.

This chapter examines the intersections between qualitative methods and digital geographies, particularly along two underlying themes: *practice*, looking at how digital tools have been adopted and adapted for qualitative data collection, analysis, and representation (including visualizations); and *meanings*, to help us understand digital lives, digital worlds, and new social/spatial engagements. I examine the mutual conditioning of digital techniques and the revitalization of qualitative geographies, qualitative GIS, and an emerging 'digital/spatial/geo-humanities', while identifying specialized resources on related debates and subfields. In the final section, I draw from my own work on two youth geography projects, separated by a decade, to demonstrate emerging shifts in the practice and meanings of digital qualitative geographies, and propose several future developments to watch.

HISTORICAL CONTEXT AND MAIN DEBATES

Geography has always had a strong tradition of qualitative research, but in the past two decades the practice of qualitative methods *and* a growing critical reflection on those practices have resulted in a robust set of methodological and epistemological developments. This can be traced, in part, to the 'critical turn' in geography from the 1970s onwards, whereby issues of social justice, diverse standpoints, and a shift in ontology (what can be known about the world) led activist scholars to develop diverse methods in line with social and political goals of equity, justice, and relevance (see Aitken and Valentine, 2006, for a detailed overview). Similarly, as traced by Corrigan (2015), humanists and phenomenologists in geography have explored the creation and meanings of place, landscape, poetics, and power for decades, using textual and visual interrogations to discern meanings. With solid critical foundations in both the social science and humanities sides of geography, and a mid-1990s critique of spatial science (Pickles, 1995), it is no surprise that the first editions of what are now essential guidebooks for qualitative methods in geography were published around the turn of the millennium. Similarly, the Qualitative Research Specialty Group of the American Association of Geographers was founded in 2000 when sufficient demand for an intellectual forum was recognized. Subsequent editions of most of the guidebooks, as well as new volumes (e.g., DeLyser et al., 2010; Gomez and Jones, 2010) and substantial journal publishing in qualitative geographies, have created a much richer library and platform for debate, inquiry, and scholarly development in qualitative geography.

The recent expansion of qualitative geography has been aided by the expansion of user-friendly tools for data collection, analysis, and representation: as new digital tools and capacities have been developed, the potential for examining "geographies produced *through*, produced *by*, and *of* the digital" (Ash et al., 2018: 27; emphasis in original) has been equally captivating to ethnographers as to quantitative modellers. In terms of (qualitative) geographies produced *through* the digital, the tools of qualitative data collection have been rapidly digitized, including digital voice recorders and cameras for interviews and focus groups, scanners for hand-drawn materials, online survey tools for open-ended responses, smartphone apps with GPS for participant diaries (travel, food, activity, etc.), and optical character recognition for digitizing the riches of the archive and making them searchable. This digitization has been incremental, unevenly adopted, and not without a certain amount of handwringing by practitioners who worry about losing something along the way – perhaps a sense of intimacy with one's data? In addition to shifting the tools of data *collection* practice, the 'digital turn' has also had significant impact on *analysis*, such as in mixed reactions of researchers to computer-aided qualitative data analysis software (see Watson and Till, 2010).

But this is not just the digitization of traditional methods of inquiry; rather, we are also seeing new techniques and approaches to qualitative information that is 'born digital', indicative of 'geographies produced *by* the digital'. These include exploring the content and geolocation of tweets (Jung, 2015; Poorthuis et al., 2016), the gendered nature of OpenStreetMap entries (Stephens, 2013) and of 'new spatial media' (Leszczynski and Elwood, 2014), and enrolling volunteered geographic information in the analysis of digitally mediated daily life (Sui et al., 2013). While many of these practices involve the *quantification* of data, there are also many qualitative operations here, such as evaluating gender bias, investigating community perceptions of 'risk', and exploring the diverse experiences, emotions, and motivations of social actors.

Finally, qualitative geographies *of* the digital may follow several threads. Consider the geographies of the physical operations that involve the capital funding, research and development, and the material production of digital technologies, fibre-optic networks, and satellite communications, which are not distillable to solely quantitative measures (Zook, 2005). Qualitative geographies *of* the digital are also seen in online and virtual worlds, through gamers' experiences of – and command over – digital environments, and in 'augmented reality' expeditions (Rutherford and Bose, 2013). Lastly, as scholars of society and space, we must attend to the ways in which digital devices and their networks (including 'smart' consumer goods such as thermostats that know when we are on our way home), computers, the internet, *and* the software code that enables them all, have shifted everyday geographic practices towards increasingly 'digital lives'. As Kitchin and Dodge (2011) argue, much of this is unseen yet vitally important to the production of *spatiality*. Qualitative digital geographies are needed to interrogate and make sense of how we produce, experience, and *know* emerging digital worlds.

The phrase 'digital geographies' conjures up the image of a computer-generated map. Indeed, as Wilson (2017) has shown, the evolution of what is now GIS was both dependent on *and* a stimulus for early digital technologies. The origin story of critical GIS (and its permutations, including qualitative GIS and public participation GIS) has been skilfully recounted in multiple places, so it will not be reviewed here (see Schuurmann, 2004; Wilson, 2017). GIS is not solely limited to the storage, analysis, and display of *quantitative* (i.e., numerical) data: numerous authors and projects have demonstrated the inherent openness of GIS to diverse data sources, the possibilities of weaving non-numerical data into the GIS itself, blending representations of quantitative and qualitative data in various digital ways, and creating analytical practices that allow different types of geographic data to rub up against each other, whether they are contradictory or serve to raise – and answer – new questions in complementary ways. These practices, as well as the abundant developments in online 'mashups' from both vernacular and research-based users, have shifted the way we think about who can map what, and thus have led to a simultaneous democratization of cartography *and* anxieties among experts about validity, 'truth', and rigour in the production of spatial visualizations.

However, as DeLyser and Sui (2014) argue in their review of qualitative and quantitative geographies in the digital age, emerging experimental cartographies represent a healthy exploration of techniques and perspectives, and a revitalization of the underlying conceptual questions of how humans engage with, produce, represent, and imagine space(s). With new tools, new ways of 'knowing', and new rhythms and practices of social, political, and economic life, qualitative digital geographies are well positioned for robust research. While such optimism is commendable, however, the demand for fresh perspectives is also necessitated in this investigation of digital life. Rose (2017: 779) argues, for example, that 'posthuman agency [is] always already co-constituted with technologies', suggesting that 'geographers must reconfigure their understanding of digitally mediated cities and acknowledge the inventiveness and diversity of urban posthuman agency'. Similarly, Leszczynski (2017: 1–2) proposes employing the 'wicked tensions' of triangulation and representativeness to 'address the ways in which the proliferation of digital materialities and practices both opens up exciting opportunities for research while also posing challenges to precisely this endeavour of meaningfully knowing and making sense of the world'. This duality of opportunity and critique guarantees a future for qualitative digital geographies, particularly as 'we're all digital [scholars] now' (Mullen, 2010).

DIGITAL/SPATIAL/GEO-HUMANITIES

New technologies and their uses in scholarship can spark new names for fields of study, even if those fields of study have a long-standing pre-digital existence. In preparing this chapter, I came to see some broad tendencies in the various terms captured in this subheading, and I make an attempt to define them here. First, 'digital humanities' has diverse meanings and is hotly contested, but basically suggests the use of digital technologies (often including quantification and heavy computational operations) to perform a range of tasks, from finding new patterns in thousands of pages of text to analysing social media using humanities approaches (Gold, 2012). In digital humanities, the debates that have raged pivot on questions such as 'whether Digital Humanities offers better ways of realizing traditional Humanities goals or has the capacity to change understandings of Humanities goals altogether' (Foley and Murphy, 2015). The humanities' 'spatial turn' generates new attention to space, place, scale, and other geographic themes, and, not surprisingly, these researchers often employ geospatial technologies and GIS. To that extent, geography has often been invoked, but few digital humanities scholars write from what might be considered a 'spatial perspective'.

Related to this, 'spatial humanities' seems to largely originate from spatial history, historical GIS, and the work of scholars involved in adopting map-related techniques in representing historical data (both quantitative and, increasingly, qualitative; see Gregory and Geddes, 2014). While researchers in this area are embracing the 'spatial turn' of humanities disciplines and animating the use of GIS in novel ways, much of the work in the spatial humanities seems to consider geography's utility to be in the tools of its trade, rather than, say, expanding critical cultural geography or historical geography's theorizing of time and space, though some work on 'deep maps' and 'spatial narratives' provides fertile ground for such theorizing (Bodenhamer et al., 2015). There is simultaneously a growing sense that visualization programs of various types that are distinctly not GIS, such as Neatline, StoryMapJS, and Adobe Illustrator, hold distinct advantages in many circumstances. As Knowles et al. (2015: 239) point out:

> Narrative mapping and the notion of deep maps both reflect a hunger to represent the meaning of place as we experience it – as an immersive, sensorily stimulating environment that is constantly changing (Massey, 1997). Although the reference systems that undergird GIS and cartography make it possible to combine source material of many kinds related to that particular place (one of the oft-noted powers of GIS), the representational models on which they are based hinder our ability to perceive and express how people experience place and space.

Third, the term 'geo-humanities' appears to have emerged as the home-grown winner among geographers themselves, represented by the eponymous publication edited by Dear et al. (2011) and the new journal, *GeoHumanities: Space, Place, and the Humanities*, produced by the American Association of Geographers, starting in 2015. In the journal, there is a clear critical spatial perspective and deep provenance of considering place and space as *primary*, rather than as a backdrop, a contextual frame of reference, or as presented via the silver platter of GIS. Cresswell (2014) states that geo-humanities represents 'a new interdisciplinary endeavor with space and place *at its heart* that links decades of critical thought following the spatial turn to new developments in our digital capabilities', yet he is also careful to trace the long-standing connections between geography and humanities, regardless of and prior to the digital capabilities of GIS (Cresswell, 2016). Similarly, the body of work presently framed as geohumanities already has a critical GIS edge, knows its deconstruction, and has embedded within it the feminist and postcolonial humanist work that prepared the field for openings into art, narrative, creativity, playfulness, juxtaposition, and experimentation (Dear et al., 2011). Thus, one might make the distinction that digital humanities and spatial humanities have digital technologies at the core of their practice, while geo-humanities has place and spatiality at the core of its theory and practice, and may or may not engage with the digital. As Peta Mitchell (in Hawkins et al., 2015: 228) succinctly states: "Although a broadly conceived GeoHumanities must take account of and engage with these spatiotechnological emergences and affordances ... it must take care not to be subsumed within a digital media/digital humanities/big data agenda that, when approached uncritically or superficially, could lead to a "restricted spatiality" (Crang, 2015) that renders space inert".

Two underlying questions continue to resonate here, and may help to distinguish these fields. First, is the goal of the research to catalogue places or movement through space (space as static backdrop or tableau), or is it to deconstruct the intersecting influences of society and space through spatially enhanced interpretation (space as produced and remade through interactions; see Crang, 2015)? Second, and related, is GIS simply a digital tool employed to reveal patterns and insights, parallel to the scraping of digitized texts for new patterns and the associated analysis by algorithm, or is a spatial perspective embraced/interrogated in a way that reflects (and possibly shifts) the ontology and epistemology of the field?

GEOGRAPHIES OF CHILDHOOD AND YOUTH

Here I draw from two of my own research projects, separated by a decade, to elucidate both the changes over time and some challenges of exploring the relationship between digital geographies and qualitative methods. When I started working in children's geographies in the early 2000s, many of the shifts noted above were in their own infancy. The Children's Urban Geographies project in Buffalo, NY (2001–2005) examined children's conceptualizations of urban space and involved many entry points for 'the digital', though they were generally opportunistic and somewhat uncritical adoptions of technology (the project is described in detail elsewhere: Cope, 2008). I review some of these intersections of digital technologies, participatory qualitative approaches, and the geographies of childhood as they emerged in that project, and then bring the empirical setting forward to another engagement with young people, in 2012, in which teen mobility was explored with more conscious attention to the role of the digital (Cope and Lee, 2016). In both projects my research team developed new digital techniques to blend qualitative data with spatial data.

In the Children's Urban Geographies project, digital approaches were part of a larger suite of tools woven into the overall goals: to learn more about the *place* of the Lower West Side of Buffalo, particularly as related to children's experiences, and to invite children to share their existing geographic knowledge and perspectives with us. We used publicly available data to map the usual cadre of neighbourhood data using GIS to become more familiar with the local area and serve as visual and contextual backdrops for participatory work.

Beyond GIS, we used digital devices, such as GPS units, digital cameras, audio recorders, and computers, with participating children to *generate* data. We were inspired by the analog children's geographies of the Detroit Geographical Expeditions (Bunge, 2011 [1971]) and digital pioneers in youth geographies such as Wridt (2004). For example, we asked children to take photos of meaningful things with digital cameras (very new in the early 2000s!) and annotate and geotag the JPG files. We taught children to use GPS units and they led neighbourhood walks while taking handwritten notes about interesting features, which we then superimposed on air photos of the area (see Cope, 2008, for an example). Using digital audio recorders, children narrated their own ghost stories about local places for a 'radio show'. One graduate student helped children find their own houses on *Google Earth*, recording their reactions to seeing a bird's-eye view of a familiar place for the first time. And we combined field excursions with photos, maps, drawings, and video to document and represent the existing conditions and the hoped-for futures of the neighbourhood through various media. These child-generated data, spatial visualizations, conversations with children, and ethnographic field observations were analysed, curated, and narrated through various media constituting exploratory digital qualitative practices. The nature of the project in turn sparked several new technological approaches: the 'imagined grid' of my PhD student, Jin-Kyu Jung, allowed him to integrate photos and other non-quantitative data directly into a visual display of a GIS rendering of demographic data (see Jung, 2009); and the iterative strategy of 'grounded visualization' that another PhD student, Ladona Knigge, and I developed allowed us to generate new digital/qualitative analyses (Knigge and Cope, 2006). The technologies we brought in not only served as a social lubricant and ice-breaker with children, but also helped generate data and develop new techniques, allowing us to jointly explore – and construct – an emerging digital geography of Buffalo childhood.

Fast-forward to 2012 and a very different project and youth population: mostly white, middle-class high school teens in suburban and rural Vermont who were plotting out their own digital geographies by combining information and communication technology with their social and material networks in order to maximize their mobility (Cope and Lee, 2016). We were interested in how teens navigate everyday life in low-density settlement areas, specifically how they managed to get from A to B without access to a car (and what difference it made when they did have a car and their driving licenses). Access to and use of cellphones clearly made a difference in teens' ability to get rides, meet up with friends, make it to work on time, and coordinate their days. While other authors had looked at how teens' cellphones eased parental concerns (e.g., Pain et al., 2005), we were also interested in the increasingly 'digital lives' of teens. We developed a new research technique called 'text review', where teens looked through their chats, direct messages, and texts on their phones and verbally recounted to us those that involved a transportation issue. Through this, we not only were able to use the digital device (phone) to *collect* data, but also gained insight into the increasingly pervasive dependence both teens and their families had on being able to connect instantly.

Projects such as these offer a view into the rapidly shifting, recursive changes wrought by both the use of digital tools in collecting and analysing data (practice) and the increasing focus on the nature and constitution of digital lives and worlds (meanings). The realm of digital youth geographies is worthy of continued attention because we are already dealing with a human population that itself was 'born digital': they have no recollection of a time before instantly and fully accessible information and communication, so not only are their everyday movements, interactions, and (Snap)chats fully logged and digitized, but also their own worldviews are already framed as digital ways of being.

POTENTIAL FUTURE DEVELOPMENTS

It is a dangerous business making any kinds of predictions of 'what's next' in a digital field, but a few emerging trends seem noteworthy. First, on the 'practice' side of qualitative digital geographies, methods of incorporating non-numerical data (text, photos, sound clips) will continue to be seamlessly woven into visualizations such as maps, charts, and timelines, and the boundaries between these will break down. New possibilities are constantly being developed from the spatially referenced GIS side (e.g., ArcGIS's Story Map functions) and from the data analysis and visualization world (e.g., mapping functions in JMP, Atlas.ti, and NVivo, and open-source cartographic display tools; see a concise review at http://dirtdirectory.org/categories/mapping). The question remains whether at some point these will converge into low-cost, easy-to-use platforms that contain both powerful mapping/visualization *and* robust qualitative data storage and analysis capabilities.

A second issue in the realm of practice involves the sticky issue of providing readers access to qualitative data in real-time. Elman and Kapiszewski (2017) are strong advocates for greater transparency in scholarship, recommending that data be 'FAIR': findable, accessible, interoperable, and reusable. They describe a not so distant future in which cheap server space enables fuller transparency of qualitative research by enabling linked, proximate access of readers to the original archival, text, or media-based data. Elman and Kapiszewski recognize potential pitfalls in this practice: researchers would have to be more savvy and responsible in data management, publishers would need to dedicate server capacity and design access mechanisms to meet ethical restrictions, and complex methods of reader authentication and permission would need to be negotiated and systematized to protect human subjects agreements. As a solution, they propose 'annotation for transparent inquiry' (ATI), which involves the collaboration of a data repository, a publisher, and the provision by authors of analytic notes, translations, excerpts, and links to data. Elman and Kapiszewski (2017; emphasis in original) claim, further, that 'the utility of ATI is premised on a counterintuitive observation: *controlling access to data will lead to more data being made accessible*'. I am intrigued by the possibilities of ATI, with its potential for better transparency and the cumulative benefits of shared data, as well as no longer having to limit the space taken by participant quotes in an article. I wonder, though, what such practices will mean for analysis and the construction of interpretations and visualizations if the raw data themselves can be readily linked to and read, as well as for scholars' labour and incompatibilities with present-day peer-review and tenure structures.

Finally, shifting to the 'meanings' portion of digital geographies, and returning to digital youth geographies as a sort of 'indicator species', it is notable that concerns about 'internet addiction' in teens have emerged. According to Cash et al. (2012: 292), who have studied internet addiction, '[a]ll addictions, whether chemical or behavioral, share certain characteristics including salience, compulsive use (loss of control), mood modification and the alleviation of distress, tolerance and withdrawal, and the continuation despite negative consequences'. While the mental health community may debate whether it is the internet itself or related behavioural addictions (e.g., gaming) and disorders such as depression and anxiety, it is clear that dominant internet companies are competing for – and thus desperate to find new ways to hold – our *attention*. Attention is a tricky beast that depends on eyes, but also brainpower, credit cards, and a community. Wilson points out that rather than bemoaning the newest generation's form of (not) paying attention, perhaps we should consider 'an awakening as to how to foster new and shared attention practices' (2015: 188). Qualitative approaches to these new (digital) worlds will surely aid this cause.

REFERENCES

Aitken, S. and Valentine, G. (eds) (2006) *Approaches to Human Geography*. London: Sage.

Ash, J., Kitchin, R. and Leszczynski, A. (2018) 'Digital turn, digital geographies?', *Progress in Human Geography*, 42(1): 25–43.

Bodenhamer, D., Corrigan, J. and Harris, T. (eds) (2015) *Deep Maps and Spatial Narratives*. Bloomington: Indiana University Press.

Bunge, W. (2011) [1971] *Fitzgerald: Geography of a Revolution*. Athens: University of Georgia Press.

Cash, H., Rae, C.D., Steel, A.H. and Winkler, A. (2012) 'Internet addiction: A brief summary of research and practice', *Current Psychiatry Reviews*, 8(4): 292–298.

Cope, M. (2008) 'Patchwork neighborhood: Children's real and imagined geographies in Buffalo, NY', *Environment and Planning, A*, 40: 2845–2863.

Cope, M. and Lee, H.Y. (2016) 'Mobility, communication, and place: Navigating the landscapes of suburban U.S. teens', *Annals of the Association of American Geographers*, 106(2): 311–320.

Corrigan, J. (2015) 'Genealogies of emplacement', in D. Bodenhamer, J. Corrigan and T. Harris (eds), *Deep Maps and Spatial Narratives*. Bloomington: Indiana University Press. pp. 54–71.

Crang, M. (2015) 'The promises and perils of a digital geohumanities', *Cultural Geographies*, 22(3): 351–360.

Cresswell, T. (2014) 'Space, place, and the geohumanities'. Available online: www.northeastern.edu/cssh/humanities/2014/11/space-place-geohumanities (accessed 1 February 2018).

Cresswell, T. (2016) 'Space, place, and geographic thinking in the humanities', Lecture at Center for Geographic Analysis Symposium, Harvard University, Cambridge, MA, 28–29 April. Available online: https://tjcresswell.com/2016/07/27/space-place-and-geographic-thinking-in-the-humanities-video (accessed 1 February 2018).

Dear, M., Ketchum, J., Luria, S. and Richardson, D. (eds) (2011) *GeoHumanities: Art, History, Text at the Edge of Place*. New York: Routledge.

DeLyser, D. and Sui, D. (2014) 'Crossing the qualitative–quantitative chasm III: Enduring methods, open geography, participatory research, and the fourth paradigm', *Progress in Human Geography*, 38(2): 294–307.

DeLyser, D., Herbert, S., Aitken, S., Crang, M. and McDowell, L. (eds) (2010) *The SAGE Handbook of Qualitative Research in Human Geography*. London: Sage.

Elman, C. and Kapiszewski, D. (2017) 'Annotating qualitative social science', *Parameters: Knowledge under Digital Conditions* (SSRC). Available online: http://parameters.ssrc.org/2017/04/annotating-qualitative-social-science (accessed 1 February 2018).

Foley, R. and Murphy, R. (2015) 'Visualizing a spatial archive: GIS, digital humanities, and relational space', *Breac: A Digital Journal of Irish Studies*. Available online: https://breac.nd.edu/articles/visualizing-a-spatial-archive-gis-digital-humanities-and-relational-space (accessed 1 February 2018).

Gold, M.K. (ed.) (2012) *Debates in the Digital Humanities*. Minneapolis: University of Minnesota Press.

Gomez, B. and Jones, J.P. (eds) (2010) *Research Methods in Geography: A Critical Introduction*. Chichester: Wiley-Blackwell.

Gregory, I. and Geddes, A. (eds) (2014) *Toward Spatial Humanities: Historical GIS & Spatial History*. Bloomington: Indiana University Press.

Hawkins, H., Cabeen, L., Callard, F., Castree, N., Daniels, S., DeLyser, D., Munro Neely, H. and Mitchell, P. (2015) 'What might GeoHumanities do? Possibilities, practices, publics, and politics', GeoHumanities, 1(2): 211–232.

Jung, J.-K. (2009) 'Computer-aided qualitative GIS: A software-level integration of qualitative research and GIS', in M. Cope and S. Elwood (eds), *Qualitative GIS: A Mixed Methods Approach*. London: Sage. pp. 115–135.

Jung, J.-K. (2015) 'Code clouds: Qualitative geovisualization of geotweets', *The Canadian Geographer/Le Géographe canadien*, 59(1): 52–68.

Kitchin, R. and Dodge, M. (2011) *Code/Space: Software and Everyday Life*. Cambridge, MA: MIT Press.

Knigge, L. and Cope, M. (2006) 'Grounded visualization: Integrating the analysis of qualitative and quantitative data through grounded theory and geo-visualization', *Environment and Planning A*, 38(11): 2021–2037.

Knowles, A., Westerveld, L. and Strom, L. (2015) 'Inductive visualization: A humanistic alternative to GIS', *GeoHumanities*, 1(2): 233–265.

Leszczynski, A. (2017) 'Digital methods I: Wicked tensions', *Progress in Human Geography*, DOI: 10.1177/0309132517711779.

Leszczynski, A. and Elwood, S. (2014) 'Feminist geographies of new spatial media', *The Canadian Geographer/Le Géographe Canadien*, 59(1): 12–28.

Mullen, L. (2010) 'Digital humanities is a spectrum, or we're all digital humanists now', *The Backward Glance*. Available online: https://lincolnmullen.com/blog/digital-humanities-is-a-spectrum-or-we8217re-all-digital-humanists-now (accessed 1 February 2018).

Pain, R., Grundy, S., Gill, S., Towner, E., Sparks, G. and Hughes, K. (2005) '"So long as I take my mobile": Mobile phones, urban life and geographies of young people's safety', *International Journal of Urban and Regional Research*, 29(4): 814–830.

Pickles, J. (ed.) (1995) *Ground Truth: The Social Implications of Geographic Information Systems*. New York: Guilford Press.

Poorthuis, A., Zook, M., Shelton, T., Graham, M. and Stephens, M. (2016) 'Using geo-tagged digital social data in geographic research', in N. Clifford, M. Cope, T. Gillespie and S. French (eds), *Key Methods in Geography*, 3rd edn. London: Sage. pp. 248–269.

Rose, G. (2017) 'Posthuman agency in the digitally mediated city: Exteriorization, individuation, reinvention', *Annals of the American Association of Geographers*, 107(4): 779–793.

Rutherford, S. and Bose, P. (2013) 'Biopower and play: Bodies, spaces, and nature in digital games', *Aether: The Journal of Media Geography*, 12: 1–29.

Schuurman, N. (2004) *GIS: A Short Introduction*. Oxford: Blackwell.

Stephens, M. (2013) 'Gender and the GeoWeb: Divisions in the production of user-generated cartographic information', *GeoJournal*, 78(6): 981–996.

Sui, D., Elwood, S. and Goodchild, M. (2013) *Crowdsourcing Geographic Knowledge: Volunteered Geographic Information (VGI) in Theory and Practice*. Dordrecht: Springer.

Watson, A. and Till, K. (2010) 'Ethnography and participant observation', in D. DeLyser, S. Herbert, S. Aitken, M. Crang and L. McDowell (eds), *The SAGE Handbook of Qualitative Research in Human Geography*. London: Sage. pp. 121–137.

Wilson, M.W. (2015) 'Paying attention, digital media, and community-based critical GIS', *Cultural Geographies*, 22(1): 177–191.

Wilson, M.W. (2017) *New Lines: Critical GIS and the Trouble of the Map*. Minneapolis: University of Minnesota Press.

Wridt, P. (2004) 'Block politics', *Children's Geographies*, 2: 199–218.

Zook, M. (2005) *The Geography of the Internet Industry: Venture Capital, Dot-coms, and Local Knowledge*. Malden, MA: Blackwell.

10

PARTICIPATORY METHODS AND CITIZEN SCIENCE

Hilary Geoghegan

INTRODUCTION

Digital technologies are changing the ways in which academic and non-academic groups explore, know, and represent the world. Diverse publics are, for example, appropriating social media to expose political tensions (Korson, 2015), mapping their local neighbourhoods to challenge social injustice (Jerrett et al., 2001), and volunteering their time and computing power to professional research projects through the practices of crowdsourcing and citizen science (Haklay, 2013a). While geography has experienced both participatory and digital turns, the links between the two have yet to receive sustained attention. In this chapter, I therefore bring participatory and digital turns into dialogue, exploring where they converge and diverge. I discuss the historical developments towards digital participatory methods through the participatory turn of geographic information science (GIScience), Web 2.0, and citizen science. I highlight some of the key challenges facing researchers working with digital technologies and how similar debates have been addressed by participatory scholars, such as privileging technology over participation, digital divides and inequalities, qualitative and quantitative approaches, and critiques of participation. I conclude with future developments around reflexive practice, participatory methods as ethical commitments, and the sub-disciplinary expansion of digital methods.

PARTICIPATORY AND DIGITAL TURNS

Participatory research involves academic researchers working *with* non-academic communities in order to collaborate and co-produce knowledge. Geographers have been doing this type of work since the 1970s, beginning with Bill Bunge's (1971) expeditions into his local area of Detroit to understand first-hand how global issues affect people's everyday lives. By the late 1990s, participatory research had been identified as a means to 'collapse the boundaries between researcher and researched' (Kitchin and Hubbard, 1999: 195) and as 'an academic praxis that is emancipatory and empowering for the participants in the research' (Fuller and Kitchin, 2004: 3). Central to this approach is the involvement of participants in the research, from defining research questions, identifying methodological approaches, analysing and interpreting data, to communicating and using the findings (Pain, 2009). Work has focused on 'effectively and ethically engaging people in processes, structures, spaces, and decisions that affect their lives, and working with them to achieve equitable and sustainable outcomes on their own terms' (Kindon, 2010: 518). Participatory methods are thus 'political and politicized' (Askins, 2017: 1), and academic interest in them is growing thanks to the rise of engagement, its impact, and widening participation agendas (Harney et al., 2016). If this popularity and its outcomes are not to be regarded as tokenistic by participants or scholars (Newton et al., 2012), researchers must have an appreciation of and commitment to the underlying principles of participatory research.

The 'participatory turn' and the methodologies that followed stemmed from critiques facing human geography relating to decolonization, marginalization, reflexivity, and the crisis of representation (Fuller and Kitchin, 2004). Critical, feminist, and postcolonial geographers argued that research is never value-free, but situated and contingent (England, 1994; Kindon, 1995), and that new approaches to data collection were required (see Fuller and Kitchin, 2004). The desire was to be less extractive and exploitative, exposing traditional hierarchies and distributions of expertise and power, and challenging who does research and whose knowledge counts and in what forms. Today, participatory research relates not only to academic researchers working with communities, but also to people who are taking local issues into their own hands and gathering data, as well as generating digital data based upon their everyday lives and online interactions with others (Purdam, 2014). Human geographers now employ a range of participatory approaches (see Pain and Francis, 2003), including participatory action research (PAR) (mrs kinpaisby, 2008; Kindon, 2010); participatory and public participation geographic information systems (P/PGIS); and, most recently, citizen science (Haklay, 2013b). The latter two approaches are closely linked to the digital turn.

Technological developments over the last 60 years, and the advent of the internet in the early 1990s, have changed the ways in which geographers do geography (Sui and Morrill, 2004). Digital technologies include: the internet; devices such as computers, laptops, smartphones, digital cameras, voice recorders, and e-book readers; social media platforms; various forms of locative and spatial media, including interactive mapping, GIS, and GPS-enabled devices; software for data collection, analysis and visualization; and 'open source' software that can be deployed for a range of projects. Such tools and associated methodological innovations have led to a wider-ranging use of participatory methods in geography, within and beyond academic settings (such as in non-governmental organizations (NGOs) and government departments), as well as encouraging communities to use research to develop their own evidence base for advocacy and activism.

For Leszczynski (2017: 1), '"Digital methods" are heuristics and techniques for identifying, capturing, managing, analysing, and theorizing materialities, social praxes, and implications of sociotechnical shifts associated with the proliferation of digital computing technologies'. Such methods employed by geographers have altered the models of data supply (Haklay et al., 2008), increasing coverage and volume (Elwood, 2008) through online data collection and submission (Catlin-Groves, 2012), remaking expertise and offering new modes of knowledge production (DeLyser and Sui, 2014), as well as asking alternative and additional research questions, with the added potential to extend the potential pool of participants and interested publics across geographical and linguistic borders (Brown and Tucker, 2017).

With respect to digital participatory methods, there have been a number of innovations, including P/PGIS (Elwood, 2008), volunteered geographic information (VGI; Goodchild, 2007), crowdsourcing (Capineri, 2016), citizen science (Haklay, 2013a), and 'open' initiatives (DeLyser and Sui, 2014). These approaches emerged in tandem with the critique and ideas that drove the participatory turn in human geography.

DIGITAL PARTICIPATORY METHODS
GIS towards P/PGIS

Associated with the spatial science of the 1960s, early geographic information systems (GIS) – namely software tools on desktop computers – enabled users to store, represent, and analyse their data spatially. 'Critical GIS' emerged in the 1990s, drawing on many of the feminist critiques developed elsewhere in human geography since the 1970s and 1980s. This critique led to a more theoretical approach in mainstream GIS and the creation of GIScience. According to Elwood (2008: 177-178):

> Critical GIS research focuses in part on the core challenges of representing and analysing spatial objects, their characteristics, and their relationships in a digital environment, and the consequences of these practices for social knowledge, representation and power (Schuurman, 1999; O'Sullivan, 2006). Critical GIS also includes GIS research and practice with an explicitly emancipatory agenda of engaging spatial technologies to disrupt socially and technologically-mediated forms of exclusion and disempowerment (Harvey et al., 2006).

The potential of spatial technologies for emancipation, exclusion and (dis)empowerment echoed commitments central to participatory geography. A new set of participatory methods with a spatial core emerged: public participation GIS (PPGIS), also referred to as participatory GIS (PGIS). It is important to note that there have been a plethora of different terms for similar practices, including participatory mapping, community-based mapping, and community-integrated mapping (for useful definition summaries, see Mukherjee, 2015). Yet these different labels are united by: (i) 'a use of Geographic Information Technologies in participatory ways to achieve a set of desired goals' (Corbett et al., 2016: 335); (ii) 'identify[ing] place attributes that range on a continuum of objective locations based on participant knowledge or experience in the study area (e.g., activities, uses, behaviours) to subjective perceptions of place including the construct of place attachment' (Brown et al., 2017: 154); and (iii) making the unprivileged visible and thereby asking new spatial questions (Pavlovskaya, 2009).

Emerging in the 1990s, P/PGIS refers to the involvement of local or non-governmental stakeholders and community members in governmental decision-making (Radil and Jiao, 2016), with participants able to process and analyse state data using a GIS (Forrester and Cinderby, n.d.). P/PGIS involves gathering data by combining methods such as focus groups and interviews with paper maps that enable research participants to capture spatial information. Using GIS software, these materials are then digitized and analysed. The main output is a digitally created map. While web-based P/PGIS is also possible, many practitioners argue that it should not replace on-the-ground participatory methods (Dunn, 2007) as web-based versions have the potential to reinforce issues of representation and authenticity that P/PGIS seeks to avoid. The use of P/PGIS enables public involvement in policy-making, often by facilitating access to data usually unavailable to participants or by collecting data from those participants, as well as assisting community groups, NGOs and others to produce an evidence base and achieve their goals.

Web 2.0, VGI and neogeography

Allied to the more recent evolution of the internet is the development of Web 2.0, defined by Catlin-Groves (2012: 5) as:

> the socially connected and interactive Internet that facilitates participatory data sharing and encourages user-generated content. This medium consists of blogs, podcasts, social networking sites, wikis, crowd-sourcing tools, and 'cloud-based' group working environments. Web 2.0 has been expanded to a mobile computing context with the proliferation of new technologies such as smart phones, laptops, and tablet computers.

The extension of Web 2.0 functionalities and practices of the user-generation of content to the geographic domain has been framed in terms of the geospatial web (geoweb) and 'neogeography' (Haklay et al., 2008). The geoweb offers a platform for public mapping practices accessible to people without a geographical, GIS, or cartography background, although the levels of skill and expertise required vary (Goodchild, 2007; Sui and DeLyser, 2012). Neogeographic practices include the production of forms of VGI ranging from public contributions to Google Earth Engine, Wikimapia, and OpenStreetMap, to geotagging social media posts through platforms such as Twitter, Instagram, Flickr, and Snapchat. While the geoweb has been heralded as participatory precisely for the ways in which it has opened up digital mapping to non-experts, the extent to which VGI may be considered to be truly 'volunteered' has been questioned, given that much of the locational data individuals generate and have generated about themselves is surreptitiously generated (Sieber and Haklay, 2015).

Participatory methods were identified earlier as 'political and politicized'; participation in P/PGIS and VGI is no different, with shifting power relations built between the state and citizen, market and citizen, researcher and citizen, and citizens themselves. Unlike GIS as a tool that participation is added to (Kar et al., 2016), the geoweb is considered by some as intrinsically participatory (Sieber et al., 2016). Of course, such participation relies on having access to a computer/smartphone and the internet. Moreover, the inclusiveness of the geoweb has been challenged by those demonstrating that the demographics of participation on platforms such as OpenStreetMap are overwhelmingly male and Caucasian (Haklay, 2013b), resulting in gender-biased representations of public spaces (wherein bars, brothels, and strip clubs are deemed legitimate categories for the kinds of places that may be added to the map, whereas childcare facilities are not; see Stephens, 2013).

Citizen science and crowdsourcing

Citizen science is the participation of non-professional volunteers in professional science projects (Wiggins and Crowston, 2011). While the roots of citizen science reach as far back as the gentleman amateur of the eighteenth century, the development of the internet and affordable networked digital devices and sensors has enabled the generation of in-field data, the online submission of vast numbers of records (Catlin-Groves, 2012), and social networking sites enabling the creation of cooperative communities (Haklay et al., 2008). Citizen science and crowdsourcing – whereby participants undertake targeted activities designed by researchers (Capineri, 2016) – offer an opportunity to gather large datasets when funding for time and qualified personnel is at a minimum. Natural science projects allied to aspects of physical geography, such as phenology, solar storms, and flooding, are further forward in this area than human geography initiatives, although citizen social science research is emerging (Purdam, 2014).

In a project on observations of homelessness, Purdam (2014: 375) asked volunteers to collect data 'about what they see around them as they go about their usual daily activities. … The volunteers were given an information briefing and research protocol but they were not formally trained social scientists'. Wiggins and Crowston (2011) suggest that '[c]itizen science represents a new type of open movement, welcoming contributions to scientific research from a diverse population of volunteers'. Notwithstanding the rise in digital technology use in the global South, for example smartphones being used for voting, sharing prices on crops, and doing remote medical operations, citizen science is mostly undertaken in the global North, and participation largely falls into the first of three categories of involvement (Bonney et al., 2009: 11):

- 'Contributory projects, which are generally designed by scientists and for which members of the public primarily contribute data';
- 'Collaborative projects, which are generally designed by scientists and for which members of the public contribute data but also may help to refine project design, analyze data, or disseminate findings'; and
- 'Co-created projects, which are designed by scientists and members of the public working together and for which at least some of the public participants are actively involved in most or all of the scientific process'.

While co-created projects are currently small in number, the emerging 'open culture' (Sui, 2014) in the form of open data and open source software is being embraced by a team of geographers and others who have developed one such project. The interdisciplinary Extreme Citizen Science (ExCiteS) research group at University College London is using digital technologies and participatory approaches to empower people to gather and use data in ways that are meaningful to them. Working in Congo and elsewhere, the ExCiteS team collaborates 'with marginalized groups, such as indigenous peoples, to support them to combine scientifically sound methods with local knowledge so they can participate more effectively in decision making processes relating to pressing issues such as deforestation, biodiversity loss and food security' (Stevens et al., 2014: 20).

KEY CHALLENGES

Digital technologies have enhanced and expanded geographical thought and praxis. Yet key challenges facing the combination of participatory methods and digital technologies remain unresolved and are likely to continue as technology advances. Benefiting from lessons learned from issues faced by participatory scholars, four key challenges are discussed in turn.

First, while the advantage of increased data availability satisfies some data-hungry researchers, many remain blind to associated issues relating to confidentiality and consent, data quality, costs of maintaining technologies, misappropriation of materials, and misrepresentation (Haklay et al., 2008). Digital technologies are not created or used in a social vacuum (Dunn, 2007) and cannot be treated as such. In their work with marginalized groups, Stevens et al. (2014: 20) identify some common issues, including 'cultural misunderstandings, inappropriate technology, misinterpretations of the purpose of engagement, misreadings of power dynamics, ineffective or divisive incentives, and various organizational issues'. Without close attention to the social and cultural consequences of employing digital technologies in participatory methods, projects and relationships may fail.

Second, given that recent research reveals that 95 percent of Americans own a mobile phone (Pew, 2017), it has been suggested that the 'digital divide' has become less relevant in the global North (Sieber et al., 2016). Instead, scholars refer to the prevalence of 'digital inequalities' (Sieber et al., 2016), whereby participation might be regarded as uneven or exclusive (Haklay et al., 2008) and in some cases exclusionary (Elwood, 2008). But there remains a significant digital divide in the global South, where smartphones are less prevalent and literacy rates are lower (Graham et al., 2014). Participatory methods have faced similar challenges around whether they are truly participatory, and in the case of digital technologies, whether they can transcend class, gender, race, and religious divisions (Radil and Jiao, 2016). The digital turn may be expanding the geographical community of potential participants, yet it does not necessarily follow that people do participate (Kar et al., 2016). This might be related to digital literacy and access, fear of technology, as well as gender/generational aspects. PGIS and some citizen science are seeking to challenge power inequalities, but there is a growing need to consider who is doing the research. By working in collaboration with community organizations on the ground, researchers can identify divisions across communities, such as technological ability, age, and access to technology, and may avoid reinforcing digital divides and inequalities.

Third, a common misconception relating to GIS is that it is purely quantitative in approach. As Pavlovskaya (2009) contends, digital spatial representation does not necessarily equate to quantitative analysis. Instead, it is about the locational and spatial information provided. The extent of people's participation in PGIS, citizen science, and other approaches has also been predisposed to quantification, with participation reduced to numbers of participants and data points entered on a map

(Sieber et al., 2016). Such misnomers and quick-win metrics fail to deliver the full potential of digital participatory methods. Drawing on the established debates and rationales within the fields of critical GIS, qualitative GIS, PGIS, and feminist GIS, Sieber et al. (2016) call for researchers to understand the deeper meaning of participation in the geoweb, and the social questions surrounding participation with and through digital technologies (Elwood, 2008).

Finally, critiques are levelled at the very nature and meaning of what constitutes digital 'participation' (Kitchin and Hubbard, 1999; Cooke and Kothari, 2001; Dunn, 2007). For Cooke and Kothari (2001: 32), '[i]n most projects "participation" is a political value to which institutions will sign up for different reasons. But it remains a way of talking about rather than doing things'. Digital technologies complicate this further by creating a communication channel between citizen and state that may not be acted upon (Sieber et al., 2016), or indeed when technologies are developed by businesses which bring their own agendas for data use (Kar et al., 2016; Leszczynski, 2017). Another issue identified by Kar et al. (2016: 297) is the form of 'passive or ambient participation' that emerges through the use of digital technologies. For example,

> we now have cell phone apps that a 'participant' can leave on while he/she anonymously moves in space-time. … Data, for example from Twitter, can be repurposed according to the developer's own needs and not the original intent of the contribution … Passivity afforded by the geoweb offers greater convenience to members of a community, both on the part of citizens and the state.

This takes us back to Sieber et al. and Elwood's call for further research on the meaning of participation.

FUTURE DEVELOPMENTS

Digital participatory methods and citizen science are opening up exciting new worlds of study that reverberate across geography, yet they raise a number of concerns. First, researchers will need to continue to be reflexive about their participatory practice. By learning from participatory geography and paying attention to the 'imbalance of power-relations between researcher and researched' (Fuller and Kitchin, 2004), scholars will be able to readily identify who is participating, how and why, the implications of participation for those individuals or communities, and what to then do with (and how to act on) the knowledge produced within and beyond the academy.

Second, participation must be understood not merely as a means of dissemination, but also as a longer-term ethical commitment to inclusivity that applies whether on the ground or through digital technologies (Shaw, 2017). While digital technologies and citizen science and crowdsourcing practices allow for rapid data collection in vast quantities, successful projects require time for development to build trust and ensure mutual benefit (Askins, 2017; Brown and Tucker, 2017). By appreciating the values that underpin participatory approaches, these activities can become more inclusive and participatory, especially when some projects require sustained participation by the same volunteers. This will also challenge the idea that digital technologies are making citizen science truly available for all (Silvertown, 2009). Indeed, citizen science still remains the pastime of the privileged few (Geoghegan et al., 2016).

Third, digital geographies are being researched by scholars from across the spectrum of geographical sub-disciplines, and this is allowing for the joining up of debates surrounding hardware, software, participation, meaning, experience, and representation. Participatory historical geography has been proposed by DeLyser (2014: 98) as 'part of progressive and liberatory research efforts', with P/PGIS and citizen science having much to offer here (Geoghegan, 2014). For example, Brown and Tucker's (2017) Quipu Project employed digital technologies and participatory storytelling to capture memory and counter-memory surrounding unconsented sterilization in Peru. In addition, digital humanities approaches which foreground digital archives and 'databases [that] include digitized books, newspapers, photos, paintings, unpublished manuscripts, music, audio recordings, transactional data like web searches, sensor data, cell-phone records, social-media postings (such as Facebook or Twitter) and much more' (DeLyser and Sui, 2013: 295) are slowly being explored and have much to learn from participatory methods and more digitally-aware disciplines.

In sum, while understanding the natural world through digital methods is well ahead of more social and cultural dimensions, digital technologies can allow us to ask critical human geography questions and to do so in ways that are emancipatory and empowering and address questions of inclusivity and participation.

Acknowledgements

I would like to thank: the editors, in particular Rob Kitchin for his feedback; and Sally Lloyd-Evans and Tara Woodyer for their comments on the global South and GIScience, respectively. The materials presented in this chapter can be attributed to activities as part of the author's ESRC Future Research Leader award: ES/K001426/2.

REFERENCES

Askins, K. (2017) 'Participatory geographies', in D. Richardson, N. Castree, M.F. Goodchild, A. Kobayashi, W. Liu and R.A. Marston (eds), *The International Encyclopedia of Geography: People, the Earth, Environment, and Technology*. Chichester: John Wiley and Sons.

Bonney, R., Ballard, H., Jordan, R., McCallie, E., Phillips, T., Shirk, J. and Wilderman, C.C. (2009) *Public Participation in Scientific Research: Defining the Field and Assessing Its Potential for Informal Science Education*. CAISE Inquiry Group Report. Center for Advancement of Informal Science Education, Washington, DC. Available online: www.birds.cornell.edu/citscitoolkit/publications/CAISE-PPSR-report-2009.pdf (accessed 1 February 2018).

Brown, G., Strickland-Munro, J., Kobryn, H. and Moore, S.A. (2017) 'Mixed methods participatory GIS: An evaluation of the validity of qualitative and quantitative mapping methods', *Applied Geography*, 79: 153–166.

Brown, M. and Tucker, K. (2017) 'Unconsented sterilisation, participatory story-telling, and digital counter-memory in Peru', *Antipode*, 49(5): 1186–1203.

Bunge, W. (1971) *Fitzgerald: Geography of a Revolution*. Cambridge, MA: Schenkman Pub. Co.

Capineri, C. (2016) 'The nature of volunteered geographic information', in C. Capineri, M. Haklay, H. Huang, V. Antoniou, J. Kettunen, F. Ostermann and R. Purves (eds), *European Handbook of Crowdsourced Geographic Information*. London: Ubiquity Press. pp. 15–33.

Catlin-Groves, C.L. (2012) 'The citizen science landscape: From volunteers to citizen sensors and beyond', *International Journal of Zoology*, 2012: 349630.

Cooke, B. and Kothari, U. (eds) (2001) *Participation: The New Tyranny?* London: Zed Books.

Corbett, J., Cochrane, L. and Gill, M. (2016) 'Powering up: Revisiting participatory GIS and empowerment', *Cartographic Journal*, 53(4): 335–340.

DeLyser, D. (2014) 'Towards a participatory historical geography: Archival interventions, volunteer service, and public outreach in research on early women pilots', *Journal of Historical Geography*, 46: 93–98.

DeLyser, D. and Sui, D. (2013) 'Crossing the qualitative–quantitative divide II: Inventive approaches to big data, mobile methods, and rhythmanalysis', *Progress in Human Geography*, 37(2): 293–305.

DeLyser, D. and Sui, D. (2014) 'Crossing the qualitative–quantitative chasm III: Enduring methods, open geography, participatory research, and the fourth paradigm', *Progress in Human Geography*, 38(2): 294–307.

Dunn, C.E. (2007) 'Participatory GIS – a people's GIS?', *Progress in Human Geography*, 31(5): 616–637.

Elwood, S. (2008) 'Volunteered geographic information: Future research directions motivated by critical, participatory, and feminist GIS', *GeoJournal*, 72(3–4): 173–183.

England, K.V. (1994) 'Getting personal: Reflexivity, positionality, and feminist research', *Professional Geographer*, 46(1): 80–89.

Forrester, J. and Cinderby, S. (n.d.) 'A guide to using community mapping and participatory-GIS'. Available online: www.tweedforum.org/research/borderlands_community_mapping_guide_.pdf (accessed 1 February 2018).

Fuller, D. and Kitchin, R. (2004) 'Radical theory/critical praxis: Academic geography beyond the academy?', in D. Fuller and R. Kitchin (eds), *Radical Theory/Critical Praxis: Making a Difference Beyond the Academy?* Vernon and Victoria, BC: Praxis (e)Press. pp. 1–20.

Geoghegan, H. (2014) 'A new pattern for historical geography: Working with enthusiast communities and public history', *Journal of Historical Geography*, 46: 105–107.

Geoghegan, H., Dyke, A., Pateman, R., West, S. and Everett, G. (2016) 'Understanding motivations for citizen science'. Available online: www.ukeof.org.uk/resources/citizen-science-resources/MotivationsforCSREPORTFINALMay2016.pdf (accessed 1 February 2018).

Goodchild, M.F. (2007) 'Citizens as sensors: The world of volunteered geography', *GeoJournal*, 69(4): 211–221.

Graham, M., Hogan, B., Straumann, R.K. and Medhat, A. (2014) 'Uneven geographies of user-generated information: Patterns of increasing informational poverty', *Annals of the Association of American Geographers*, 104(4): 746–764.

Haklay, M. (2013a) 'Citizen science and volunteered geographic information: Overview and typology of participation', in D.Z. Sui, S. Elwood and M. Goodchild (eds), *Crowdsourcing Geographic Knowledge*. Dordrecht: Springer. pp. 105–122.

Haklay, M. (2013b) 'Neogeography and the delusion of democratization', *Environment and Planning A*, 45(1): 55–69.

Haklay, M., Singleton, A. and Parker, C. (2008) 'Web mapping 2.0: The neogeography of the GeoWeb', *Geography Compass*, 2(6): 2011–2039.

Harney, L., McCurry, J., Scott, J. and Wills, J. (2016) 'Developing "process pragmatism" to underpin engaged research in human geography', *Progress in Human Geography*, 40(3): 316–333.

Jerrett, M., Burnett, R.T., Kanaroglou, P., Eyles, J., Finkelstein, N., Giovis, C. and Brook, J.R. (2001) 'A GIS–environmental justice analysis of particulate air pollution in Hamilton, Canada', *Environment and Planning A*, 33(6): 955–973.

Kar, B., Sieber, R., Haklay, M. and Ghose, R. (2016) 'Public participation GIS and participatory GIS in the era of GeoWeb', *Cartographic Journal*, 53(4): 296–299.

Kindon, S. (1995) 'Dynamics of difference', *New Zealand Geographer*, 51(1): 10–12.

Kindon, S. (2010) 'Participation', in S. Smith, R. Pain, S.A. Marston and J.P. Jones (eds), *The SAGE Handbook of Social Geographies*. London: Sage. pp. 517–545.

Kitchin, R.M. and Hubbard, P.J. (1999) 'Research, action and "critical" geographies', *Area*, 31(3): 195–198.

Korson, C. (2015) 'Political agency and citizen journalism: Twitter as a tool of evaluation', *Professional Geographer*, 67(3): 364–373.

Leszczynski, A. (2017) 'Digital methods I: Wicked tensions', *Progress in Human Geography*, DOI: 0309132517711779.

mrs kinpaisby (2008) 'Taking stock of participatory geographies: Envisioning the communiversity', *Transactions of the Institute of British Geographers*, 33: 292–299.

Mukherjee, F. (2015) 'Public participatory GIS', *Geography Compass*, 9(7): 384–394.

Newton, J., Franklin, A., Middleton, J. and Marsden, T. (2012) '(Re-)negotiating access: The politics of researching skills and knowledge for "sustainable communities"', *Geoforum*, 43(3): 585–594.

Pain, R. (2009) 'Introduction: Doing social geographies', in S. Smith, R. Pain, S.A. Marston and J.P. Jones (eds), *The SAGE Handbook of Social Geographies*. London: Sage. pp. 507–515.

Pain, R. and Francis, P. (2003) 'Reflections on participatory research', *Area*, 35(1): 46–54.

Pavlovskaya, M. (2009) 'Non-quantitative GIS', in M. Cop and S. Elwood (eds), *Qualitative GIS: A Mixed Methods Approach*. London: Sage. pp. 13–37.

Pew (2017) 'Mobile fact sheet'. Available at: www.pewinternet.org/fact-sheet/mobile (accessed 1 February 2018).

Purdam, K. (2014) 'Citizen social science and citizen data? Methodological and ethical challenges for social research', *Current Sociology*, 62(3): 374–392.

Radil, S.M. and Jiao, J. (2016) 'Public participatory GIS and the geography of inclusion', *Professional Geographer*, 68(2): 202–210.

Shaw, J.A. (2017) 'Where does the research knowledge lie in participatory visual processes?', *Visual Methodologies*, 5(1): 51–58.

Sieber, R.E. and Haklay, M. (2015) 'The epistemology(s) of volunteered geographic information: A critique', *Geo: Geography and Environment*, 2(2): 122–136.

Sieber, R.E., Robinson, P.J., Johnson, P.A. and Corbett, J.M. (2016) 'Doing public participation on the geospatial web', *Annals of the American Association of Geographers*, 106(5): 1030–1046.

Silvertown, J. (2009) 'A new dawn for citizen science', *Trends in Ecology & Evolution*, 24(9): 467–471.

Stephens, M. (2013) 'Gender and the GeoWeb: Divisions in the production of user-generated cartographic information', *GeoJournal*, 78(6): 981–996.

Stevens, M., Vitos, M., Altenbuchner, J., Conquest, G., Lewis, J. and Haklay, M. (2014) 'Taking participatory citizen science to extremes', *IEEE Pervasive Computing*, 13(2): 20–29.

Sui, D. (2014) 'Opportunities and impediments for open GIS', *Transactions in GIS*, 18(1): 1–24.

Sui, D. and DeLyser, D. (2012) 'Crossing the qualitative–quantitative chasm I: Hybrid geographies, the spatial turn, and volunteered geographic information (VGI)', *Progress in Human Geography*, 36(1): 111–124.

Sui, D. and Morrill, R. (2004) 'Computers and geography: From automated geography to digital earth', in S.D. Brunn, S.L. Cutter and J.W. Harrington (eds), *Geography and Technology*. New York: Springer. pp. 81–108.

Wiggins, A. and Crowston, K. (2011) 'From conservation to crowdsourcing: A typology of citizen science', in *HICS '11: Proceedings of the 2011 44th Hawaii International Conference on System Sciences*. Washington, DC: IEEE Computer Society.

11

CARTOGRAPHY AND GEOGRAPHIC INFORMATION SYSTEMS

David O'Sullivan

INTRODUCTION

The default form of the map today is a web map, viewed on a phone or other internet-enabled device, responsive to the location and movement of its viewer, often overlaid with information tailored to the particular user. Underpinning the production of such maps are digital cartography and geographic information systems (GIS). The former can be thought of as the theories, practices, and institutions that combine to produce maps of all kinds (today's paper maps are also digital products), while the latter are the computational infrastructure that underpins the storage, manipulation, management, and analysis of geospatial data. GIS exists on traditional desktop software platforms, and more commonly now on distributed computing systems, whether in client–server, peer-to-peer, or cloud architectures. Digital cartography and GIS share some common ancestry in the spatial science of the late 1950s and early 1960s. Experiences with learning to program, computer punch cards, and the frustrations of limited computing resources loom large in accounts of this period (see the many reminiscences in Stimson, 2008), and make clear that this was when geography made its first steps towards computation and the digital.

For many, digital cartography and GIS are synonymous. They are certainly related, but their parallel evolution as fields of study and of practice since the Second World War is complicated, and has often been more separate than is assumed. These interrelated but distinct histories may originate in cartography's long-standing dual identity as both science *and* craft (see, for example, Brewer, 1994), as compared with the more self-consciously academic path of GIS, especially following its reinvention as geographical information *science* (GIScience), which explicitly sought to emphasize theoretical underpinnings over practical applications (Goodchild, 1992). Maintaining this distinction proved impossible (Wright et al., 1997), especially under sustained critique from social theory (Pickles, 1995), and the recognition that GIS, like cartography, is embedded in communities of training and practice has become a cornerstone of *critical GIS* (Schuurman, 2000). Fittingly, research communities of practice, particularly feminist geographers (McLafferty, 2002; Schuurman, 2002; Warren, 2004) and proponents of participatory GIS, have been prominent in advancing the critical GIS enterprise. These developments have narrowed the gap between digital cartography and GIScience at the same time as cartography has metamorphosed and blended with visualization, and also become more reliant on digital tools and infrastructure. Such inheritances from social theory and radical critique are important to understand as digital cartography and GIS themselves become pillars of newly emerging digital geographies (Ash et al., 2018).

In this chapter I attempt to trace a little more of the parallel evolution sketched above, attending particularly to the points of connection between digital cartography and GIS and their mutual influences. It is especially interesting to note the far-reaching impact that the experience of interactive map exploration, so central to 'doing GIS', has had on the evolution of the contemporary digital map into spatial and locative media and location-based services; on the accompanying growth of internet-based mapping and location-based applications/services and associated spatial technologies (collectively termed the *geoweb*; see Leszczynski and Wilson, 2013); and on the collaborative building of the geoweb by its users, through *neogeography* and *volunteered geographic information* (VGI; see Elwood, 2008). This evolution in turn raises numerous questions concerning individual autonomy and surveillance by both states and corporations (Elwood and Leszczynski, 2011).

HISTORICAL CONTEXT: BRAIDED STREAMS

While the history of cartography is an established subdiscipline, convincing, synthetic accounts of the emergence, widespread dissemination, and uptake of GIS remain only partially written. Cartography's intimate entanglement with capitalist modernity, the exercise of state power, and colonialism, is widely acknowledged.

These themes are explored in considerable depth and nuance in the mammoth multi-volume *History of Cartography* project (Harley et al., 1987-[2022]). The critical tradition in cartographic studies was initiated by Harley (1989) and Wood (1992) and was insistent, against the claims to neutrality of self-styled 'scientific' cartographers, that mapping is irrevocably intertwined with power relations. The long-term influence of these insights is borne out both by its later influence on critical GIS (Crampton and Wilson, 2015) and by the reach of critical cartography studies beyond geography, with contributions from historians and others (see, for example, Schulten, 2012). As a result, connections between the development of mapping and survey techniques and colonial concerns with the subdivision and exploitation of land, with military campaigns, and with the bureaucratic management of population have been explored in depth (see, for example, Carroll, 2006).

By contrast, GIS's relationship to central axes of power has not been well elucidated. Smith (1992) declared the Gulf War of 1990–1991 the first 'GIS war', but this gesture towards a military history behind GIS is largely unexplored, and Smith's (1992: 258) argument that 'the time is ripe for a critical and contextual history of GIS beyond existing internalist treatments' remains relevant a quarter of a century later. The youth of GIS (decades) compared with cartography's longevity (millennia) perhaps makes for an unfair comparison, but even so, the military roots of GIS have received scant attention other than in general overviews by Cloud (2002) and Clarke and Cloud (2000). Bill Rankin's *After the Map* (2016) sketches a history of the Global Positioning System (GPS), a military technology in its inception and for years after its introduction into service (see also Propen, 2005). But Rankin (2016: 18) explicitly disavows relating his story to an account of GIS: 'the rise of electronic mapping and GIS … is barely part of my story at all. As other historians have shown these are hugely important developments with serious political (and territorial) implications'. Yet Rankin references no 'other historians', and his off-hand bracketing of 'electronic mapping and GIS' as synonymous is typical.

Other links from state power to GIS have been sketched in (barely) more detail in accounts of the development of the Dual Independent Map Encoded (DIME) file format developed for the computerization of the 1970 US Census (Chrisman, 2006: 13; Weiss, 1988). Coming from another direction, McHaffie (2002) offers insights in his work on automation of map production at the US Geological Survey during the mid-twentieth century. McHaffie's account makes clear that larger socio-political and economic forces meshed with institutional interests were at work than Smith's 'internalist' accounts would suggest. Other accounts emphasize innovative work at particular university laboratories. Chrisman's (2006) history of the Harvard Computer Graphics Laboratory offers fascinating glimpses of the often haphazard and stuttering emergence of now common approaches to the representation of map data in computers. Many innovations do not appear in the published literature and important individual contributions thus remain under-appreciated. For example, Chrisman (2006: 22) acknowledges the work of several women programmers on the SYMAP software, including Betty Benson, Marion Manos, and Kathleen Reine, names probably unfamiliar to present-day GIScientists (the parallel with the forgotten work of Britain's 'map girls' is unmistakable; see Maddrell, 2008). Of interest in such accounts is how software and the associated work practices, data formats, and so on, quickly acquire a logic, embedding assumptions about best solutions and approaches, and producing strong path dependencies in GIS (see Sheppard, 1995). Another of Smith's disparaged accounts (Tomlinson, 1988: 252) emphasizes the separation between the automation of map production and GIS development: 'In general, early automatic cartographic systems were not established to facilitate geographical analysis and in many cases severely inhibited such analysis.' Tomlinson (1988: 252) nevertheless recognizes that many cartographic conventions were effectively baked in to GIS from its earliest inception, given that '[t]he analysis of the information contained in maps was of the essence'.

While these accounts have their limitations, they usefully clarify the importance of manipulating, analysing and visualizing conventional cartographic representations of the world (i.e., maps) as a drive behind GIS from the outset. Other emerging streams of thinking about space and its quantitative representation and analysis were not prioritized: 'These developments [of quantitative geographic methods] made little impact on the early development of automatic cartography or geographic information systems' (Tomlinson, 1988: 252).

So, what are we to make of the tangled relationship between digital cartography and GIS? I want to emphasize four aspects. First, as already suggested, much of the present form of GIS originates in its adoption of a *cartographic model of the world*. Second, an important way that GIS has acted back on cartography is in the emergence of maps as *temporary* artefacts, produced not as end-products but as fleeting moments in an interactive *process of mapping*. Third, bringing us closer to the present, is the emergence of *the internet as a platform for mapping and GIS*, a platform that blurs distinctions between the digital maps and GIS. Fourth, a development with high current visibility, and with likely important effects into the future, is the *increasing salience of code* as the 'moving parts' of maps and GIS. Each of these is explored further in the following sections.

A CARTOGRAPHIC MODEL OF THE WORLD

GIS has embodied a cartographic model of the world from its earliest inception. Elements that compose traditional maps, particularly various kinds of line work (points, lines, or polygons), are the building blocks of GIS data. Much ingenuity in the 1970s and 1980s was dedicated to encoding and standardizing these elements in computer file formats and data structures within GIS platforms, and these remain influential as a spatial data *infrastructure* (Easterling, 2014) through standards such as the geography object model in the Open Geospatial Consortium's (2011) geographic markup language. One departure from the cartographic object approach is the raster data model, where the world is understood as a continuous sensed field of measurements (as a grid of cells), perhaps most commonly in remote-sensed imagery. The relationship between raster and vector data models remains awkward even if debates as to their relative merits have subsided (Couclelis, 1992) and integration of the approaches remains limited, with most GIS treating datasets of each type as distinct layers relatable to one another by various spatial operations, but otherwise distinct.

One half of GIS's great leap forward in the 1990s was the linking of cartographic data structures to relational databases (the other was the emergence of powerful computer graphics; see the next section). Integration with relational databases is explicit in the name of the long-time industry-leading product Arc/INFO. By the time this innovation occurred, it was widely considered a commercial necessity (Dangermond and Lowell, 1988). Relational databases are centrally concerned with rationalizing the storage and management of datasets to prevent inconsistencies between records, an important consideration for owners of corporate databases. A relational database consists of a set of tables, each itself a collection of records, each record representing a particular object of interest. Each record in a table consists of a series of fields or attributes with stored values that together describe the object represented. The relational aspect refers to the way that records in different tables can be related to one another via key or index fields. Adding cartographic objects to this framework yields the now familiar menu of spatial queries such as polygon overlay, point-in-polygon queries, buffering of spatial objects, and the associated repertoire of spatial joins central to GIS analysis.

The bifurcated geometric object plus relational database/raster layer model, broadly standard across GIS platforms by the end of the 1990s, can paint a compelling picture of the world, although much is missing. Most obviously absent are temporality and change, and time as a consequence remains a challenge for GIScience, in spite of considerable research over many years (Langran, 1992; Peuquet, 2003; Yuan et al., 2014). Also difficult to satisfactorily address in the standard framework are uncertainty, ambiguity, meaning, and more qualitative aspects of phenomena, and these aspects are central concerns of GIScience research. These representational limitations are unfortunate from a theoretical geographic perspective, given the degree to which such considerations play into key concepts like place, neighbourhood, or region. In large measure, these limitations are a direct consequence of the association between the early development of GIS and cartographic representations.

MAPPING AS A HIGHLY INTERACTIVE PROCESS

Whatever the evident representational limitations, as Dangermond and Lowell (1988: 310) comment, 'GIS technology and cartography are powerful tools because they allow us to deal with abstraction rather than reality'. This power became more apparent through the 1990s when the graphical capabilities of readily available desktop computers allowed researchers to interactively explore mapped data. This experience was distilled into a new way to think about maps and mapping in Alan MacEachren's notion of 'cartography cubed' (MacEachren, 1994). MacEachren posits a three-dimensional space (the cube) of map use, with dimensions from 'revealing unknowns to presenting knowns', from 'private to public', and, most crucially in the present context, from 'low to high interaction'. According to MacEachren, maps were (and are) increasingly used in contexts of high map–user interaction where there is no final 'best' map, but the map user frequently changes what is displayed on the screen, overlaying different maps, changing map symbolization and colour schemes, and so on. Subsequent developments have seen such insider practices of highly interactive map use, previously limited to researchers, become quotidian as digital maps have diffused widely. MacEachren's perspective has been taken up in arguments by critical geographers that a proper understanding of maps, perhaps all maps at all times, but certainly today's digital maps, requires seeing them not as end products, but as processual entities always coming into existence through use (Kitchin and Dodge, 2007). The archetypical map of today is the smartphone navigation or location-based service app, constantly updating in response both to the changing demands and location of the phone's user and, less obviously, but no less significantly, the algorithmically encoded agenda of the app provider.

THE INTERNET AS A MAPPING PLATFORM

Of course, indispensable to the digital map as interactive process has been the emergence of the World Wide Web and, more recently, the mobile geoweb as mapping platforms (Leszczynski, 2012). Although maps on the web were commonplace from the mid-1990s, the impact of the internet on map use and map design has only slowly been realized (see Peterson, 2003). This may be because early web maps were slow, being generated at the server and delivered to client applications (usually a web browser) as low-resolution images, and other approaches emulating individually manipulable GIS layers tended, if anything, to be even slower. The breakthrough that changed everything was the 'slippy map' introduced by Google in 2005, which, along with the virtual globe Google Earth, generated huge excitement (Crampton, 2009). The potential of the slippy map interface became apparent with the launch of Apple's iPhone in 2007, when the key ingredients of today's interactive and immersive digital maps, combined with location-based services, were in place. The twin developments of a comprehensive virtual 'mirror world' (Google Earth and its competitors) and ubiquitous computing (smartphones and the internet of things) were anticipated in their broad outlines (see Gelernter, 1991; Weiser, 1991), but the details of how they might emerge, and the degree to which location and digital mapping have been central to their evolution, were not widely anticipated.

The front-end of modern digital maps (slippy maps on phones) is immediately apparent and clearly evokes MacEachren's world of high-interaction, fleeting map use. Countless maps are made, used, and discarded every second. It is important to note the significant loss of control of the map's end user in this setting compared with MacEachren's expert users. At some broader scale, perhaps MacEachren's experts do not have much autonomy, since they are likely working on projects or timescales not of their own choosing. However, up close, in the moment of map use, their freedom to explore and change the map (in ways beyond panning and zooming) is greater than the usual experience of a smartphone map user, whose map interactions are also affected by the not always clear agenda of the map provider.

The geoweb brings such questions of control and ownership to the fore in all stages of digital map production. Much less visible than the slippy map is how the back-end production of maps has changed, and how the ownership of the means of map production has also shifted. Most digital maps have been built by for-profit companies, drawing on and extending published data and available imagery, together with local knowledge. In many cases, these data sources are further augmented by data 'volunteered' by platform users (Elwood, 2008). A parallel, alternative digital map ecosystem has been developed based entirely on such volunteer, crowd-sourced methods in the shape of OpenStreetMap (Haklay, 2010) and forms the basis for both for-profit mapping by companies unable to build their own maps, and non-profit projects. These developments have seen optimistic utopian claims made about the democratization of access to digital mapping, although it is clear that many problems of access and control remain (Stephens, 2013). It is noteworthy that none of these endeavours challenge the dominant cartographic object model embedded in GIS.

THE INCREASING SALIENCE OF CODE

The convergence of digital maps and GIS in online platforms increasingly foregrounds their nature as digital artefacts. Maps and geospatial data increasingly exist – *can* exist – only in the context of digital infrastructure, and are themselves an increasingly important component part of that infrastructure, constitutive of and embedded within it. The implications of this development remain unclear. Here I briefly note two aspects, neither new in itself, both enduring concerns in critical GIS, but which may now have become even more important for digital geographic pedagogy as a consequence.

The first is the question of the degree to which cartographic/geographic education should engage with programming and software engineering, or, as has become shorthand for these, 'code'. Web maps can be made without learning code, but fluency in their construction can only be accomplished by developing programming skills. This confronts anyone delivering 'Mapping 101' classes with challenges in terms of what to expect of students, even beyond the technical issues that remain. A question I regularly pose in my own introductory class is, 'If digital mapmaking has become a branch of computer programming, what can geographers contribute to the process?' and it is this challenge, rather than the narrow technical (if difficult) challenge of how to approach teaching code, that is more urgent. Geographers have developed a rich variety of conceptual tools for thinking about space and place. Critically considering how these conceptual tools do or do not mesh with, or how they might extend those available in digital mapping is centrally important. Here, the historical connections between mapping and GIS, and the limitations of cartographic models of the world, become important jumping-off points.

Closely related is a second aspect, ably discussed in a recent article by Elwood and Wilson (2017), concerning the ethics of mapping and spatial analysis, and how this theme can be embedded in student experiences of mapping from the outset, and not treated as a postscript to otherwise technically focused syllabuses. The overriding concern here is that mapping be understood as an embodied and socially embedded process. With digital maps increasingly ubiquitous media, conveying this idea is in some ways easier than when the authoritative paper map as disembodied, finished artefact was more prominent; but also harder, when digital maps present themselves as somehow magically 'just there', conjured out of thin air.

POSSIBLE FUTURES

Given the rapidity of change in digital mapping, speculating about even near-future developments is a doomed enterprise. It is difficult from the vantage point of the present to see major recent trends reversing anytime soon. The digital map as a (usually) market-mediated window on the world that guides users through a personalized landscape of 'real-world' consumption opportunities in much the same way that web search engines do the internet, is already well-established in spite of its novelty. To what extent the digital map is a geographical 'filter bubble' (Pariser, 2011) and precursor to an augmented-reality, all-encompassing 'code/space' (Kitchin and Dodge, 2011) is difficult to determine. Challenges to and developments in social norms around concepts such as privacy (see, for example,

Elwood and Leszczynski, 2011), and perhaps even more fundamental notions such as autonomy and freedom of choice, seem very likely. Whether and how these developments can be resisted or subverted to more emancipatory ends remains uncertain in the absence of far-reaching changes to an emerging surveillance capitalism (Zuboff, 2015). Such change surely entails a reimagining of digital maps as vehicles for exploration and understanding of their worlds on users' own terms and under users' conscious control. Much current work in GIScience stems from the limits of the cartographic object model, and its difficulty in accommodating time, uncertainty, ambiguity, meaning and other human notions, and might find use in such digital maps. If that is to be the case then, as with critical GIS, digital geographies must extend beyond critique, to the exploration and development of critically engaged practice.

REFERENCES

Ash, J., Kitchin, R. and Leszczynski, A. (2018) 'Digital turn, digital geographies?', *Progress in Human Geography*, 42(1): 25–43.

Brewer, C.A. (1994) 'Color use guidelines for mapping and visualization', in A.M. MacEachren and D.R.F. Taylor (eds), *Visualization in Modern Cartography*. Oxford: Pergamon Press. pp. 123–147.

Carroll, P. (2006) *Science, Culture, and Modern State Formation*. Berkeley: University of California Press.

Chrisman, N.R. (2006) *Charting the Unknown: How Computer Mapping at Harvard Became GIS*. Redlands, CA: Esri Press.

Clarke, K.C. and Cloud, J.G. (2000) 'On the origins of analytical cartography', *Cartography and Geographic Information Science*, 27(3): 195–204.

Cloud, J.G. (2002) 'American cartographic transformations during the Cold War', *Cartography and Geographic Information Science*, 29(3): 261–282.

Couclelis, H. (1992) 'People manipulate objects (but cultivate fields): Beyond the raster-vector debate in GIS', in A. Frank, I. Campari and U. Formentini (eds), *Theories and Methods of Spatio-temporal Reasoning in Geographic Space*. Berlin: Springer. pp. 65–77.

Crampton, J.W. (2009) 'Cartography: Maps 2.0', *Progress in Human Geography*, 33(1): 91–100.

Crampton, J.W. and Wilson, M.W. (2015) 'Harley and Friday Harbor: A conversation with John Pickles', *Cartographica: The International Journal for Geographic Information and Geovisualization*, 50(1): 28–36.

Dangermond, J. and Lowell, K.S. (1988) 'Geographic information systems and the revolution in cartography: The nature of the role played by a commercial organization', *Cartography and Geographic Information Science*, 15(3): 301–310.

Easterling, K. (2014) *Extrastatecraft: The Power of Infrastructure Space*. London: Verso.

Elwood, S. (2008) 'Volunteered geographic information: Key questions, concepts and methods to guide emerging research and practice', *GeoJournal*, 72(3–4): 133–135.

Elwood, S. and Leszczynski, A. (2011) 'Privacy, reconsidered: New representations, data practices, and the geoweb', *Geoforum*, 42(1): 6–15.

Elwood, S. and Wilson, M.W. (2017) 'Critical GIS pedagogies beyond "Week 10: Ethics"' *International Journal of Geographical Information Science*, 31(10): 2098–2116.

Gelernter, D.H. (1991) *Mirror Worlds, or, The Day Software Puts the Universe in a Shoebox: How It Will Happen and What It Will Mean*. New York: Oxford University Press.

Goodchild, M.F. (1992) 'Geographical information science', *International Journal of Geographical Information Systems*, 6(1): 31–45.

Haklay, M. (2010) 'How good is volunteered geographical information? A comparative study of OpenStreetMap and Ordnance Survey datasets', *Environment and Planning B: Planning and Design*, 37(4): 682–703.

Harley, J.B. (1989) 'Deconstructing the map', *Cartographica: The International Journal for Geographic Information and Geovisualization*, 26(2): 1–20.

Harley, J.B., Woodward, D., Malcolm Lewis, G., Edney, M.H., Pedley, M.S., Kain, R.J.P. and Monmonier, M. (eds) (1987–[2022]) *The History of Cartography*. Chicago: University of Chicago Press.

Kitchin, R. and Dodge, M. (2007) 'Rethinking maps', *Progress in Human Geography*, 31(3): 331–344.

Kitchin, R. and Dodge, M. (2011) *Code/Space: Software and Everyday Life*. Cambridge, MA: MIT Press.

Langran, G. (1992) *Time in Geographic Information Systems*. London: Taylor & Francis.

Leszczynski, A. (2012) 'Situating the geoweb in political economy', *Progress in Human Geography*, 36(1): 72–89.

Leszczynski, A. and Wilson, M.W. (2013) 'Guest editorial: Theorizing the geoweb', *GeoJournal*, 78(6): 915–919.

MacEachren, A.M. (1994) 'Visualization in modern cartography: Setting the agenda', in A.M. MacEachren and D.R.F. Taylor (eds), *Visualization in Modern Cartography*. Oxford: Pergamon Press. pp. 1–12.

Maddrell, A. (2008) 'The "Map Girls": British women geographers' war work, shifting gender boundaries and reflections on the history of geography', *Transactions of the Institute of British Geographers*, 33(1): 127–148.

McHaffie, P. (2002) 'Towards the automated map factory: Early automation at the U.S. Geological Survey', *Cartography and Geographic Information Science*, 29(3): 193–206.

McLafferty, S.L. (2002) 'Mapping women's worlds: Knowledge, power and the bounds of GIS', *Gender, Place and Culture: A Journal of Feminist Geography*, 9(3): 263–269.

Open Geospatial Consortium (2011) 'OpenGIS implementation specification for geographic information – Simple feature access – Part 1: Common architecture'. Available at: www.opengeospatial.org/standards/sfa (accessed 14 August 2018).

Pariser, E. (2011) *The Filter Bubble: What the Internet Is Hiding from You*. New York: Penguin Press.

Peterson, M.P. (ed.) (2003) *Maps and the Internet*. London: Elsevier.

Peuquet, D.J. (2003) *Representations of Space and Time*. New York: Guilford Press.

Pickles, J. (ed.) (1995) *Ground Truth: The Social Implications of Geographic Information Systems*. New York: Guilford Press.

Propen, A.D. (2005) 'Critical GPS: Toward a new politics of location', *ACME: An International E-journal for Critical Geographies*, 4(1): 131–144.

Rankin, W. (2016) *After the Map: Cartography, Navigation, and the Transformation of Territory in the Twentieth Century*. Chicago: University of Chicago Press.

Schulten, S. (2012) *Mapping the Nation: History and Cartography in Nineteenth-Century America*. Chicago: University of Chicago Press.

Schuurman, N. (2000) 'Trouble in the heartland: GIS and its critics in the 1990s', *Progress in Human Geography*, 24(4): 569–590.

Schuurman, N. (2002) 'Women and technology in geography: A cyborg manifesto for GIS', *The Canadian Geographer/Le Géographe Canadien*, 46(3): 258–265.

Sheppard, E.S. (1995) 'GIS and society: Towards a research agenda', *Cartography and Geographic Information Systems*, 22(1): 5–16.

Smith, N. (1992) 'History and philosophy of geography: Real wars, theory wars', *Progress in Human Geography*, 16(2): 257–271.

Stephens, M. (2013) 'Gender and the geoweb: Divisions in the production of user-generated cartographic information', *GeoJournal*, 78(6): 981–996.

Stimson, R.J. (2008) 'A personal perspective from being a student of the quantitative revolution', *Geographical Analysis*, 40(3): 222–225.

Tomlinson, R.F. (1988) 'The impact of the transition from analogue to digital cartographic representation', *Cartography and Geographic Information Science*, 15(3): 249–262.

Warren, S. (2004) 'The utopian potential of GIS', *Cartographica: The International Journal for Geographic Information and Geovisualization*, 39(1): 5–16.

Weiser, M. (1991) 'The computer for the 21st century', *Scientific American*, 265(3): 94–104.

Weiss, M.J. (1988) *The Clustering of America*. New York: Harper & Row.

Wood, D. (1992) *The Power of Maps*. New York: Guilford Press.

Wright, D.J., Goodchild, M.F. and Proctor, J.D. (1997) 'Demystifying the persistent ambiguity of GIS as "tool" versus "science"', *Annals of the Association of American Geographers*, 87(2): 346–362.

Yuan, M., Atsushi, N. and Bothwell, J. (2014) 'Space–time representation and analytics', *Annals of GIS*, 20(1): 1–9.

Zuboff, S. (2015) 'Big other: Surveillance capitalism and the prospects of an information civilization', *Journal of Information Technology*, 30(1): 75–89.

12

STATISTICS, MODELLING, AND DATA SCIENCE

Dani Arribas-Bel

INTRODUCTION

We live in exciting times. As the data revolution unfolds, many of its consequences are becoming more apparent. From self-driving cars to language translation, to smarter cities, the effects of the automated generation of datasets about human activity are having tangible impacts on our daily lives, both positive – creating insights and efficiencies that enhance business, government, and civic life (see, for example, Mayer-Schönberger and Cukier, 2013) – and not so positive, exacerbating inequalities, increasing surveillance and eroding privacy, and tightening regulation and control (e.g., O'Neil, 2016). The data revolution is also having profound effects on how we come to know and understand the world. As Kitchin (2014) notes, 'Big Data and new data analytics are disruptive innovations which are reconfiguring in many instances how research is conducted'. The relevant part of that quote in the context of this chapter is *new data analytics*. The age of datafication (Schutt and O'Neil, 2013) is starting to have profound implications for the type of quantitative analytics we develop and deploy to understand the world. This shift is already in motion, and the avid reader of social science journals will have started to see hints of and references to it in the form of terms such as 'data science' and 'machine learning'. This transformation will only increase as data and new tools become ever more prevalent, reaching a point where they will become so pervasive and embedded in the geographer's toolbox that they will probably lose any distinctiveness.

This chapter is concerned with this broad epistemological trend in the context of geography and, more particularly, with respect to geographically inspired quantitative methods. It has been argued that geography is currently undergoing a 'digital turn' (Ash et al., 2018). One of its likely consequences is that anything that happens in the 'digital' will more easily propagate and resonate in geographical spheres. The chapter argues that this will be the case when it comes to techniques to model spatial data. In particular, the key message conveyed is that, as we immerse ourselves more and more deeply in a world of abundant data, much of which is georeferenced, the community interested in spatial modelling techniques and statistics will have to adapt from traditional approaches to stay relevant. Part of this evolution will involve repurposing the contributions made in the past decades by the GIScience and geocomputation literatures for the big data age. A non-trivial aspect of this process will also involve stepping out of the comfort zone of quantitative geography and bridging over to the disciplines of computer science, machine learning/artificial intelligence, and data science.

Of course, cross-pollination between geography and mathematically inspired fields such as statistics is nothing new (see, for example, Bunge, 1962; Fotheringham, 1998; Miller and Goodchild, 2015). Part of my argument will be that the disciplines the field will need to engage with more intensely will shift from those more statistically orientated to those more computational in nature. A useful term in this context will be 'data science', a vague but rapidly growing domain at the intersection of statistics, computer science, and software engineering. This chapter explores several aspects of this shift. The next section reviews the recent past of both traditional spatial modelling and data science. In the following section, the case for a merger of the two perspectives is made and illustrated with an example. The chapter finishes with three predictions about what the near future of modelling in geography will look like.

HISTORICAL CONTEXT

To understand where statistics and modelling are today within geography, it is useful to locate where in the discipline most of the contributions have occurred as well as what are the external influences that will more likely have an effect in the near future (or, in fact, are already impacting it). As we will see, the 'digital' represents an important component throughout. In fact, it is fair to say that quantitative geography and related subfields such as geocomputation (Fotheringham, 1998; Longley et al., 1998) and GIScience (Goodchild, 1991, 1992), the main home for statistics and modelling in geography, have played an important role in instigating the 'digital turn' documented in Ash et al. (2018). To a large extent, this prominence is explained by the integral reliance of these sub-domains on computers and digital representations from their inception: indeed, without the 'digital', there is no such thing as geocomputation and quantitative analysis becomes incredibly time-consuming or impossible. Beyond simply relying on computers, geographical statistics and modelling have turned this dependence into an opportunity to develop methods which produce results without a parallel in an analog world. For example, some of the more modern geographically weighted methods go beyond a digital version of standard 'analog' techniques into methods that it would not be possible to conceive of without the power of modern computing. In this process, new techniques build such features at their core, creating effectively 'digital-native' approaches.

From a statistical perspective, it is fair to say that the standard quantitative methods currently taught and used in mainstream geography derive in large part from traditional statistics and frequentist probability theory (e.g., Harris, 2016; Rogerson, 2014). Building on this foundation, quantitative geographers, GIScientists and geocomputation practitioners have collaborated with spatial statisticians (e.g., Cressie, 2015; Ripley, 2005) to build an entire body of statistical techniques which place space and location at the centre of the analysis. This is possible by formally representing location and spatially mediated interactions within a statistical framework. The result is a set of methods that are able not only to account for the fact that the units of study are located somewhere, but also to exploit it, extracting insight into the underlying mechanisms that give rise to such interactions in the first place.

It is important to highlight that, just like much of the traditional statistics upon which they are based, most of these methods rely on very sophisticated mathematical devices that exploit the properties of probability theory to be able to reach meaningful conclusions in a computationally efficient way. It is also important to emphasize that, as children of an age of scarce data and limited computing, these methods rely on making assumptions and imposing exogenous structure on the modelling approach, both of which are usually derived from theoretical models. Although there have been calls to widen this view to incorporate more computationally intensive and less restrictive methods (see Openshaw, 1983, for an almost visionary perspective and Fotheringham, 1998, for a later consideration), their influence to this day has been limited.

Coming from a very different perspective, the last few years have seen the rise of data science (DS; Peng and Matsui, 2015; Schutt and O'Neil, 2013) as an established discipline. Although its origins are hard to pinpoint, DS as a term began with the rise of internet companies in the early 2000s (Weinberger, 2011) and the realization that the data they were creating through server logs were potentially profitable but not in their raw form. The industry's response was to blend computational statistics with computer science (in particular with machine learning, which focuses on methods capable of flexibly extracting structure from the data and using it to make predictions in an automated fashion), software/database engineering, and some visualization and storytelling to turn raw logs into actionable insights. From user click rates to customer segmentation, to server load balancing, DS is portrayed as the answer to convert data into better business decisions. Since then, the DS approach to data has expanded, accompanying the explosion of data into several areas of industry, policy, and science. In the social sciences, this has taken the form of computational social science (CSS; Lazer et al., 2009) which is starting to permeate more intensively, branching out into sub-disciplines. In geography, CSS is being taken up by the communities formed around GIScience and geocomputation which, together with influences from DS, are giving rise to new approaches that could be named geographic data science. For the purpose of this chapter, it is important to highlight in what sense DS differs from the more traditional approach to data analysis championed mostly by standard statistics. There are several ways to draw this distinction; all are probably misleading in some way, but also capture some useful aspect. Two seem particularly relevant to elaborating a comparison with the methods pushed forward from the GIScience and geocomputation communities: first, in the trade-off between mathematical 'trickery' and computational brute force, DS clearly leans towards the latter; and second, because of the abundance of both data and computer power, DS typically imposes fewer assumptions on the structure of both the data and functional forms estimated in the models deployed. There are other key differences, chief among them probably the shift of focus from inference to prediction (brilliantly summarized in Mullainathan and Spiess, 2017, as $\hat{\beta}$ versus $\hat{y}$) but, for the sake of the discussion below, I will concentrate on the first two.

CURRENT DEBATES

It is highly likely that the two perspectives described above will increasingly engage in more intense interaction, and that DS will have an ever-growing influence on new developments in statistics and modelling within geography. As mentioned above but not always presented in such a way, quantitative geography and GIS have always been inherently digital, facilitated by the development of digital computers since the 1950s. What DS is newly bringing to this picture is an infusion of modern computational approaches and digitally native data that is changing the nature of the 'digital' in the domain. On the one hand, the questions DS has expanded to consider often have a clear spatial dimension, and data scientists are beginning to experiment with tools and concepts very familiar to both GIScientists and geocomputation scholars.

As an example of this, the Carto company, which has become very popular in the last few years, brands itself as a location intelligence service, where tools from traditional GIS are moved online to interact with more standard DS tools. On the other hand, elements very familiar to the usual data scientist are starting to make their way into quantitative geography.

To illustrate some of the advantages and challenges this interaction between statistics and modelling in geography and DS poses, I will use an empirical example. In an article called 'The Spoken Postcodes', Arribas-Bel (2015) considers two long-standing questions for quantitative geographers: the concept of neighbourhood and the modifiable areal unit problem (MAUP; Openshaw and Taylor, 1979). The MAUP is a spatial version of an ecological fallacy, with two components (a scale problem and a zoning problem), wherein false inferences can be made about a location depending on how the data is aggregated geographically. Using a combination of a machine learning algorithm and a dataset with georeferenced tweets, the program is able to redraw meaningful neighbourhoods in the city of Amsterdam based on the language mix of the tweets of each area. The exercise highlights how fluid the idea of neighbourhood can be, and how much flexibility is afforded by the combination of new forms of data with modern computing power.

Before getting into the output of the analysis, let us consider the situation one would face traditionally. Small-area urban studies usually need to use administrative geographies to obtain data points within a given city. In the case of the Netherlands, the most common administrative unit is the postcode, which can be seen in Figure 12.1 for the municipality of Amsterdam. As the map makes clear, postcodes delineate space in a regular and neat fashion: they all take up a similar area and are aligned as closely as possible to a grid, given the irregularities that come with an ancient city such as Amsterdam. Whether a given study is interested in income inequalities, ethnic diversity or the social effects of pollution, in the large majority of cases, they are stuck with these administrative boundaries. And yet, very few researchers would agree they match the underlying process of interest, potentially giving rise to the MAUP.

Now consider Figure 12.2, which presents the neighbourhood delineation based on Twitter languages. Before delving into the differences, let us describe how the map was constructed. Using a smaller area unit (the five-digit postcode, instead of the more common four-digit level), the language profile is derived by obtaining the proportion of tweets in each of the major languages in the dataset. For example, for a location in the city centre, this could be an almost equal share between Dutch and English, with a bit less of Turkish, and a higher than usual share of other languages such as German and French. This profile would reflect the centre's role as a tourist hub. In contrast, a small postcode in the west, where there is a large population with a Turkish background, might display most of its tweets split

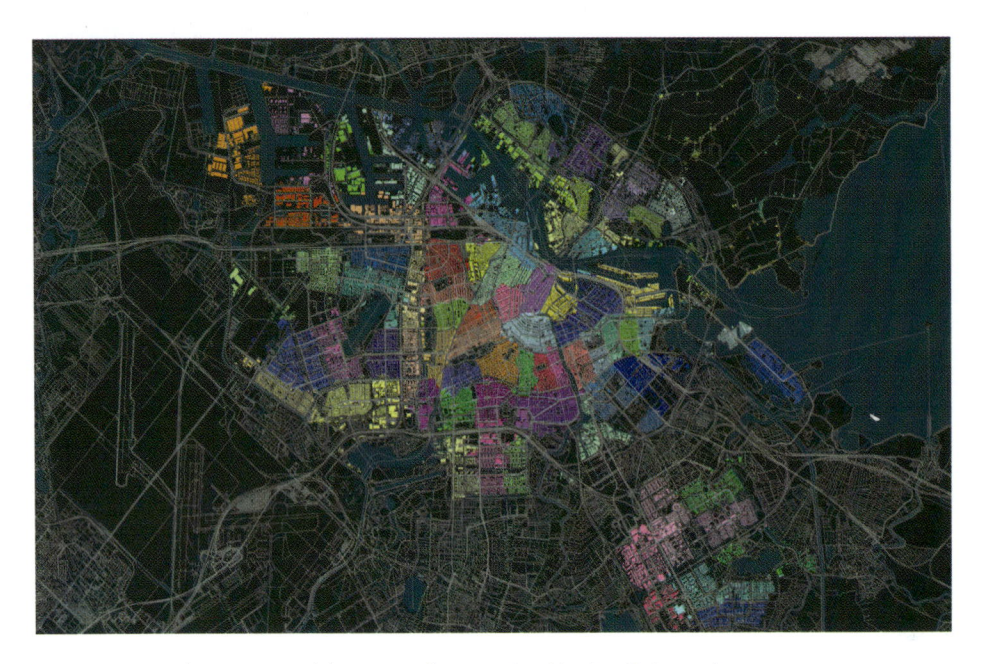

Figure 12.1 Administrative delineation of postcodes (Arribas-Bel, 2015)

between Dutch and Turkish. In sum, by obtaining language shares at a very fine-grained scale, we obtain the building blocks of more meaningful neighbourhoods; that is, of areas with a consistent profile – of language in this case. But the building blocks by themselves are not neighbourhoods. Neighbourhoods represent larger (contiguous) areas sharing the same 'essence' or, in this case, language profile. This is obtained by grouping the five-digit postcodes so that similar and contiguous areas are joined. This process of aggregation is called regionalization (Duque et al., 2007) and has a long tradition in quantitative geography because it represents one of the most robust solutions to the MAUP. Using the automated zoning procedure (Openshaw, 1977), the approximately 1100 small postcodes are aggregated into 81 regions, about the same number as the official four-digit postcodes in Figure 12.1. The result is displayed in Figure 12.2. Instead of the regular and orderly administrative boundaries, the result is a much more chaotic layout where some areas are very large (e.g., the neighbourhood of Bijlmer in the south east) while others seem to be tiny outliers in the middle of a larger, more uniform area (e.g., small parts in green, west of the city centre).

The point of including the spoken postcodes example is to highlight the extent to which DS is already being incorporated into geographical modelling, and the degree to which that integration shows advantages, but also poses significant challenges. Let us start with positive aspects. The use of new forms of data

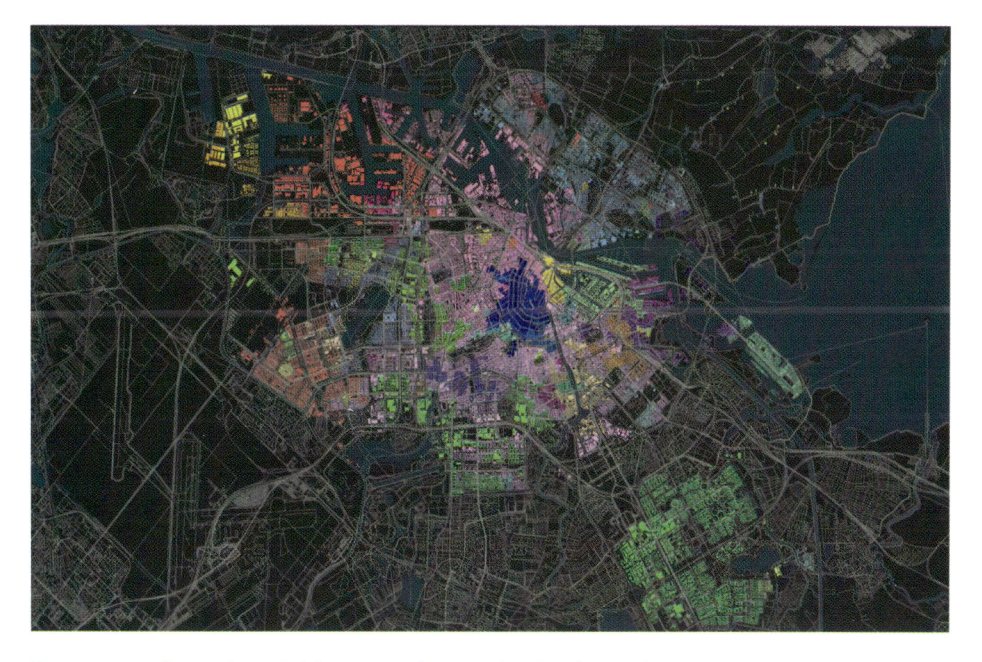

Figure 12.2 Tweet-based delineation of postcodes (Arribas-Bel, 2015)

(Twitter in this case), one of the signature elements of DS, enables a brand new perspective on a long-standing question, that of what a neighbourhood is and how we can define it. It does not mean the answer is definitive or entirely correct, but it does provide a tool to think in new ways that were not possible before. Secondly, tweets *per se* do not make neighbourhoods; it is the combination of data with explicitly spatial techniques that makes the delineation possible. In this context, it is useful to point out that the method itself is not new, but, as with much machine learning, it is experiencing a renaissance powered by the abundance of data and computer power, which is allowing these techniques to produce results that were not possible when they were originally proposed.

Finally, a note of caution is in order. Despite the new possibilities DS and related advances afford us, it is important to highlight some of the main challenges they embody. These have been detailed more extensively elsewhere (e.g., Arribas-Bel, 2014; Kitchin, 2014), so I will only discuss them in brief. Besides the computational skills required to carry out the analysis (beyond those of the traditionally trained geographer), there are important questions to consider about self-selection bias and representativity of the sample used. Not everyone tweets, and not everyone even owns a smartphone. What does this mean for the representations we are building of cities based on these datasets? Divides and inequalities existing at the data collection stage will inevitably be carried over to the final products of the analysis.

FEASIBLE FUTURES

The two previous sections should give the impression that, far from static, the state of affairs in statistics and modelling within geography is undergoing significant changes. It follows that the field will, in a few years' time, potentially have a different look about it compared to today. Here, I review three main trends I consider will gain relevance in the coming years (some of them are already under way), shaping how we do statistics and modelling within geography.

Data, data, data

The first trend relates to the pervasive presence and influence of data as a key factor underlying the development of new methods. To understand this statement, it is useful to consider how the increase of cheap computer power in the 1990s gave rise to what could be seen as a 'local revolution' in spatial statistics (Fotheringham, 1997; Haining, 2014) – the proliferation of statistical methods specifically designed to study spatial heterogeneity and departures from the global trend. In a similar fashion, the abundance of data with extraordinary granularity over space, time, or both is likely to spur the development of methods that can take explicit advantage of these characteristics to allow for insights unavailable through traditional methods, crafted in a time of scarce and coarse data. Examples of this include methods that do not require pre-imposed spatial structure (as in the example in the previous section), that accommodate real-time data points (e.g., streaming techniques), or that allow incremental updates as new batches of data become available (e.g., online learning approaches).

Equations versus CPUs

As reviewed in Efron and Hastie (2016), much of the history of statistics in the twenty-first century can be interpreted as a shift from an approach that depends on stricter assumptions and more efficient computations to one that relies on the power of modern computers to produce more flexible and automated inference devices. To some extent, a similar shift has also affected the subfield of spatial statistics and, in my view, will only increase over the next few years. As DS is heavily inspired by computer science and machine learning principles, greater interaction between DS and geography will lead to a more (geo)computational statistics, in the Fotheringham (1998) sense of one 'in which the computer plays a pivotal role'. An aspect I believe will require further consideration is how this shift should translate into changes in the geography curriculum. My view is that, parallel to what other disciplines are proposing (see Hardin et al., 2015, for the case of statistics), this should encompass a similar shift in the expected learning outcomes, emphasizing computational literacy over pure mathematical prowess.

Thinking machines

My final prediction relates to the previous two but takes their conclusions one step further. As we move into a world where data is so abundant that it allows for extremely flexible models which can be computed thanks to unprecedented cheap computer power, we might start seeing instances where insights are suggested by algorithms rather than humans. To be sure, the day when we state a research question and the computer responds with the desired analysis still belongs to the realm of science fiction. What I am imagining, however, is a situation where the researcher presents the computer with a set of data and only a very loose set of assumptions and/or expectations, and the computer returns a variety of 'suggestions' for the researcher to examine. This approach by no means falls into what Kitchin (2014) calls the empiricist approach, the view that big data by itself can replace science altogether. Rather, this is exploratory data analysis (Tukey, 1977) taken to the next level, and is thus much closer to what the same book proposes as 'data-driven science'.

An excellent example of this approach is the case of AlphaGo (Silver et al., 2016), a computer program written by DeepMind, a subsidiary of Alphabet (the holding company of Google). In 2016, AlphaGo beat Lee Sedol, widely considered as the best player of Go, an ancient Chinese board game. This feat was possible by the combination of a large dataset of past games played by several humans and, crucially, by the application of a neural network algorithm that was able to extract the essence of the game and use it to generate new moves that eventually took it to victory. What is useful about this example in the context of this chapter is that, once the program was trained, the sets of strategies that it started generating were not necessarily a repetition or combination of those in the original dataset, but included approaches that surprised even seasoned players. It has been argued that those new strategies, once studied and understood, will probably spur a new generation of players who are significantly better at Go. Now consider how that could play out if, instead of an ancient board game, we 'taught' computers to, for example, identify income inequalities from satellite images (which, by the way, are being generated at a record frequency and quality). You could train an algorithm to detect different levels of, say, income based on characteristics engrained in the pixels from the imagery. The output might not only produce accurate estimates, as compared to those obtained from satellite images and more traditional approaches such as regression (e.g., Arribas-Bel et al., 2017), but could potentially shed light on factors humans had not previously explored, and thus become the seed for new theories.

CONCLUSION

In conclusion, statistics and modelling in geography are undergoing important changes and experiencing substantial shifts as a result of an increasing interaction with broader developments in the 'digital', in particular data science. As a result, the field is expected to become more data-driven, less mathematical, and more computational, evolving into a geographic data science hybrid. This process will enable the leveraging of the full potential and benefits of the data revolution already in progress. Taking these trends together, the field is likely to look rather different in a few years' time, much more integrated methodologically with other computational areas with which there has been historically little interaction. This is to be celebrated as it will create a space for exchange, and will enable collaboration and cross-pollination in terms of methods, tools, and practices. This shift is also likely to redefine what it means to be a statistical and computational geographer, bringing it much closer to the figure of a data scientist. In this context, it is important that the current geographic community of modellers adapt and evolve to remain relevant in the field. If they do not, they run the risk of being overtaken by other fields with computational skills but little geographical expertise. This would be highly undesirable for two main reasons: first, geographers' work would likely be relegated to a secondary role; but, second and more importantly, many of the advances the geographical community has developed over the years to deal with well-known problems would end up being rediscovered and reinvented in a fairly inefficient and unfair process. As such, we live in exciting times.

Acknowledgements

I would like to thank Alec Davies and Sam Comber, from the Geographic Data Science Lab at the University of Liverpool, for helpful comments on a previous version. All remaining errors are my sole responsibility.

REFERENCES

Arribas-Bel, D. (2014) 'Accidental, open and everywhere: Emerging data sources for the understanding of cities', *Applied Geography*, 49: 45–53.

Arribas-Bel, D. (2015) 'The spoken postcodes', *Regional Studies, Regional Science*, 2(1): 458–461.

Arribas-Bel, D., Patino, J.E. and Duque, J.C. (2017) 'Remote sensing-based measurement of Living Environment Deprivation: Improving classical approaches with machine learning', *PLoS ONE*, 12(5): e0176684. Available at: https://doi.org/10.1371/journal.pone.0176684 (accessed 1 February 2018.

Ash, J., Kitchin, R. and Leszczynski, A. (2018) 'Digital turn, digital geographies?', *Progress in Human Geography*, 42(1): 25–43.

Bunge, W. (1962) *Theoretical Geography*. Lund Studies in Geography Series C: General and Mathematical Geography, No. 1. Lund: Gleerup.

Cressie, N. (2015) *Statistics for Spatial Data*. Hoboken, NJ: John Wiley & Sons.

Duque, J.C., Ramos, R. and Suriñach, J. (2007) 'Supervised regionalization methods: A survey', *International Regional Science Review*, 30(3): 195–220.

Efron, B. and Hastie, T. (2016) *Computer Age Statistical Inference*. Cambridge: Cambridge University Press.

Fotheringham, A.S. (1997) 'Trends in quantitative methods I: Stressing the local', *Progress in Human Geography*, 21(1): 88–96.

Fotheringham, A.S. (1998) 'Trends in quantitative methods II: Stressing the computational', *Progress in Human Geography*, 22(2): 283–292.

Goodchild, M.F. (1991) 'Geographic information systems', *Progress in Human Geography*, 15(2): 194–200.

Goodchild, M.F. (1992) 'Geographical information science', *International Journal of Geographical Information Systems*, 6(1): 31–45.

Haining, R. (2014) 'Spatial data and statistical methods: A chronological overview', in M. Fischer and P. Nijkamp (eds), *Handbook of Regional Science*. Berlin: Springer. pp. 1277–1294.

Hardin, J., Hoerl, R., Horton, N.J., Nolan, D., Baumer, B., Hall-Holt, O., Murrell, P., Peng, R., Roback, P., Temple Lang, D. and Ward, M.D. (2015) 'Data science in statistics curricula: Preparing students to "think with data"', *American Statistician*, 69(4): 343–353.

Harris, R. (2016) *Quantitative Geography: The Basics*. London: Sage.

Kitchin, R. (2014) 'Big data, new epistemologies and paradigm shifts', *Big Data & Society*, 1(1). DOI: 2053951714528481.

Lazer, D., Pentland, A., Adamic, L., Aral, S., Barabasi, A.L., Brewer, D., et al. (2009) 'Life in the network: The coming age of computational social science', *Science*, 323(5915): 721–723.

Longley, P.A., Brooks, S., Macmillan, W. and McDonnell, R. (1998) *Geocomputation: A Primer*. Chichester: Wiley.

Mayer-Schönberger, V. and Cukier, K. (2013) *Big Data: A Revolution that Will Transform How We Live, Work, and Think*. London: John Murray.

Miller, H.J. and Goodchild, M.F. (2015) 'Data-driven geography', *GeoJournal*, 80(4): 449–461.

Mullainathan, S. and Spiess, J. (2017) 'Machine learning: An applied econometric approach', *Journal of Economic Perspectives*, 31(2): 87–106.

Openshaw, S. (1977) 'A geographical solution to scale and aggregation problems in region-building, partitioning and spatial modelling', *Transactions of the Institute of British Geographers*, 2(4): 459–472.

Openshaw, S. (1983) 'From data crunching to model crunching: The dawn of a new era', *Environment and Planning A*, 15: 1011–1013.

Openshaw, S. and Taylor, P.J. (1979) 'A million or so correlation coefficients: Three experiments on the modifiable areal unit problem', *Statistical Applications in the Spatial Sciences*, 21: 127–144.

O'Neil, C. (2016) *Weapons of Math Destruction: How Big Data Increases Inequality and Threatens Democracy*. New York: Crown Publishing Group.

Peng, R.D. and Matsui, E. (2015) *The Art of Data Science: A Guide for Anyone Who Works with Data.* Victoria, BC: Leanpub.

Ripley, B.D. (2005) *Spatial Statistics.* Hoboken, NJ: John Wiley & Sons.

Rogerson, P.A. (2014) *Statistical Methods for Geography: A Student's Guide.* London: Sage.

Schutt, R. and O'Neil, C. (2013) *Doing Data Science: Straight Talk from the Frontline.* Sebastopol, CA: O'Reilly Media.

Silver, D., Huang, A., Maddison, C.J., Guez, A., Sifre, L., Van Den Driessche, G., et al. (2016) 'Mastering the game of go with deep neural networks and tree search', *Nature*, 529(7587): 484–489.

Tukey, J. (1977) *Exploratory Data Analysis.* Reading, MA: Addison-Wesley.

Weinberger, D. (2011) *Too Big to Know.* New York: Basic Books.

PART III
DIGITAL CULTURES

13

MEDIA AND POPULAR CULTURE

James Ash

INTRODUCTION

Media and popular culture have become an important area of concern for digital geographies. Of course, geographers were interested in media and popular culture prior to their expression in digital forms. There has been a whole suite of work on a variety of analog media such as film (Cresswell and Dixon, 2002; Aitken and Dixon, 2006), television (Hay, 1993; Christophers, 2009), photography (Kinsman, 1995; Larsen, 2005), radio (Pinkerton, 2008; Pinkerton and Dodds, 2009) and comic books (Dittmer, 2010; Gallacher, 2011), among others (for an overview, see Dittmer et al., 2014). Alongside these analog media, geographers have also investigated a number of born digital forms of media and popular culture, such as videogames (Ash and Gallacher, 2011), digital cinema (Jackman, 2015), image memes (Rose, 2016) and Graphics Interchange Format (GIF) images, which can be looped to create short animations (Ash, 2015).

What unites these different forms of media is that they are now, for the most part, accessed via distinct digital platforms. These platforms include image sharing apps and sites such as Instagram, video-sharing platforms such as YouTube and videogame digital distribution sites such as Steam. These platforms not only involve the creation of new forms of content, such as memes and GIFs, but also remediate many of the analog forms of media and popular culture mentioned above. For instance, analog forms of media such as comics and graphic novels are now sold as digital Portable Document Format (PDF) files via app-based platforms such as Marvel Unlimited, and movies recorded on celluloid are streamed on platforms such as Netflix as digital H.264/AVC files. With the remediation of analog content into digital formats and the emergence of new digital formats in mind, this chapter focuses on contemporary media and popular culture as less a series of distinct objects tied to particular mediums and more a set of overlapping and interconnected platforms and services that can be accessed on a variety of devices. For example, movies from a video-streaming service such as Netflix can be played on tablets, personal computers, smartphones, smart televisions, and games consoles. In a similar way, an image-sharing service such as Instagram can be accessed through a dedicated smartphone app, or a responsive webpage and images from the site can be embedded onto Facebook, Twitter and other social media sites.

Despite the rise and ubiquity of digital platforms, very few geographers working on media have examined how platforms are shaping the production and consumption of popular culture. For the sake of this chapter, popular culture can be understood as the 'everyday practices, experiences and beliefs of what has been called "the common people" – that overwhelming proportion of society that do not occupy positions of wealth and power' (Burgess and Gold, 2016: 3) – although of course, wealthy and powerful people can still enjoy popular culture. From this perspective, media are key to popular culture because people spend so much time engaging with media, which in turn influences their everyday conduct and beliefs about the world around them.

Addressing the absence of work on digital platforms by geographers, this chapter argues that researchers need to attend to the material specificity and logics of these platforms if they want to understand the changing geographies of media and popular culture. To make this claim, the rest of the chapter demonstrates how digital platforms, services and devices are producing new, and reshaping existing, forms of popular culture. Specifically, the chapter investigates how digital platforms are altering the contours of popular culture in three main ways. First, digital technologies are enabling new types of content to be produced and shared. Second, these platforms and services generate new micro-cultures associated with this content. Third, and finally, these micro-cultures create the potential for intensive affects between different groups of people, individuals, and objects, which serve as a new kind of currency that is central to the impact of digital media on popular culture and vice versa.

THE RISE OF DIGITAL PLATFORMS

Digital platforms shape the type of content that is produced and who produces it. The type of content produced is based on the platforms business model, where, '[t]o a greater-or-lesser extent, different platform types attempt to enrol participants who are figured not as "consumers" but as "users" who "co-create value"' (Langley and Leyshon, 2017: 17; see also Srnicek, 2017). Langley and Leyshon (2017: 13) term these types of service a form of platform capitalism, where platforms are defined as 'a discrete and dynamic arrangement defined by a particular combination of socio-technical and capitalist business practices'. Langley and Leyshon outline five different types of platform, three of which are relevant to our discussion of digital media and popular culture. These are: online exchange markets, which sell products and services through 'physical distribution, downloads, and streaming', such as Amazon, Apple, Spotify, and Ebay; social media and user-generated content that act as a 'host for user communities to post content', such as Facebook and YouTube; and crowdfunding, which acts as a 'marketplace for donation, pledging, lending or investing money', such as Kickstarter and Indiegogo (Langley and Leyshon, 2017: 16).

The technical aspects of these platforms are key to the type of content created and in turn the success and popularity of the platform as a whole. For instance, as Langley and Leyshon (2017: 21) argue in relation to YouTube:

> when YouTube became rapidly established during the latter half of 2005 as the go-to video content-hosting platform, it quickly outstripped Google Video which was launched contemporaneously. YouTube featured an interface that was extremely popular with users because digital content could be uploaded in almost any format, whereas Google Video required potential users to first download software that would standardise the format of their uploads. The ease and flexibility of the act of uploading ensured that the YouTube platform filled up with content, which in turn attracted audiences, and then advertisers. Google purchased YouTube in October 2006 at a cost of $1.65 billion.

DIGITAL PLATFORMS AND THE LOGICS OF CONTENT CREATION

Within the business models of platforms, authors or makers do not tend to work directly for a central studio or publisher, as in television, radio, film, and videogames, but become self-employed 'content creators' who earn money directly from advertising that is automatically linked to the content they generate or by selling products to users through the medium of the platform (Kim, 2012; Smith et al., 2012; Burgess and Green, 2013).

This business model, alongside each platform's internal rules and dynamics, shapes the type and style of content created and even encourages the development of new genres of media. In the case of YouTube, one can point to how it can automatically allocate video and banner adverts to videos and allow the uploader to receive a share of the revenue from the number of people who viewed these adverts. There is no limit to the allocation of adverts, meaning that users can upload as many videos as they want, whenever they want, and increase their advertising income from doing so. In turn, this led to the rise of the genre of daily video logging (vlogging). Daily vloggers film, edit, and upload a vlog every day to their YouTube channel. Some channels may focus on general everyday-life vlogs (e.g., Casey Neistat), while others may focus on a particular theme, activity or practice, such as skateboarding (e.g., John Hill) or travelling (e.g., Louis Cole). The necessity to film, edit, and upload engaging content every day that is necessary to create loyal viewers, both utilizes emerging forms of digital technology and provides the impetus for the creation of innovative techniques of filming, editing, and montage (Longhurst, 2009; Laurier, 2015). For example, the popular vlogger Casey Neistat uses a drone to film himself riding around the streets of New York on his electric skateboard. In doing so, he is travelling to his destination, as well as controlling the drone and framing the shot that will ultimately be edited into his vlog.

Beyond the quantity and frequency of videos, the logic of the platform also shapes the length of vloggers' videos. For instance, YouTubers realized that by creating videos longer than 10 minutes, YouTube would add more adverts to their video, thus enabling the content creator to earn more ad revenue. This resulted in videos just over 10 minutes in length becoming the norm for vloggers and thus shaping the medium of vlogging as a form of cultural expression (Snickars and Vonderau, 2009). As the simple example of YouTube demonstrates, the logic of platforms shapes the kind of content that is created on every level and in doing so transforms the environment in which popular culture is shared and disseminated.

Alongside the creation of new genres and styles of media, crowdfunding sites such as Kickstarter and Indiegogo enable the production of pre-existing forms of media that could not exist without these platforms. Take, for example, the crowdfunding campaign surrounding the videogame *Shenmue 3*. First released on the Sega Dreamcast in 2001, the *Shenmue* series was designed as an 11-chapter experience, with all chapters planned for release on the Dreamcast console. However, after the first two instalments of the game saw moderate commercial success, Sega pulled out of the console market, meaning the series was left unfinished. In the intervening years, the game picked up a cult following, with web forums such as shenmuedojo.net and YouTube channels such as shenmuedojo providing in-depth analysis of the games', as well as hosting video walkthroughs and music playlists from the games' soundtracks. In turn, several petitions were set up on change.org to demonstrate the demand for a third instalment of the game. This continued fan outcry encouraged the creator of *Shenmue*, Yu Suzuki, to launch a Kickstarter campaign to develop the game. The Kickstarter asked backers to fund $2 million of development, and anything raised over that amount would enable a series of stretch goals that would add features to the final delivered game.

The Kickstarter campaign was successful, finishing in July 2015 with 69,320 backers pledging over $6 million. The crowdfunded nature of *Shenmue 3*'s development not only allowed the game to be developed when major publishers would not invest, but also directly fed into and influenced the structure of the product itself. As Yu Suzuki put it in an interview after the Kickstarter campaign: 'for the Kickstarter, the architecture of the game was based on a scalable structure that could be adapted to the changes in budget. I can continually receive feedback from the backers through the entire process, which in turn helps to focus the development' (Sillis, 2016). In the case of *Shenmue 3*, whole sections of the final game would be either present or absent depending on the number of stretch goals reached. Here, the development of the game is intimately tied to the digital platforms upon which the funding for the game's development was raised. Beyond *Shenmue 3*, one could examine a similar transformation of the production of popular culture in relation to a range of other media such as crowdfunded music albums, board games or graphic novels on a range of platforms such as Patreon and Prosper. In any of these examples, it is clear that the digital nature of platforms has radically transformed both what kind of popular culture is produced and how it is produced.

DIGITAL PLATFORMS AND MICRO-CULTURES

As platforms lead a shift in the type of media content that is created and who creates it, this also results in the production of a highly diverse, yet specific set of micro-cultures. These cultures can be organized around particular channels, feeds, accounts or creators associated with specific products, hobbies, political orientations or skilled practices. What makes micro-cultures unique is that they can consist of anywhere between a few hundred and a few million people who follow the same creator, feed, account or channel, and these people may never meet one another face-to-face. Nonetheless, these micro-cultures create durable practices that are specific to that culture, such as the development of slang that is particular to the comments sections on a user's account, or through the use of a hashtag associated with that user, which is employed across a variety of platforms (Marwick, 2013). Understanding how platform users engage with and form these micro-cultures is an important topic of study for geographers interested in digital media and popular culture, because their comments, likes, and responses to content produced by others is key to the formation, circulation, and regulation of the content that enters into popular culture.

DIGITAL PLATFORMS, MICRO-CULTURES, AND AFFECT

The development of micro-cultures enabled by platforms can lead to the creation of new types and intensities of affective attachment between platform users and digital content (Balance, 2012; Kuntsman, 2012). Affect refers to the sensations, moods, and feelings actualized by an encounter with different objects and materials. These affective intensities are expressed in a number of ways, from practices of internet trolling, to meme culture and the creation and dissemination of GIFs. These practices are important for those interested in the geographies of media and popular culture because they increasingly influence how world events are experienced and understood (Meek, 2012).

As Pedwell (2017: 160) argues, images and graphical memes shared on social media can generate an affective power, which are 'enabled by the linked dynamics of amplification and participation'. For Pedwell (2017: 160), these affects are 'by their very nature, propagative … in making some small, yet notable, modification to a previous visual contribution'. For instance, we can consider how Twitter and other social media platforms enabled the rise and spread of the Pepe the Frog meme from its origins on the 4chan message board to an international symbol of the alt-right movement in the USA.

Pepe the Frog was created as a character in an internet comic strip by Matt Furie that was uploaded to the Myspace social network platform in 2005. Users of the 4chan message board appreciated the humour of the comic strip and Pepe's image was regularly used in memes and avatars on 4chan. At the same time, and coincidentally, several sub-boards on the 4chan site became an emerging meeting ground for the alt-right movement. As Malmgren (2017: 12) explains:

> Pepe the Frog's connection to the 'alt-right'… dates back to a late-night/pol/thread from the beginning of 2016. When one poster noticed that GOP consultant Cheri Jacobus had tweeted that 'the green frog symbol is what white supremacists use in their propaganda,' they were amused that someone would think such a thing. After some conversation about how the meme had been coopted by 'normies' (one user noted that Katy Perry had recently tweeted a Pepe), the thread decided to make Jacobus's observation true, in order to reclaim 4chan's intellectual property and ensure that nobody would want to be associated with the depressed green frog.

For Malmgren (2017: 12), the use of Pepe as a meme says a lot about the alt-right movement itself. As he puts it:

for the bulk of the 'alt-right' base, the embrace of an oppressive and violent politics has just been another way of having fun by pissing people off … a significant portion of the 'alt-right' base simply gets a rise out of pushing MSNBC to run segments on racist memes, or the Anti-Defamation League to add 4chan slang to its hate symbol database.

In other words, while the alt-right may have committed leaders who have specific ideological goals, many of the people who circulate these memes are not interested in developing an actual political movement. Rather, their goal is the proliferation of affect itself in order to agitate and stoke tension with little fear of reprisal or consequence (on Pepe the Frog, see also Applegate and Cohen, 2017).

In a rather different vein, we can also consider how users remix and rework existing content from popular culture such as films or video into new forms that circulate through different platforms for other purposes. For instance, looping GIF animations that can be embedded on Twitter, Facebook, and Instagram are often used to provide an amusing visual means for displaying how the user feels about a particular post or image to elicit some sensation or affect from the viewer. As Ash (2015: 126) argues, 'the very editing of [GIFs] creates new resonances and rhythms of sensation, which can potentially generate new affects'. Ash discusses the designer Micaël Reynaud, who uses photos to create time-lapse GIFs, such as a cat yawning on a lawn. In relation to a GIF of a loaf rising in an oven, 'these GIFs might invoke proprioceptive feelings of stickiness or warmth in the viewer's body as the dough thickens and rises, changing density, shape, and texture' (Ash, 2015: 130). Furthermore, the constant looping of these GIFs 'can induce affects of grip, grab … and holding in the muscles, as viewers try to examine, grasp, and visually immobilize the organized sensation of the constantly repeating image' (Ash, 2015: 130).

In the example of the yawning cat GIF, Ash suggests that the GIF might also affect the user on the 'level of involuntary memory, uniting past and present sensations into novel combinations. Past experiences of touching animal fur, or particular experiences with grass, might unite to generate a new affect of tiredness, as viewers watch the cat yawn while it sits on the grass' (Ash, 2015: 130). The examples of both image memes and GIFs suggest that affect, in terms of how it is produced, circulated, and experienced, is now a key currency of micro-cultures on various digital platforms, regardless of why the content linked to these affects is created. Geographers interested in media would therefore be wise to attend to these affects and how they come to be circulated on platforms because they have the potential to form the basis of so many people's experiences, conduct, and beliefs about the world around them.

STUDYING DIGITAL PLATFORMS AND POPULAR CULTURE

This chapter has pointed to a number of ways in which digitization is altering the relationship between media and popular culture. I argued that much of media and popular culture, in the West at least, is being produced and consumed via the materialities and logics of platforms, such as Facebook, YouTube, Twitter, Instagram, and so on. These platforms alter the type of media content that is created and how it is circulated. In turn, these platforms shape how media enter into popular culture through the generation of micro-cultures. Specifically, platforms generate micro-cultures organized around intensities of affect, and affect becomes the key currency through which content gains the power to travel, engage, and provoke people.

Previous work in geography on media and popular culture focused on particular mediums, such as television, radio, and cinema, and the distinct types of content these mediums produced. However, the rise of digital platforms challenges the notion that mediums and media are indelibly linked. Rather than differentiating between media as distinct types of content that are tied to a particular format, this chapter has suggested that digital geographers interested in media and popular culture should attend to the specificity of the logics and materialities of particular platforms and services. By identifying the types of content produced, how it is shared, the types of micro-cultures this content enables, and how this content affects people, geographers can begin to analyse how digital technologies are transforming the relationship between media, popular culture and the geographies of everyday life.

REFERENCES

Aitken, S.C. and Dixon, D. (2006) 'Imagining geographies of film', *Erdkunde*, 60(4): 326–336.

Applegate, M. and Cohen, J. (2017) 'Communicating graphically mimesis, visual language, and commodification as culture', *Cultural Politics*, 13(1): 81–100.

Ash, J. (2015) 'Sensation, networks, and the GIF: Toward an allotropic account of affect', in K. Hillis, S. Paasonen and M. Petit (eds), *Networked Affect*. Cambridge, MA: MIT Press. pp. 119–135.

Ash, J. and Gallacher, L.A. (2011) 'Cultural geography and videogames', *Geography Compass*, 5(6): 351–368.

Balance, C.B. (2012) 'How it feels to be viral me: Affective labor and Asian American YouTube performance', *WSQ: Women's Studies Quarterly*, 40(1–2): 138–152.

Burgess, J. and Gold, J. (2016) 'Place, the media and popular culture', in J. Burgess and J. Gold (eds), *Geography, the Media and Popular Culture*. London: Routledge. pp. 1–33.

Burgess, J. and Green, J. (2013) *YouTube: Online Video and Participatory Culture*. Oxford: John Wiley & Sons.

Christophers, B. (2009) *Envisioning Media Power: On Capital and Geographies of Television*. Lanham, MD: Lexington Books.

Cresswell, T. and Dixon, D. (2002) *Engaging Film: Geographies of Mobility and Identity*. Lanham, MD: Rowman & Littlefield Publishers.

Dittmer, J. (2010) 'Comic book visualities: A methodological manifesto on geography, montage and narration', *Transactions of the Institute of British Geographers*, 35(2): 222–236.

Dittmer, J., Craine, J. and Adams, P.C. (2014) *The Ashgate Research Companion to Media Geography*. Farnham: Ashgate.

Gallacher, L.A. (2011) '(Fullmetal) alchemy: The monstrosity of reading words and pictures in shonen manga', *Cultural Geographies*, 18(4): 457–473.

Hay, J. (1993) 'Invisible cities/visible geographies: Toward a cultural geography of Italian television in the 90s', *Quarterly Review of Film & Video*, 14(3): 35–47.

Jackman, A. (2015) '3-D cinema: Immersive media technology', *GeoJournal*, 80(6): 853–866.

Kim, J. (2012) 'The institutionalization of YouTube: From user-generated content to professionally generated content', *Media, Culture & Society*, 34(1): 53–67.

Kinsman, P. (1995) 'Landscape, race and national identity: The photography of Ingrid Pollard', *Area*, 300–310.

Kuntsman, A. (2012) 'Introduction: Affective fabrics of digital cultures', in A Karatzogianni and A. Kuntsman (eds), *Digital Cultures and the Politics of Emotion*. London: Springer. pp. 1–17.

Langley, P. and Leyshon, A. (2017) 'Platform capitalism: The intermediation and capitalization of digital economic circulation', *Finance and Society*, 3(1): 11–31.

Larsen, J. (2005) 'Families seen sightseeing: Performativity of tourist photography', *Space and Culture*, 8(4): 416–434.

Laurier, E. (2015) 'YouTube: Fragments of a video-tropic atlas', *Area*, 48(4): 488–495.

Longhurst, R. (2009) 'YouTube: A new space for birth?', *Feminist Review*, 93(1): 46–63.

Malmgren, E. (2017) 'Don't Feed the Trolls', *Dissent*, 64(2): 9–12.

Marwick, A. (2013) *Status Update: Celebrity, Publicity, and Branding in the Social Media Age*. New Haven, CT: Yale University Press.

Meek, D. (2012) 'YouTube and social movements: A phenomenological analysis of participation, events and cyberplace', *Antipode*, 44(4): 1429–1448.

Pedwell, C. (2017) 'Mediated habits: Images, networked affect and social change', *Subjectivity*, 10(2): 147–169.

Pinkerton, A. (2008) 'A new kind of imperialism? The BBC, Cold War broadcasting and the contested geopolitics of South Asia', *Historical Journal of Film, Radio and Television*, 28(4): 537–555.

Pinkerton, A. and Dodds, K. (2009) 'Radio geopolitics: Broadcasting, listening and the struggle for acoustic spaces', *Progress in Human Geography*, 33(1): 10–27.

Rose, G. (2016) 'Rethinking the geographies of cultural "objects" through digital technologies: Interface, network and friction', *Progress in Human Geography*, 40(3): 334–351.

Sillis, B. (2016) 'Kickstarting Shenmue 3 and the return of Ryo', *Redbull.com*. Available at: www.redbull.com/en/games/stories/1331775510544/shenmue-3-yu-suzuki-interview (accessed 1 February 2018).

Smith, A.N., Fischer, E. and Yongjian, C. (2012) 'How does brand-related user-generated content differ across YouTube, Facebook, and Twitter?', *Journal of Interactive Marketing*, 26(2): 102–113.

Snickars, P. and Vonderau, P. (eds) (2009) *The YouTube Reader*. Stockholm: National Library of Sweden.

Srnicek, N. (2017) *Platform Capitalism*. Cambridge: Polity Press.

14

SUBJECT/IVITIES

Sam Kinsley

INTRODUCTION

This chapter explores subjects/subjectivities in relation to digital geographies. I begin from the premise that there is no distinctly digital 'subject' or 'subjectivity'. Rather, the forms of subject or subjectivity studied as 'digital' are homologous with and bound up with wider understandings of those concepts. 'The subject' as an abstract catch-all figure can be attributed with the ability to act and is often characterized as the vessel for the identities, personhood, and experiences of different and diverse individuals. Indeed, a key concern expressed about the growth of (big) data-driven 'personalization' and surveillance is that it propagates monolithic data-based subjectivities (Amoore, 2013; Lupton, 2016; Thrift, 2011). In this sense, the 'ontological' entity of 'subject' appears to supplant the multiple, messy, forms of subjective experience; and both of these perhaps displace or elide wider discussions about agency (cf. Barnett, 2005; Jones, 2008). Digital media, networks, and technologies, of course, help to produce and bring into relief subjectivities, but it is not helpful, I argue, to consider these as essentially distinct from other, perhaps 'non-digital', subjectivities. Instead, we can productively see 'the digital' as a lens through which to examine emotional, legal, and political personhood and various forms of subjective experience.

There are three ways we can usefully understand 'the subject' and subjectivity to study 'digital' geographies. First, what is called 'the subject' is a conceptual figure, exemplified in discussions of the abstract figure of the digitally discretized, legally differentiated or surveilled individual. Second, particular kinds of role and responsibility can be understood as 'subject positions'. These are characterized by particular 'statistical doubles' (Rouvroy and Berns, 2013) represented in data and often governing the various ways we are addressed by companies or government. Third, the term 'subject' can refer to modes of experience as 'subjectivities', often addressed as the feelings and sensibilities of living with digital technologies, such as social media 'memes' (Wilson, 2015a) or fitness trackers (Pink and Fors, 2017). It should be stressed that these are not static categories; in a variety of geographical research they are all considered ongoing processes (Pile, 2008).

Subjectivities, in the three forms outlined above, are intimately linked to digital technology. We negotiate the performance of our identity through conditions of mediation, from government-issued personal identity codes to messages on WhatsApp. In turn, we come to understand who and what belongs and who is 'other' through digital media, from social media to the promise of smart cities – who we 'are' is often negotiated through mediation. We assume particular forms of status or receive responsibilities, and afford those qualities to organizations that may act autonomously, from companies to 'intelligent agents'. All of these issues may be discussed in terms of the figure of a 'subject', or the qualities of (more or less 'human') experience in terms of 'subjectivity'. Subjectivities in digital media geographies figure in more-or-less contrasting but sometimes overlapping accounts. These might be encapsulated as a surveilled individual (human) experience calculated by 'algorithms' into data, on the one hand, and expressions of mediated, yet still 'affective' and perhaps more than human, spatial experience, on the other.

To unpack the relationship between 'digital geographies' and subjectivity, this chapter consists of two main parts. First, I suggest that much geographical research explores how digital technologies generate particular forms of digital subject, through processes of abstraction and datafication. Most common is the data-based subject, subjectified through a population (through governmental or corporate surveillance) but, equally, atomized within herself as 'fractionated subject[s]' (Amoore, 2013: 8). Second, I interrogate the ways in which digital geographers explore what comes to count as a subject within various digital systems and processes and how this work might be further developed.

DATA AND THE SUBJECT OF SURVEILLANCE

Geographical research of 'digital' phenomena often uses variants of a digitally discretized figure that either imply or explicitly articulate a 'digital' subject or 'digital' modes of subjectivity. Such a subject, or modes of subjectivity, are often associated with codifications of (personal) identity and activity in data, often in significant volume. The capture, processing, and acting upon this data are often automated, for example performed by 'algorithms'. In such accounts, individuals are sometimes figured as outcomes of processes of 'subjectification' (Rose, 1998), which are more or less coercive and derived from governmental techniques

(Lemke, 2002). There are broadly two often used understandings of data-'derived' subjectivities. First, the data representations of a given individual are proximate to them, actions that play out in relation to the data derivative map onto the 'person'. For example, an individual travelling through an airport may be profiled using various forms of surveillance, resulting in a risk score that triggers some kind of action at a security checkpoint (see, for example, Amoore, 2013). This way of interrogating data-oriented subjective experience is mostly, therefore, 'personalized' in some way – it is concerned with a given person (subject). Second, the data representations are more free-floating, they feed back and forth into aggregate data, and form categorizations, or types, of people – we might see these as 'subject-positionings'. For example, users of shopping websites are often categorized according to their purchase history and receive recommendations on that basis, and there are many forms of market segmentation 'used to generate stable images of individual and group attitudes and motivations' (Barnett and Mahony, 2016: 367). Of course, as Rouvroy and Berns (2013) observe, there is both a figuring of an individual and wider profiling of types at the same time.

Particular geographies have been examined where data-driven subject-positionings are made visible. Borders, or places where bordering gets performed, are a key site of study. Amoore (2006, 2013) explores the ways in which people are broken up into atomized calculable risk factors, which we might call subject-positions, such as 'student', 'muslim' and 'woman', and through these 'dividing practices' … 'the subject becomes objectivised' (Amoore, 2006: 339). The recording, sorting, and profiling of individuals and populations according to biometric data anchors identity in bodily characteristics, which are used to govern the mobilities of different biometrically defined subject-positions (Amoore, 2006). As both Adey (2004a) and Amoore (2006) highlight, mobility becomes a defining factor in discerning both the subject-positions that emerge from such forms of profiling and the kinds of spatial experiences and the kinds of subjectivities that become performed with and in relation to such forms of surveillance. Indeed, Adey (2004b) argues that such forms of profiling and sorting, of governmentalizing subject-positions, were a prototype for wider reconfigurations of public space (a point echoed, albeit with different emphasis, by Graham, 2010). The figure of the 'migrant' is often used in such debates and for ways of understanding how the experiences and capacities of mobility are monitored and governed (Amoore, 2006; see also Bhabha, 1994). The body that moves across borders is fractioned through information technology-led systems, like the US VISIT programme, into 'ever-more finite categories of life – degrees of safe and dangerous, vulnerable and durable, mobile and restricted, identifiable and unidentified, verifiable and unverified and so on' (Amoore, 2013: 12). Accordingly, the subject as 'bare life' (Agamben, 1998) is an influential framing, in which 'living is reduced to calculability' (Amoore, 2006: 348). In doing so, the individual 'subject' is differentiated as a series of statistical selves, or subject-positions, represented in data. In the case of a 'migrant', these are 'dividing practices in which the subject is broken up into calculable risk factors both within herself (such as, for example, "student" and "muslim" and "woman") and necessarily also in relation to others (as, for example, "alien", "immigrant" or "illegal")' (Amoore, 2006: 339). Rouvroy and Berns' (2013) theorization of 'algorithmic governmentality' has proven an influential means of interrogating these 'statistical doubles'. They argue that through computational sorting, 'individual subjects are in fact avoided, to the extent that this creates a sort of statistical "double" of both subjects and "reality"' (Rouvroy and Berns, 2013: 167). Everyday things, from bank cards to bus tickets, hold a currency in these 'doublings' (Dodge and Kitchin, 2005). The bank card and mass transit cards (such as London's Oyster and Seoul's Upass) both uniquely index particular forms of transaction that can be a proxy for a given person, in their travel and in their exchange of money. Beyond tracking movement, the logs of such activity can feed into other measures such as credit scoring. Leszczynski (2015) identifies a double 'fear' of both: not being represented in data, so in some way missing out in the computational sorting that, she argues, increasingly structures life opportunities (such as credit scores), and also being represented in data in overly revealing and intimate ways (see also Leszczynski and Crampton, 2016).

Geographers have argued that the mappings of individuals into digitally discretized subject-positions produce and derive from forms of 'spatial big data', not only the GPS-enabled 'geotagging' of social media content, but also wider voluntary and passive disclosures of locational information (Leszczynski, 2015). Indeed, not only have the 'subjects' of data-gathering practices been concerned about representation and representativeness but so too have researchers within geography. Leszczynski (2017: 5) articulates debates around triangulating data sources and 'the extent to which data trails [are] considered representative of the socio-spatial phenomena that … analyses purport to inform, and the representativeness of the populations and subjectivities that are abstracted into these data flows'. More broadly, concerns about the surveillance of intimate details of life have long been discussed as constituting new forms of subjective experience. From relatively early in their development, the 'technological family' of geographic information systems has arguably been implemented to perform the kinds of 'statistical doubling' into subject-positions discussed above (Curry, 1997). The combining together of surveillance systems to produce more detailed 'doublings' has been analysed as a 'surveillant assemblage' (Haggerty and Ericson, 2000). Building from this work, geographers have developed a rich picture of how surveillant, 'data-doubling', systems become normalized (Wood, 2017) and how our experiences of everyday technology use can become predicated upon them (Evans and Perng, 2017). For example, through the use of, and perhaps reliance upon, self-tracking devices such as FitBit for fitness, we can become habituated to forms of commercial surveillance (Pink and Fors, 2017). These can also become linked to access to affordable healthcare and employment (Lupton, 2016). At the same time, writers such as Kitchin (2017; see also Part 3 of Kitchin et al., 2017) point to how less intrusive alternatives are being developed.

The consequences of data-driven subject-positionings are normatively figured as negative, apparently leading to experiences of less privacy, less personal choice and less exposure to different viewpoints. 'Attention' is an interesting diagnostic for both subject-positioning and subjective experience. 'Economies of attention' (Crogan and Kinsley, 2012) and related subjectivities are explored as a significant result of 'datafication' and 'dataveillance' (Graham and Wood, 2003; van Dijck, 2014). We are both categorized according to what we pay attention to and our attention is sought or 'filtered' according to those categorizations. Our attention, and wider practices of media use, are theorized in two key ways that say something about mediated subjective experience. First, attention is figured, by some, as a form of 'work' (echoing Smythe, 1981). Data about our media use has value to advertisers. Following Marxian analysis, we can be alienated from our attention work, dispossessed of its value, and the products of that apparently free labour are sold to advertisers. This has been the focus of several analyses of an 'attention economy', in which 'labour itself becomes "a subset of attention, one of the many kinds of possible attention potentially productive of value"' (Clough, 2003, citing Beller, 1998). For example, Wilson (2015b) analyses and contributes to the community mapping practices of non-profit organizations in furthering their responses to social justice issues such as food security. The data community organizers produce and the kinds of actions they enable, Wilson (2015b) argues, draw upon and produce a significant amount of 'attention-work', in the form of engagement with social media such as Facebook and YouTube, which reconfigures the kinds of subject-positions that volunteers and community organizers must adopt. Second, some have identified brain and nervous activity itself as an object or site of politics, with a neural conception of attention becoming a key issue. In her work on the practices and rationales of psychological governance, Pykett (2015) has highlighted the ways in which particular neuroscientific knowledge practices – such as in the increasingly mediated built environment through 'neuroarchitecture' (2015: 87) – have informed the development of policy, not least in relation to the smart cities agenda (2015: 95), constructing a range of normative subject-positionings. Both conceptualizations of an 'attention economy' advance familiar subject-positions and modes of subjective experience. On the one hand, attention-as-work puts us all in a proletarian position (Stiegler, 2012): we are 'working' even when at leisure (Marazzi, 2008; Terranova, 2012). Indeed, Ash (2012) has outlined the ways in which leisure activities such as playing videogames are designed to capture players' attentions and 'modulate affect' as a strategy for commercial success. On the other hand, attention as a neural condition, open to discipline or control, positions us as subjects of governmentality performed not only by states but also by large transnational corporations such as Facebook and Google (cf. Amoore, 2006; Bucher, 2012). If the subjective experiences of 'algorithmic governmentality' are according to forms of 'categorical suspicion', the subjective experiences of an attention economy are akin to 'categorical seduction' (Bauman and Lyon, 2013). The overarching character of 'digital' subject-positions is how individuals are both sorted and aggregated, thus a key facet of 'digital' subjectivities must then be who counts.

WHO COUNTS AS A (DIGITAL) SUBJECT?

An ongoing challenge for researchers of digital geographies is to discern who counts as a 'subject', who is enrolled in subject-positions, and what forms of subjective experience we should study. I identify three key concerns for geographers studying digital subject/ivities to negotiate: changing, perhaps new, forms of mediated subjective experience; normative negotiations of subject-positions in different domains; and epistemic shifts in legal and socio-technical understandings of who is accorded the status of 'subject'. First, it can be difficult to identify stable digital phenomena and the subjective experiences through which they may be performed. Perhaps due to our own 'statistical doubling' through academic metrifications, geographers sometimes overgeneralize and try to describe generic 'digital' experiences, such as the experience of Facebook or Twitter. Yet there may be significant diversity in the experience of a given social media platform or messaging app, such as the racialized use of hashtags on Twitter that can both facilitate 'anti/racist humour, sentiment and social commentary' and become 'instrumental in producing networked subjects which have the capacity to multiply the possibilities of being raced online' (Sharma, 2013: 46). The experience and performance of difference with/through digital media are complex (see Maragh, 2016; McLean and Maalsen, 2013) and need further attention. In particular, the ways in which automated systems propagate long-standing inequalities along lines of difference (e.g., NARMIC and American Friends Service Committee, 1982) warrant greater geographical scrutiny. So, accounts of subjective experiences of 'digital geographies' could make such differences more visible. Digital geographies could and should become more 'intersectional' (Noble and Tynes, 2016).

Second, the kinds of roles, or subject-positions, we assume within society may also evolve, disappear, and/or be replaced. A key area already being addressed is work. Work in a 'digital economy' influences subjective experience and forms of subject-positioning. Digital mediation has led to the blurring of roles alongside an extension of workplaces, a greater intensity and intimacy of working experiences, and a blurring of the status of what it means to be a 'worker' and how that labour is (not) valued (see Richardson, 2018). Airbnb 'hosts', for example, become positioned through performances of domesticity and hospitality that become conventional but do not necessarily form part of their remuneration. In doing so, a 'host's' intimate sphere (their home) becomes a workplace (Molz, 2012). Both academic and public debates have addressed work in relation to automation. We are told that 'the robots are coming' (Horton, 2015), which results in a 'crisis of abstract labour' (Holloway, 2010) or, worse, large-scale unemployment. Nevertheless, research shows everyday geographies of automation illustrate long-standing labour issues along lines of difference that demand further scrutiny (Bear and Holloway, 2015). Furthermore, what we consider to be 'automated' often may be, in actuality, the work of 'menial' digital work, arranged through platforms like Amazon's Mechanical Turk, often set in contradistinction to skilled 'innovative' labour (Irani, 2015). With the growth in the precariousness of work, enabled by networked infrastructures, the subject-positionings of 'digital' labour should be of concern (see Chapter 16).

Third, 'who' is accorded the status of 'subject' in light of automation and digital mediation is becoming a more intensively studied question. The rise of automation and 'artificial intelligence', actually and fictionally, prompts questions about agency and ownership. If 'robots' fulfil roles as carers, servants or sex 'workers' and if we grant or apportion 'them' agency and yet own 'them', questions arise about the legal and moral status of these 'robots' (cf. Bryson, 2010; Danaher, 2016). Likewise, the location of responsibility should fully automated weapons systems be deployed to take lives remains a deeply contentious issue (see Bhuta et al., 2016). As Casino (2016) notes, there are significant questions concerning the ethics of care in relation to automation. Furthermore, with the increases in the technical capacities for simulation, questions are prompted about the status of 'lifelike' automated simulations of our selves after death. The cultural and legal status of these representations is already a contested issue (D'Rozario, 2016). Rather than retreat from what may seem fanciful discussions concerning the status of (more or less) speculative subject-positions, 'digital geographies' should perhaps engage with their attendant geographical imaginations. A significant gap in the current calls for a consideration of the affective affordances, techno-bodily relation, and imaginings of automation (pace Bissell and Casino, 2017) is the agential and ethical/moral status of the automata, or 'robots', that are planned or are being introduced. An ongoing challenge is to tread the fine line between critical analysis of automation and how it is narrated or predicted and (inadvertently) affirming a technological determinism.

CONCLUSION

This chapter has examined how conceptualizations of a figure of 'the subject', 'subject positions', and subjective experience are usefully explored in and through 'digital' geographies. I began with the contention that there is no distinctly digital 'subject' or 'subjectivity'. Instead, I have sought to show how emotional, legal, and political personhood and various forms of subjective experience are integral to 'digital' geographies, but not essentially distinct. In particular, I have highlighted how subject-positionings produced and performed through digital technologies are framed in geographical research through understandings of calculation and statistics. Multiple, surveillant, data-derived representations of us as individuals are used to classify, govern, and sell to us individually and in categorized groups. Particular subject-positions thus emerge from such data practices that can perpetuate existing political economic iniquities, but have the potential to be otherwise. Our attention is said to be measured, modelled, and commoditized in an 'attention economy'. Ongoing research into automation and the subjective experiences of digital media, among other themes, render 'who' counts of pressing concern. It is tempting to see 'the digital' in this light as dystopian, but that risks a form of 'justifactory' or 'methodological' technological determinism (Wyatt, 2008: 174-175). While I argue there may not be essentially 'digital' subjectivities, there remain fruitful lines of inquiry for opening out the subject-positions and subjectivities through digital geographies. In this chapter I have identified three key concerns for 'digital' geographers to negotiate: first, mediated subjective experiences have (sometimes rapidly) changing forms, contingent upon complex sociotechnical systems of production and use; second, negotiating the norms of subject-positions in different domains; and third, ongoing shifts in legal and socio-technical understandings of 'who' is accorded the status of 'subject'.

REFERENCES

Adey, P. (2004a) 'Secured and sorted mobilities: Examples from the airport', *Surveillance and Society*, 1: 500–519.

Adey, P. (2004b) 'Surveillance at the airport: Surveilling mobility/mobilising surveillance', *Environment and Planning A*, 36: 1365–1380.

Agamben, G. (1998) *Homo Sacer: Sovereign Power and Bare Life*. Palo Alto, CA: Stanford University Press.

Amoore, L. (2006) 'Biometric borders: Governing mobilities in the war on terror', *Political Geography*, 25: 336–351.

Amoore, L. (2013) *The Politics of Possibility: Risk and Security beyond Probability*. Durham, NC: Duke University Press.

Ash, J. (2012) 'Attention, videogames and the retentional economies of affective amplification', *Theory, Culture & Society*, 29: 3–26.

Barnett, C. (2005) 'Ways of relating: Hospitality and the acknowledgement of otherness', *Progress in Human Geography*, 29: 5–21.

Barnett, C. and Mahony, N. (2016) 'Marketing practices and the reconfiguration of public action', *Policy & Politics*, 44: 367–382.

Bauman, Z. and Lyon, D. (2013) *Liquid Surveillance: A Conversation*. Cambridge: Polity Press.

Bear, C. and Holloway, L. (2015) 'Country life: Agricultural technologies and the emergence of new rural subjectivities', *Geography Compass*, 9: 303–315.

Beller, J. (1998) 'Capital/cinema', in E. Kaufman and K.J. Heller (eds), *Deleuze and Guattari: New Mappings in Politics, Philosophy and Culture*. Minneapolis: University of Minnesota Press. pp. 77–95.

Bhabha, H. (1994) 'Frontlines/borderposts', in A. Bammer (ed.), *Displacements: Cultural Identities in Question*. Indianapolis: Indiana University Press. pp. 269–272.

Bhuta, N., Beck, S., Geiß, R., Hin-Yan, L. and Kreß, C. (2016) *Autonomous Weapons Systems: Law, Ethics, Policy*. Cambridge: Cambridge University Press.

Bissell, D. and Casino, V.J.D. (2017) 'Whither labor geography and the rise of the robots?', *Social & Cultural Geography*, 18: 435–442.

Bryson, J.J. (2010) 'Robots should be slaves', in Y. Wilks (ed.), *Close Engagements with Artificial Companions: Key Social, Psychological, Ethical and Design Issues*. Amsterdam: John Benjamins Publishing. pp. 63–74.

Bucher, T. (2012) 'A technicity of attention: How software "makes sense"', *Culture Machine*, 13: 1–23.

Casino, V.J.D. (2016) 'Social geographies II', *Progress in Human Geography*, 40: 846–855.

Clough, P.T. (2003) 'Affect and control: Rethinking the body "beyond sex and gender"', *Feminist Theory*, 4: 359–364.

Crogan, P. and Kinsley, S. (2012) 'Paying attention: Towards a critique of the attention economy', *Culture Machine*, 13: 1–29.

Curry, M.R. (1997) 'The digital individual and the private realm', *Annals of the Association of American Geographers*, 87: 681–699.

D'Rozario, D. (2016) 'Dead celebrity (deleb) use in marketing: An initial theoretical exposition', *Psychology & Marketing*, 33: 486–504.

Danaher, J. (2016) 'Human enhancement, social solidarity and the distribution of responsibility', *Ethical Theory and Moral Practice*, 19: 359–378.

Dodge, M. and Kitchin, R. (2005) 'Codes of life: Identification codes and the machine readable world', *Environment and Planning D: Society & Space*, 23: 851–881.

Evans, L. and Perng, S.-Y. (2017) 'Spatial knowledge and behaviour', in R. Kitchin, T. Lauriault and M.W. Wilson (eds), *Understanding Spatial Media*. London: Sage. pp. 169–177.

Graham, S. (2010) *Cities Under Seige: The New Military Urbanism*. London: Verso.

Graham, S. and Wood, D.M. (2003) 'Digitizing surveillance: Categorization, space, inequality', *Critical Social Policy*, 23: 227–248.

Haggerty, K. and Ericson, R. (2000) 'The surveillant assemblage', *British Journal of Sociology*, 51: 605–622.

Holloway, J. (2010) 'Cracks and the crisis of abstract labour', *Antipode*, 42: 909–923.

Horton, R. (2015) 'The robots are coming'. A Deloitte Insight report. London: Deloitte LLP.

Irani, L. (2015) 'The cultural work of microwork', *New Media & Society*, 17: 720–739.

Jones, O. (2008) 'Stepping from the wreckage: Geography, pragmatism and anti-representational theory', *Geoforum*, 39: 1600–1612.

Kitchin, R. (2017) 'Leveraging finance and producing capital', in R. Kitchin, T. Lauriault and M.W. Wilson (eds), *Understanding Spatial Media*. London: Sage. pp. 178–187.

Kitchin, R., Lauriault, T. and Wilson, M.W. (2017) *Understanding Spatial Media*. London: Sage.

Lemke, T. (2002) 'Foucault, governmentality, and critique', *Rethinking Marxism*, 14: 49–64.

Leszczynski, A. (2015) 'Spatial big data and anxieties of control', *Environment and Planning D: Society and Space*, 33: 965–984.

Leszczynski, A. (2017) 'Digital methods I: Wicked tensions', *Progress in Human Geography*, DOI: 10.1177/0309132517711779.

Leszczynski, A. and Crampton, J. (2016) 'Introduction: Spatial Big Data and everyday life', *Big Data & Society*, 3(2). DOI: 10.1177/2053951716661366.

Lupton, D. (2016) *The Quantified Self*. Cambridge: Polity.

Maragh, R.S. (2016) 'Our struggles are unequal', *Journal of Communication Inquiry*, 40: 351–369.

Marazzi, C. (2008) *Capital and Language: From the New Economy to the War Economy*. Cambridge, MA: MIT Press.

McLean, J. and Maalsen, S. (2013) 'Destroying the joint and dying of shame? A geography of revitalised feminism in social media and beyond', *Geographical Research*, 51: 243–256.

Molz, J. (2012) 'CouchSurfing and network hospitality: "It's not just about the furniture"', *Hospitality & Society*, 1: 215–225.

NARMIC and American Friends Service Committee (1982) *Automating Apartheid: U.S. Computer Exports to South Africa and the Arms Embargo*. Philadelphia: National Action/Research on the Military-Industrial Complex/American Friends Service Committee.

Noble, S.U. and Tynes, B.M. (2016) *The Intersectional Internet: Race, Sex, Class, and Culture Online*. New York: Peter Lang.

Pile, S. (2008) 'Where is the subject? Geographical imaginations and spatializing subjectivity', *Subjectivity*, 23: 206–218.

Pink, S. and Fors, V. (2017) 'Being in a mediated world: Self-tracking and the mind-body-environment', *Cultural Geographies*, 24(3): 375–388.

Pykett, J. (2015) *Brain Culture: Shaping Policy through Neuroscience*. Bristol: Policy Press.

Richardson, L. (2018) 'Feminist geographies of digital work', *Progress in Human Geography*, 42(2): 244–263.

Rose, N. (1998) *Inventing Ourselves: Psychology, Power and Personhood*. Cambridge: Cambridge University Press.

Rouvroy, A. and Berns, T. (2013) 'Algorithmic governmentality and prospects of emancipation: Disparateness as a precondition for individuation through relationships?', *Réseaux*, 177: 163–196.

Sharma, S. (2013) 'Black Twitter? Racial hashtags, networks and contagion', *New Formations*, 78: 44–64.

Smythe, D.W. (1981) 'On the audience commodity and its work', in D.W. Smythe (ed.), *Dependency Road: Communications, Capitalism, Consciousness and Canada*. Norwood, NJ: Ablex. pp. 22–51.

Stiegler, B. (2012) 'Relational ecology and the digital pharmakon', *Culture Machine*, 13.

Terranova, T. (2012) 'Attention, economy and the brain', *Culture Machine*, 13.

Thrift, N. (2011) 'Lifeworld Inc. and what to do about it', *Environment and Planning D: Society & Space*, 29: 5–26.

van Dijck, J. (2014) 'Datafication, dataism and dataveillance: Big data between scientific paradigm and ideology', *Surveillance and Society*, 12: 197–208.

Wilson, M.W. (2015a) 'Morgan Freeman is dead and other big data stories', *Cultural Geographies*, 22: 345–349.

Wilson, M.W. (2015b) 'Paying attention, digital media, and community-based critical GIS', *Cultural Geographies*, 22: 177–191.

Wood, D.M. (2017) 'Spatial profiling, sorting and prediction', in R. Kitchin, T. Lauriault and M.W. Wilson (eds), *Understanding Spatial Media*. London: Sage. pp. 225–235.

Wyatt, S. (2008) 'Technological determinism is dead; long live technological determinism', in E.J. Hackett, O. Amsterdamska, M. Lynch, J. Wajcman and W.E. Bijker (eds), *The Handbook of Science and Technology Studies*. Cambridge, MA: MIT Press. pp. 165–180.

15

REPRESENTATION AND MEDIATION

Gillian Rose

INTRODUCTION

The concept of representation first gained a significant foothold in the discipline of geography in the late 1980s, as part of the 'new cultural geography'. As geographers began to engage with the 'cultural turn' taking place across the social sciences more broadly, the notion of representation was elaborated by a number of cultural geographers who drew on a particular tradition of British Marxist thought (Burgess, 1990; Cosgrove, 1984; Cosgrove and Daniels, 1989; Jackson, 1989). The concept spread across the discipline and became a key term for explorations of the cultural construction of social reality, operationalized through interpretive readings of cultural and other kinds of texts (Barnes and Duncan, 1992). Representation, then, was part of the intellectual context into which a new kind of interest in digital geographies emerged in the late 1990s. Although geographers had been using digital technologies such as geographic information systems and statistical analysis packages as research tools for decades, the earliest sustained discussions by geographers of what was then called cyberspace or virtual space appeared in the late 1990s and focused on digital forms of information communication technologies (ICTs) (Bingham et al., 1999, 2001; Crang et al., 1999; Graham and Marvin, 2001; Holloway et al., 2000; Kitchin, 1998).

The next part of this chapter explores how some of those digital geographies deployed the concept of representation. However, representation and its theoretical baggage were never quite sufficient to attend to the full range of changes being enacted through digital technologies. As ICTs rapidly evolved during the

1990s – from smartphones and social media platforms to big data and ubiquitous computing – representation was outflanked as an analytical tool (as indeed was cultural geography as a sub-discipline adequate to their analysis, it could be argued; Rose, 2016). As both digital technologies and scholarship on digital geographies expanded, another term became more frequently used as a way of understanding the effects of those technologies: *mediation*. The third section of this chapter examines some key discussions of digital mediation and considers the relationship between mediation and representation. The fourth section speculates on future developments.

REPRESENTATION AND DIGITAL GEOGRAPHIES

'Representation' can be both a process and an object. As a process, it refers to the way in which humans interpret their experiences of the world by giving them meaning. 'Our concepts, images and emotions "stand for", or represent, in our mental life, things which are or may be "out there" in the world' (Hall, 2013: xx). Representation as a process might thus be characterized as an intermediary between entities, and more specifically as a process of meaningful symbolization or signification. As a concept, then, representation makes a theoretical distinction between what is represented and its representation. Representation can also describe objects. In books like Cosgrove's *Social Formation and Symbolic Landscape* (1984) and Duncan's *The City as Text* (1990), geographers took objects such as landscape paintings, maps, and architecture as representations which interpreted the world in certain ways. Cultural geographers were particularly interested in interpreting the meanings given to material locations (cities, landscapes, nations) but also the representations of those geographies in cultural texts such as novels, films, and travel guides. Such material objects were understood as imbued with meanings, values, ideas, and feelings which needed careful interpretation to understand their significance, particularly in terms of the social identities and relations that they assumed or contested. Who, where, and what was represented, how, and with what effects, were key questions for the new cultural geography.

Both understandings of representation – as process and object – were used by geographers interested in ICTs. As Bingham (1999) and Kitchin (1998) note, in the late 1990s the notion of 'cyberspace' was being widely discussed in magazines, memoirs, manuals, films, television programmes, and so on. Several of the geographers interested in the spatialities of new computer-mediated communication considered how these popular discussions were representing cyberspace in particular kinds of ways. Many such popular discussions made a clear distinction between the cyberspace produced by digital communication technologies and the 'real' space of everyday human experience, a binary representation that many geographers challenged (Crang et al., 1999; Madge and O'Connor, 2005). Bingham (1999) described this separation as the most recent version of the technological sublime, a long-standing and totalizing interpretation of new technologies which turned on technological fetishism and determinism, all of which enacted a masculinist position of knowledge and/as power. Kneale (1999) discussed the influential novels of William Gibson, particularly *Neuromancer* (1984), and described them as 'tools used by authors and readers to make sense of [cyber] space' (Kneale, 1999: 206). For Kneale, this resulted in cyberspace being represented as, for example, kinetic and synaesthetic, and this particular representation worked to enact a powerful masculinist colonizing gaze over a new territory, with 'a certain conservatism' detected in the readers who tend to replicate that gaze (Kneale, 1999: 219). A decade later, on the cusp of another wave of fascination with new digital technologies – this time ubiquitous computing, big data, and smart cities – a similar critique was made by Kinsley (2010) in his discussion of vision videos made by large digital corporations. Treating the videos in part as 'representational artefacts', he argued that they anticipate very particular kinds of futures and thus enact a specific politics of anticipation (Kinsley, 2011; see also Rose, 2017b).

As well as discussions of the representation of digital technologies, the notion of representation has also been brought to bear on the ways in which digital technologies are themselves used to make representations (Kitchin and Dodge, 2011: 111–134). Sometimes these digital artefacts mimic the products of older visual technologies. Some attention has been given to computer-generated images on billboards advertising new urban development projects, for example, which draw on the conventions of advertising, architectural photography, and aerial photography, and which picture 'imaginaries of place circumscribed through resolutely corporate and privatized productions' (Jackson and della Dora, 2011: 308; see also Degen et al., 2017). Geographers have also begun to study some of the social media platforms established over the past decade, such as YouTube. Several studies suggest that many YouTube videos replicate existing social relations. In her study of birthing videos, for example, Longhurst (2009: 48) concluded that 'power relations in cyber/space reflect and reinforce power relations in "real" space. … YouTube does not sit outside of normative expectations of what constitutes an "acceptable" representation of birth, but rather functions to reflect and reinforce these expectations', with most videos picturing conventional understandings of a 'good' birth (see also Casino and Brooks, 2015: 475). Studies of other digital media platforms concur. It has been argued that participatory mapping using Google Earth can reiterate existing racialized urban landscapes (Crutcher and Zook, 2009) and that photographs on Flickr represent Western images of the world (Lambio and Lakes, 2017), while studies of Wikipedia have noted the uneven distribution of both the coverage of Wikipedia pages (Graham et al., 2014) and the writers of these pages (Graham et al., 2015).

Attention is also now being paid to the representations embedded in new forms of the digital visualization of spaces and places. Digital animations of future cities (Rose, 2017b), hurricanes (Woodward et al., 2015), computer games (Ash, 2009; Moran and Etchegoyen, 2017), smartphone applications (Leszczynski and Elwood, 2015), and spatial media activism (Elwood and Leszczynski, 2013; Hawkins and Silver, 2017) have all been discussed in terms of representation as a practice undertaken by specific actors that create specific versions of the world. While much of this work emphasizes how digital representation 'continues to reflect the contours and divisions of the offline world in which its creators live' (Crutcher and Zook, 2009: 524), other work suggests that the participatory nature of many digital technologies can be harnessed in order to create representations of place that challenge dominant interpretations. For instance, digital mapping tools (Crampton, 2013), augmented reality mobile apps (see, for example, Koeck and Warnaby, 2015; Liao and Humphreys, 2014), digital film making and sharing (Dickens and Butcher, 2016), and i-documentaries (Harris, 2017) have all been interpreted as being able to contest prevailing representations of different spaces and places.

DIGITAL GEOGRAPHIES AND MEDIATION

Embedded in the notion of representation is a particular understanding of what is distinctive about human beings. Representation emerged from a form of cultural theory that assumed a distinction between human biology and culture. As Hall (2013: xix) puts it, the practice of meaning making is distinct from 'what is simply biologically driven'. In other words, for Hall, makers and interpreters of meanings are human through and through, even when humans create and use technology to make this meaning. As a by-product of this explicit humanism, accounts of representation also focused on how meaning could be contested by humans – indeed, Barnett (2004) criticized cultural geography for constantly presuming to find 'resistance' to hegemonic representations. This focus on the human agency that drives representation as a practice has fed through to much digital geographical work. There are persistent references to the work of fantasy, imagination, and desire, for example, in discussions of how specific technologies are given meaning by their users (Boulton and Zook, 2013; Kinsley, 2010).

However, other work by digital geographers has been particularly concerned precisely with an absence of human agency in representational practices. This is particularly the case among geographers interested in the processes of digital data search (Graham et al., 2013; Shelton, 2017). This body of work uses the term 'representation' to refer to the way in which data selectively represent the real world. Power here is understood in terms not so much of what forms of social identities and relations are reproduced as of who it is that controls the algorithmic means of producing representations (Kinsley, 2015; Leszczynski, 2012; Thatcher et al., 2016).

Some of this interest in non-human forms of agency – in the agency of code and algorithms – is indebted to quite different philosophical traditions from the humanist Marxism favoured by cultural geographers (Rose, 2017a). Accounts of the 'sentient city', for example, use Deleuzian accounts of affect to emphasize the agency of software and its 'automatic production of space' (Thrift and French, 2002). Dense webs of sensors, algorithms, protocols, and databases are described as producing 'the world of "local intelligence" in which everyday spaces become saturated with computational capacities, thereby transforming more and more spaces into computationally active environments able to communicate within and with each other' (Thrift and French, 2002: 315). In this work, the human is 'no longer modelled on the individual psyche but on mimetic waves of sentiment which are able to move … rapidly through populations' (Thrift, 2009: 122). Such an account is explicitly non-representational and, perhaps partly as a consequence of its lack of interest in representations, has been criticized for a lack of concern with the ways in which different kinds of humans are constituted by and with digital technologies (Rose, 2017a).

A shift in the objects that make up digital geographies, from fixed screens and computers to smart devices and environmentally embedded sensors (Crampton, 2009; Leszczynski, 2015), has also encouraged a move away from notions of 'representation'. Given the ubiquity of spatial media, many geographers are arguing that spatial media cannot only represent social life; rather, social life must happen through spatial media. Instead of brokering human relations with the world (by representing it), spatial media actively constitute both self and world. Humans do not engage with digital technologies through representations of them, nor are digital technologies representational intermediaries between humans and the world. Rather, from this perspective, digital technologies appear as a constitutive condition of social life.

The result of these empirical changes in digital technology, in many areas of digital geographies scholarship, has been a preference for the concept of 'mediation' rather than 'representation' and for 'affect' rather than 'meaning' as its consequence. Writing in 2015, Leszczynski explored both mediation as a process and digital spatial media as a noun. Mediation as a process resolutely refuses the distinction between the real and its representation (Kember and Zylinska, 2012). In so far as it is attentive to questions of meaning, mediation assumes that the world is no longer *represented* by cultural objects, but is *produced* at multiple sites, between hardware, software, and humans. Meaning making is therefore less a matter of resistance and more one of reinvention by recombination (Rose, 2017a), productivity (Hartley, 2012) or 'distributed feedback' (McQuire, 2016: 45).

As a noun, mediation refers to the materiality of specific media, and Leszczynski also used the term in this sense to describe the specificities of digital spatial media: 'their modifiability (or malleability), independence of content from instantiating technologies, hybridity, interactivity, portability, intimacy, and the ways in which they organize, subsume, and position presences, people, and practices in (relation to) networks' (Leszczynski, 2015: 738). While other accounts of digital spatial media emphasize somewhat different aspects (see, for example, McQuire, 2016), there is a sense in these discussions of digital spatial media that meaning is extended, spreadable (Jenkins et al., 2013), and multiple. It is performed and materialized at specific sites; it is accessed, made to travel, searched for, modified, patched, and laboured over in an uneven, variable, and frictional network held together by diverse forms of work.

This digital geographical scholarship on mediation rejects representation as a process. However, representation does linger on in some of this work as a noun referring to a certain class of objects, albeit ones that now need to be seen rather differently. No longer stable cultural texts, representations as mediated *objects* need to be understood as carrying the traces of their digitality with them (Rose, 2016). Longhurst's (2016) account of mothers' digitally mediated communication with their children describes different technologies being used to convey different kinds of messages, for example, so that the meanings of the texts and images sent are inflected by the specificities of digital devices and media. In their study of the creation of computer-generated images as part of an urban design project, Rose et al. (2014) also embed digital qualities into their understanding of imagery, arguing that digital images need to be understood as an unstable, crafted assemblage of components generated in different places by different actors (see also November et al., 2010; Rose et al., 2015). In digital spatial media, then, it might be concluded that the meaning of text or imagery 'is itself and more' (Dean, 2010: 115), residing in both its significations and the specific qualities of its digitality.

FUTURE DIRECTIONS

This account of representation, mediation, and digital geographies has suggested that the field of digital geographies concerned with digital forms of communication frames its object of study according to both theoretical and technological shifts. Clearly both those kinds of shifts will continue into the future. Certainly there are many digital meaning-making technologies whose mediations – representational or otherwise – have barely been addressed by geographers. This is particularly true of social media platforms and their immense and complex geographies of production, encounter, and circulation. Images, sounds, and texts about places are made in and travel through highly differentiated networks, by many different people, and are seen, heard, and read in many different ways. Other such technologies – including those that promise augmented, virtual, and interactive realities – are about to go mainstream. Geographers need to be much more engaged with these technologies as they mediate many everyday lives. To conclude on a note of caution, geographers must also not neglect to examine the ways in which new and old forms of social difference and power are represented and mediated by digital technologies. Accounting for social difference and power was a key concern of the new cultural geography, and its focus on representation formed the basis of its cultural politics. Even if this cultural politics could on occasion descend into caricature, with power always being met by resistance, accounting for social differentiation and its effects should remain absolutely central in future digital geographical scholarship.

REFERENCES

Ash, J. (2009) 'Emerging spatialities of the screen: Video games and the reconfiguration of spatial awareness', *Environment and Planning A*, 41(9): 2105–2124.

Barnes, T.J. and Duncan, J.S. (eds) (1992) *Writing Worlds: Discourse, Text and Metaphor in the Representation of Landscape*. London: Routledge.

Barnett, C. (2004) 'A critique of the cultural turn', in J.S. Duncan, N.C. Johnson and R.H. Schein (eds), *A Companion to Cultural Geography*. Oxford: Blackwell. pp. 38–48.

Bingham, N. (1999) 'Unthinkable complexity? Cyberspace otherwise', in M. Crang, P. Crang and J. May (eds), *Virtual Geographies: Bodies, Space and Relations*. London: Routledge. pp. 244–260.

Bingham, N., Valentine, G. and Holloway, S. (1999) 'Where do you want to go tomorrow? Connecting children and the Internet', *Environment and Planning D: Society and Space*, 17(6): 655–672.

Bingham, N., Valentine, G. and Holloway, S. (2001) 'Life around the screen: Re-framing young people's use of the internet', in N. Watson and S. Cunningham-Burley (eds), *Reframing Bodies*. London: Palgrave Macmillan. pp. 228–243.

Boulton, A. and Zook, M. (2013) 'Landscape, locative media, and the duplicity of code', in N.C. Johnson, R.H. Schein and J. Winders (eds), *The Wiley-Blackwell Companion to Cultural Geography*. Chichester: Wiley. pp. 437–451.

Burgess, J. (1990) 'The production and consumption of environmental meanings in the mass media: A research agenda for the 1990s', *Transactions of the Institute of British Geographers*, 15(2): 139–161.

Casino, V.J.D. and Brooks, C.F. (2015) 'Talking about bodies online: Viagra, YouTube, and the politics of public(ized) sexualities', *Gender, Place & Culture*, 22(4): 474–493.

Cosgrove, D.E. (1984) *Social Formation and Symbolic Landscape*. London: Croom Helm.

Cosgrove, D.E. and Daniels, S.G.H. (eds) (1989) *The Iconography of Landscape: Essays on the Symbolic Representation, Design and Use of Past Environments*. Cambridge: Cambridge University Press.

Crampton, J. (2009) 'Cartography: MAPS 2.0', *Progress in Human Geography*, 33(1): 91–100.

Crampton, J. (2013) 'Mappings', in N.C. Johnson, R.H. Schein and J. Winders (eds), *The Wiley-Blackwell Companion to Cultural Geography*. Chichester: Wiley. pp. 423–436.

Crang, M., Crang, P. and May, J. (eds) (1999) *Virtual Geographies: Bodies, Spaces, Relations*. London: Routledge.

Crutcher, M. and Zook, M. (2009) 'Placemarks and waterlines: Racialized cyberscapes in post-Katrina Google Earth', *Geoforum*, 40(4): 523–534.

Dean, J. (2010) *Blog Theory: Feedback and Capture in the Circuits of Drive*. Cambridge: Polity.

Degen, M., Melhuish, C. and Rose, G. (2017) 'Producing place atmospheres digitally: Architecture, digital visualisation practices and the experience economy', *Journal of Consumer Culture*, 17(1): 3–24.

Dickens, L. and Butcher, M. (2016) 'Going public? Re-thinking visibility, ethics and recognition through participatory research praxis', *Transactions of the Institute of British Geographers*, 41(4): 528–540.

Duncan, J.S. (1990) *The City as Text: The Politics of Landscape Interpretation in the Kandyan Kingdom*. Cambridge: Cambridge University Press.

Elwood, S. and Leszczynski, A. (2013) 'New spatial media, new knowledge politics', *Transactions of the Institute of British Geographers*, 38(4): 544–559.

Gibson, W. (1984) *Neuromancer*. London: Gollancz.

Graham, M., De Sabbata, S. and Zook, M.A. (2015) 'Towards a study of information geographies: (Im)mutable augmentations and a mapping of the geographies of information', *Geo: Geography and Environment*, 2(1): 88–105.

Graham, M., Hogan, B., Straumann, R.K. and Medhat, A. (2014) 'Uneven geographies of user-generated information: Patterns of increasing informational poverty', *Annals of the Association of American Geographers*, 104(4): 746–764.

Graham, M., Zook, M. and Boulton, A. (2013) 'Augmented reality in urban places: Contested content and the duplicity of code', *Transactions of the Institute of British Geographers*, 38(3): 464–479.

Graham, S. and Marvin, S. (2001) *Splintering Urbanism: Networked Infrastructures, Technological Mobilities and the Urban Condition*. London: Routledge.

Hall, S. (2013) 'Introduction', in S. Hall, J. Evans and S. Nixon (eds), *Representation*. London: Sage. pp. xvii–xxvi.

Harris, E. (2017) 'Introducing i-docs to geography: Exploring interactive documentary's nonlinear imaginaries', *Area*, 49(1): 25–34.

Hartley, J. (2012) *Digital Futures for Cultural and Media Studies*. Chichester: John Wiley.

Hawkins, R. and Silver, J.J. (2017) 'From selfie to #sealfie: Nature 2.0 and the digital cultural politics of an internationally contested resource', *Geoforum*, 79: 114–123.

Holloway, S.L., Valentine, G. and Bingham, N. (2000) 'Institutionalising technologies: Masculinities, femininities, and the heterosexual economy of the IT classroom', *Environment and Planning A*, 32(4): 617–633.

Jackson, M.S. and della Dora, V. (2011) 'Spectacular enclosures of hope: Artificial islands in the Gulf and the urban present', in R. Shields, O. Park and T. Davidson (eds), *Ecologies of Affect: Placing Nostalgia, Desire and Hope*. Waterloo, Ontario: Wilfrid Laurier University Press. pp. 293–316.

Jackson, P. (1989) *Maps of Meaning: An Introduction to Cultural Geography*. London: Unwin Hyman.

Jenkins, H., Ford, S. and Green, J. (2013) *Spreadable Media*. New York: New York University Press.

Kember, S. and Zylinska, J. (2012) *Life after New Media: Mediation as a Vital Process*. Cambridge, MA: MIT Press.

Kinsley, S. (2010) 'Representing "things to come": Feeling the visions of future technologies', *Environment and Planning A*, 42(11): 2771–2790.

Kinsley, S. (2011) 'Anticipating ubiquitous computing: Logics to forecast technological futures', *Geoforum*, 42(2): 231–240.

Kinsley, S. (2015) 'Memory programmes: The industrial retention of collective life', *Cultural Geographies*, 22(1): 155–175.

Kitchin, R. (1998) *Cyberspace: The World in the Wires*. Chichester: Wiley.

Kitchin, R. and Dodge, M. (2011) *Code/Space: Software and Everyday Life*. Cambridge, MA: MIT Press.

Kneale, J. (1999) 'The virtual realities of technology and fiction: Reading William Gibson's cyberspace', in M. Crang, P. Crang and J. May (eds), *Virtual Geographies: Bodies, Space and Relations*. London: Routledge. pp. 205–221.

Koeck, R. and Warnaby, G. (2015) 'Digital chorographies: Conceptualising experiential representation and marketing of urban/architectural geographies', *Architectural Research Quarterly*, 19(2): 183–192.

Lambio, C. and Lakes, T. (2017) 'Placing of photos on the internet: Critical analysis of biases on the depictions of France and Afghanistan on FLICKR', *Geoforum*, 82: 21–25.

Leszczynski, A. (2012) 'Situating the geoweb in political economy', *Progress in Human Geography*, 36(1): 72–89.

Leszczynski, A. (2015) 'Spatial media/tion', *Progress in Human Geography*, 39(6): 729–751.

Leszczynski, A. and Elwood, S. (2015) 'Feminist geographies of new spatial media', *The Canadian Geographer/Le Géographe canadien*, 59(1): 12–28.

Liao, T. and Humphreys, L. (2014) 'Layar-ed places: Using mobile augmented reality to tactically reengage, reproduce, and reappropriate public space', *New Media & Society*, 17(9): 1418–1435.

Longhurst, R. (2009) 'YouTube: A new space for birth?', *Feminist Review*, 93(1): 46–63.

Longhurst, R. (2016) 'Mothering, digital media and emotional geographies in Hamilton, Aotearoa New Zealand', *Social & Cultural Geography*, 17(1): 120–139.

Madge, C. and O'Connor, H. (2005) 'Mothers in the making? Exploring liminality in cyber/space', *Transactions of the Institute of British Geographers*, 30(1): 83–97.

McQuire, S. (2016) *Geomedia: Networked Cities and the Future of Public Space*. Cambridge: Polity Press.

Moran, D. and Etchegoyen, L. (2017) 'The virtual prison as a digital cultural object: Digital mediation of political opinion in simulation gaming', *Environment and Planning A*, 49(2): 448–466.

November, V., Camacho-Hübner, E. and Latour, B. (2010) 'Entering a risky territory: Space in the age of digital navigation', *Environment and Planning D: Society and Space*, 28(4): 581–599.

Rose, G. (2016) 'Rethinking the geographies of cultural "objects" through digital technologies: Interface, network and friction', *Progress in Human Geography*, 40(3): 334–351.

Rose, G. (2017a) 'Posthuman agency in the digitally mediated city: Exteriorization, individuation, reinvention', *Annals of the American Association of Geographers*, 107(4): 779–793.

Rose, G. (2017b) 'Screening smart cities: Managing data, views and vertigo', in P. Hesselberth and M. Poulaki (eds), *Compact Cinematics: The Moving Image in the Age of Bit-Sized Media*. London: Bloomsbury Academic. pp. 177–184.

Rose, G., Degen, M. and Melhuish, C. (2014) 'Networks, interfaces, and computer-generated images: Learning from digital visualisations of urban redevelopment projects', *Environment and Planning D: Society and Space*, 32(3): 386–403.

Rose, G., Degen, M. and Melhuish, C. (2015) 'Looking at digital visualisations of urban redevelopment projects: Dimming the scintillating glow of unwork', in S. Jordan and C. Lindner (eds), *Cities Interrupted: Visual Culture, Globalisation and Urban Space*. London: Bloomsbury. pp. 105–120.

Shelton, T. (2017) 'The urban geographical imagination in the age of Big Data', *Big Data & Society*, 4(1): DOI: 2053951716665129.

Thatcher, J., O'Sullivan, D. and Mahmoudi, D. (2016) 'Data colonialism through accumulation by dispossession: New metaphors for daily data', *Environment and Planning D: Society and Space*, 34(6): 990–1006.

Thrift, N. (2009) 'Different atmospheres: of Sloterdijk, China, and site', *Environment and Planning D: Society and Space*, 27(1): 119–138.

Thrift, N. and French, S. (2002) 'The automatic production of space', *Transactions of the Institute of British Geographers*, 27(3): 309–335.

Woodward, K., Jones, J.P., Vigdor, L., Marston, S.A., Hawkins, H. and Dixon, D. (2015) 'One sinister hurricane: Simondon and collaborative visualization', *Annals of the Association of American Geographers*, 105(3): 496–511.

PART IV
DIGITAL ECONOMIES

16

LABOUR

Mark Graham and Mohammad Amir Anwar

INTRODUCTION

David Harvey once famously noted that work is inherently place-based because, in contrast to capital, 'labour-power has to go home every night' (Harvey, 1989: 19). Work has traditionally been tethered to place: a farmer tilling a field; a hunter hunting prey; a factory worker operating a machine; a homeworker cooking and cleaning in a house. All these activities have required workers to be physically proximate to the object or output of their labour.

This relationship between workers and place became more complicated once the raw material that people were working with was information – something that could be manipulated remotely. The tool was no longer just a spade, a plough, or a machine in a factory, but rather devices that could store and instantaneously transmit information. A worker always performs work in the time and place that they inhabit, but all of a sudden their work is also simultaneously done somewhere else.

This meant that an important link between workers and the object of their work was severed. If workers can do information-based work that can be quickly transmitted around the world, then that work can, in theory, be done from anywhere and by anyone who has access to the right machines and connectivity. When you file a complaint because the train was late or call an airline to request a special meal on your flight, the workers who handle your request could be either down the road from you or on the other side of the planet. We have a mass migration of labour without the migration of workers (Standing, 2016).

Does this mean that geography no longer matters to digital work? Not exactly. This chapter draws on our previous empirical research into digital labour to outline how geography matters, and who it matters for in a world of increasingly digital work. The contemporary geography of digital labour can be used to exploit workers, but we also argue that it opens up distinct possibilities for digital workers to recreate their own worlds of work.

HISTORICAL CONTEXTUALIZATION: OLD AND NEW SILK ROADS

In contemporary scholarship, the term 'digital labour' has been used to describe a huge variety of activities: clickwork done in people's homes, call centre work in large offices, editing a Wikipedia article, and even uploading a photograph to social media from a phone (Graham, 2012; Fuchs, 2013; Scholz, 2013). This chapter is concerned with the kind of digital labour that is both income-generating and digitally intensive (rather than just delivered over digital networks).[1] In order to adequately discuss the nature of digital labour, it is useful to first outline what is and is not new about digital work.

Since the advent of trade, long and complicated global production networks have existed, with workers on one side of the planet labouring to make things that would be sold and used on the other side without coming in contact with their consumers. For instance, two thousand years ago, the Silk Road allowed Roman glassware to be sold in China and Chinese silk to be sold in the Roman Empire. Now the advent of contemporary technologies has changed the temporality of such relationships: a Kenyan rose grower who picks and packages her flowers on a Monday on the shores of Lake Naivasha could have her products bought and displayed in a home in Rome by the end of the week.

In both moments and modes of production, and everything in between, there is a spatial division of labour at play (Massey, 1998). In other words, there is a functional division of labour between different parts of the world. With exceptions, due to highly uneven geographies of transportation technologies, the further away a production site is from the end consumers in a global production network, the longer it takes to deliver goods. This means some non-perishable goods can be produced at great distances from sites of consumption (e.g., coal or cars), while more perishable goods are produced closer to home (e.g., dairy products). Many other factors undoubtedly also come into play (e.g., regulatory environments, regional specializations, commodifiability of goods, etc.), but the point remains that there has traditionally been an important relationship between what was produced and where it is produced and consumed.

In both cases, it is also noteworthy that while sites of production (and associated labour) could be spread out across the planet, some types of service work remained relatively geographically bound to the places in which it was used or consumed.

While a Chinese silk weaver and a Kenyan rose grower can both perform thousands of miles from a Roman consumer, a Roman shopkeeper (based Rome) is still needed to sell those goods. Put differently, some jobs carried with them an inherent geographic stickiness.

The rise of digital labour has seen these two commonalities change. First, for digital work, the link between distance and time has been almost completely severed. Proximity between employers, workers, and clients now has almost no impact on how quickly a digital product or service can be delivered. Second, for many types of service work, geography has become less sticky. The modularization, commodification, and standardization of work tasks (Scott, 2001), the creation of markets for digital work, and advances in automation all present ways to sever the ties between service work and particular places.

These two changes have been apparent in the two most significant moments in the history of digital labour. A first wave of digital labour arose in the 1980s. Western firms began outsourcing their non-core business functions to low-wage locations (Taylor and Bain, 2008). By the 1990s, countries like India and the Philippines were home to millions of workers who were carrying out service work for predominantly Western clients. Those workers, however, almost always were employed in the local labour market by an outsourcing firm that had a physical presence there.

A second wave of digital labour appeared much more recently in the form of 'cloud work' (Graham et al., 2017a). Cheap computers and connectivity have drastically lowered the costs of some of the means of production, creating an enormous potential labour pool. Unlike the first wave that involved outsourcing between different firms and organizations, digital work platforms (such as Upwork.com and Freelancer.com) can now match big firms, small businesses, and individual clients directly with workers and small enterprises anywhere. A small business in London, for instance, can now directly hire a worker in Kenya to make a website for them. Work is always inherently done at the worker's physical location, but it simultaneously can be done or delivered to any other connected part of the globe, allowing workers to escape some of the constraints of their local labour markets. Unlike a farmer or a factory worker, today's digital workers have far less need to be physically proximate to the object of their labour.

DIGITAL LABOUR

Today there are close to 50 million people who have registered with digital work platforms in a market that has surpassed $4 billion of transactions (Kuek et al., 2015). All of those potential workers, of course, must go home every night. They still have to interface with a physical machine, which they – at some point – plug into a physical wall somewhere. But an ability to quickly transmit, mediate, or co-perform work in other places does mean that something has changed. Despite being tethered to the places in which they live, workers can now do digital work that originates anywhere.

While this has brought jobs to millions that might not have been available in their local labour markets, some of our research group's previous research highlights significant issues for workers that arise (little or no bargaining power, discrimination, precariousness, and poor skill development; Graham et al., 2017a). Many of the identified issues are related to the huge oversupply of labour power. Graham et al. (2017b) show that on one of the world's biggest platforms, there are often ten times as many online job seekers as there are workers who successfully manage to get a job (in some African countries, this number is even higher). This oversupply of labour has the effect of pushing down labour costs and restricting the ability of workers to bargain for better conditions. Furthermore, because of the ways platforms are designed, competition rather than collaboration between workers is encouraged. Workers are classed as independent workers rather than employees and are made to feel like relatively atomized entrepreneurs competing for gigs in a global market, rather than employees or workers who share key commonalities, deserve some of the rights of employees, and who might benefit from collective organization and bargaining. Workers recognize that they are often relatively atomized competitors in global markets, being aware that if they do not do a job at the rates and conditions at which it is offered, then someone else will (Graham et al., 2017a).

As ever more people from low-income countries join the internet,[2] this creates a worrying state of affairs. Clients located primarily in high-income countries can force workers from around the world (in rich and poor countries) to compete with one another in a giant labour market. Unless the supply of jobs on digital work platforms outstrips the supply of labour, new workers will find themselves locked into an increasingly difficult cycle of competition with one another. In other words, the spatial configuration of digital work and digital workers might ultimately lead to a race to the bottom.

The production of space

One way of thinking about the current configurations of digital labour is as a deliberate construction of contemporary capital. Capitalism is inherently crisis ridden, and in order to overcome its crises and survive, capital creates a physical landscape (Harvey, 1978) or produces space in its own image (Smith, 1984; Lefebvre, 1991). David Harvey (2003) referred to such processes as 'spatio-temporal fixes'. There are two meanings of 'fix' here: first, a literal meaning as fixing capital in place in physical forms (factories or transportation infrastructure); and second, a metaphorical meaning, as in a solution to crises in capitalism through spatial organization of capital and specific strategies to address those crises. In other words, fixes represent capitalism's ability to create a landscape (only to have it destroyed at a subsequent point in time) so that profits are made, albeit temporarily. Fixes lead to newer contradictions, introducing new rounds of spatio-temporal fixes (Harvey, 2014). Thus, fixes can be understood as a never-ending search for both the internal and external transformation of capitalism through 'geographical expansion and geographical restructuring' (Harvey, 2001: 24).

Specifically, capital or labour surpluses get exported and moved to deal with those crises. A company in the United States seeking lower labour costs would, for instance, locate a factory in a low-wage location such as Mexico. Many of these fixes allowed space to be produced in very particular ways, putting workers from around the world in competition with one another. This rendered workers in the original locations relatively immobile, with little bargaining power to extract better working conditions.

Digital labour certainly presents a new kind of fix that generates a reserve army of labour (such as students, the retired, and the unemployed in low- and middle-income countries). But is this a fix that is fundamentally different in nature from previous ones, in an interconnected world economy?

The networking of the world relies on fixed forces of production (for instance, the global networks of submarine fibre-optic cables). Once these infrastructures are in place, a fix at a scale never before possible has been brought into being. If capital produces space in its image, and does so by building upon successive waves of fixes, can space continue to be remade in a world of full connectivity? Unlike previous fixes, perhaps the global nature of this one means that geographic expansions are no longer possible; perhaps we ultimately reach a point where everybody and everything are connected.

This could be the final fix for labour: a system where workers are tethered and atomized, and pitted against each other in one giant market[3] where their labour is bought and sold as a commodity, one where firms that outsource work are able to draw on an infinite pool of tethered workers.[4] It could be a virtual fix in which capital no longer needs to be frozen into place (Green and Joseph, 2015), and in which labour surpluses can be exported without exporting labourers, thus affording workers little voice and little power. How do we avoid this? How do we instead build a world that is co-created by workers?

Digital space? Whose digital space?

Here is it useful to draw on Andrew Herod's (2001) *Labor Geographies*, in which he distinguishes between the geography of labour (i.e., the distribution of labour, something that tends to portray workers in a passive way) and labour geographies (which portray workers as active agents able to create and manipulate space to their own advantages). Herod notes that in the process of simply ensuring that the spatial fixes needed for workers to reproduce themselves are in place, they too shape the geography of capitalism. He therefore takes issue with descriptions like the one above that deprive workers of agency. While it is true that capital can produce space, so too can labour.

Herod (2001) showed, for instance, how a New York City garment workers' union successfully shaped city planning laws to protect jobs, and how a North American dockers' union was able to resist the relocation of the freight-handling industry from the unionized coast to cheaper locations inland. Both strategies were more than simple stories of global capital creating a world in its own image, instead involving large coalitions of organized workers shaping the built environment together to bring about economic geographies that better serve their interests.

But if capital or labour are to produce new economic spaces, and those spaces in turn constrain and enable what is and is not possible, we should do more to understand the emerging digital spaces of work. The contemporary global network of digital labour is an inherently geographical project. Following Herod's prompt, we therefore need to understand not just how current digital geographies are created, but also how workers can actually produce new kinds of digital labour geographies themselves in order to envision new ways in which they can be recreated.

We propose two ways of thinking about the spaces of digital labour. First, there is the vision that digital technologies can actually bring into being an entirely new ontic space: a 'world that is both everywhere and nowhere, but it is not where bodies live' (Barlow, 1996). In other words, digital tools and technologies create a new plane of existence – a *digitally distinct space* that is 'both fixed in a distinct digital location, and simultaneously accessible from anywhere' (Graham, 2015: 870).

A second way of envisioning the digital spaces of labour is as something that augments already existing spatial relations. Here *digitally augmented space* is not pre-existing, but is rather the 'indeterminate, unstable, context dependent and multiple realities brought into being through the subjective coming-togethers in time and space of material and virtual experience' (Graham et al., 2013: 465). Instead of creating any sort of ontologically distinct space, digital tools here augment our experiences. These augmentations sometimes involve reconfiguring relative positionalities by changing spatial and temporal frictions, but they never totally transcend the material world.

RETHINKING THE SPACES OF DIGITAL LABOUR

Instead of arguing that one of these approaches may be more useful than the other, we wish to show how they can both be useful for rethinking digital labour geographies in different ways. Labour's own digital spatial fixes can be brought into being with both worldviews.

If we think of digital space as being digitally distinct, we must first ask what the nature of this space is. The markets that platforms create are the digital spaces, and these spaces are not just inherently non-public, but are also entirely created by actors who do not necessarily have workers' best interests at heart. In contrast to Herod's (2001) vision that there can be a 'labor's spatial fix', every facet of these spaces is designed from the bottom-up by capital. There is literally no space for workers to create a space.

Yet even here, there are ways workers can create their own fixes. One is to look to the history of the picket line. A picket line is generally a protest outside of a place of work in order to stop people going in. It is a way of shutting down the means of production. In the context of digital labour, it could be argued that most workers actually control the means of production (their computers). But it is rather the means of distribution and sites of consumption that they seem to have no control over. We could therefore look to picketing tactics to think through how sites of distribution and consumption can be blockaded. Instead of physically blocking a shop or an office, we could use tactical media approaches to picket the digital presence of a firm (Lovink, 2002). Think, for instance, of how political activists use 'Google bombing': manipulating search engines to display the desired answers to certain queries (the most famous example of this being results related to US President Bush returned in response to the query 'miserable failure'). If a digital firm is its digital presence, then despite how controlled digital spaces are, tactical media approaches offer suggestions on how to block, barricade, and refix space. These approaches will not shut down a company, but might provide a sufficient amount of disruption to make client/company tactics to extract the absolute most work for the absolute minimum cost less viable.

A vision of a digitally distinct space also offers opportunities to move past the idea that digital workers are atomized alienated competitors. If digital workers can converge into a digital space, doing so offers opportunities for horizontal collaboration rather than purely competition between workers. Digital workers already collaborate to find jobs, support one another, and share strategies to deal with clients and administrators. Workers might be geographically isolated, but they are using digital tools to co-convene and digitally congregate. Any effective future worker resistance is likely to be based on the ability of workers to do this. However, many workers do ultimately always remember their scattered material geographies: that instead of being immersed in a space of co-presence with fellow workers, huge distances separate them and workers are willing and able to undercut them.

It is therefore useful to move beyond the digitally distinct vision and frame digital labour as something that happens in digitally augmented spaces. Digital labour here happens not in some abstract space, but instead in the huge diversity of homes, offices, public, and private space in which work is carried out. What opportunities does an augmented view of work afford workers who wish to create their own labour geographies?

Seeing the world as digitally augmented initially helps to distinguish between geographically sticky work (e.g., driving) and non-sticky work (e.g., data entry). Workers doing geographically sticky work have inherent advantages when it comes to trying to build collective action (in the UK, for instance, striking delivery workers used apps to order food in order to make contact with fellow workers).

Workers doing non-sticky digital labour do not have these same advantages. As mentioned earlier in this chapter, some workers feel that they have no bargaining power because they see digital tools as connecting and creating an almost infinite pool of labour supply. However, Graham et al. (2017b) show that the fact that digital work can be carried out from anywhere does not necessarily mean that it will. Different types of digital work concentrate in particular places. Clients, too, have a concentrated geography. A handful of countries are home to a majority of them. For example, more than 50 percent of the jobs posted on five of the biggest English-language platforms come from employers/clients based in the United States (Kässi and Lehdonvirta, 2016), whilst freelancers from the United States, India, and the Philippines make up almost half of all the workers who have earned $1 or more on Upwork, the world's biggest online work platform.

Understanding the economic topologies and geographies of the digitally augmented landscapes that workers and clients bring into being allows bottlenecks and weak points to be identified. If, say, online personal assistants know that a third of the world's work happens in the Philippines, then they have some of the same advantages that exist in the context of sticky work. This does not negate the weak structural-economic power of those workers, but it presents collaborative opportunities that would not exist if those workers were truly scattered around the planet. While it is true that there is a large global reserve supply of labour, it remains the case that, for most job types, labour is both not as commoditized as many buyers of it would hope it to be, and operates with a 'just in time' temporality, making it hard to quickly shift large parts of global value chains from one part of the world to another (see Silver, 2003, for a similar argument).

Realizing the potential for localized coalitions of workers is one way of highlighting bottlenecks and chokepoints in the economic landscape. It opens up possibilities for coalitions of workers to threaten to withdraw labour, and limits the ability of clients to spatially switch work.

Understanding the material geographies of digital labour can also help in devising ways to better regulate it. Perhaps due to its transnational nature, much of today's digital labour is unbound by regulations. Clients rarely pay attention to rules on the books in workers' countries of origin. Although some workers thrive in this environment, it can hurt more vulnerable workers – who are the very people regulation should be designed to protect. If digital labour is seen to take place in a global digital market, some would argue that the reason why it is largely unregulated is that it is unregulatable.

To counter this idea, we can recognize that digital work is not global. Rather, it is international. It has clear concentrations, and always/inherently falls under the jurisdiction of at least one place. This opens up possibilities for workers and their allies to take action in specific jurisdictions that end up reshaping the economic geographies of digital work.

CONCLUSIONS

The networking of the world has not rendered geography irrelevant – far from it. Clients now have access to a globally dispersed pool of workers tethered to their homes. This state of affairs presents a worrying and precarious situation for digital workers. In this chapter, we have argued that a spatial division of labour has been constructed in which digital labour is traded as a commodity at a global scale by placing workers in competition with one another in a way that undermines the power of workers.

However, the geographic landscapes of digital labour that we see are not an inevitable outcome of the spread of digital technologies to every corner of the world. This chapter also argues that possibilities exist for what Herod (2001) refers to as 'labor geographies': spatial fixes created by and for workers that challenge the idea that atomized competition is an inevitability. Two very different ontologies – 'digitally distinct space' and 'digitally augmented space' – can be used to build those strategies.

This is not just an argument about semantics. Workers, unions, and regulators are all using outdated concepts to try and make sense of a contemporary world of work. If we are to build a fairer world of work, we are going to need new language and new concepts for networks, processes, and organizations of digital labour, for strikes, for picket lines, and for coalitions of, and collaborations between workers. These concepts will shape how we understand digital labour and how we envision 'paths to the possible'.

Strategically deploying those spatial ontologies reveals sites at which the proactive geographical praxis of workers can reshape the geographies of labour. Workers do not necessarily need global campaigns to match the global reach of platforms and clients – instead, they need to understand the nodes at which the local can influence the non-local. Workers carry the power to dismiss the idea that digital labour represents a final hegemonic spatial fix in which they have no agency due to atomization and the commodification of work. Reconceptualizing the geographies of digital labour and digital labour geographies reveals the remaining possibilities for collective action, for labour's own spatial fixes, and for a reshaping of the very landscapes of digital work.

Notes

1. Specifically, we focus on work that is: predominantly digitally-based (i.e., work that is based on the manipulation of digital data in some form), digitally intensive (the value is primarily created from the manipulation of digital data), potentially non-geographically proximate (i.e., work that can, in theory, be done from anywhere), and income-generating (rather than, say, the act of updating a social media profile).
2. At the time of writing there are 3.5 billion internet users on the planet, and 2017 will be the first year in which more than half of the world's population is connected to the global network. Due to saturation in high-income countries, most of the new growth in internet use will come from people in low- and middle-income countries.
3. It is worth noting that almost all successful digital work platforms are owned and run by profit firms (usually backed by venture capital).
4. Even though the costs of some of the means of production have been drastically reduced, only a few firms have tightened their grip on the means of distribution (admittedly an integral part of the means of production), a situation that affords them great power.

Acknowledgements

The authors would like to thank Alex Wood and Kat Braybrooke for their feedback on earlier drafts. This research was supported by the International Development Research Centre (grant number 107384–001), and the European Research Council under the European Union's Seventh Framework Programme for Research and Technological Development (FP/2007–2013, ERC Grant Agreement no. 335716).

REFERENCES

Barlow, J.P. (1996) 'A declaration of the independence of cyberspace', Electronic Frontier Foundation. Available at: www.eff.org/cyberspace-independence (accessed 1 February 2018).

Fuchs, C. (2013) 'Theorising and analysing digital labour', *Political Economy of Communication*, 1(2): 3–27.

Graham, M. (2012) 'The knowledge based economy and digital divisions of labour', in V. Desai and R.B. Potter (eds), *Companion to Development Studies*, 3rd edn. Abingdon: Routledge. pp. 189–194.

Graham, M. (2015) 'Contradictory connectivity: Spatial imaginaries and technomediated positionalities in Kenya's outsourcing sector', *Environment and Planning A*, 47(4): 867–883.

Graham, M., Hjorth, I. and Lehdonvirta, V. (2017a) 'Digital labour and development', *Transfer: European Review of Labour and Research*, 23(2): 135–162.

Graham, M., Lehdonvirta, V., Wood, A., Barnard, H., Hjorth, I. and Simon, D.P. (2017b) *The Risks and Rewards of Online Gig Work At the Global Margins*. Oxford: Oxford Internet Institute. Available at: www.oii.ox.ac.uk/publications/gigwork.pdf (accessed 30 January 2018).

Graham, M., Zook, M. and Boulton, M. (2013) 'Augmented reality in the urban environment', *Transactions of the Institute of British Geographers*, 38(3): 464–479.

Green, D.M. and Joseph, D. (2015) 'The digital spatial fix', *tripleC*, 13(2): 223–247.

Harvey, D. (1978) 'The urban process under capitalism: A framework for analysis', *International Journal of Urban and Regional Research*, 2(1–3): 101–131.

Harvey, D. (1989) *The Condition of Postmodernity*. Oxford: Blackwell.

Harvey, D. (2001) 'Globalization and the "spatial fix"', *Geographische Revue*, 2: 23–30.

Harvey, D. (2003) *The New Imperialism*. Oxford: Oxford University Press.

Harvey, D. (2014) *Seventeen Contradictions and the End of Capitalism*. London: Profile Books.

Herod, A. (2001) *Labor Geographies*. New York: Guilford.

Kässi, O. and Lehdonvirta, V. (2016) 'Building the Online Labour Index: A tool for policy and research', paper presented at the 19th ACM Conference on Computer Supported and Collaborative Work (CSCW 2016) workshop on The Future of Platforms as Sites of Work, Collaboration and Trust, San Francisco.

Kuek, C., Paradi-Guilford, C., Fayomi, T., Imaizumi, S. and Ipeirotis, P. (2015) *The Global Opportunity in Online Outsourcing*. Washington, DC: World Bank Group.

Lefebvre, H. (1991) *The Production of Space*, trans. D.N. Smith. Oxford: Blackwell.

Lovink, G. (2002). *Dark Fiber*. Cambridge, MA: MIT Press.

Massey, D. (1998) *Spatial Divisions of Labor*. New York: Routledge.

Scholz, T. (2013) *Digital Labor*. New York: Routledge.

Scott, A.J. (2001) 'Capitalism, cities, and the production of symbolic forms', *Transactions of the Institute of British Geographers*, 26(1): 11–23.

Silver, B. (2003) *Forces of Labor*. Cambridge: Cambridge University Press.

Smith, N. (1984) *Uneven Development, Nature, Capital and the Production of Space*. Oxford: Blackwell.

Standing, G. (2016) *The Corruption of Capitalism: Why Rentiers Thrive and Work Does Not Pay*. London: Biteback.

Taylor, P. and Bain, P. (2008) 'United by a common language? Trade union responses in the UK and India to call centre offshoring', *Antipode*, 40(1): 131–154.

17

INDUSTRIES

Matthew Zook

INTRODUCTION

Digital industries are deeply embedded in the spaces and practices of daily life. We engage with them every time we send/receive a text, we rely on them to socialize, and we use them to search for answers and directions. Much of the terminology describing digital technologies uses geographic metaphors – cyberspace, information superhighways, virtual worlds, etc. Yet, these key geographies undergirding everyday activities are often overlooked by researchers and the public.

Digital industries are the assemblages of hardware, infrastructure, and software applications that comprise and are used by the internet and other information networks, as well as the social and economic networks essential for their development, production, and circulation. Digital industries come in many forms. Closest to the end user are applications such as social media, search, mapping, and other services we use to manage our daily lives. These utilities run on various digital platforms, including desktop and laptop computers, smart city infrastructures, and mobile phones. These devices in turn generate and transfer data packets via cable, WiFi, or mobile systems to the routers and switches of internet service providers (ISPs), private/state networks, and telecom operators. These packets are routed locally and globally via a complex infrastructure of network exchange points, fibre-optic cables, and satellite connections relying on software protocols such as TCP/IP[1] and DNS[2] to successfully traverse the network. The difference in temporal scales between human observation and digital functions helps hide these complex, distributed assemblages momentarily brought into being for each text we send and every e-mail we receive. The simple and smoothed results that we see in response to clicking a link or starting an app belie the dizzying array of processes, relations, and geographies we set in motion.

Even the more human-centred connections we make – direct communication with a friend or family member – often involve unexpectedly digitally-mediated geographies. The e-mail, text, or video chat may be viewed on one's local device, but it also resides on a server farm hundreds of miles away and is eventually archived in longer-term storage on yet another farm. Other configurations such as firewalled and password-protected private networks and encrypted anonymous networks (such as TOR) spanning the globe are also part of these digital geographies. In short, digital industries enable and directly participate in a vast increase in the scale, scope, and variety of information created and used in society and the economy (Castells, 1996). And yet, despite its centrality, the visibility of these industries is low, especially as our use of digital technologies has shifted from physically tethered connections – computing centres with desktop machines – to mobile connections that we carry around in our pockets.

It is important to combat this obfuscation or veiling of digital industries because their ability to shape spatialities at the level of the individual through to the geographies of the global economy is central to place-making in our current world. As we use digital technologies every day – an online purchase from an eBay seller hundreds of kilometres away or instant message with a customer support representative on the other side of the globe – we are making complex geographies that transcend the material places of our homes, work, and neighbourhoods. In so doing, we construct a 'global sense of place' (Massey, 1991) defined not solely by proximity but by our connections, the bundles of disparate relations and moments in space-time made through our everyday digital practices. Moreover, the differentiated ability to project techno-power shapes the terms under which lives are lived and locales are enrolled into global systems (Sheppard, 2002). For example, smartphone users must accept the terms and conditions of service that shift control and ownership of personal information to media companies who then resell this data to third parties, or share it with security arms of the state. This chapter begins by tracing the historical origins of digital industries. It then uses three lenses through which to render the geographies of digital industries visible: locating digital industries; democratizing the use of digital industries; and digital industries and the production of space.

HOW DIGITAL INDUSTRIES CAME TO BE

As language, cave paintings, and the earliest forms of writing attest, information and information sharing have long been part of human society. These technologies shaped social activities, organization, and spaces. These forms of communication, however, were initially embodied in human physicality (how far sounds such as shouting or drumming could carry), and eventually were ensconced in physical objects such as clay tablets or letters that required transportation from one location to another. It was not until the advent of the telegraph (and later the telephone) in the nineteenth century that information transfer was split from materiality (Standage, 1998). Physical infrastructures remained essential – the dots and dashes of Morse code required the copper wires and wooden poles holding them up to traverse distances – but the physical (and geographical) constraints on movement of information were fundamentally altered by these technological changes.

The integration and use of these nineteenth-century information communication systems offer an important parallel to the digital geographies of the current era. Fischer's (1994) social history of the telephone provides a rich accounting of societal expectations for telephones in the late nineteenth century in the United States. Originally seen (and marketed) as a tool for business, the telephone was also perceived as a possible intruder into certain spaces such as those of the home. At the time of its introduction, questions were asked as to how it might alter the sense of privacy and allow outside influences and interference into personal and family lives. Although the value of the phone for socialization was established in the decades after its introduction – in no small part because of aggressive phone company marketing – there was originally little envisioned space for such a frivolous use of the technology. It was also a time of geographic difference, with farmers setting up their own cooperative phone systems as cities enjoyed a greater availability of telecommunications services relative to rural areas. This rural–urban divide is still seen in digital industries today.

Like the telephone, the internet was also a decades-long project developed for particular uses before integrating into the fabric of daily life. The predecessor to the internet, ARPANET, emerged from the US government and military response to the technological achievements of the Soviet Union. It first became operational in 1971 using a packet switching design developed to ensure the survivability of the communications system. The initial four nodes of ARPANET (clustered largely in California) slowly extended to a small network of computer science centres across the USA to increase remote access to the scarce resource of mainframe computers. This interconnection across space and platforms created a key challenge of integrating a system comprised of many different machines and operating systems (Abbate, 2000). This problem was solved by the development of the TCP and IP protocols which set the technological foundation (an ability to network networks) behind the ARPANET, which eventually became the internet. Later networks – such as CSNET, BITNET and NSFNET– used TCP/IP to connect to the network of networks, and the roll-out of personal computers and local area networks during the 1980s added further momentum.

By 1990, the internet had shifted from academic and government-funded systems to private operations increasingly populated by the general public. Alongside this transformation of the infrastructure, new software – Veronica, Gopher and Archie – made command line interfaces more intuitive. These themselves were eventually surpassed by the World Wide Web and the graphic browser. As these changes drew more and more people onto the internet, its role as a platform for socialization moved to the forefront, echoing the earlier evolution of the adoption of the telephone.

GEOGRAPHIES OF DIGITAL INDUSTRIES

This brief history sets the stage for identifying three lenses through which to trace the geographies of digital industries and their effects. First, just as the roll-out of the telephone created urban–rural difference, digital industries have specific and multiple geographies that shape the societies and spaces in which they act. Second, the distinct spatialities of digital industries impact people's ability to participate in activities ranging from digitally mediated socializing to mapmaking. Third, the geographies of digital industries help enact certain kinds of power and agency in the production of our social and economic spaces.

Locating digital industries

Together, all the elements of digital industries – from software applications to mobile devices to fibre-optic networks to server farms – have distinct materialities and spatialities. Given the broad definition of digital industries used in this chapter, locating digital industries involves tracing the geographical footprints and physical extents of digital infrastructures. This requires data on the pathways of fibre-optic cables, clouds of WiFi connectivity, production of content, server farms, and the locations and movement of users. However, metrics on digital industries are not regularly captured as part of national census surveys or other state sources.

Collecting reliable data on the physical location and extent, capacity, and utilization of digital industries was particularly important during the early 1990s to respond to a common trope that digital industries would bring about the 'death of distance' or the end of geography (Cairncross, 1997). The substance behind this trope was that easier and faster communications would fundamentally alter the conditions of work, allowing firms to restructure with little concern for location while simultaneously allowing workers to move anywhere. This simplistic formulation was readily critiqued (see Graham, 1998); space and distance remain relevant as they are enrolled in and affect the ways that technologies are deployed to structure global and local economies, organize societies, and exercise political power.

The challenge for researchers is marking and understanding the spatial and societal effects of these new technologies. There is a long and rich history of analyses that measure and visualize the virtual landscapes of digital industries (see Dodge and Kitchin, 2001), with most deploying the norms of cartography to 'map the internet'. These mapping practices emphasize infrastructures, and include representations of cable routes with lines varying in colour and thickness,[3] as well as representations of digital activities such as domain name registrations (Zook, 2000) and tweets as points, shaded polygons, or hexbins (see Poorthuis et al., 2017).

Representations of material digital infrastructures, however, need not be (nor have they been) limited to conventional cartography. In particular, topological representations of networks that do not seek to touch down in Euclidean space are useful in showing connectivity between nodes such as friends on Facebook or the path of a data packet as it moves across the internet. One of the earliest examples of this type of map was the Internet Mapping Project (Burch and Cheswick, 1999) which used traceroute paths – the routes of connection between computers on the internet – to visualize the overall network. The resulting visualization was a dense network graph showing the interconnections of the internet and could be used for a number of topics from designing more efficient routing to graph theory. Moreover, other types of visualization conventions, including chord diagrams, bubble charts, and three-dimensional rendering, can provide important 'mappings' of the materiality of digital industries. For example, CAIDA's[4] chord diagram[5] of IP topology shows peering relationships between major ISPs across geographies that are vital in ensuring smooth flows of internet traffic. While these visualizations are difficult for laypeople to interpret, they help network engineers better understand the structural relationships within the infrastructure of the internet.

Many of these visualizations that trace the spatial materiality of digital industries are generated by individuals or small enterprises; that is, there is no official map of the internet generated by a singular authority. The ability of multiple and small-scale actors to locate digital industries through maps and other data-driven visualizations is made possible by unprecedented access to historically unconventional data sources, such as from social media platforms, afforded through scripts and APIs.[6] However, precisely because these visualizations are contingent upon access to data, an ability to render them is often challenged by enclosures of these datastores through firewalls, password protection, and ownership by private platforms such as Facebook. The diverse motivations that inform the production of these maps also means that they are constructed at many scales and sometimes come with a clear propagandistic purpose, marketing or normalizing the diffusion of a new technology. For example, the popularity of Twitter and other social media maps of cultural and political phenomena[7] reinforces their popularity to the benefit of the company which developed and manages the platform.

Diverse motivations aside, all of these mappings are useful towards establishing that geography and distance matter profoundly for digital industries. Thus, while firms within digital industries promote a rhetoric of ubiquitous and uniform connectivity (e.g., mobile phone companies touting functionality in over 200 countries), it is readily evident that the geography of the material elements of such connectivity is much more complex. The death of distance may be often expected but never comes. New technologies – from the first telephone to the latest smartphone – overlay existing patterns of connectivity and disconnection, cost, infrastructure, and power, shaping the geographies of global connection and marginalization. For example, the first undersea telegraph cables were laid in the 1850s between the UK and Europe, and then North America. This pattern of strong connectivity, particularly relative to less connected regions such as sub-Saharan Africa, remains evident today in the networks of fibre-optic cables, many of which retrace (and thereby further solidify) early trans-oceanic telegraph routes.

Democratizing digital industries

In addition to spatially locating the materialities of digital industries, it is also important to understand how these industries are adopted by societies. Even though ARPANET, the precursor to the internet, was designed for remotely accessing computers, it also generated other, originally unanticipated uses. E-mail was a relatively early application, but ARPANET systems also housed some of the first computer games (such as *Oregon Trail* and *Star Trek*) as well as the first distributed computer discussion board, Usenet (Abbate, 2000). The user-operators of the early ARPANET also developed novel processes for negotiating technical change (such as the introduction of the TCP/IP protocols) within digital industries. Many of the people developing ARPANET were graduate students who prudently developed the Requests for Comments (RFC) system for introducing proposals for technical innovation without sounding too final and cutting off discussion (Abbate, 2000). This system for public input was so successful that RFCs remain the means by which new technical standards are introduced and debated by the Internet Engineering Task Force (IETF), which sets the operation protocols used on the internet.

While the origins of the internet, such as the RFC system, contribute to an ethos of openness in contemporary digital industries (e.g., the open data movement and free and open-source software), digital industries are not uniform or equally accessible to all. Digital divides – in connectivity, broadband access, linguistic representation, and cultural attitudes to digital participation – remain. Moreover, variations in skill sets – what might be termed 'developer divides' – create differences between those merely using the technologies of digital industries and those able to engage in deep technical hacking, that is, reconfiguration of technologies and industries (Haklay, 2013).

For example, when volunteered geographic information (VGI) and neogeography[8] first appeared in the mid-2000s, some such as Turner (2006) trumpeted the democratizing power of open-source technologies for mapping. While neogeography and VGI certainly challenged existing professional cartographic practices (Goodchild, 2007), it was also evident that other issues complicated any simple democratization narrative (Elwood, 2010; Haklay, 2013). Haklay (2013) argues that despite expectations for more equitable engagement with mapping, neogeography does not *de facto* redistribute power within society. There remain distinct patterns in terms of those who are able to access and influence these technologies. Haklay (2013) found that the majority of contributors to a crowdsourced mapping project were white, English-speaking men. Elsewhere, Stephens (2013) documents the gendered disparities within the hierarchical organization of the same project which contributed to gendered biases in which kinds of places actually get mapped. Similarly, the enrolment of many more (though not all) people in the use of digital technologies does not simply equate with a democratization of the spatial representation of places. For example, standard Google Maps searches for information about a place are ranked by Google's opaque algorithms, ensuring that some places rise to the top of the results chain and others remain buried in obscurity. Zook and Graham (2007) document how keyword searches in Google Maps highlight certain interests over others; for example, a search for pizza in Lexington, Kentucky prominently featured chain restaurants over local establishments. Similar simplistic expectations (and critiques) have also coalesced around the emergence of big data (Anderson, 2008; boyd and Crawford, 2012).

The issue of democratization – greater participation in, but not greater influence over the design of mapping technology or geocoded content – is exacerbated by the partial roll-back of the state from the mapping enterprise and digital industries' leveraging of crowdsourcing approaches to content generation that are often premised on free labour (Leszczynski, 2012). Indeed, private actors – most notably corporations – take leading and powerful roles in shaping the use of new technologies that channel use towards certain predetermined ends that serve the profit motive, a process that Zook and Graham (2007) call 'Google governance'.[9] As a result, the terms under which individuals choose to participate are highly structured. For example, the user agreements for many apps and most social media require that users allow the service providers to record and reuse their data in often opaque ways, leading Leszczynski and Elwood (2015) to argue that data is better characterized as extracted rather than volunteered.

Another example of how digital industries are reconfiguring social relations is the ongoing changes to how labour and capital interact. Not only are new jobs emerging – web design, search engine optimization, social media marketing – but also digital industries have proven essential for the emergence of new forms of distantiated labour such as is exemplified by Amazon's Mechanical Turk platform. These systems allow companies to advertise short information-processing jobs that

workers from around the world bid upon, resulting in very low wages (G
et al., 2017). Related are other platforms that have emerged from the digital in
tries that reorganize work via the called sharing economies in which labou is
moved from regular salaried positions into freelance or independent contractor
status (Cockayne, 2016). While much of the industry rhetoric promoting these
work relationships highlights aspects of 'freedom' and 'opportunity' of this reorganization of work, this use of digital technologies also has the fortuitous (from
capital's perspective) effect of sidestepping many existing regulations. The net
effect of this new use is that risk and costs previously borne by companies have
been shifted to workers, many of whom are in new locations. Much like neogeography's promise of democratizing mapping, the social and spatial effects are never
simplistic and uniform, and there are profound concerns that these benefits will
only accrue to those already fortuitously situated within the global economy.

Digital industries producing space

A final key theme through which to engage the geographies of digital industries
is their role and power in the production of space. As Graham (1998: 174) notes,
'[p]ower over space and power over telecommunications networks go hand in
hand'. Originating in the materiality of digital industries (as discussed above),
more recently attention has focused on the power of software (or code) to produce
spaces in particular ways. For example, Thrift and French (2002: 309) discuss how
software embedded in buildings, vehicles, and personal digital devices 'act[s] as a
means of providing a new and complex form of automated spatiality' contributing
to the production of everyday places. Thrift and French also note the power of
software to reshape the entire economy. Using the example of the diffusion of
spreadsheet software through business and other settings, they argue that more
than a simple refinement of an existing technology – the paper sheets used by
earlier generations of accountants – this product of digital industries has resulted
in an entirely new mindset focused on constant and reiterative scenario-testing.
This has contributed to the rise of styles of governance encouraging businesses
(and other institutions such as higher education) to focus more tightly on resource
optimization and revenue maximization than was previously the case.

The contribution of digital industries to the production of space is also evident
in Graham's (2005) argument that 'software-sorting' is fundamental to the ordering
of space (and the people who inhabit it) by determining who is able to access a
range of goods and services, and even specific spaces. This role of code in shaping
spaces was further expanded by Kitchin and Dodge's (2011) formulation of code/
space. Carefully eschewing software determinism, Kitchin and Dodge provide
detailed audits of the powerful roles code plays in daily life, with particular attention paid to how control over daily spaces is negotiated and resisted.

A common concern is how these products of digital industries will shift and perhaps concentrate power, a far different expectation than the liberating or democratizing rhetoric discussed earlier. For example, Graham (2005) points to the likelihood that existing socio-spatial divides and classifications will be digitally cemented rather than undermined, such as a bad credit score that hinders an individual's economic opportunities. Sheppard (2002: 319) also notes the 'remarkable persistence and path dependence' surrounding changes resulting from information technologies. The economic advantages of the undersea telegraph cable that first allowed information exchange between the USA and the UK in the nineteenth century have persisted to today, while other locations (e.g., sub-Saharan Africa) enjoy much less connectivity. While digital industries regularly produce new and disruptive technologies (such as the spreadsheet), the power of these changes often plays out along standard trajectories of privilege that enable certain actors to exert control over the new spaces that emerge. For example, as software becomes ever more integrated into tools and equipment (such as tractors), the long-standing practices of self-repair, tinkering, and do-it-yourself run foul of password protections and digital copyrights. This has produced new global geographies of resistance, such as American farmers relying on software hacks developed in eastern Europe to subvert software locks placed on their tractors by the manufacturer for repairs, rather than depending upon more expensive and less responsive repair people from dealerships (Koebler, 2017).

These concerns extend well beyond tractor repair, with serious implications for how daily socialization and economic actions are surveilled and shaped. Given the centrality of digital industries to everyday life, it is almost impossible to avoid entanglement with these powerful technologies and their influence on the production of space. However, this power is not absolute, and individuals and groups can resist through tactics of avoidance, hacking, blocking, and masking, as well as other techniques (see Kitchin and Dodge, 2011). This can include efforts to surveille state actors – such as documenting civilians killed by police in the USA or online contingent workers sharing information about the quality of work offered by different employers.[10] The effects of these kinds of transgressions and subversion are complex; often, they are not universally available but accrue to certain individuals and situations. Thus, 'hacking code/space' can work to confound the power of code over daily life, but the interconnectivity of digital industries also means that the resulting impacts are often distributed widely and inequitably (Zook and Graham, 2018).

NEXT STEPS FOR DIGITAL INDUSTRIES

In conclusion, the geographies of digital industries are shaped at many scales – from the local to the global – by the individual, the corporation, the state, and society at large. This was true during the nineteenth-century roll-out of the telephone, and if anything, these patterns have only become more profound. The embedding of locational affordances within all types of digital artefacts (devices, hardware, software) engendered by the geospatial web during the 2000s will only grow deeper as the internet of things develops and state and corporate actors amass ever larger databases on the movements, opinions, and actions of individuals.

A key struggle within digital geographies has been working to incorporate these technologies into the traditional concerns of geography, space, place, and scale. How do emergent digital technologies change these concepts both theoretically and in everyday lived experiences? How can we use these concepts to understand these new phenomena and their effects?

Notes

1. The Transmission Control Protocol (TCP) and Internet Protocol (IP) set the standards for how data is packaged and transmitted across the internet.
2. The Domain Name System (DNS) translates the numerical identifications for computers on the internet into more easily remembered domain names such as Google.com.
3. TeleGeography is a good (although by no means the only) example of these types of maps. The most recent version is available at www.submarinecablemap.com.
4. Center for Applied Internet Analysis, www.caida.org.
5. See www.caida.org/research/topology/as_core_network.
6. An application programming interface (API) allows automatic access to data (e.g., tweets, posts), according to rules set by the provider.
7. See www.floatingsheet.org.
8. VGI is the creation of spatial data by individuals, often but not necessarily non-experts (see Goodchild, 2007), and neogeography is the use of mapping tools for personal and community projects by non-traditional mappers (Turner, 2006).
9. Google governance refers to the ability of dominant platforms – operating systems, applications, or hardware devices – to control what is seen or can be done by users.
10. See mappingpoliceviolence.org and https://turkopticon.info.

REFERENCES

Abbate, J. (2000) *Inventing the Internet*. Cambridge, MA: MIT Press.
Anderson, C. (2008) 'The end of theory: The data deluge makes the scientific method obsolete', *Wired*, 23 June. Available at: www.wired.com/2008/06/pb-theory (accessed 1 February 2018).

boyd, d. and Crawford, K. (2012) 'Critical questions for big data', *Information, Communication and Society*, 15(5): 662–679.

Burch, H. and Cheswick, B. (1999) 'Mapping the internet', *Computer*, 32(4): 97–98.

Cairncross, F. (1997) *The Death of Distance: How the Communications Revolution Will Change Our Lives*. Boston: Harvard Business School Press.

Castells, M. (1996) *The Rise of the Network Society: The Information Age – Economy, Society and Culture Volume I*. Oxford: Blackwell.

Cockayne, D.G. (2016) 'Sharing and neoliberal discourse: The economic function of sharing in the digital on-demand economy', *Geoforum*, 77: 73–82.

Dodge, M. and Kitchin, R. (2001) *Atlas of Cyberspace*. Harlow: Addison-Wesley.

Elwood, S. (2010) 'Geographic information science: Emerging research on the societal implications of the geospatial web', *Progress in Human Geography*, 34(3): 349–357.

Fischer, C.S. (1994) *America Calling: A Social History of the Telephone to 1940*. Berkeley: University of California Press.

Goodchild, M. (2007) 'Citizens as sensors: The world of volunteered geography', *GeoJournal*, 6(4): 211–221.

Graham, M., Hjorth, I. and Lehdonvirta, V. (2017) 'Digital labour and development: Impacts of global digital labour platforms and the gig economy on worker livelihoods', *Transfer: European Review of Labour and Research*, 23(2): 135–162.

Graham, S. (1998) 'The end of geography or the explosion of place? Conceptualising space, place and information technology', *Progress in Human Geography*, 22(2): 165–185.

Graham, S. (2005) 'Software-sorted geographies', *Progress in Human Geography*, 29(5): 562–580.

Haklay, M. (2013) 'Neogeography and the delusion of democratisation', *Environment and Planning A*, 45(1): 55–69.

Kitchin, R. and Dodge, M. (2011) *Code/Space: Software and Everyday Life*. Cambridge, MA: MIT Press.

Koebler, J. (2017) 'Why American farmers are hacking their tractors with Ukrainian firmware', *Motherboard*, 22 March. Available at: https://motherboard.vice.com/en_us/article/xykkkd/why-american-farmers-are-hacking-their-tractors-with-ukrainian-firmware (accessed 1 February 2018).

Leszczynski, A. (2012) 'Situating the geoweb in political economy', *Progress in Human Geography*, 36(1): 72–89.

Leszczynski, A. and Elwood, S. (2015) 'Feminist geographies of new spatial media', *The Canadian Geographer/Le Géographe canadien*, 59(1): 12–28.

Massey, D. (1991) 'A global sense of place', *Marxism Today*, 35(6): 24–29.

Poorthuis, A., Zook, M., Shelton, T., Graham, M. and Stephens, M. (2017) 'Using geotagged digital social data in geographic research', in N. Clifford, M. Cope, T. Gillespie and S. French (eds), *Key Methods in Geography*, 3rd edn. London: Sage. pp. 248–268.

Sheppard, E. (2002) 'The spaces and times of globalization: Place, scale, networks, and positionality', *Economic Geography*, 78(3): 307–330.

Standage, T. (1998) *The Victorian Internet: The Remarkable Story of the Telegraph an Nineteenth Century's On-line Pioneers*. London: Weidenfeld & Nicolson.

Stephens, M. (2013) 'Gender and the GeoWeb: Divisions in the production of user-generated cartographic information', *GeoJournal*, 78(6): 981–996.

Thrift, N. and French, S. (2002) 'The automatic production of space', *Transactions of the Institute of British Geographers*, 27(3): 309–335.

Turner, A. (2006) *Introduction to Neogeography*. Sebastopol, CA: O'Reilly Media.

Zook, M.A. (2000) 'The web of production: The economic geography of commercial internet content production in the United States', *Environment and Planning A*, 32(3): 411–426.

Zook, M. and Graham, M. (2007) 'The creative reconstruction of the Internet: Google and the privatization of cyberspace and DigiPlace', *Geoforum*, 38(6): 1322–1343.

Zook, M. and Graham, M. (2018) 'Rethinking the code of global capitalism: Relational code/spaces and airline hacking', *Transactions of the Institute of British Geographers*, DOI: 10.1111/tran.12228.

18

SHARING ECONOMY

Lizzie Richardson

INTRODUCTION

New market actors such as Uber and Airbnb, premised on digital technologies and service delivery, have emerged to alter existing economic relations across sectors and industries, predominantly although not exclusively in the global North. The *sharing economy* describes two distinctive aspects of economic activity facilitated by these actors. First, they operate through a digital platform that enables efficient, multi-sided user exchanges, which can bypass traditional business-to-consumer relationships. Sharing economy platforms are intermediaries that produce, secure, and coordinate the connections for economic exchange between users (both client and service provider) as 'strangers' who may be geographically proximate or distant. An example of this technology for multi-sided exchange is the ground-transportation brokering service Uber, which connects 'riders' (clients) with a 'driver' (service provider) to provide them with a lift. Second, the ease and immediacy of the horizontal exchanges facilitated through the platform are intended to provide short-term access to previously underutilized resources such as transport, space, or skills. These digital market actors therefore shift consumption practices away from ownership, and simultaneously open up opportunities for new forms of service provision. An example of this access-based model is the short-term accommodation platform Airbnb which enables 'hosts' (occupants of private residences) to rent out overnight accommodation space to 'travellers'. These dimensions of multi-sided exchange and access-based consumption are considered to be constitutive of 'sharing' in so far as they mark a shift away from hierarchical structures of exchange and ownership models of consumption.

However, the extent and manner of change attributable to these new market actors, and thus whether 'sharing' is an appropriate catch-all term to describe them, are open to debate. Engagement with these broad questions constitutes much of the nascent geographical scholarship in this area. Providing an overview of this work, this chapter will first offer some historical context for both the term 'sharing economy' and the digital economic activities that it encompasses. It will then outline three emerging areas of interest for geographical research on the sharing economy and these new market actors: the discourse of sharing, the role of the digital platform, and the possibilities of a politics of sharing orientated around distribution. It finishes by pointing towards future developments.

THE SHARING ECONOMY IN HISTORICAL CONTEXT

The term 'sharing economy' cannot be easily attributed to a single source. Its emergence should be understood in relation to the appearance of associated vocabularies for describing changing norms of consumption and exchange enabled through digital technologies. These include 'collaborative consumption', as coined by Rachel Botsman in her 2010 TED talk,[1] and the 'access-based economy' (Bardhi and Eckhardt, 2012). One origin story for the connection specifically between (digital) 'sharing' and 'economy' can be traced to Benkler's (2004: 330–331) notion of 'sharable goods', and what he termed 'sharing as a mode of economic production'. He outlined that there are particular types of goods that have a systematic 'overcapacity' compared to their owner's requirements. For example, a car owner may not need to use their vehicle most of the time, meaning that potential usage exceeds actual usage. Benkler suggests that this overcapacity – this underutilized driving time – is best distributed through 'social sharing'. Social sharing is characterized by decentralized and networked forms of participation that are motivated by reasons other than market-dictated prices. Crucially, social sharing can be pursued by weakly connected participants or even total strangers, and for Benkler it is this possibility that holds the greatest economic promise in digitally networked environments.

Returning to the example of the car as a 'sharable good', digital technologies have enabled the reconfiguration and extension of models of shared car usage, such as car clubs and ride sharing. ZipCar is illustrative of the former, enabling users on personal mobile devices to locate and pay for short-term car rental of vehicles located nearby. BlaBlaCar, a car pooling platform, exemplifies the latter through connecting travellers with drivers going to the same destination who have unoccupied seats in their vehicles. While not limited to any singular notion of the digital, Benkler's (2004) argument is that the relative economic role of sharing changes with technology. Any given class of technologies imposes threshold constraints upon the effectiveness, but do not determine the volume, of sharing. Such technology-dependent alterations to modes of consumption can be illustrated through two antecedents to contemporary digital sharing activity examined by geographers.

The first is the rise of 'e-commerce' at the turn of the millennium, which was heralded as a change to the geographies of retail. E-commerce refers to electronic non-store retailing through the internet and the attendant geographies of physical storage and distribution that support this (Currah, 2002; Murphy, 2007). Geographers identified two key e-commerce business models. One was the 'pure-play' e-tailers, consisting of innovative companies using 'disruptive technology' to 'create new business models' that were perceived as a threat to existing retailers (Wrigley et al., 2002: 182). An example of this model is Amazon.com, which eschewed retail store networks for warehouses. These businesses could circumvent and deconstruct the value chains of traditional retailers in ways more recently echoed by the intermediary functions of contemporary sharing economy platforms. The other was the 'bricks and clicks' retailers that had an existing store network and were developing systems to enable consumers to purchase goods online (Murphy, 2003). The UK grocery retailer Tesco was an early example of this model, building from an existing store network to offer home delivery through an online ordering system. A key challenge for both models was how to furnish the quick response demanded by online ordering through sufficiently sophisticated logistical systems of storage, picking, and delivery of goods (Wrigley and Currah, 2006). These 'problems of space and time' (Murphy, 2003: 1176) remain the focus of new market actors associated with 'on-demand' consumption that provide last-mile urban logistics, such as Uber and Deliveroo, the online restaurant delivery platform.

The second antecedent, and that which has received less explicit attention in geographical scholarship, is the role of the internet in forms of peer-to-peer exchange. This has primarily focused on how peer-to-peer networks have altered conventional geographies of distribution, such as Leyshon's (2003, 2009) examination of the changing spaces of music production and consumption. The circulation of music through user-friendly MP3 file exchange systems such as Napster initially bypassed 'copyright capitalism' (Leyshon, 2003), and later the sharing of music and video on MySpace and YouTube became a channel for distribution of 'home' recorded content as digital recording rigs became more affordable. These possibilities of democratizing production and gifting as a mode of consumption are present in some contemporary discussions of access-based usage through sharing economy platforms, where market-mediated transactions occur but no transfer of ownership takes place. New market actors enabled by contemporary digital technologies must be understood within the context of shifting norms of consumption denoted by the term 'sharing', and also within this longer history of the changing geographies of retail and distribution through the internet. The next section will consider how geographers have asked whether sharing is an appropriate label for these digital market actors.

THE DISCOURSE OF SHARING

There are questions concerning the relationship between the discourse or language of the sharing economy and practices of new digital market actors. The core problem lies in defining the nature of the transformation to economic activities implied by the term 'sharing'. Two sets of questions in relation to this arise in popular as well as academic debates. The first are those concerned with identifying novelty. These questions ask whether sharing is new or, put another way, what difference the digital makes to the emergence of sharing as a unique mode of economic exchange. The starting point for this line of inquiry is that sharing has always existed in forms of gifting, barter, and non-monetary exchange that lie outside of market-driven price systems (Waite and Lewis, 2017). This has led to attempts to create typologies to distinguish between different forms of sharing exchange. Taking food sharing as an example, Davies et al. (2017) illustrate the complexity of activities of exchange, outlining the variety of organizational forms for sharing (including for profit, social enterprise, co-op, charity, etc.) that might combine with different practices of sharing (such as gifting, selling (for profit and not for profit), collecting, bartering, etc.).

The second set of questions are concerned with veracity. These interrogate the truth or reality of sharing as a label for the economic activities brokered by digital technologies. Such questions challenge the accuracy of claims that digital technologies can produce alternative or non-capitalist forms of economic activity. Echoing Morozov's (2013) accusation that the sharing economy is 'neoliberalism on steroids', Martin (2016), for example, argues that the sharing economy may just as easily be thought of simultaneously as a nightmarish form of capitalism and as a pathway to sustainability through reducing resource consumption (Frenken and Schor, 2017). In a similar vein, Belk (2014: 11) makes a distinction between what he terms 'sharing' and 'pseudo-sharing', suggesting that the latter is a business relationship masquerading as communal sharing. He offers four examples of models of such pseudo-sharing: long-term renting and leasing; short-term rental; online sites 'sharing' your data; and online, facilitated barter economies. Belk (2014: 14) does nonetheless suggest that there are a number of 'true sharing forms' that have emerged via Web 2.0, including 'online facilitated hospitality' where he points to Couchsurfing (see Molz, 2012).

Some geographers have taken a post-structuralist approach to shift the focus away from these questions of the novelty and veracity of the sharing economy. Their intervention begins from the position that the economy does not have an 'essential' identity and is instead constituted by sets of discourses and practices that produce a 'virtual' (economic) world and its object (Thrift, 2005). In other words, the economy comprises multiple arrangements of the simulations and models in combination with the activities to which they refer (Mitchell, 2008). Rather than trying to assess the extent to which digital market actors are transformative or authentic, the interest here lies in how and with what implications the economy is *constructed* as shared. In this vein, Cockayne (2016) shows how the trope of sharing is used by entrepreneurs and software developers in San Francisco's digital media sector to encourage and dissuade particular combinations of labouring and social practices. His argument is that the discourse of sharing is not incidental to these digital economic practices but is rather co-produced alongside them, and has significant implications for the normalization of activities that devalue labour under digital capitalism. This is further nuanced in Richardson's (2015) framing of the sharing economy as a performance that operates both as part of the capitalist economy and as an alternative to it. Drawing on understandings of economic diversity, she suggests that there is a performative promise to the deployment of the 'sharing economy' that might bring about alternative and potentially more socially just economic practices. While not directly challenging this, Cockayne (2016) points to the necessity of attending to the differentiated deployments of sharing in understanding the variegated activities of and through digital platforms to assess the ways in which they might alter existing economic practices. The operations of these digital platforms have accordingly begun to receive more attention from geographers, examined in the next section.

THE ROLE OF THE DIGITAL PLATFORM

The digital platforms of the sharing economy can seemingly simply be understood as that which connects different stakeholders (i.e., clients, providers) of a resource or service. However, as Gillespie (2010: 349) has noted, the term 'platform' is both specific enough to mean something, yet vague enough to work across multiple audiences, such that 'to call one's online service a platform is not a meaningless claim, nor is it a simple one'. Regarding their operations, platforms extend the intermediary logics of the above noted e-commerce developments in the 1990s that used the distance-shrinking capacities of the internet to solve coordination problems in market exchange. However, rather than understood as neutral infrastructure or conduit, Langley and Leyshon (2017: 19) argue that the operations of platforms 'actively induce, produce and programme circulations'. Thus, they suggest that the novelty of the platform lies not in its role in intermediating connection between parties in an already existing economic exchange, but rather in its capacities to actively curate connectivity so as to produce novel forms of value generation. This means targeting the value resulting from the network effects of user co-creation; the 'peer-to-peer' or multi-sided market possibilities offered by the platform.

A key basis for this platform model of revenue generation is through new forms of categorization and exclusion that preclude notions of a democratic, collaborative economic transformation between 'the peers' and the corporation, termed by Chase (2015) 'the Inc'. In other words, it is in the interests of platform entities such as Airbnb to encourage usage through the guise of an inclusive, participatory culture to attract and grow a substantial user base, because it is through the coordination and regulation of such usage that they generate value. The most notable forms of categorization are the reputational economies that have grown up as a means for standardizing circulations between distributed users in the network, of which Airbnb provides a useful example. After enrolling users – whether as guests or hosts – through a user verification programme (including the provision of identity documents), Airbnb enables transactions on the basis of user-generated profiles and reviews. These profiles have a reputational 'currency' in that they provide 'traceable and verifiable records' reflected in both the 'quantity and quality of received reviews' (Stabrowski, 2017: 332). The logic is that the wisdom of the crowd provides checks and balances: reviewers are expected to be honest as they themselves do not want to receive a bad review. In the case of Airbnb, the company argues that this reputation economy improves existing (informal) hospitality practices because it allows users 'to screen each other and create a safer, more transparent environment during those transactions' (Hantman, 2015, in Stabrowski, 2017: 332).

As Langley and Leyshon (2017: 20) suggest, these reputational devices contribute to the appearance of the sharing economy as a near perfect market, 'where participants have access to almost fully disclosed information on the other parties'. However, participation in such an economy, and the defining terms of such reputational transparency, are dictated by the Airbnb platform, which thus also benefits from the further transactions generated as users try to build their reputations. This curation of connectivity of the digital platform therefore differs from e-commerce websites and mobile apps which provide only an additional channel for revenue by intermediating exchange in two-sided markets, rather than an entirely new source. It is this capacity to generate additional value that has led to the neologism 'platform capitalism' (Lobo, 2014). This term challenges narratives of the sharing economy as diverse and redistributive, and instead suggests that the platform points to new tendencies for concentrated accumulation within capitalism that hinder any move towards a 'post-capitalist' future (Srnicek, 2017). Such concentrations of

..c in the hands of the owners of the platform have led to experiments ..i cooperativism: new decentralized networks that are enabling people . their data with each other without relying on the corporate cloud (for ..iples, see Scholz, 2016). This interest in cooperativism has also been fuelled by ..e working conditions of providers in the sharing economy, discussed below.

SHARING AS DISTRIBUTION?

If sharing is understood nominally as a form of exchange, this invites a critical approach to the digital economy that emphasizes a politics of distribution. Such a politics foregrounds the organization of social life around the ways wealth is shared out, rather than through its production. This latter politics of production has historically centred political economy around the paid labour of able-bodied men supported by the unpaid reproductive work of women. In contrast, a distributive political economy would focus on the myriad ways in which existing wealth could be divided up and transferred through social relations that sustain and thus reproduce society (Ferguson, 2015). Yet despite this possibility for a reorientation of political approach, much of the popular and academic critical debate concerning the sharing economy has been directed through a politics of production. It has focused on the category of labour and questions of worker (or 'provider') agency and exploitation. There is certainly good reason for this focus, given the duplicitous nature of such work. The forms of labour associated with digital platforms such as Uber are framed as flexible, meaning that the worker has the possibility to choose when to work. However, this also means that work (i.e., income) is not necessarily there when the worker wants it (Scholz, 2016).

This problem is compounded by the employment status of those whose work is brokered through digital platforms. Major platform companies have argued that those who provide services through their technology are self-employed contractors. This means that Uber drivers do not benefit from the securities afforded to workers who have employee status. The categorization of self-employment is rendered more problematic because the promised benefits of flexibility and independence are often not realized. For example, Ravenelle (2017) details how sharing economy workers are held to certain behaviour and responsiveness requirements set by the companies through which they access work. Uber drivers are expected to maintain a minimum 'star' approval rating (4.6 out of 5 stars) and to accept 80 percent of ride requests; failure to do so can result in the deactivation of their account and thus their ability to secure work through the platform. For those platforms where the client gets to pick from various service providers, Ravenelle (2017) highlights the power of the company's platform design to determine which providers are shown to clients (consumers) and how this visibility also governs the parameters of providers' availability. To illustrate this, she uses the example of TaskRabbit, a platform through which 'taskers' (workers willing to do piecemeal work, or 'tasks') offer their services to do odd jobs or 'gigs' for clients. A recent change to the platform ended task bidding on work and instead required task workers (the 'Taskrabbits') to list their availability in four-hour blocks and to respond to task assignments within 30 minutes.

In the cases of both Uber and TaskRabbit then, the platform owner plays a significant role in determining the volume of work and the manner in which such work is distributed. Despite being nominally self-employed, the conditions of activity that establish providers as workers resemble many of those that define the category of employee. However, the insecurities of income associated with this self-employed status do not necessarily correlate with low income overall for those working through the platforms. Indeed, Schor (2017) argues that it is precisely because many sharing economy providers have income from other sources that they are able to do such work. Her research suggests that this results in a 'crowding out' of workers with low educational attainment who have traditionally done much of the manual work that these more privileged providers are now doing. With this in mind, it is worth returning to the question of what it might mean to approach the sharing economy through a politics of distribution. Whether resulting in underpaid work or underworked labour, sharing economy platforms tend towards uneven distributions of income at best. Yet, by bringing such work into view – that which has historically been insecure, underpaid or simply not recognized as labour – the sharing economy exposes the significant role of such activity in producing social life, as has long been shown by feminist scholarship (see Richardson, 2018). The 'sharing economy' therefore poses the question of whether production should remain the primary site for political articulation when opportunities for a 'gig' are manifold but such activity alone does not supply sufficient income on which to live. Rather than being limited to current operations of the profit-orientated digital platforms, then, the 'sharing economy' might serve as a reminder that 'it is necessary always to hold open the possibility of change' (Massey, 1995: 286).

FUTURE DEVELOPMENTS

In popular and academic debate beyond geography, the problems and possibilities of new digital market actors associated with the sharing economy are likely to continue. Regarding the problems, this will result in further attempts to regulate the activities of platforms such as Uber and Airbnb in geographically specific ways, as these companies adjust their business models to suit the specificities of particular (urban) markets. Therefore, understanding the variegated practices through which these platform companies undermine different regulatory regimes across their distinct markets of (present/future) operation is likely to be a continuing research theme. In relation to the possibilities, there will also be continued attempts to 'harness' the opportunities offered through such new market actors for shared access to resources, together with additional opportunities for income. Geographical research will contribute to such site-specific policy debates (Kent and Dowling, 2013), not least through providing more nuanced accounts of how sharing practices take place.

Note

1. www.ted.com/talks/rachel_botsman_the_case_for_collaborative_consumption

REFERENCES

Bardhi, F. and Eckhardt, G. (2012) 'Access-based consumption: The case of car sharing', *Journal of Consumer Research*, 39(4): 881–898.

Belk, R. (2014) 'Sharing versus pseudo-sharing in Web 2.0', *Anthropologist*, 18(1): 7–23.

Benkler, Y. (2004) 'Sharing nicely: On sharable goods and emergence of sharing as a modality of economic production', *Yale Law Journal*, 114(2): 273–358.

Chase, R. (2015) *Peers Inc: How People and Platforms Are Inventing the Collaborative Economy and Reinventing Capitalism*. New York: Public Affairs.

Cockayne, D.G. (2016) 'Sharing and neoliberal discourse: The economic function of sharing in the digital on-demand economy', *Geoforum*, 77: 73–82.

Currah, A. (2002) 'Behind the web store: The organisational and spatial evolution of multichannel retailing in Toronto', *Environment and Planning A*, 34(8): 1411–1441.

Davies, A., Donald, B., Gray, M. and Knox-Hayes, J. (2017) 'Sharing economies: Moving beyond binaries in a digital age', *Cambridge Journal of Regions, Economy and Society*, 10(2): 209–230.

Ferguson, J. (2015) *Give a Man a Fish: Reflections on the New Politics of Distribution*. Durham, NC: Duke University Press.

Frenken, K. and Schor, J. (2017) 'Putting the sharing economy into perspective', *Environmental Innovation and Societal Transitions*, 23(June): 3–10.

Gillespie, T. (2010) 'The politics of "platforms"', *New Media & Society*, 12(3): 347–364.

Kent, J. and Dowling, R. (2013) 'Puncturing automobility? Carsharing practices', *Journal of Transport Geography*, 32: 86–92.

Langley, P. and Leyshon, A. (2017) 'Platform capitalism: The intermediation and capitalization of digital economic circulation', *Finance and Society*, 3(1): 11–31.

Leyshon, A. (2003) 'Scary monsters? Software formats, peer-to-peer networks, and the spectre of the gift', *Environment and Planning D: Society and Space*, 21(5): 533–558.

Leyshon, A. (2009) 'The software slump?: Digital music, the democratisation of technology, and the decline of the recording studio sector within the musical economy', *Environment and Planning A*, 41(6): 1309–1331.

Lobo, S. (2014) 'Auf dem Weg in die Dumpinghölle', *Spiegel Online*, 3 September. Available at: www.spiegel.de/netzwelt/netzpolitik/sascha-lobo-sharing-economy-wie-bei-uber-ist-plattform-kapitalismus-a-989584.html (accessed 17 July 2017).

Martin, C.J. (2016) 'The sharing economy: A pathway to sustainability or a nightmarish form of neoliberal capitalism?', *Ecological Economics*, 121: 149–159.

Massey, D. (1995) 'Thinking radical democracy spatially', *Environment and Planning D: Society and Space*, 13(3): 283–288.

Mitchell, T. (2008) 'Rethinking economy', *Geoforum*, 39(3): 1116–1121.

Molz, G. (2012) 'CouchSurfing and network hospitality: "It's not just about the furniture"', *Hospitality & Society*, 1(3): 215–225.

Morozov, E. (2013) 'The "sharing economy" undermines workers' rights', *Financial Times*, 14 October. Available at: www.ft.com/content/92c3021c-34c2-11e3-8148-00144feab7de (accessed 2 February 2018).

Murphy, A. (2003) '(Re)solving space and time: Fulfilment issues in online grocery retailing', *Environment and Planning A*, 35(7): 1173–1200.

Murphy, A. (2007) 'Grounding the virtual: The material effects of electronic grocery shopping', *Geoforum*, 38: 941–953.

Ravenelle, A. (2017) 'Sharing economy workers: Selling, not sharing', *Cambridge Journal of Regions, Economy and Society*, 10(2): 281–295.

Richardson, L. (2015) 'Performing the sharing economy', *Geoforum*, 67: 121–129.

Richardson, L. (2018) 'Feminist geographies of digital work', *Progress in Human Geography*, 42(2): 244–263.

Scholz, T. (2016) *Uberworked and Underpaid: How Workers Are Disrupting the Digital Economy*. Cambridge: Polity Press.

Schor, J.B. (2017) 'Does the sharing economy increase inequality within the eighty percent? Findings from a qualitative study of platform providers', *Cambridge Journal of Regions, Economy and Society*, 10(2): 263–279.

Srnicek, N. (2017) *Platform Capitalism*. Cambridge: Polity Press.

Stabrowski, F. (2017) '"People as businesses": Airbnb and urban micro-entrepreneurialism in New York City', *Cambridge Journal of Regions, Economy and Society*, 10(2): 327–347.

Thrift, N. (2005) *Knowing Capitalism*. London: Sage.

Waite, L. and Lewis, H. (2017) 'Precarious irregular migrants and their sharing economies: A spectrum of transactional laboring experiences', *Annals of the American Association of Geographers*, 107(4): 964–978.

Wrigley, N. and Currah, A. (2006) 'Globalizing retail and the "new e-conomy": The organizational challenge of e-commerce for the retail TNCs', *Geoforum*, 37(3): 340–351.

Wrigley, N., Lowe, M. and Currah, A. (2002) 'Retailing and e-tailing', *Urban Geography*, 23(2): 180–197.

19

TRADITIONAL INDUSTRIES

Bruno Moriset

INTRODUCTION

Centuries-old sectors such as retail, banking, and manufacturing are being 'disrupted' by digitization. Digitization describes the process by which core services, processes, and practices become partially or thoroughly replaced by computing technologies. Beyond information technology (IT) and other 'natively digital' industries, the economy as a whole is being transformed by digitization, which blurs the lines between traditional sectors, drives the globalization of value chains, and shapes the geography of industries and firms. E-commerce and cloud computing have been commoditized. Big data, additive technology, virtual reality, the internet of things, machine learning, and artificial intelligence are opening the doors to a global transformation that is simultaneously igniting fears about the possible vanishing of millions of jobs as they are replaced by robots and algorithms (Frey and Osborne, 2017). New and emerging business models, goods, and services are not only replacing but also actively displacing business actors and entities who have dominated markets and sectors for decades, transforming the very nature of the sectors into which they are moving and taking on competitors.

This chapter begins by identifying three ways in which the digital transforms and impacts traditional industries: it blurs the boundaries between industrial sectors of the economy; it is acting as a 'general purpose technology'; and it is driving the globalization of value chains. The second half of the chapter examines how three specific, centuries-old industries – retail, finance, and manufacturing – are being disrupted by digitization. The chapter concludes by summarizing the geographic implications of digitization, which do not necessarily diminish the general tendency towards the spatial polarization of high value-added business, skilled jobs, investment capital, and wealth.

TRADITIONAL INDUSTRIES AND THE TRANSFORMATIVE NATURE OF THE DIGITAL

The digital economy and the blurring of boundaries between industries

There is no universal definition of the digital economy (Malecki and Moriset, 2008). However, one defining characteristic of the rise of the digital economy is the blurring of boundaries between economic sectors. Examples abound. Amazon, an online retailer, is a leader in cloud computing services and drone delivery, and recently acquired the grocery chain Whole Foods. Telecom companies like Orange in France, and T-Mobile in Poland, offer banking services. Alphabet,[1] Uber, and Apple are poised to become automobile manufacturers through their initiatives in autonomous vehicle engineering.

Worldwide, information technology (IT) spending[2] in 2017 is projected to be worth $3.5 trillion (Gartner, Inc., 2017), or approximately 5 percent of global gross domestic product. However, the actual extent of the digital economy is larger if we consider the digitization of value chains beyond natively digital or digital-centric industries. The McKinsey Global Institute (2015) ranks industries according to a 'Digitization Index' (Table 19.1) based on the share of IT spending in operating costs, the weight of IT in firms' assets, and the share of tasks which are computerized. Finance, media, and advanced manufacturing rank among the highly digitized. Sectors moderately digitized overall – such as retail, transportation, and hospitality – also include 'digital champions' such as Amazon, Uber, and Airbnb. However, even sectors with the lowest digitization ranking have become digital to some extent. Farmers and fishermen in developing countries may not be equipped with the GPS-guided tractors and boats common in advanced economies, but they use mobile phones to market their products more efficiently, or to receive weather and agricultural reports (Jensen, 2007).

The nature of economic transformations driven by the dissemination of IT across traditional industries has been discussed in terms of *disruption* or *uberization*. Disruption describes a process whereby a smaller company with fewer resources is able to successfully challenge established incumbent businesses (Christensen et al., 2015). The rise of Airbnb, founded in 2008, which has changed the nature of the accommodation industry, is a textbook example of disruption. The term 'uberization' was coined by Maurice Lévy, former CEO of the advertising agency Publicis,[3] to signal the roll-out of digital platforms across traditional sectors of the economy, as epitomized by the upheaval in the taxi industry created by ride-hailing mobile applications like Uber and its competitors. Digital technologies not only drive disruption, but have become 'general purpose' technologies essential to innovation across all industries.

Table 19.1 Digitization levels across business sectors in the USA

Digitization level	Sectors
1	Information and communication technologies
2	Media; professional services; finance and insurance
3	Wholesale trade; advanced manufacturing; oil and gas; utilities
4	Real estate; education; retail trade; personal services; government
5	Chemicals and pharmaceuticals; basic goods manufacturing Transportation and warehousing; health care
6	Mining; construction; entertainment and recreation; hospitality; agriculture

Source: McKinsey Global Institute (2015: 5).

'General purpose technology' and digital convergence

Key digital technologies such as semiconductors are regarded as 'general purpose technologies' (GPTs), as once were steam machines and electricity. They are considered 'general purpose' in that they demonstrate the potential for continuous improvement (as suggested by Moore's law); utility across a wide range of sectors (semiconductors are everywhere, from cars to household appliances); and strong innovation complementarities with other sectors (for example, the rise of biotechnology and genomics relies on big data and fast computing – see Marx, 2013) (Bresnahan and Trajtenberg, 1995). Semiconductors' continuous improvement in power and miniaturization was instrumental to the advent of the smartphone, the iconic device of the digital society, and the epitome of the digital convergence

(Yoffie, 1996). Smartphones have integrated once distinct analog devices such as telephones, clocks, agendas/calendars, maps, newspapers, record players, cameras, and televisions. The smartphone is now a platform on which industries such as mail, telecommunications, retail, media, gaming, and banking also converge. These kinds of IT-enabled complementarities and convergence give birth to new markets and business ecosystems. For example, the action camera popularized by GoPro comprises a multi-billion-dollar market that has flourished at the crossroads of social demand (self-promotion on Facebook), digital media (YouTube, Snapchat), technical improvements (polycarbonates, optics, data storage), and the growth of tourism and outdoor activities.

The globalization of IT-driven value chains: Outsourcing and offshoring

Enormous computing power and data storage capacity, and cheap broadband connectivity, have further driven the organizational and geographic unbundling of value chains (Ge et al., 2004). Value chains consist of a series of linked actions (e.g., research and development (R&D), raw materials extraction, manufacturing, marketing, delivery) aimed at the creation of value in terms of the amount of money that end-consumers are willing to pay for a good or service (Porter, 1985). The coordinating power of the digital has increased the complexity and scope of the locational portfolios of companies, their affiliates, and contractors. Digital technologies in supply chains and logistics (such as inventory management software, barcode scanning and GPS tracking for delivery) reduce uncertainty and delays. This favours the growth of a fine-grained division of labour. Cost considerations and the search for economies of scale have fuelled the offshoring of parts of the production process in emerging or developing countries, notably China for manufacturing and India for services. This phenomenon has caught the eyes of the media, stirring up political controversies and attracting the attention of geographers (Peck, 2017). Advanced telecommunications have enabled the real-time delivery of a wide range of IT services to business units, headquarters, and customers across multiple locations around the world. The spectrum of business process outsourcing (BPO)[4] services open to offshoring is wide: R&D, testing, design, architecture, financial and legal services, accounting, marketing and customer relations, education, and medical services. This 'collapsing of time and space', whereby these services may be delivered remotely from abroad, has given birth to multi-billion-dollar industries in diverse countries such as India, the Philippines, and Israel.

THREE INDUSTRIES DIGITALLY DISRUPTED: RETAIL, FINANCE, AND MANUFACTURING

E-commerce and the crisis of 'brick-and-mortar' retail

According to eMarketer,[5] worldwide e-commerce reached $1.9 trillion in 2016, 8.7 percent of total retail spending. The largest market is China, with online sales worth $582 billion in 2015 (Deloitte, 2016). From 2001 to 2015, e-commerce sales in the USA increased tenfold, to $340.4 billion, a 7.2 percent market share (US Census Bureau, 2017). Meanwhile, brick-and-mortar shopping struggles for survival, notably in the USA, where newspapers rival in superlatives about the decline of physical retail.[6] Sears, an iconic department store chain with 140,000 employees, was on the verge of bankruptcy in 2017 after losing $7.3 billion in the previous five years.[7] Macy's Inc. announced the closure of 68 stores in 2017 and the layoff of about 10,000 employees.[8] Shopping malls are in serious decline, notably in the USA: there is a 'dead mall' entry in Wikipedia, and a website dedicated to dead shopping malls, www.deadmalls.com.

The digital disruption is not singularly to blame for the difficulties experienced by the retail industry as a whole. In America, the intensifying polarization of wealth and the squeezing of middle-class family incomes must also be taken into account. But e-commerce is nevertheless the biggest, immediate challenge traditional retailers are facing, and their transformation towards 'brick and click' (also known as 'click and collect'), multichannel shopping is a matter of survival (Wrigley and Currah, 2006). Walmart, the world's largest company by measures of employment and revenue ($481 billion in 2016), acknowledges that '[c]onsumers are increasingly embracing shopping online and through mobile commerce applications' and that it must 'build and deliver a seamless shopping experience across the physical and digital retail channels'.[9] The digital transformation of retail is captured by 'the epic battle' between Walmart and Amazon (Heller, 2016). The two companies are 'on a collision course': in 2016, Walmart acquired JetCom, an online retailer, and on 16 June 2017, Amazon announced it will acquire Whole Foods, an American chain of upscale grocery stores (Bose and Dastin, 2017). Despite low returns for shareholders, Amazon's market valuation is twice that of Walmart ($462 billion versus $228 billion as of 30 June 2017).[10] These low returns are explained by Amazon's prioritization of growth as much of its net cash resulting from operations is invested in infrastructure and technology.[11]

Fulfilment and logistics are the cornerstone of e-commerce (Murphy, 2003). Sophisticated web platforms and trustworthy payment systems are required to reach customers, provide them with a customized shopping experience, and secure their loyalty. However, swift delivery of goods while keeping inventories as low as possible is about warehouses, aircraft (and soon drones), trucks and vans, and congestion-free roads. By the end of 2016, Amazon operated worldwide nearly 160 million square feet (about 15 million square metres) of fulfilment facilities (data centres and warehouses). This is the equivalent of 840 Walmart supercentres. From its beginnings, the cornerstone of Amazon's strategy has been to decrease delivery time. Subscribers to its Prime programme benefit from free, two-day delivery, and same-day delivery across 5000 American cities.[12] This discussion of e-commerce stresses the ways in which geography still matters. In countries with poor physical infrastructures and congested cities, like India, the 'last mile' (the last leg of delivery to customers) has become a nightmare for e-retailers. Amazon's recent acquisition of Whole Foods shows that the convergence towards a multichannel model of retail has increased the value of location for brick-and-mortar stores, supermarkets, and supercentres, used as distribution centres and depots, but only where they are easily accessible and strategically distributed across distribution networks.

Digital finance: A paradoxical geography

Since the invention of the bill of exchange, money trading has been at the vanguard of capitalist 'time-space compression' (Harvey, 1999). Dealing with an intangible substance, modern finance has superficially epitomized the mythical 'end of geography' (O'Brien, 1992). Societies are on the way to becoming cashless. In 2015, 98 percent of payments in Sweden were made through credit cards and mobile apps such as Swish[13] (Henley, 2016). In India, the government is vigorously promoting digital payments through the Cashless India programme.[14]

The provision of remote access to banking services via desktops or smartphones has prompted some to predict a collapse of retail banking (Kessler, 2016). Banks in Western countries are closing branches. Bank of America, which has 21 million customers active online, has closed 1400 of 6000 branches since 2007 (Wadhwa, 2016). This consolidation process is pushed by the competition incumbent banks are facing from technology start-ups (or 'fintechs') and IT giants such as Apple, Alphabet, and Facebook (USA), or Tencent and Alibaba (China), which turn to financial services to increase revenues they make from their platforms' billion of users. According to a report by Citigroup (2016), fintechs may grab 17 percent of banking revenues in the USA and Europe by 2023. In China, they have passed the 'tipping point' and surpass incumbent banks by the number of clients.

However, the rise of online banking and fintech is unlikely to beget the hollowing out of employment in the finance industry. It is more likely that these will reinforce the current shift from routine jobs to more specialized, highly skilled jobs. In the USA, finance is not forecast to shrink, but rather to add 500,000 jobs to the economy between 2014 and 2024 (US Bureau of Labor Statistics, 2017).

Nevertheless, branch closures are visible in these employment projections: the bank teller workforce is projected to shrink by 7.7 percent. This will likely be compensated for by the rise of occupations requiring high skills or face-to-face contact with customers such as analysts (11.7 percent), credit counsellors (15.5 percent), and personal financial advisors (29.6 percent).

The finance sector captures a central paradox that characterizes the geography of the digital economy (Moriset and Malecki, 2009): although transactions via computers or mobiles are nearly ubiquitous, high-end services concentrate in major financial centres such as London, New York, Tokyo, and Hong Kong. Spatial concentration of a fully digital sector is counter-intuitive because IT makes it possible to offer services from abroad irrespective of the location of capital. The geography of advanced financial services (currency and securities trading, asset management) is production-driven rather than market-driven in several ways. First, there is the competition for talents. Clark (2015) explains how the availability of 'star' professionals is instrumental to the prominence of London in asset management services. In addition to the urban amenities which highly paid professionals demand, London and its region host world-class universities and finance-oriented curricula (Hall and Appleyard, 2009). The presence of major financial institutions fuels a highly competitive labour market which, in turn, attracts the best specialists from abroad. Second, there is the quest for 'informational asymmetries'[15] resulting from 'urban buzz' (Storper and Venables, 2004), which reduce uncertainty and increase returns from operations. Third, the digital technology itself (algorithmic, data centres, optical networks) requires agglomeration in its search for economies of scale and low latency[16] in high-frequency trading (Wójcik et al., 2017). However, these agglomeration externalities produce their full effect only if they are leveraged by favourable legal environments, like those resulting from the deregulation of financial markets – or the 'Big Bang' – which occurred in the UK in 1986 (Snyder et al., 2006).

Manufacturing and the industrial internet

The latest advances in digital technology may be the starting point of a great turn in the history of industrial production, notably in 'advanced manufacturing': aerospace, automobiles, energy, medical equipment, and machinery. Several neologisms with overlapping meanings describe the industrial future: the 'industrial Internet' (General Electric and Accenture, 2015), 'cybermanufacturing' (Lee et al., 2016), and 'industry 4.0' (Germany Trade and Invest, 2014).

Until the present, computer-aided operations in R&D, supply chains, and production lines were separated in time and space. Today, the tendency is towards the integration of value-chain bricks into a product life cycle, managed like a systemic loop 'from the first idea of a product all the way through until it is retired and disposed of' (Stark, 2015: 1). Feedback from end-customers and information from after-sales services are analysed in real-time and drive continuous improvements at the design or mass-production stages. Much greater changes are potentially driven by the rise of 'the internet of things' (IoT), which paves the way for 'the industrial internet'. In the IoT, the flow of data captured, channelled, stored, and analysed originates from things as diverse as cars, closed-circuit television cameras, home appliances, heating, ventilation, and air conditioning systems, or the blades of a turbine. Machine-to-machine connections are likely to grow from 3.3 billion in 2013 to 10.5 billion by 2019 (Cisco Systems, 2015). As captured by an industry report produced by General Electric and Accenture (2015), 'the Industrial Internet enables companies to use sensors, software, machine-to-machine learning and other technologies to gather and analyze data from physical objects or other large data streams – and then use those analyses to manage operations and in some cases to offer new, value-added services'.

In 2013, General Electric launched a platform for cybermanufacturing, Predix, which may be understood as a potential 'Facebook for machines'. Predix is the product of an ecosystem (Agarwal and Brem, 2015) shared with IT companies such as AT&T (wireless communications), Cisco (collaborative tools), Amazon (cloud infrastructure), and Accenture (development and commercialization). The transformation of an old industrial conglomerate into a data-centric and software-centric company which employs approximately 13,000 software engineers (Agarwal and Brem, 2015) illustrates the blurring of the boundaries between manufacturing and services, or the 'servitization' of manufacturing (Rymaszewska et al., 2017).

The example of Rolls-Royce Plc., a British jet engines manufacturer, shows how the predictive capacity of the IoT drives the servitization of manufacturing. According to the company's annual report (Rolls-Royce Holdings plc, 2016), 52 percent of the revenue of the Civil Aerospace Division in 2015 came from services such as engines' real-time monitoring ('engine health management'). Data acquired by sensors on in-flight engines are transmitted for monitoring and diagnosis to the Rolls-Royce operation centre in Bristol. Feedback from analysis of this data subsequently drives benefits to the entire value chain: the design of more reliable and fuel-efficient engines, a streamlining of the maintenance schedule, and the elimination of unnecessary, unexpected inspections and repairs (Marr, 2015).

Cybermanufacturing, robotics and the IoT have received much attention in Germany, the birthplace of the 'Industrie 4.0' initiative, a 'strategic initiative' aimed at 'establish[ing] Germany as a lead market and provider of advanced manufacturing solutions'.[17] Germany boasts the strongest industrial base of any advanced economy, but its workforce is ageing, and the shortage of skilled workers is a systemic problem (it is worth noting that Japan, a leading country in robotics, faces similar challenges). In this context, to remain innovative and to maintain an edge over its competitors, Germany's industries must upgrade and embrace digitization. The implementation of Industrie 4.0 could have significant geographic effects. It could drive a process of 're-shoring', bringing production once transferred to emerging Asia back to western Europe or the USA. Additive technology (3D printing) could reduce the need for remote sourcing of components (Gress and Kalafsky, 2015). The demand for flexibility, customization, and quick delivery could favour the emergence of 'smart factories' located in the core of main markets. Adidas's 'Speed Factory' in Ansbach (Bavaria), opened in mid-2017, is a fine example. Robots and 3D printers will produce 500,000 pairs of sneakers a year, offering customers a short time to delivery and an unprecedented choice of sizes, forms, colours, and fabrics (*The Economist*, 2017).

CONCLUSION: GEOGRAPHY PREVAILS

The implications of the digital transformation of traditional industries are difficult to capture in all their magnitude. IT implementation has a vast 'disruptive' potential in education, health and medicine, and transportation, to name only a few sectors. Yet whatever the trajectory of disruptive innovations and their effects across both emerging and traditional industries, geography remains central to these developments and our understanding of their effects.

First, the importance of location has not diminished. The existence of localized clusters (Delgado et al., 2014) in all industries has not been seriously challenged. It is noteworthy that Tesla, Inc., one of today's most 'disruptive' ventures in the automobile industry, is headquartered in Palo Alto, California, the heart of Silicon Valley.[18] Cross-sectoral, IT-driven convergences and complementarities, and the 'stickiness' of technology venture capital, favour large cities' industrial and research ecosystems where firms at different stages of development, from start-ups to behemoths like General Electric, Amazon, and Citigroup, can finance their development, get in touch with high-end service providers, and easily recruit engineers and scientists.

Second, digitization favours polarization in large cities, or 'metropolization', rather than dispersion. Community malls are squeezed between e-commerce and Walmart's supercentres. In the banking industry, most branch closures happen in small and medium-sized cities, or peripheral communities, where household incomes and profitability are lower. The upgrading of financial services, and the competition to attract talent, increase the geographic concentration of operations. In India, the growth of IT-enabled services – which are true distance-breakers – favours 'tech cities' such as Bangalore, Noida, and Gurgaon, while rural areas are left behind. Languishing rustbelts and rural areas in developed countries, and now in China, tell a similar story.

In the end, there are few reasons to think that information technology will lessen in the foreseeable future the premium given to face-to-face contacts (Leamer and Storper, 2001), which is the *raison d'être* of creative hubs and technology clusters in the digital economy.

Notes

1. The parent company of Google.
2. Includes data centres, enterprise software, digital devices (smartphones, PCs), IT services, and communications services.
3. *Financial Times*, 14 December 2014.
4. Business process outsourcing (BPO) is the subcontracting of tangible or non-tangible tasks in the production process (part manufacturing, machine maintenance, computer system management, etc.) to a third-party company. Outsourcing is a legal concept which does not carry any geographic meaning. If a task is processed in a country outside of where the ordering firm is located, it is said to be 'offshore'.
5. www.emarketer.com/Article/Worldwide-Retail-Ecommerce-Sales-Will-Reach-1915-Trillion-This-Year/1014369
6. www.nbcnews.com/business/consumer/retail-wreck-over-1-000-stores-close-single-week-n767556
7. Sears Holdings Corporation (2017) Form 10-K Annual Report for the fiscal year ended January 28, 2017. US Securities and Exchange Commission, Washington, DC. Available at: www.sec.gov/Archives/edgar/data/1310067/000131006717000005/shld201610k.htm (accessed 3 February 2018).
8. Macy's, Inc. (2017) Press release, 4 January. Available at: http://phx.corporate-ir.net/phoenix.zhtml?c=84477&p=irol-newsArticle&ID=2234057 (accessed 16 May 2018).
9. Wal-Mart Stores, Inc. (2017) Form 10-K Annual Report for the fiscal year ended January 31, 2017. US Securities and Exchange Commission, Washington, DC. Available at: www.sec.gov/Archives/edgar/data/104169/000010416917000021/wmtform10-kx1312017.htm (accessed 16 May 2018).
10. See https://finance.yahoo.com/quote/AMZN/ and https://finance.yahoo.com/quote/WMT.
11. Amazon.com, Inc. (2017) Form 10-K Annual Report for the fiscal year ended December 31, 2016. US Securities and Exchange Commission, Washington, DC. Available at: www.sec.gov/Archives/edgar/data/1018724/000101872417000011/amzn-20161231x10k.htm (accessed 2 February 2018).
12. www.amazon.com/Prime-FREE-Same-Day-Delivery/b?node=8729023011
13. Founded in 2012, Swish has attracted 5.4 million users, more than half of the country's total population (www.getswish.se).

14. http://cashlessindia.gov.in
15. Informational asymmetry occurs when one party holds more or better information than the other.
16. Latency, measured in milliseconds, is the delay between the command of an operation at one point of the network and its reception at another point. It is a function of the speed of light through fibre-optics and, therefore, of the distance.
17. www.gtai.de/GTAI/Navigation/EN/Invest/industrie-4-0.html
18. The main factory is in Fremont, CA.

REFERENCES

Agarwal, N. and Brem, A. (2015) 'Strategic business transformation through technology convergence: Implications from General Electric's industrial internet initiative', *International Journal of Technology Management*, 67(204): 196–214.

Bose, N. and Dastin, J. (2017) 'With Whole Foods, Amazon on collision course with Wal-Mart', *Reuters*, 18 June. Available at: www.reuters.com/article/us-whole-foods-m-a-amazon-com-walmart-idUSKBN1990HH (accessed 16 May 2018).

Bresnahan, T.F. and Trajtenberg, M. (1995) 'General purpose technologies: Engines of growth?', *Journal of Econometrics*, 65(1): 83–108.

Christensen, C.M., Raynor, M.E. and McDonald, R. (2015) 'What is disruptive innovation?', *Harvard Business Review*, December. Available at: https://hbr.org/2015/12/what-is-disruptive-innovation (accessed 2 February 2018).

Cisco Systems, Inc. (2015) 'The zettabyte era: Trends and analysis'. Available at: www.cisco.com/c/en/us/solutions/collateral/service-provider/visual-networking-index-vni/vni-hyperconnectivity-wp.pdf (accessed 2 February 2018).

Citigroup Inc. (2016) Citi GPS: Digital disruption. *Citi GPS: Global Perspectives and Solutions*, 31 March. Available at: www.privatebank.citibank.com/home/fresh-insight/citi-gps-digital-disruption.html (accessed 16 May 2018).

Clark, G.L. (2015) 'The components of talent: Company size and financial centres in the European investment management industry', *Regional Studies*, 50(1): 168–181.

Delgado, M., Porter, M. and Stern, S. (2014) 'Clusters, convergence, and economic performance', *Research Policy*, 43(10): 1785–1799.

Deloitte (2016) 'China e-retail market report 2016'. Available at: www2.deloitte.com/content/dam/Deloitte/cn/Documents/cip/deloitte-cn-cip-china-online-retail-market-report-en-170123.pdf (accessed 2 February 2018).

Frey, C.B. and Osborne, M.A. (2017) 'The future of employment: How susceptible are jobs to computerisation?', *Technological Forecasting and Social Change*, 114(C): 254–280.

Gartner, Inc. (2017) 'Gartner Worldwide IT spending forecast Q1 2017'. Available at: www.gartner.com/technology/research/it-spending-forecast (accessed 2 February 2018).

Ge, L., Konana, P. and Tanriverdi, H. (2004) 'Global sourcing and value chain unbundling'. Available at: www.mccombs.utexas.edu/faculty/prabhudev.konana/globalsourcing.pdf (accessed 2 February 2018).

General Electric and Accenture (2015) 'Industrial Internet Insights Report for 2015'. Available at: www.ge.com/digital/sites/default/files/industrial-internet-insights-report.pdf (accessed 2 February 2018).

Germany Trade and Invest (2014) 'Industrie 4.0: Smart manufacturing for the future'. Available at: www.gtai.de/GTAI/Content/EN/Invest/_SharedDocs/Downloads/GTAI/Brochures/Industries/industrie4.0-smart-manufacturing-for-the-future-en.pdf?v=8 (accessed 2 February 2018).

Gress, D.R. and Kalafsky, R.V. (2015) 'Geographies of production in 3D: Theoretical and research implications stemming from additive manufacturing', *Geoforum*, 60: 43–52.

Hall, S. and Appleyard, L. (2009) 'City of London, city of learning? Placing business education within the geographies of finance', *Journal of Economic Geography*, 9(5): 597–617.

Harvey, D. (1999) 'Time-space compression and the postmodern condition', in M. Waters (ed.), *Modernity: Critical Concepts*, Volume 4. Abingdon: Routledge. pp. 98–118.

Heller, L. (2016) 'The battle between Walmart and Amazon will be epic', Forbes.com, 30 October. Available at: www.forbes.com/sites/lauraheller/2016/10/30/the-battle-between-walmart-and-amazon-will-be-epic/#11e7068a56ee (accessed 2 February 2018).

Henley, J. (2016) 'Sweden leads the race to become cashless society', *The Guardian*, 4 June. Available at: www.theguardian.com/business/2016/jun/04/sweden-cashless-society-cards-phone-apps-leading-europe (accessed 2 February 2018).

Jensen, R. (2007) 'The digital provide: Information (technology), market performance and welfare in the South Indian fisheries sector', *Quarterly Journal of Economics*, 122(3): 879–924.

Kessler, A. (2016) 'The uberization of banking', *The Wall Street Journal*, 29 April. Available at: www.wsj.com/articles/the-uberization-of-banking-1461967266 (accessed 2 February 2018).

Leamer, E. and Storper, M. (2001) 'The economic geography of the Internet age', *Journal of International Business Studies*, 32: 641–665.

Lee, J., Bagheri, B. and Jin, C. (2016) 'Introduction to cyber manufacturing', *Manufacturing Letters*, 8: 11–15.

Malecki, E.J. and Moriset, B. (2008) *The Digital Economy: Business Organization, Production Processes and Regional Developments*. Abingdon: Routledge.

Marr, B. (2015) 'How big data drives success at Rolls-Royce', *PC Portal*, 3 June. Available at: http://pcportal.us/how-big-data-drives-success-at-rolls-royce (accessed 2 February 2018).

Marx, V. (2013) 'Biology: The big challenges of big data', *Nature*, 498: 255–260.

McKinsey Global Institute (2015) 'Digital America: A tale of the haves and have-mores'. Available at: www.mckinsey.com/industries/high-tech/our-insights/digital-america-a-tale-of-the-haves-and-have-mores (accessed 2 February 2018).

Moriset, B. and Malecki, E.J. (2009) 'Organization vs space: The paradoxical geographies of the digital economy', *Geography Compass*, 3(1): 256–274.

Murphy, A. (2003) '(Re)solving space and time: Fulfilment issues in online grocery retailing', *Environment and Planning A*, 35(7): 1173–1200.

O'Brien, R. (1992) *Global Financial Integration: The End of Geography*. London: Pinter.

Peck, J. (2017) *Offshore: Exploring the Worlds of Global Outsourcing*. Oxford: Oxford University Press.

Porter, M.E. (1985) *Competitive Advantage: Creating and Sustaining Superior Performance*. New York: Free Press.

Rolls-Royce Holdings plc (2016) *Annual Report 2016*. Available at: www.rolls-royce.com/~/media/Files/R/Rolls-Royce/documents/annual-report/rr-2016-full-annual-report.pdf (accessed 5 June 2017).

Rymaszewska, A., Heloa, P. and Gunasekaran, A. (2017) 'IoT powered servitization of manufacturing – an exploratory case study', *International Journal of Production Economics*, 192: 92–105.

Snyder, M. et al. (2006) *Big Bang 20 Years On: New Challenges Facing the Financial Services Sector*. London: Centre for Policy Studies. Available at: www.cps.org.uk/files/reports/original/111028101637-20061019EconomyBigBang20YearsOn.pdf (accessed 2 February 2018).

Stark, J. (2015) *Product Lifecycle Management: 21st Century Paradigm for Product Realisation*. Geneva: Springer International.

Storper, M. and Venables, A.J. (2004) 'Buzz: Face-to-face contact and the urban economy', *Journal of Economic Geography*, 4(4): 351–370.

The Economist (2017) 'Adidas's high-tech factory brings production back to Germany', *The Economist*, 14 January. Available at: www.economist.com/news/business/21714394-making-trainers-robots-and-3d-printers-adidass-high-tech-factory-brings-production-back (accessed 2 February 2018).

US Bureau of Labor Statistics (2017) 'Occupational employment and job openings data 2014 and projected 2024'. Available at: www.bls.gov/emp/ep_table_107.htm (accessed 2 February 2018).

US Census Bureau (2017) 'Estimated annual US retail trade sales'. Available at: www.census.gov/retail/index.html#ecommerce (accessed 2 February 2018).

Wadhwa, T. (2016) 'America's biggest banks are closing hundreds of branches', *Business Insider*, 23 October. Available at: www.businessinsider.com/bank-branches-around-the-world-are-shrinking-in-favor-of-digital-models-2016-10 (accessed 2 February 2018).

Wójcik, D., MacDonald-Korth, D. and Zhao, S.X. (2017) 'The political–economic geography of foreign exchange trading', *Journal of Economic Geography*, 17(2): 267–286.

Wrigley, N. and Currah, A. (2006) 'Globalizing retail and the "new e-conomy": The organizational challenge of e-commerce for the retail TNCs', *Geoforum*, 37: 340–351.

Yoffie, D.B. (1996) 'Competing in the age of digital convergence', *California Management Review*, 38(4): 31–53.

PART V
DIGITAL POLITICS

20

DEVELOPMENT

Dorothea Kleine

INTRODUCTION

It is easy to argue that digitalization has had a profound impact on almost all societies globally. An estimated 47 percent of the global population are now using the internet (International Telecommunication Union (ITU), 2016), and digitalization is increasingly permeating existing patterns of social, economic, political and cultural activity. However, an estimated 3.9 billion people do not have access to the internet (ITU, 2016) and an estimated 2 billion do not have a mobile phone (GSMA, 2017). Digital divides, defined as the uneven spread of information and communication technologies (ICTs) across countries and within societies (Norris, 2001), persist, and they tend to follow existing axes of exclusion along, for instance, lines of class, gender, education, and age, as well as between urban and rural areas and between income-rich and income-poor countries.

Scholars of 'development' draw a useful distinction between 'development as an immanent and unintentional process' and 'development as an intentional activity' (Cowen and Shenton, 1998). International development practice and the interdisciplinary field of development studies have been focused on the latter. The normative question of what then is to be understood by development has been highly contested, with divergent perspectives emphasizing, for instance, economic growth; basic needs; equity; freedom, capabilities and the ability to choose; and rights-based approaches (for a useful introduction to development theories, see Willis, 2011). Some, including myself, have argued that development from a freedom, well-being, and sustainability perspective is still taking place everywhere and thus all countries are 'developing countries' regardless of whether they are in the global South or North (Kleine, 2013). The UN Sustainable Development Goals,[1] adopted in 2015, are designed for all countries globally. However, for many commentators 'development' remains something which happens in the global South.

'Digital development' and 'ICT4D' (information and communication technologies for development), then, are labels for the interdisciplinary field of action and scholarship where the digital and intentional development efforts intersect. From the perspective of international development, digital tools have the potential to transform humanitarian aid, the delivery of services to marginalized communities, the amplification of the voice of the less powerful, as well as campaign efforts and civic activism. Scholars from a variety of disciplines, including information systems, computer science, development studies, geography, politics, economics, and anthropology, have engaged with this field from positions ranging from observation, critique, theorization, evaluation, and synthesis to participatory action research and co-production. This chapter will offer a short and unavoidably incomplete overview of this expanding area, highlighting some core issues and offering an outlook on emerging themes.

A BRIEF LOOK BACK

There exists a historical entanglement between notions of progress, colonialism, geopolitics, international cooperation, and technology. The contested space of international development practice has been drawing on technical innovations for decades. Practitioners recognized the power of devices such as radio and television in development efforts when packaging public health messages in soap operas or providing agricultural information via radio. More recently, in step with the dot-com boom of the late 1990s, the then UN General Secretary Kofi Annan called in 1997 for the use of ICTs in 'agriculture, health, education, human resources and environmental management, or transport and business development'. He optimistically concluded that 'the consequences could really be revolutionary' (Annan, 1997). Such techno-optimism was widespread at the time and was further bolstered by relevant UN conferences. The dual UN World Summit on the Information Society in 2003 and 2005 brought together government delegations, business representatives, multilateral and bilateral development actors, non-governmental organizations, civil society campaigners, and activists from 174 countries – over 19,000 participants in all (Kleine and Unwin, 2009).

Typical domains for interventions encompassed ICTs for business and enterprise, education and rural development, as well as e-government and e-health (Unwin, 2009). Examples include telemedicine; agricultural price and weather information services; and, more generally, telecentres which offered access to the internet and training on a no-cost or highly subsidized basis. However, academics examining the many ICT4D initiatives concluded that the majority failed (Heeks, 2002), potentially for technical reasons but often also because the social context in which the technology was meant to be embedded had not been taken into account sufficiently. Meanwhile, initiatives such as One Laptop per Child (OLPC) emerged, where a team of computer scientists and educators at MIT designed a ruggedly built, simple laptop with a target cost of $100 which they proposed could improve the educational chances of disadvantaged children in 'developing countries' who suffered from poor-quality schooling. The OLPC caught the imagination of some politicians who in key cases like Rwanda, Uruguay, and Peru ordered hundreds of thousands of machines. Critics pointed out that the OLPC initiative did not work sufficiently with teachers; was too focused on the artefact of the laptop, not the process of learning; neglected the costs of repair, maintenance, and teacher training in its model; and came with high opportunity costs for countries which already had strained education budgets (Villanueva-Mansilla, 2015).

Meanwhile, many countries had drawn up national systemic and multi-sector digital strategies and in some cases succeeded in building successful multi-stakeholder partnerships. For example, in the 2000s Chile, a country of 18 million inhabitants, connected all its schools to the internet and successfully trained over 600,000 out-of-school adults in basic computer skills, with the most training courses taking place in government-run telecentres (Kleine, 2009). Telecentres seemed to lose in significance as mobile phones became one of the fastest growing technologies in history. In 1997 there were 215 million mobile phone subscriptions globally (ITU, 1999); now there are an estimated 5 billion (GSMA, 2017). Access to mobile phones is far more achievable for income-poor people than access to the internet and, increasingly, mobile is the way most people in the global South access the internet for the first time. Mobiles now form a multi-purpose tool which has become central to many people's lives. People can receive agricultural information or health advice on their mobile phones. One of the best-known success stories is M-Pesa, the Kenyan mobile money system which allows customers of the market-dominating Safaricom network to transfer money digitally. In a country where the rural poor have limited access to formal banking, and international and urban-to-rural remittance flows are common, M-Pesa has proved highly popular. Replicating the success of M-Pesa has proven difficult in countries where the telecommunications or financial markets are more fragmented (Donovan, 2015).

Digital technologies based on mobiles have now widely permeated development practice, from using social media for disaster response to using mobile phone cameras and telemedicine phone apps in diagnostics. Debates among development practitioners and scholars were once framed in unhelpful binaries of whether, for instance, money should be spent on either internet access or water pumps. Today, digital sensors attached to water pumps allow for measuring water quality, monitoring use, auto-reporting failures, and triggering repair team visits. Digital dashboards can provide village water committees with data to inform their deliberations. Instead of a false choice between priorities (water or internet connectivity), the hybrid and intertwined nature of the socio-technical systems of water and data flows has become evident. The challenge remains how to implement such systems in ways that are socially and culturally appropriate as well as technically and financially sustainable.

THEORETICAL APPROACHES

Alongside more applied scholarly approaches where researchers have advised, co-designed, co-implemented or evaluated specific interventions, there has been a growing set of theoretical perspectives on digital development/ICT4D. Theories of innovation and adoption have filtered into digital development/ICT4D from different disciplines and often focus on technology adoption and user practices. Institutional theory scholars have drawn attention to the societal structures, organizational change, and evolving social norms and discourses related to the digital (e.g., Avgerou, 2003). A number of scholars have drawn on structuration theory to further conceptualize practices and the relationship between cultural values and technology (e.g., Walsham, 2002). Scholars have applied actor network theory perspectives (e.g., Stanforth, 2006), drawing attention to the way ICT devices are itemized and fetishized while their efficacy actually depends on much wider and complex socio-technical systems. From a development perspective, researchers have sought to understand digitalization from the vantage point of competitive advantage (e.g., Heeks, 2006), from stakeholder analysis (e.g., Bailur, 2006), the livelihoods framework (e.g., Duncombe, 2006), and feminist development studies (e.g., Buskens, 2010). Further, there is a rich vein of ICT4D theorization (e.g., Garnham, 1999; Gigler, 2004; Zheng and Walsham, 2008; Kleine, 2010) building on the capabilities approach to development which argues that local people's freedoms to live 'the lives they have reason to value' (Sen, 1999: 293) should be central and that these freedoms are not just economic, but also social, political, and cultural (Kleine, 2013). These scholars argue that digitalization can offer powerful tools for expanding such freedoms, but that it can also have detrimental effects. Above all, they contend that the question of what is meant by 'development' and what kinds of future people themselves desire must take precedence over questions of the practical implementation of any specific digital technologies.

KEY DEBATES

There are several ongoing core controversies concerning the relationship between digital technologies and development. These include debates over the effects of digital interventions, dimensions of access, the design of digital initiatives, environmental questions, and data ethics.

Immanent effects versus interventions

Firstly, some critics of ICT4D argue that the associated over-optimistic hype of digital solutionism underplays the way that uneven capitalist development is reinforced by digitalization (Murphy and Carmody, 2015). Using the distinction between immanent and intentional development, they argue that the immanent effects of digitalization far outweigh the intentional effects and indeed that celebrating small-scale successes of intentional development will risk drawing attention away from deep structural disadvantages. For instance, small-scale enterprises in South Africa and Tanzania might benefit from more price information or efficient communication with their suppliers and customers via mobile phone. However, they still face trade barriers, poor road infrastructure, and operate in low-skill, low-wage environments.

Others would argue that while the immanent effects are indeed of a much greater magnitude, using digital tools and data in efforts to reduce global inequalities is acceptable, as long as the hype is countered so as to not over-promise and obscure the existing structural economic injustices. Indeed, a progressive perspective of ICT4D includes using data and digital technologies to visualize and monitor inequality and support campaigning and organizing for change.

Dimensions of access

A key concern for the field of digital development is the question of uneven access to the internet and digital technologies. Gerster and Zimmermann (2003) conceptualize the core dimensions of access as availability, affordability, and skills. Internet connectivity and mobile phone coverage are unevenly distributed, with poorer and less populated areas frequently under-served. Linked to this is affordability, which encompasses the cost of access and the cost of ownership of specific devices. Social norms around access, affordability, and quality of use differ. For instance, the less powerful members of the household (frequently women) will often have to borrow a phone or be passed on old phones which the more powerful household members (frequently men) no longer want. In order to reduce the cost of use, some people will carry multiple SIM cards and/or handsets to use the cheapest provider for the time of day. 'Flashing' is also popular – a practice of letting somebody else's phone ring a fixed number of times without them responding. The number of rings can be an agreed message, which in this way can be conveyed at zero cost.

Skills also affect the quality of use of digital devices. Even SMS messages on feature phones require literacy in the language in which they are sent. Much of the content online is in English and other dominant languages, thus limiting the information available to users with less formal education speaking only local languages. Digital literacy is required to use desktops, tablets, and smartphones.

The gender digital divide persists, and globally it is estimated that women are proportionally 12 percent less likely to be online than men (International Telecommunication Union, 2017). Apart from inequalities in availability, affordability, and skills, there are norms on the uses of time and space which affect online use (Kleine, 2013). Here it is impossible to generalize, as the axes of privilege and disadvantage intersect in complex ways between and within societies. Men tend to have fewer care responsibilities and greater autonomy over their time than women and girls and thus more free time to access the internet and use digital devices. However, the time pressures of a young lower-caste woman in rural India providing care duties for her siblings, and an upper-caste, urban married woman in Bangalore relying on servant labour are radically different, and so will their media usage be. Class/caste, urban–rural, education, gender, age, marital status, differential ability, and other axes of difference all intersect and impact on the availability of free time which in turn affects participation online.

Other geographers have further noted that the spaces of access matter. Telecentres have fixed locations and set opening times. This makes it harder for women to visit, particularly where there are social norms restricting women's mobility to the house and house-bound tasks. Mobile phones and cheap individual access can be seen as liberating, as they do not require women to leave the house, but at the same time the empowering aspect of congregating with other women and sharing experiences can be affected. Further, mobile phones have become battlegrounds of gender politics in the household. A study by GSMA (2015) showed that among respondents in Niger, 86 percent of women and 79 percent of men agreed that it was acceptable for a husband to check the numbers on his wife's mobile phone, while only 58 percent of women and 45 percent of men agreed it was acceptable for the wife to check numbers on her husband's phone. Access to digital technologies does not by itself have the power to shift gender inequality, which is deeply entrenched in social attitudes.

Design principles

The design of digital development projects has come some way since earlier phases which were characterized by a high failure rate. Lessons have been learned and different international communities of practice have developed design principles which cumulated in the 2015 Principles for Digital Design. These have been endorsed by over 54 organizations and key donors, including the United Nations Development Programme, Unicef, the World Bank, Swedish International Development Cooperation Agency (SIDA), USAID and the Bill and Melinda Gates Foundation. The principles are as follows:

1. Design with the user.
2. Understand the existing ecosystem.
3. Design for scale.
4. Build for sustainability.
5. Be data driven.
6. Use open standards, open data, open source and open innovation.
7. Reuse and improve.
8. Address privacy and security.
9. Be collaborative.[2]

These principles remain contested, and the list of endorsing organizations is interesting for both its presences and absences. There are certainly some principles which, had they been followed before, would have gone a long way to reduce the failure rate of ICT4D projects. For instance, 'Design with the user' is the belated lesson for ICT4D which could have been learned earlier if the participatory turn which started in development practice in the 1970s had been heeded. There is much that can be broadly welcomed but, in particular, principles 3 and parts of 6, the emphasis on scalability and on open-source technologies, are being critiqued, since local contexts may require different approaches.

Inherent environmental unsustainability

One of the inherent challenges in digital development is that the business models behind the devices on which many interventions depend are environmentally unsustainable (Vallauri, 2009). Mobile phones contain minerals which have often been sourced from states where their trade fuels internal armed conflict, such as in the Democratic Republic of Congo (Epstein and Yuthas, 2011). In the global North, mobile phone operators entice their customers to discard their 'old' handset every two years or less. Mandatory software updates force users to upgrade to devices with greater computing power. This leads to substantial e-waste, which is frequently shipped to the global South where it is disposed of or stripped into its components and recycled under conditions which often endanger worker health, water, and soil. Thus, devices which are used to accelerate progress towards the UN Sustainable Development Goals[3] can also have negative impacts for human well-being and the environment. A hopeful counter-example is FairPhone,[4] a Dutch-based initiative seeking to source, build, and distribute an 'ethical' phone produced to high environmental and social standards. With a much higher device price and just over 100,000 units produced so far (Apple has sold over a billion iPhones), FairPhone remains a path-breaking initiative but a niche product which is also unobtainable for those on low incomes or most customers in the global South.

Data ethics

As digital technologies are integrated and leveraged for humanitarian aid and service delivery, they offer unprecedented possibilities for traceability and customized support for individual beneficiaries. Traceability is related to the difficulties arising from non-transparent and complex supply chains, for example food aid deliveries which can be prone to loss, corruption, nepotism, and favouritism. Using supply-chain radio frequency identification (RFID) technology to trace food deliveries can improve traceability, while elsewhere RFID traceability on medications reduces the risk of counterfeit medication being introduced into supply chains.

In health service delivery, storing medical data (e.g., the birth weight, vaccinations and medical check-ups of a child) on a chip card or mother's mobile phone, and linking this to SMS service reminders, can in principle do much to improve medical services for children. SMS reminder systems for patients who are HIV positive and need to remember to take anti-retroviral medication can save lives. In general, data capture in service delivery can do much to enable impact monitoring, real-time decision-making, and agile responses.

However, the cybersecurity measures around such systems are often much less thought through than for similar services in the global North. This is in part due to the urgency of needs experienced by frontline healthcare practitioners, but also to a host of other factors, including a 'can do' bias which drives practitioners and many action researchers, including Northern engineers and computer scientists, to implement solutions first and ask questions later; the lack of awareness of or capacity to deal with data ethics; the concentration of limited resources on a system 'without frills'; and looser data protection legislation and enforcement in many countries of the global South.

FUTURE DEVELOPMENTS

Looking ahead, digitalization is having a potent impact on many intervention domains, yet simultaneously its very force, pervasiveness, and disruptive character give rise to new risks.

The mainstreaming of digital development

Digital development, or ICT4D, used to be seen with some suspicion by many development practitioners and scholars who assumed it was a fashionable topic which would soon fade away as the next 'development trend' came along. Instead, digital technologies and data have become ubiquitous in international development and have been largely mainstreamed into initiatives. Water and sanitation, agriculture, business development, education, healthcare – most areas of service delivery today rely on some form of digital tools. Examples include the internet of things and sensor technology providing many future opportunities for monitoring based on machine-to-machine communication, while raising questions of data surveillance. Disaster relief work relies on custom-made platforms as well as Twitter, WhatsApp, and Facebook. Development advocacy and fundraising campaigns take advantage of social media and digital platforms.

Among the many challenges arising from this is one of capacity building: development practitioners and local partners need to have technical knowledge even if they only oversee or commission technical tasks including software development or hardware repair. The use of digital tools also creates new comprehensive, non-deletable, and newly combinable big data footprints, while many development actors, including multilateral and bilateral agencies and non-governmental organizations, have not yet fully updated their data protection policies.

The digitalization of economies

In societies with many young people looking for work, often with limited education and skills, increased automation may carry the risk of more widespread job losses and unemployment. Governments have sought to instead capitalize on new digital labour markets. However, these risk a race to the bottom as low-paid digital-related tasks are globally distributed to atomized digital workers (Graham et al., 2017). At the top end, innovation hubs like Nairobi's feted iHub are supported by development agencies, foundations, and large corporations such as Google and Facebook. In many capital cities across Africa, there are now similar co-working spaces that have been successful in bringing digital entrepreneurs and innovators together to develop digital start-ups and forge a new image of certain African cities as hotbeds of technology entrepreneurship, such as Nairobi's 'Silicon Savannah'. Models vary from Silicon Valley type incubators offering competitive seed-funding to start-ups, to spaces of formal and informal capacity building and simply co-working spaces (Kelly and Firestone, 2016). There is as yet insufficient evidence of their impact, but research has shown that they are often dominated by young male entrepreneurs (Jiménez and Zheng, 2018), with women in IT professions founding their own support networks (Roberts, 2016). African tech hubs are located in urban centres and cater mainly to urban, educated, middle-class young people, so far only reaching a very small percentage of the millions of unemployed and underemployed in sub-Saharan Africa.

Reduced internet freedom and increased data surveillance

Another major trend to watch is the trend in ongoing reduction in internet freedom, the closing down of anonymized online spaces, and the increased tracing and recording of online activity. It is estimated that two-thirds of the world's internet users live under government censorship, and internet freedom is being reduced year after year (Freedom House, 2016). Progressive development causes, including press and media freedom, democratic rights and human rights advocacy, women's rights groups, LGBT+ support networks, indigenous rights, and humanitarian help for refugees regardless of their legal status, are impacted by the various mechanisms by which states are policing and de-anonymizing communications. The issue is complicated as terrorists and criminals use the same tools to remain anonymous as protest movements, political dissenters, and support networks for persecuted minorities do. In addition, many digital development projects rely on people's right to access the internet freely, but few countries have enshrined this as a right, such as France, Estonia, Finland, and Costa Rica. Other digital rights include data protection, privacy, and freedom of expression. On the other hand, 'digital-by-default' is driven by government and the private sector, and risks marginalizing those who cannot or do not want to use ICTs and leave a digital footprint (Unwin, 2017). Actors in the digital rights movement are effectively defending basic rights and choices on which much of freedom- and well-being-related digital development relies.

CONCLUSION

This chapter has offered a compressed overview of key issues and debates in the interdisciplinary area of digital development/ICT4D research and praxis, demonstrating how it is both rapidly expanding and highly contested. Digital technologies and related data flows are reshaping societies and are increasingly integrated in a wide range of intentional development interventions. They can act as 'amplifiers' (Toyama, 2011) and thus can lead to existing social inequalities being retraced and increased. In other cases, digital innovations have amplified positive development effects. While new technical innovations change the risks and opportunities that present themselves, the fundamental question that needs to be continuously asked remains: what kind of 'development' is being promoted and who has been empowered to co-shape that vision?

Notes

1. See www.un.org/sustainabledevelopment/sustainable-development-goals.
2. See https://digitalprinciples.org/principles.
3. See https://sustainabledevelopment.un.org/sdgs.
4. See www.fairphone.com.

REFERENCES

Annan, K. (1997) 'Secretary General stresses international community's objective of harnessing informatics revolution for benefit of mankind'. Geneva: Commission on Science and Technology for Development 'Inter-Agency Project on Universal Access to Basic Communication and Information Services', 3rd Session, E/CN.16/1997/Misc.3.

Avgerou, C. (2003) 'IT as an institutional actor in developing countries', in S. Krishna and S. Madon (eds), *The Digital Challenge: Information Technology in the Development Context*. Aldershot: Ashgate. pp. 44–62.

Bailur, S. (2006) 'Using stakeholder theory to analyze telecenter projects', *Information Technologies and International Development*, 3(3): 61–80.

Buskens, I. (2010) 'Agency and reflexivity in ICT4D research: Questioning women's options, poverty, and human development', *Information Technologies and International Development*, 6: 19–24.

Cowen, M. and Shenton, R. (1998) 'Agrarian doctrines of development', *Journal of Peasant Studies*, 25(2): 49–76.

Donovan, K. (2015) 'Mobile money', in R. Mansell, P.H. Ang, C. Steinfeld, S. van der Graaf, P. Ballon, A. Kerr, J.D. Ivory, S. Braman, D. Kleine and D.J. Grimshaw (eds), *The International Encyclopedia of Digital Communication and Society*. Malden, MA: Wiley-Blackwell. pp. 619–626.

Duncombe, R. (2006) 'Using the livelihoods framework to analyze ICT applications for poverty reduction through microenterprise', *Information Technologies and International Development*, 3(3): 81–100.

Epstein, M.J. and Yuthas, K. (2011) 'Conflict minerals: Managing an emerging supply-chain problem', *Environmental Quality Management*, 21(2): 13–25.

Freedom House (2016) 'Silencing the messenger: Communication apps under pressure', *Freedom on the Net 2016*. Washington, DC: Freedom House. Available at: https://freedomhouse.org/report/freedom-net/freedom-net-2016 (accessed 3 February 2018).

Garnham, N. (1999) 'Amartya Sen's "capabilities" approach to the evaluation of welfare: Its application to communications', in A. Calabrese and J.C. Burgelman (eds), *Communication, Citizenship and Social Policy – Rethinking the Limits of the Welfare State*. Lanham, MD: Rowman & Littlefield.

Gerster, R. and Zimmermann, S. (2003) *Information and Communication Technologies (ICTs) for Poverty Reduction?* Bern: Swiss Agency for Development Cooperation.

Gigler, B.S. (2004) 'Including the excluded – can ICTs empower poor communities? Towards an alternative evaluation framework based on the capability approach', paper presented at the Fourth International Conference on the Capability Approach, Pavia, Italy.

Graham, M., Hjorth, I. and Lehdonvirta, V. (2017) 'Digital labour and development: Impacts of global digital labour platforms and the gig economy on worker livelihoods', *Transfer: European Review of Labour and Research*, 23(2): 138–162.

GSMA (2015) *Bridging the Gender Gap: Mobile Access and Usage in Low- and Middle-Income Countries*. London: GSMA. Available at: www.gsma.com/mobilefor development/wp-content/uploads/2016/02/GSM0001_03232015_GSMAReport_NEWGRAYS-Web.pdf (accessed 3 February 2018).

GSMA (2017) *The Mobile Economy 2017*. London: GSMA. Available at: www.gsma.com/mobileeconomy (accessed 3 February 2018).

Heeks, R. (2002) 'Information systems and developing countries: Failure, success and local improvisations', *Information Society*, 18(2): 101–112.

Heeks, R. (2006) 'Using competitive advantage theory to analyze It sectors in developing countries: A software industry case analysis', *Information Technologies and International Development*, 3(3): 5–34.

International Telecommunication Union (ITU) (1999) *World Telecommunication Development Report 1999*. Geneva: ITU. Available at: www.itu.int/pub/D-IND-WTDR-1999 (accessed 19 May 2018).

International Telecommunication Union (ITU) (2016) *ICT Facts and Figures*. Geneva: ITU. Available at: www.itu.int/en/ITU-D/Statistics/Documents/facts/ICTFactsFigures2016.pdf (accessed 31 October 2017).

International Telecommunication Union (ITU) (2017) *Mobile Phone Subscriptions per 100 Inhabitants*. Geneva: ITU. Available at: www.itu.int/ITU-D/ict/statistics/ict/graphs/internet.jpg (accessed 31 October 2017).

Jiménez, A. and Zheng, Y. (2018) 'Tech hubs, innovation and development', *Information Technology for Development*, 24(1): 95–118.

Kelly, T. and Firestone, R. (2016) 'How tech hubs are helping to drive economic growth in Africa', background paper for the World Development Report 2016: Digital Dividends. Available at: http://documents.worldbank.org/curated/en/626981468195850883/How-tech-hubs-are-helping-to-drive-economic-growth-in-Africa (accessed 30 May 2017).

Kleine, D. (2009) 'The ideology behind the technology: Chilean microentrepreneurs and public ICT policies', *Geoforum*, 40(2): 171–183.

Kleine, D. (2010) 'ICT4What? Using the choice framework to operationalise the capability approach to development', *Journal of International Development*, 22(5): 674–692.

Kleine, D. (2013) *Technologies of Choice: ICTs, Development and the Capabilities Approach*. Cambridge, MA: MIT Press.

Kleine, D. and Unwin, T. (2009) 'Technological revolution, evolution and new dependencies: What's new about ICT4D?', *Third World Quarterly*, 30(5): 1045–1067.

Murphy, J. and Carmody, P. (2015) *Africa's Information Revolution: Technical Regimes and Production Networks in South Africa and Tanzania*. Malden, MA: Wiley.

Norris, P. (2001) *Digital Divide: Civic Engagement, Information Poverty, and the Internet Worldwide*. Cambridge, MA: Harvard University Press.

Roberts, T. (2016) 'Women's use of participatory video technology to tackle gender inequality in Zambia's ICT sector', in *Proceedings of the Eighth International Conference* on *Information and Communication Technologies and Development (ICTD '16)*. New York: Association for Computing Machinery. Available at: https://doi.org/10.1145/2909609.2909673 (accessed 3 February 2018).

Sen, A. (1999) *Development as Freedom*. Oxford: Oxford University Press.

Stanforth, C. (2006) 'Using actor-network theory to analyze e-government implementation in developing countries', *Information Technologies and International Development*, 3(3): 35–60.

Toyama, K. (2011) 'Technology as amplifier in international development', in *Proceedings of the 2011 iConference* (iConference '11). New York: ACM. pp. 75–82.

Unwin, T. (2009) *ICT4D*. Cambridge: Cambridge University Press.

Unwin, T. (2017) *Reclaiming Information and Communication Technologies for Development*. Oxford: Oxford University Press.

Vallauri, U. (2009) 'Beyond e-waste: Kenyan creativity and alternative narratives in the dialectic of end-of-life', *International Review of Information Ethics*, 11(10): 20–24.

Villanueva-Mansilla, E. (2015) 'One Laptop Per Child (OLPC) strategy', in R. Mansell, P.H. Ang, C. Steinfeld, S. van der Graaf, P. Ballon, A. Kerr, J.D. Ivory, S. Braman, D. Kleine and D.J. Grimshaw (eds), *The International Encyclopedia of Digital Communication and Society*. Malden, MA: Wiley-Blackwell. pp 674–679.

Walsham, G. (2002) 'Cross-cultural software production and use: A structurational analysis', *MIS Quarterly*, 26(4): 359–380.

Willis, K. (2011) *Theories and Practices of Development*, 2nd edn. London: Routledge.

Zheng, Y. and Walsham, G. (2008) 'Inequality of what? Social exclusion in the e-society as capability deprivation', *Information Technology and People*, 21(3): 222–243.

21

GOVERNANCE

Rob Kitchin

INTRODUCTION

Geographers have long been interested in how societies and places are governed, both with respect to how sovereign states (embodied in local, regional, and national governments and state agencies) manage civil society and markets within their territories, and to how businesses, third-sector bodies (e.g., non-governmental organizations (NGOs), charities), and the general public seek to regulate domains and maintain social order (Herod et al., 2002). Indeed, traditional governmental structures, policies, and legislative bodies are just one component of governance, with many other actors increasingly playing a role in managing social and spatial relations, sometimes in conjunction with or on behalf of the state, or independently. This relationship appears to be in flux at present as the relations between sovereign states, the market, and civil society are renegotiated and blurred, with a shift from centralized and bureaucratic forms of regulation and government to a plurality of coexisting and overlapping networks and partnerships that work at different scales from the local to the global.

As I discuss in this chapter, digital technologies have contributed to this flux by introducing a variety of new means to manage and govern society and have transformed the governmentality at work in important ways. For Foucault (1991), governmentality is the logics, rationalities, and techniques that render societies governable and enable government and other agencies to enact governance. The nature of governmentality mutates over time, and periodically its form can shift fundamentally in character – for example, in the shift from a feudal society to modern society, wherein more systematized means for managing and regulating individuals through centralized and institutionalized bureaucracy were introduced. For many analysts, the digital era of ubiquitous computing (the proliferation of digital devices and computation being embedded into previously dumb objects and being made available everywhere through mobile access to information and communications technology networks), big data (massive amounts of real-time streams of data) and machine learning (computers being able to learn from data and autonomously extract value from them) is producing a similar seismic shift in how societies are managed and controlled. I begin by briefly placing the role of digital technology in government and governance in historical context. I then discuss more contemporary forms of digital governance and how it is changing the practices of security, policing, government administration and operations, and relations between companies and consumers. In the final section I consider how technocratic, algorithmic, automated, and predictive systems are transforming governmentality, shifting disciplinary modes of governance to control and anticipation.

INITIAL FORMS OF DIGITAL GOVERNANCE

Since the 1950s and the birth of digital computing, computation has been deployed by governments in the global North for the purposes of managing populations. Computers were used within bureaucracies to construct, store, manage, and process data for the purposes of administration and the delivery of services. The use of such systems was limited in scope and extent due to cost and technical requirements, but their use formed the bedrock for later developments. Similarly, supervisory control and data acquisition systems were rolled out to monitor and control utility and other infrastructures and to manage city services, with electromagnetic sensors and analog cameras deployed across a network to monitor performance and information flowing to and from centralized control rooms. In the late 1960s, cybernetic thinking, in which it was believed that governance and policy issues could be more effectively managed computationally, was applied to some elements of government. Cities, for example, were envisioned as consisting of a system of systems that could be digitally mediated (Forrester, 1969). Each system, it was argued, could be broken down into its constituent parts and processes, be modelled and simulated to capture its essence, and these models used to plan and operate its functions. Early deployments, however, failed to produce optimal solutions because how cities work proved more complex, contingent, and socio-political than the models permitted (Flood, 2011). As Light (2003) details, the approach adopted in cybernetics and other technology-led approaches to city management sought to adapt military technologies to civilian contexts, and in so doing shifted the rationality of urban management and governance towards technocratic solutions.

In the 1980s and 1990s, as personal computers started to pervade central and local government, the use of computation in governance extended rapidly, for the purposes of both administration and operational delivery. The key geographical technology embedded in government at this time was geographic information systems (GIS) used to document and analyse land use and the spatial constitution of city assets, population, and economy and to aid decision-making and resource allocation. Technologies designed to regulate citizens' spatial behaviour, such as traffic management systems, were also deployed in most cities around the world, enabling the real-time monitoring of traffic flow and the control of traffic light sequencing, and predictions of likely outcomes under different scenarios. With the roll-out of the internet in the 1990s and 2000s, there was a large investment in e-government (the delivery of services and interfacing with the public via digital channels) and e-governance (managing citizen activity using digital tools) and a related reorganization and reduction in government offices. In addition, the first attempts at digitally-facilitated, community-orientated, participatory democracy – public electronic networks – were rolled out, aimed at improving public debate and making decision-making more transparent, as well as new direct channels to access politicians via e-mail and bulletin boards (Kitchin, 1998). The internet also enabled the proliferation of networked surveillance systems, notably digital video cameras and various forms of digital snooping (of e-mail, mobile phones, databases, etc.) in order to monitor and discipline citizens (Lyon, 1994). As well as being a means through which to govern society, the internet itself became a new space to be governed, with a myriad of new customary laws and formal rules and regulations being put in place to police online behaviour (Lessig, 1999; Dodge and Kitchin, 2000).

Throughout each of these developments, geographers both contributed to the development of the technologies, undertaking fundamental and applied research, and sought to understand their societal implications. For example, early quantitative geographers built models for policy formulation, and there has been an ongoing debate with respect to the development, use, and politics of GIS. From the vantage point of the present, the geographies produced by digital technologies and their use in governance form the basis for some interesting contemporary historical geography, as the work of Jennifer Light (2003), Joe Flood (2011), Matthew Wilson (2017), Trevor Barnes (2014), Simone Natale and Andrea Ballatore (2017) and others attests. However, rather than explore further the historical development of how the digital reshaped geographies of governance, in the remainder of the chapter I concentrate attention on the contemporary period.

DIGITAL GOVERNANCE OF SOCIO-SPATIAL RELATIONS

The confluence of new digital technologies and techniques – cloud computing, big data, and machine learning – is transforming how people and places are governed. In short, the roll-out of ubiquitous computing and the production of big data are broadening and deepening the ability to capture fine-grained information about the behaviour and actions of individuals and systems. New data analytics can then be used to extract insight using machine learning and artificial intelligence techniques, including data mining, pattern recognition, modelling, simulation, and prediction, to adapt and control systems to mediate and regulate further behaviour. The generation and use of big data for governance purposes is most obvious with respect to security and policing, but also increasingly pervades how governments manage daily operations and the interface with citizens, and how companies seek to influence and nudge consumer behaviour. In this section, I detail various ways in which digital technologies are impacting on governance; in the following section, I set out how they are shifting the nature of governmentality.

The era of ubiquitous computing has radically transformed the volume, range, and granularity of the data being generated about people and places, radically deepening the surveillance of society. Digital technology inherently produces data through their use, and when these technologies are networked the data are easily shared. As more and more aspects of everyday life become mediated by networked digital technologies, more and more data are captured about the people using them or who are visible to their 'gaze' (e.g., people passing by a camera or sensor). The extent of the surveillance and dataveillance (surveillance through data records) being practised means that people are not only having their activities captured, but they are also subject to almost continuous geosurveillance (Kitchin, 2015) in which their location and movement are routinely tracked in a number of ways, for example by:

- controllable digital high-definition closed-circuit television (CCTV) cameras (increasingly used with facial recognition software);
- smartphones that track phone location via cell masts, GPS, or WiFi connections, sharing data with the mobile phone company and app developers;
- other smart devices such as GPS-enabled fitness trackers and smart watches;
- sensor networks that capture and track phone identifiers such as MAC addresses;
- smart card tracking that captures the scanning of barcodes/RFID chips of cards used to enter buildings or travel on public transport;
- vehicle tracking using automatic number plate recognition cameras, unique ID transponders for automated road tolls and car parking, on-board GPS;
- other staging points such as the use of automatic teller machines, credit card use, metadata tagging of photos uploaded to the internet, geotagging of social media posts;
- electronic tagging of children and paroles with GPS tracking devices;
- shared calendars that provide the date, time and location of meetings.

Importantly, as Leszczynski (2017) notes, the capture and circulation of these data are:

- indiscriminate and exhaustive (involve all individuals, objects, transactions, etc.);
- distributed (occur across multiple devices, services, and places);
- platform independent (data flow easily across platforms, services, and devices);
- continuous (data are generated on a routine and automated basis).

Such datafication has profound effects with respect to privacy. People are now subject to much greater levels of intensified scrutiny than ever before. Moreover, the pervasiveness of digitally-mediated transactions and surveillance, plus the increasing use of unique identifiers to access services (e.g., names, usernames, passwords, account numbers, addresses, e-mails, phone details, credit card numbers, smart card IDs, license plates, faces), means that it is all but impossible to live our everyday lives without leaving digital footprints (traces we leave ourselves) and shadows (traces captured about us). Further, these data enable a lot of inference to be made beyond the data generated to reveal insights that have never been disclosed. Those to whom the data refer often have little control over the data generated, their form, extent, or how they are used.

Importantly, these data enable the refinement of existing modes of governance and the production of new modes. For example, it becomes possible for state agencies such as the police and security services to routinely monitor the views (via social media, e-mail, messaging, phone conversations), associations (social networks), activities, and locations of populations. As the revelations of Wikileaks, Edward Snowden, and other whistleblowers have demonstrated, there has been a step change in the extent and nature of state-led surveillance and securitization in many nations (e.g., the various programmes of the US National Security Agency and UK Government Communications Headquarters). As well as being analysed for strategic intelligence, the data are analysed to identify who might pose a potential security threat. Beyond special operations to target suspected terrorists, where such security screening becomes most obvious to us is in international travel and border control (Amoore, 2006). Passing through an airport now involves the multiple checking of identity (at check-in, security checkpoints, boarding, immigration) via documents and biometric measures (as well as tagging, scanning, and tracking of baggage), with information cross-referenced against other government databases, in which there are very limited rights for passengers to query or to appeal decisions to deny travel or entry (Kitchin and Dodge, 2006). Increasingly, such screening also involves predictive profiling that analyses communications, associations, and locations in order to forecast levels of risk as to who should receive additional scrutiny. In effect, air travel passengers are funnelled through a closed, closely monitored physical and data security apparatus designed to ensure they act as what Foucault (1991) termed 'docile bodies' (compliant passengers who act as required with no resistance to authority).

Such data is also useful to everyday policing when conjoined to data analytics. As well as enhancing surveillance and creating a databank of material and new tools to search for evidence when a crime has occurred (e.g., conducting facial recognition on digital CCTV), data are now being used to guide operations and conduct predictive policing. For example, a number of police forces have invested heavily in new command-and-control centres that employ enhanced and extensive multi-instrumented surveillance (e.g., high-definition CCTV, drone cameras, sensors, community reporting) to direct on-the-ground policing (as well as act as a deterrent to criminal acts) (Wiig, 2017). In addition, police forces monitor the communications of known activists and agitators to try and anticipate and control social unrest. When protesters do gather, police will seek to keep abreast of activists' plans by scanning social media and identifying and tracking the mobile phones of leaders within radio-cell grids, using a form of 'digital kettling' to isolate protestors into a contained area (Paasche, 2013). A number of forces are now also using predictive policing to identify potential future criminals and to direct the patrolling of areas based on an analysis of historical crime data, arrest records, and the known social networks of criminals (Stroud, 2014), though such an approach has been critiqued as effectively reproducing racial profiling (Harcourt, 2006).

Beyond security and policing, big data and analytics are used by the state for the purposes of public administration and managing operations. All nation states conduct biopolitics, seeking to monitor and manage populations and their entitlements (to services, welfare, housing, health, etc.) and compliance with laws and regulations (attending school, paying taxes, obeying traffic rules). Increasingly, more and more interactions with the state are conducted online, directly interfacing with government services and databases. Analytics are applied to these databases to identify potential cheats and reduce fraud. Such systems also work to monitor the performance of government itself, with data being used to assess the efficiency and effectiveness of programmes and policies, and to design new ways of delivering services (Kitchin, 2014). In terms of operations, new digital technologies are transforming how services are configured and deployed. For example, sensors in rubbish bins monitor how full they are, communicating that information to waste management services so that garbage trucks only visit those that need emptying. With respect to traffic management, dense networks of cameras and inductive loop sensors monitor the flow of traffic across a road system, automatically adjusting traffic light sequencing to try and minimize congestion and keep traffic flowing, with this information also being communicated to the public via apps and radio to try and nudge them to take alternative routes or forms of transport (Coletta and Kitchin, 2017).

In addition to states, companies now routinely generate data with respect to all aspects of their business, including their customers and their patterns of consumption, using the information to influence behaviour, assess risk, predictively profile, and socially and spatially sort consumers. Companies seek to monetize their data by more effective micro-targeting of advertising, or nudging consumers into purchases, or by selling the data to data brokers who consolidate and repackage data into new products and offer a variety of data services (e.g., people and place profiling; search and background checks; assessments of creditworthiness; provision of tracing services; undertaking predictive modelling as to what individuals might do under different circumstances or how much risk a person constitutes). Data brokerage is a multi-billion-dollar industry with vast quantities of data and derived information being rented, bought, and sold daily across a variety of markets – retail, financial, public administration, health, tourism, logistics, business intelligence, real estate, private security, political polling, and so on (Kitchin, 2014). One such data brokerage company, Acxiom, is reputed to have constructed a databank concerning 500 million active consumers worldwide, with about 1500 data points per person, and claims to be able to provide a '360-degree view' on consumers, meshing offline, online and mobile data (Singer, 2012). Data brokers contribute to forms of governance through social and spatial sorting – creating profiles of citizens and (potential) customers as to the likely value or worth of an individual, or their credit risk and how likely they are to pay a certain price or be able to meet payments. While the aim is to provide customers with personalized treatment, including dynamic pricing that reflects their preferences and worth, it is also used by vendors to reduce risk by identifying which individuals to marginalize and exclude, for example denying credit, housing, and career opportunities. Through the practices of geodemographics, data brokers also profile places and spatially sort locations with respect to investment (Harris et al., 2005).

FROM DISCIPLINE TO CONTROL AND ANTICIPATION

For many scholars, the increasing use of digital technologies for the purposes of governance is shifting the nature of governmentality – that is, the underlying logics and mechanisms as to how governance is organized and works. The contention is that governance is becoming more technocratic, algorithmic, automated, and predictive in nature (Kitchin and Dodge, 2011). Technocratic forms of governance presume that social systems can be measured, monitored, and treated as technical problems which can be addressed through technical solutions. That is, it is possible to effectively tackle the management of populations and social problems, and to deliver services, through computational systems rather than through other governance mechanisms such as regulation, policy, social partnerships, and community development. These technocratic systems are underpinned and driven by algorithms that process and assess data feeds and determine outcomes based upon their underlying rule-set. Increasingly, these algorithmic machines work in automated, autonomous, and automatic ways (Dodge and Kitchin, 2007) with human oversight being limited to three levels of participation (Docherty, 2012):

- human-in-the-loop – the system identifies and selects decisions, but people perform the key decision-making and actioning role;
- human-on-the-loop – the system is automated, making key decisions and acting on them but under the oversight of a human operator who can actively intervene;
- human-out-of-the-loop – the system is automated and makes decisions and acts on them without human input or interaction.

Automated systems often employ machine learning and seek to learn from the outcome of previous decisions, and they also predict how people will behave and act on that prediction (Amoore, 2013). Within such automated systems, the rules for acting on data and making decisions are black-boxed and thus lack transparency and accountability. As such, they can be Kafkaesque in terms of how they work; for example, no-fly lists where people are not informed as to why they have been placed on the list, yet nor can they argue against the decision.

The effect of technocratic, algorithmic, automated, and predictive systems is to shift governmentality from disciplinary forms towards social control and anticipatory governance. Foucault (1991) argued that governmentality in the late twentieth century – through its interlocking apparatus of institutions, administration, law, technologies, social norms, and spatial logics – exercised a form of disciplinary power designed to corral and punish transgressors and instil particular habits, dispositions, expectations, and self-disciplining. A key aspect of disciplinary governmentality is that people know that they are subject to monitoring and enrolment in calculative regimes (e.g., bureaucracies that monitor and reward them) and thus self-regulate their behaviour accordingly to avoid incurring penalties. Technologies such as CCTV are thus disciplinary in nature, designed to make people act appropriately for fear of being witnessed transgressing, and punished.

In the twenty-first century, the implementation of algorithmic forms of governance that process big data has greatly intensified the extent and frequency of monitoring and shifted the governmental logic from surveillance and discipline to capture and control (Deleuze, 1992). Here, people become subject to constant modulation through software-mediated systems, such as a transport network controlled by an intelligent transport system, or checking in online for a flight, in which their behaviour is explicitly or implicitly steered or nudged rather than being (self-) disciplined. Governmentality is no longer solely about subjectification (moulding subjects and restricting action) but also about control (modulating affects, desires and opinions, and inducing action within prescribed comportments) (Braun, 2014). Rather than power being spatially confined and periodic (at set times in set places, such as schools and work), systems of control are distributed, interlinked, overlapping, and continuous, enabling institutional power to creep across technologies and pervade the social landscape. For example, as Davies (2015) notes with respect to Hudson Yards, a smart city development in New York that is being saturated with sensors and embedded computation, residents and workers will be continually monitored and modulated across the entire complex by an amalgam of interlinked systems. The result will be a quantified community with numerous overlapping calculative regimes designed to produce a certain type of social and moral arrangement, rather than people being regulated into conformity within institutional enclosures.

As detailed by Amoore (2013), the rationality of algorithmic governmentality is also rooted in possibilities – calculating potential future outcomes to direct action in the present. Anticipatory governance uses predictive analytics to forecast future risk and to produce appropriate responses. Predictive policing, identifying the possible location of future criminal acts and who might perpetrate them, is one example. Social and spatial sorting is another. In such cases, a person's data shadow does more than follow them; it precedes them, seeking to anticipate behaviours that may never occur yet have real consequences (e.g., being subject to more stop and search; not being able to travel overseas; being denied a job or a place to live) (Harcourt, 2006). The worry for some is that new forms of 'data determinism' are emerging, in which individuals are judged and treated not only on the basis of what they have done but also based on predictions of what they might do in the future (Rameriz, 2013).

It should be noted that the tactics and techniques of governmentality in contemporary society are highly varied, for example utilizing a range of technologies, each of which can be configured and deployed in different ways. More fundamentally, the nature of governmentality can be diverse, with several related and overlapping forms of governmentality enacted and promoted by different entities (state bodies, companies, communities) at work at the same time. Indeed, Ong (2006) argues that contemporary governmentalities associated with neoliberalism are not uniform and do not possess universal global logics. Rather, they have mutable logics which are abstract, mobile, dynamic, entangled, and contingent, being translated and operationalized in diverse, context-dependent ways. Just as disciplinary power never fully replaced sovereign power, control is likely to supplement rather than becoming dominant to discipline (Davies, 2015). In turn, power, governmentality, and governance are resisted and alternative forms of social relations are enacted through more participatory forms of community development (see Chapter 22).

CONCLUSION

Since the first digital computers, the forms and modes of governance have adapted to take advantage of computation. With the advent of ubiquitous computing, big data, cloud computing, and machine learning, the practices of governance have become thoroughly digital in nature, in turn changing the nature of contemporary governmentality. We now live in age of algorithmic and anticipatory governance in which huge amounts of data are generated with respect to our everyday actions, movements and views, with computational systems processing and acting upon these data to make decisions that manage, discipline, control, and nudge our behaviours. Governance is becoming increasingly technocratic, automated, and predictive in nature, and many more actors are involved beyond the state, such as companies, public–private partnerships, NGOs, and community bodies. Geographers are particularly interested in how the digital age is transforming the governance of socio-spatial relations and producing new spatialities and mobilities. There is still, however, much theoretical and empirical research needed to more fully understand how different digital technologies – e-government systems, city operating systems, performance management systems, urban dashboards, centralized control rooms, surveillance systems, predictive policing, coordinated emergency response, intelligent transport systems, logistics management, smart grids and smart meters, sensor networks, building management systems, app-controlled smart appliances – are reshaping the rationalities, logics, and practices of governance and producing new modes of governmentality, and how these are being resisted and contested by citizens. Such work is important if we are to comprehend and challenge the politics and economics driving technocratic and algorithmic governance and think of alternative ways of benefiting from digital technologies while minimizing some of their pernicious effects (see Chapters 22 and 23).

REFERENCES

Amoore, L. (2006) 'Biometric borders: Governing mobilities in the war on terror', *Political Geography*, 25(3): 336–351.

Amoore, L. (2013) *The Politics of Possibility: Risk and Security Beyond Probability*. Durham, NC: Duke University Press.

Barnes, T.J. (2014) 'What's old is new, and new is old: History and geography's quantitative revolutions', *Dialogues in Human Geography*, 4(1): 50–53.

Braun, B.P. (2014) 'A new urban dispositif? Governing life in an age of climate change', *Environment and Planning D: Society and Space*, 32(1): 49–64.

Coletta, C. and Kitchin, R. (2017) 'Algorhythmic governance: Regulating the "heartbeat" of a city using the Internet of Things', *Big Data & Society*, 4(2). DOI: 10.1177/2053951717742418.

Davies, W. (2015) 'The chronic social: Relations of control within and without neoliberalism', *New Formations*, 84/85: 40–57.

Deleuze, G. (1992) 'Postscript on the societies of control', *October*, 59: 3–7.

Docherty, B. (2012) *Losing Humanity: The Case against Killer Robots*. New York: Human Rights Watch. Available at: www.hrw.org/sites/default/files/reports/arms1112_ForUpload.pdf (accessed 17 November 2015).

Dodge, M. and Kitchin, R. (2000) *Mapping Cyberspace*. London: Routledge.

Dodge, M. and Kitchin, R. (2007) 'The automatic management of drivers and driving spaces', *Geoforum*, 38(2): 264–275.

Flood, J. (2011) *The Fires: How a Computer Formula, Big Ideas, and the Best of Intentions Burned Down New York City and Determined the Future of Cities*. New York: Riverhead.

Forrester, J.W. (1969) *Urban Dynamics*. Cambridge, MA: MIT Press.

Foucault, M. (1991) 'Governmentality', in G. Burchell, C. Gordon and P. Miller (eds), *The Foucault Effect: Studies in Governmentality*. Chicago: University of Chicago Press. pp. 87–104.

Harcourt, B.E. (2006) *Against Prediction: Profiling, Policing and Punishing in an Actuarial Age*. Chicago: Chicago University Press.

Harris, R., Sleight, P. and Webber, R. (2005) *Geodemographics, GIS and Neighbourhood Targeting*. Chichester: Wiley.

Herod, A., O'Tuithail, G. and Roberts, S. (eds) (2002) *Unruly World? Globalization, Governance and Geography*. London: Routledge.

Kitchin, R. (1998) *Cyberspace: The World in the Wires*. Chichester: John Wiley and Sons.

Kitchin, R. (2014) *The Data Revolution: Big Data, Open Data, Data Infrastructures and Their Consequences*. London: Sage.

Kitchin, R. (2015) 'Spatial big data and the era of continuous geosurveillance', *DIS Magazine*. Available at: http://dismagazine.com/issues/73066/rob-kitchin-spatial-big-data-and-geosurveillance (accessed 3 February 2018).

Kitchin, R. and Dodge, M. (2006) 'Software and the mundane management of air travel', *First Monday*, 11(9). Available at: http://firstmonday.org/ojs/index.php/fm/article/view/1608 (accessed 3 February 2018).

Kitchin, R. and Dodge, M. (2011) *Code/Space: Software and Everyday Life*. Cambridge, MA: MIT Press.

Lessig, L. (1999) *Code and Other Laws of Cyberspace*. New York: Basic Books.

Leszczynski, A. (2017) 'Geoprivacy', in R. Kitchin, T. Lauriault and M. Wilson (eds), *Understanding Spatial Media*. London: Sage. pp. 235–244.

Light, J.S. (2003) *From Warfare to Welfare: Defense Intellectuals and the Urban Problems in Cold War America*. Baltimore, MD: Johns Hopkins University Press.

Lyon, D. (1994) *The Electronic Eye: The Rise of the Surveillance Society*. Oxford: Polity Press.

Natale, S. and Ballatore, A. (2017) 'Imagining the thinking machine: Technological myths and the rise of Artificial Intelligence', *Convergence: The International Journal of Research into New Media Technologies*. DOI: 10.1177/1354856517715164.

Ong, A. (2006) *Neoliberalism as Exception: Mutations of Citizenship and Sovereignty*. Durham, NC: Duke University Press.

Paasche, T.F. (2013) 'Coded police territories: 'Detective software' investigates', *Area*, 45(3): 314–320.

Rameriz, E. (2013) 'The privacy challenges of big data: A view from the lifeguard's chair', *Technology Policy Institute Aspen Forum*, 19 August. Available at: http://ftc.gov/speeches/ramirez/130819bigdataaspen.pdf (accessed 11 October 2013).

Singer, N. (2012) 'You for sale: Mapping, and sharing, the consumer Genome', *New York Times*, 17 June. Available at: www.nytimes.com/2012/06/17/technology/acxiom-the-quiet-giant-of-consumer-database-marketing.html (accessed 6 February 2018).

Stroud, M. (2014) 'The minority report: Chicago's new police computer predicts crimes, but is it racist?', *The Verge*, 19 February. Available at: www.theverge.com/2014/2/19/5419854/the-minority-report-this-computer-predicts-crime-but-is-it-racist (accessed 17 July 2014).

Wiig, A. (2017) 'Secure the city, revitalize the zone: Smart urbanization in Camden, New Jersey', *Environment and Planning C: Politics and Space*, 36(3): 403–422.

Wilson, M.W. (2017) *New Lines: Critical GIS and the Trouble of the Map*. Minneapolis: Minnesota University Press.

22

CIVICS

Taylor Shelton

THE EMERGENCE OF DIGITAL CIVICS

The rapid growth and prevalence of digital technologies in recent decades has often been heralded as an inherently democratizing force, providing citizens with new ways of interacting with one another and organizing towards collective goals. With prominent cases such as the US presidential campaigns of Howard Dean in 2004 and Barack Obama in 2008 and the massive protests against repressive political regimes during the Arab Spring of 2011, examples abound of the increasingly important role played by digital technologies in facilitating citizen participation and political organizing. That being said, there are numerous reasons to doubt that the most important effect of these digital technologies is a trend towards democratization.

Persistent inequalities in access to digital technologies and the skills to use them – whether across race, gender, age, disability, income or geography – mean that significant numbers of people are not even able to access such tools, much less use them for socially beneficial, altruistic ends. Similarly, it is evident that many of the same technologies heralded for their role in prominent political protest can be just as readily used for the purposes of surveilling and repressing political dissidents. Despite the fact that this popular narrative around democratization is a good deal more complicated than typically assumed, digital technologies are undoubtedly playing an important role in shaping politics and governance across multiple scales, especially with respect to the way citizens are enrolled in such processes and allowed to participate in them.

This chapter reviews some of the key ways that civic engagement and public participation have become increasingly digitized and data-driven. But rather than engaging in debates over the democratic potential of digital technologies, it is arguably more productive to look at the range of ways that this emerging 'digital civics' is reconfiguring how we conceptualize and practise citizenship in the era of big data. First, the chapter discusses how citizenship is increasingly defined in relation to data and data practices, and how these redefinitions have precipitated larger changes in the way citizenship is conceptualized and operationalized. Second, the chapter identifies three ongoing, interrelated changes to the digital civics landscape that are worthy of greater attention moving forward. These include the *spatialization* of digital civics, the *corporatization* of digital civics, and the growing prominence of *oppositional uses* of digital civics that seek to challenge the social and political status quo.

THE DATAFICATION OF CITIZENSHIP

As digital technologies are seen less and less as technologies for communication, they are increasingly viewed as platforms for producing and analysing massive amounts of data about any number of social processes. Given this shift, scholars have also turned to understanding what this increasing 'datafication' of social life means for different realms. As an outcome of this emerging research agenda into data and society, scholars have identified two key effects of digital technologies on citizenship: first, the performance of citizenship is increasingly oriented around data; and second, this focus on data results in a redefinition of citizenship and where it is located.

While many of the most prominent examples of digital technologies being incorporated into forms of governance and politics are adopted by large institutions, these technologies are simultaneously directed at citizens and processes of civic participation. This dynamic is highlighted in designer Dan Hill's (2013) call for a shift from 'smart cities' to 'smart citizens', which attempts to valorize the more piecemeal, bottom-up and citizen-driven ways that technology is being used to effect change in local communities. Townsend (2014: 25) puts the smartphone at the centre of these efforts, arguing that '[t]hese devices are both a new lens on the dynamic life of the city around us, and the remote controls we can use to activate the world at a distance'. While the ability to access information about the city on the go, or even provide feedback and additional information to the city itself, can allow for new ways of interacting with each other and our environment, this dynamic has also had broader ramifications for how we actually conceptualize and practise citizenship.

For Jennifer Gabrys (2014: 34), '[m]onitoring and managing data in order to feed back information into urban systems are practices that become constitutive of citizenship. Citizenship transforms into citizen sensing, embodied through practices undertaken in response to (and communication with) computational environments and technologies'. That is, the definition and performance of 'good' citizenship is tied to citizens using the technologies in their hands or pockets in order to contribute data back to their city or to the public at large. Whether this is through a more active and deliberate contribution like using local issue-reporting applications or even through a more passive participation of allowing one's self to be tracked by sensors embedded in the built environment without raising complaints about privacy, the end result is that '[t]he citizen is a data point, both a generator of data and a responsive node in a system of feedback' (Gabrys, 2014: 38). Regardless of what particular form this data takes or what issue it seeks to address, it is through being made into data that citizens (and their experiences, opinions and concerns) are made to 'matter' (Wilson, 2011a).

But turning civic participation into a process defined by data does not inexorably lead to greater efficiency or responsiveness to citizen concerns. If anything, this process ultimately works to limit the scope of citizen participation, often foreclosing the possibility of proposing or even creating radical alternatives, while channelling action into the much more limited realm of increasing the efficiency of different processes through informational interventions. As Wilson (2011b) describes in the case of a neighbourhood indicators project in Seattle, the codification of urban social problems into discrete categories can allow some problems to go unnoticed while surface-level manifestations are treated in isolation from their broader causes. For Wilson (2011b: 370), 'this move to place these assessment technologies in the hands of residents worked to shift citizens away from complaint systems and into reporting systems'. That being said, Offenhuber (2015) has shown that not all reporting systems are made equal, with the design of such applications allowing (or at times discouraging) more contentious and critical comments about community issues. So, even as citizens are almost uniformly responsibilized through data – shifting the onus for collecting and analysing data in order to make and enact policy from the state onto citizens – the forms this responsibility takes are decidedly limited.

At the same time as the scope of citizenship is reduced to being, and contributing, data points, so too are the terms of citizenship being reconfigured through this focus on data. Indeed, in many ways it is not the actual data itself that is most important, but rather how data helps to further reorient social structures and processes. One of the most frequently discussed manifestations of this new digital civics is the civic hackathon, one-off events that bring together teams of citizen technologists to work intensely on a given civic problem for a short period of time. But as a growing body of literature suggests, these events rarely produce meaningful technological outputs, and are instead focused on shaping the broader discourse around certain social problems and providing motivation for continued involvement in technology-centric forms of citizen participation (cf. DiSalvo et al., 2014; Lodato and DiSalvo, 2016; Robinson and Johnson, 2016; Schrock, forthcoming). This distinction is important, as Leszczynski (2016) argues that it is necessary to focus not only on the particular forms that data takes in the context of governance practices, but also on the ways that data helps to create particular visions of the future. And just as civic apps structure what civic and political participation can look like in the present and future, so too do hackathons, which Schrock (forthcoming) argues tend towards fundamentally 'conservative civic visions'. That is, the vision of the future offered up by these ostensibly participatory events is a kind of technocratic, instrumental rationality that continues to privilege the role of data in urban governance (Perng and Kitchin, 2018), and, despite the limited track record in producing meaningful products out of such data, focuses on certain kinds of technological and design products that ultimately foreclose critical inquiry into the issues at hand (Gregg, 2015; Lodato and DiSalvo, 2016; Schrock, forthcoming).

This increasingly prominent understanding of citizenship *vis-à-vis* data has also worked to redefine *who* is a citizen and how citizenship is defined spatially. In particular, there is a shift away from citizenship as a formal legal status defined through place-based identities. As technical expertise, especially the ability to manipulate data, is increasingly valorized, those who possess this expertise are given a privileged seat at the proverbial table, even when they do not possesses the formal legal status of citizenship (or even residence) in a given place. As Shelton and Lodato (in press) demonstrate in the case of smart cities programmes in Atlanta, this privileging of technical expertise leads to an inability on the part of municipal officials to grapple with the specifics of who citizens are and what their needs may be, as citizens *without* such technical acumen are largely excluded from planning and decision-making processes in favour of experts who make decisions on their behalf. Ultimately, citizenship is defined less by the actual places where one holds the legal status of citizenship and more by the kinds of expertise that one can contribute, regardless of place of origin, residence or personal investment in a given locality. At the same time, the spaces where citizenship is presumed to exist are also being reconfigured, privileging hackathons or the digital spaces of apps and open data portals, while material public spaces are being made less accessible to citizens. Citizen protest and participation in these more conventional locations are seen to be disruptive to the social order, rather than constitutive of it, a fact that has been demonstrated by responses to the Black Lives Matter and Occupy protests in recent years. But as citizenship has increasingly become defined and reconfigured in relation to the discourses and practices of digital data, so too have these changes begotten further shifts in how citizenship and civic participation are being practised. The following sections attempt to trace three emerging trends within digital civics that are deserving of future attention.

THE SPATIALIZATION OF DIGITAL CIVICS

The first emerging trend is the increasing *spatialization* of digital civics. As civic participation is increasingly mediated by the digital, so too are these digital traces increasingly tied explicitly to geography. This explosion of spatial data has meant a growth in mapping tools and platforms, data dashboards and dynamic visualizations to be used in civic participation processes so as to demonstrate the fundamental connection between space, place, and social processes. Whether described as neogeography, volunteered geographic information, or the geoweb, this more spatially explicit manifestation of the broader Web 2.0 ethos (Johnson and Sieber, 2012) means that more conventional ways of thinking about and representing geographic processes are becoming more central to the broader civic imaginary. These practices range from attaching locational data to the kinds of issue-reporting application described above, to using simple web maps to raise awareness about a given issue of local importance, or the use of more complex spatial analytical techniques and representations to make the case for civic action. At the same time, these new spatial technologies are also working to reshape the way people interact with maps and spatial data, providing something of an inadvertent response to long-standing critiques of mapping as privileging masculinist, imperialist and Cartesian knowledges, instead allowing for a wider range of epistemological and ontological approaches to be realized within digital mapping (Elwood, 2008; Warf and Sui, 2010; Elwood and Leszczynski, 2013).

Though the emergence of these new platforms and forms of data means that spatial information has become more readily accessible and more variegated in form, Haklay (2013) has cautioned against viewing this quantitative growth with a qualitative shift in how these technologies are able to be used by everyday people. So, despite the promise of this more spatially explicit iteration of digital civics of allowing for greater engagement with place-specific issues as originally suggested by Goodchild (2007), these technologies have done little to overcome long-standing barriers that mean that the voices of well-educated, relatively affluent, white men are overrepresented in such platforms. As Haklay (2013: 66) argues,

> [t]he main error in the core argument of those who promote it as a democratic force is the assumption that, by increasing the number of people who utilise geographic information in different ways and gain access to geographic technology, these users have been empowered and gained more political and social control ... neogeography has merely opened up the collection and use of this information to a larger section of the affluent, educated, and powerful part of society.

THE CORPORATIZATION OF DIGITAL CIVICS

This limited potential for a deeper democratization of digital technology has undoubtedly been shaped by the simultaneous *corporatization* of digital civics.

Emerging in conjunction with the spatialization of civic participation, the increased need for technical expertise in order to enact these kinds of digital spatial platforms and processes means that corporate technology vendors are stepping in to facilitate on behalf of, or at least in conjunction with, local governments. But this moment extends beyond what Leszczynski (2012) describes as the neoliberalization of mapping, with the state and other more-or-less public institutions being replaced by private corporations in the provision of spatial information. Now, because of the centrality of spatial data to the practice of datafied citizenship described above, the act of civic engagement itself requires the participation, if not beneficence, of technology corporations.

Key players in the mapping industry, including market-leader Esri and relative newcomers Mapbox and Carto, have all launched some type of municipal government or civic participation programme or platform in recent years (Carto, 2015; Poon, 2016; Turner, 2016). While many of these programmes seem targeted at providing a combination of software services and technical expertise to city governments in need, the controversial ride-hailing app Uber has taken a different approach with its municipal government outreach. Recognizing that the *data* collected by the platform is extremely valuable to municipal governments in attempting to understand the everyday mobilities of urban residents, Uber appears to be providing limited access to its proprietary data as a way of extracting concessions from local governments who have previously been keen to regulate such ride-hailing apps (Poon, 2017). Even the most visible institution in the ostensibly non-profit wing of the digital civics space, Code for America, has played an active role in spinning off the projects from its fellowship programme into for-profit tech start-ups, with platforms like LocalData and CivicInsight emerging out of the Detroit and New Orleans fellowship teams and their work on data platforms for analysing vacant properties in these respective cities.

For some municipalities invested in becoming 'smarter' and more data-driven, it is only through partnerships with these kinds of corporations that such goals can be realized. Whether through direct procurement or more mutually beneficial partnership agreements, cities not only require the technology and services provided, but also seek to acquire the reputational capital that comes with such public–private partnerships. For example, in Louisville, Kentucky, the Metro government has not only sought to participate in a variety of technical assistance programmes provided through non-profits like Code for America, Bloomberg Philanthropies, the Rockefeller Foundation, and others, but also developed partnerships with for-profit companies like IBM, OpportunitySpace, MySidewalk, Asthmapolis, and LocalData. This kind of corporatization of digital civics is, in many ways, a result of the fact that most municipal governments do not have the internal capacity necessary to do the kind of data-intensive work being promoted, especially in an era of fiscal austerity. Instead, they turn to the external institutions where this kind of expertise is increasingly concentrated. But this process ends up in a self-reinforcing cycle, where local capacity and expertise are never built, but instead continually outsourced to private companies (often located in an entirely different city or state) who are able to extract money from local government, while also continuing to privilege technological solutions to intensely *social* problems.

EMERGING OPPOSITIONAL USES OF DIGITAL CIVICS

But just as digital civics, like so many other areas of social life, has been increasingly colonized by technology corporations and an overarching neoliberal ethos, so too has there been a counter-movement to claim the potential for these technologies to act as a means towards more radical and emancipatory ends. Rather than reinforcing corporate power, encouraging the roll-back of governmental services, and enshrining the value of technical expertise, these emerging *oppositional uses* of digital civics seek to challenge the social and political status quo. These projects demonstrate that in an era where data is increasingly privileged as the primary means by which citizenship is expressed, data can be just as usefully used by citizens for their own purposes, even serving as the grounds on which broader political claims are made (Taylor et al., 2014; Shelton et al., 2015; Le Dantec et al., 2016). Drawing, if at times implicitly, on a longer history of counter-mapping (cf. Peluso, 1995), these more confrontational and contentious uses of digital data and mapping technologies seek to demonstrate that these tools do not inherently lead to the kinds of problematic understandings of social and spatial processes and naturalization of social inequality and stigma common among more institutional iterations of digital technologies (cf. Shelton, 2017; Jefferson, 2018). Instead, they use data analysis and visualization to promote critical, counter-hegemonic understandings of, and interventions for, any number of social problems.

Among those issues most frequently targeted by this 'counter data' movement has been the global housing crisis. From the Bay Area's Anti-Eviction Mapping Project[1] to Detroit's Property Praxis[2] and the translocal investigations of Inside Airbnb,[3] these more oppositional iterations of digital civics show its potential to challenge, not just reinforce, existing social hierarchies. While these projects are powerful in part because of the compelling interactive visualizations they have produced, they are also important in so far as they help to break the long-assumed link between mapping and spatial analytical methods with a kind of naïve logical positivism (Wyly, 2009). None of these projects purport to be neutral, simply describing the world as it is through quantitative data. Instead, they all bring a particular political position to bear on the data and resulting analyses, which redirects the conversation about these issues from what might simply appear to be the case, to the underlying levers of technology-based gentrification processes, tax foreclosure and property speculation that are wreaking havoc on residents and housing markets in these places.

Despite being enabled by and articulated through digital technology, these emerging contentious forms of digital civics echo the roots of 'civics' in the pre-digital mapping and urban fieldwork of Patrick Geddes and other early social reformers (Guldi, 2017). Indeed, they also represent a realization of Sieber and Johnson's (2015) more contemporary call for open data to go beyond just the provision of data as an end in itself, and towards open data as a means of furthering agendas of inclusion and participation. So, even as many of these projects operate less from the frame of open data or civic technology, and more from the position of using these technologies as a means towards articulating radical alternatives to the status quo, they mobilize many of the same tools and approaches as more institutionally based forms of digital civics, highlighting the flexibility of these technologies within different social and organizational contexts and the contradictions in how the growing importance of data is reshaping citizenship and civic participation.

Notes

1. www.antievictionmap.com
2. www.propertypraxis.org
3. www.insideairbnb.com

REFERENCES

Carto (2015) 'Urban insights: An analysis of the future of our cities and technology', White Paper. Available at: http://go.cartodb.com/hubfs/SmartCitiesWhitePaper.pdf (accessed 3 February 2018).

DiSalvo, C., Gregg, M. and Lodato, T. (2014) 'Building belonging', *interactions*, 21(4): 58–61.

Elwood, S. (2008) 'Volunteered geographic information: Future research directions motivated by critical, participatory, and feminist GIS', *GeoJournal*, 72(3–4): 173–183.

Elwood, S. and Leszczynski, A. (2013) 'New spatial media, new knowledge politics', *Transactions of the Institute of British Geographers*, 38(4): 544–559.

Gabrys, J. (2014) 'Programming environments: Environmentality and citizen sensing in the smart city', *Environment and Planning D: Society and Space*, 32(1): 30–48.

Goodchild, M. (2007) 'Citizens as sensors: The world of volunteered geography', *GeoJournal*, 69(4): 211–221.

Gregg, M. (2015) 'Hack for good: Speculative labour, app development and the burden of austerity', *Fibreculture Journal*, 25: 183–201.

Guldi, J. (2017) 'A history of the participatory map', *Public Culture*, 29(1): 79–112.

Haklay, M. (2013) 'Neogeography and the delusion of democratisation', *Environment and Planning A*, 45(1): 55–69.

Hill, D. (2013) 'On the smart city; or, a "manifesto" for smart citizens instead', *Cityofsound*, 1 February. Available at: www.cityofsound.com/blog/2013/02/on-the-smart-city-a-call-for-smart-citizens-instead.html (accessed 3 February 2018).

Jefferson, B.J. (2018) 'Predictable policing: Predictive crime mapping and geographies of policing and race', *Annals of the American Association of Geographers*, 108(1): 1–16.

Johnson, P.A. and Sieber, R.E. (2012) 'Motivations driving government adoption of the geoweb', *GeoJournal*, 77(5): 667–680.

Le Dantec, C.A., Appleton, C., Asad, M., Rosenberger, R. and Watkins, K. (2016) 'Advocating through data: Community visibilities in crowdsourced cycling data', in A. Golub, M.L. Hoffmann, A.E. Lugo and G.F. Sandoval (eds), *Bicycle Justice and Urban Transformation: Biking for All?* Abingdon: Routledge. pp. 70–85.

Leszczynski, A. (2012) 'Situating the geoweb in political economy', *Progress in Human Geography*, 36(1): 72–89.

Leszczynski, A. (2016) 'Speculative futures: Cities, data, and governance beyond smart urbanism', *Environment and Planning A*, 48(9): 1691–1708.

Lodato, T.J. and DiSalvo, C. (2016) 'Issue-oriented hackathons as material participation', *New Media & Society*, 18(4): 539–557.

Offenhuber, D. (2015) 'Infrastructure legibility – a comparative analysis of open311-based citizen feedback systems', *Cambridge Journal of Regions, Economy and Society*, 8(1): 93–112.

Peluso, N.L. (1995) 'Whose woods are these? Counter-mapping forest territories in Kalimantan, Indonesia', *Antipode*, 27(4): 383–406.

Perng, S.Y. and Kitchin, R. (2018) 'Solutions and frictions in civic hacking: Collaboratively designing and building wait time predictions for an immigration office', *Social & Cultural Geography*, 19(1): 1–20.

Poon, L. (2016) 'Helping smart cities harness big data', *CityLab*, 29 September. Available at: www.citylab.com/life/2016/09/how-mapbox-will-help-smart-cites-tackle-urban-challenges/502241 (accessed 3 February 2018).

Poon, L. (2017) 'Finally, Uber releases data to help cities with transit planning', *CityLab*, 11 January. Available at: www.citylab.com/transportation/2017/01/finally-uber-releases-data-to-help-cities-with-transit-planning/512720 (accessed 3 February 2018).

Robinson, P.J. and Johnson, P.A. (2016) 'Civic hackathons: New terrain for local government-citizen interaction?' *Urban Planning*, 1(2): 65–74.

Schrock, A. (forthcoming) '"Hackathons with no hacking": Civic hackathons and the performance of innovation', in C. Watkins (ed.), *Rethinking the Innovation Economy: Exploring the Future of Technology, Social Inequality, and Creative Labor*. New York: Routledge. Available at: www.dropbox.com/s/d6ji0gq9tgiqt46/hackathons%20with%20no%20hacking-public%20draft%20with%20edits.pdf?dl=0 (accessed 17 May 2018).

Shelton, T. (2017) 'The urban geographical imagination in the age of Big Data', *Big Data & Society*, 4(1). DOI: 10.1177/2053951716665129.

Shelton, T. and Lodato, T. (in press) '"Actually existing smart citizens": Expertise and (non)participation in the making of the smart city', paper presented at Creating the Smart City Workshop, Maynooth University, Maynooth, Ireland, *City*.

Shelton, T., Zook, M. and Wiig, A. (2015) 'The "actually existing smart city"', *Cambridge Journal of Regions, Economy and Society*, 8(1): 13–25.

Sieber, R.E. and Johnson, P.A. (2015) 'Civic open data at a crossroads: Dominant models and current challenges', *Government Information Quarterly*, 32(3): 308–315.

Taylor, A.S., Lindley, S., Regan, T. and Sweeney, D. (2014) 'Data and life on the street', *Big Data & Society*, 1(2). DOI: 10.1177/2053951714539278.

Townsend, A. (2014) 'To know thy city, know thyself', in D. Hemment and A. Townsend (eds), *Smart Citizens*. Manchester: FutureEverything. pp. 23–26. Available at: http://futureeverything.org/ideas/smart-citizens-publication (accessed 3 February 2018).

Turner, A. (2016) 'Data-driven citizenship', *Esri Insider*, 27 September. Available at: https://blogs.esri.com/esri/esri-insider/2016/09/27/data-driven-citizenship (accessed 3 February 2018).

Warf, B. and Sui, D. (2010) 'From GIS to neogeography: Ontological implications and theories of truth', *Annals of GIS*, 16(4): 197–209.

Wilson, M.W. (2011a) 'Data matter(s): Legitimacy, coding, and qualifications-of-life', *Environment and Planning D: Society and Space*, 29(5): 857–872.

Wilson, M.W. (2011b) '"Training the eye": Formation of the geocoding subject', *Social & Cultural Geography*, 12(4): 357–376.

Wyly, E. (2009) 'Strategic positivism', *Professional Geographer*, 61(3): 310–322.

23

ETHICS

Linnet Taylor

INTRODUCTION

For every action there is always an equal and opposite reaction. In the case of datafication, this counterweight has been the notion of *data ethics* (Floridi and Taddeo, 2016), which has developed as an intersection between various contributing fields of philosophy and social science, including information ethics (Floridi, 2013) and critical data studies (Dalton and Thatcher, 2014), but also, importantly, geography. The ethical dimensions of geography are an active and ongoing debate: Smith (1997) identified a 'moral turn' in the field in the late 1990s that touched both on human geography concerns such as migration and politics and on ethics with regard to physical geography, something that has gained importance as climate change and environmental justice become central concerns in geography. Writing a decade later, Popke (2009) argued for an affective ethics on the part of geographers, one that can take into account collectives and solidarity in relation to space – this notion can be seen underlying recent work on 'smart cities' such as that of Hatuka and Toch (2017).

Related fields such as geographies of development also help us to understand what an ethics of digital geography might be. The initiation of the Human Development Index in 1990 provided geographers with new conceptual tools to research social and economic inequality, a conceptual shift that was then supplemented by geographic information systems (GIS) tools in the 2000s (Porter and Purser, 2008), and by new data sources over the course of the 2010s (United Nations, 2014). These new sources, particularly mobile phones, also pose ethical problems for digital geography in terms of research methods and power asymmetries (Taylor, 2016a), and are giving rise to calls for new research priorities in geographical ethics that can inform ethics in other fields dealing with digital data (Dalton et al., 2016).

Through these debates geographers have played an important role in developing the conceptual basis for data ethics, particularly around issues of positionality, research methods, and data sources. One of the tasks data ethics is increasingly engaging with is interrogating the power asymmetries that have accompanied the rise of ubiquitous connectivity and big data analytics (Taylor and Broeders, 2015; Hatuka and Toch, 2017). By drawing attention to the human impacts of datafication, data ethics broadly aims to understand how moral choices are made with regard to data systems, but also the politics and history of data systems (Dalton et al., 2016) and how those shape and determine power asymmetries and conflicting understandings.

The new digital data sources present some important challenges for geographers. These challenges, which evolve out of known problems such as positionality and inclusivity, both require new thinking and offer insights into what good geographic research is in general. Issues that are central to the ethics of digital geographic research include positionality and inclusiveness, for example Kwan's (2015) work on the analysis of experienced space and Sen et al.'s (2015) on the discursiveness of location data as ground truth; Lauriault and Mooney's (2014) practical and ethical interrogation of volunteered and crowdsourced data, and Georgiadou et al.'s (2016) deconstruction of GIS metadata in development. As Schuurman (2009) points out, focusing on these kinds of digital geography tends to demand qualitative, rather than mainly quantitative, research. How can this be reconciled with big (spatial) data and the opportunities it brings? This apparent conflict may underlie Elwood and Wilson's (2017) observation that the technical demands of learning GIS tend to make geography students resist engaging with the ethical implications of their work.

One of the objects of study at the centre of digital geography's contribution to ethics is the smart city. This chapter will use the example of smart city data to examine some of the ethical concerns relating to today's digital geographies. What Dalla Corte et al. (2017: 81) term the 'instrumented urban environment' involves a collaboration between public and private sector actors, infrastructures, and practices in the production of the sensed, and sensing, environment. City authorities do not have the capacity to engineer an environment full of sensors, nor do they have sufficient data scientists to analyse the data produced by them. Instead, they contract with commercial firms, other administrative authorities, and academic researchers to get, and analyse, data about the city and its functioning. This multifaceted public–private interface is sometimes citizen-facing and open to analysis, but often becomes opaque to both the public and to researchers who may use the data the city generates (Kitchin, 2016a), making it difficult to track and to govern the collection, handling, and storing of data, and to understand the possible ethical impacts of using that data.

Kitchin (2016b) has outlined the ethical implications of the change in the way data is generated and the questions that are asked of it in the smart city, with a focus on privacy and awareness on the part of citizens. This chapter will not cover the same ground. In order to draw out the particular problems that face those aiming to use 'smart city data' as a research tool, I will use a descriptive lens to analyse how ethics is portrayed and presented in relation to the datafication of urban space. I will argue that if we seek to understand how decisions are made and justified, and which actors claim to be the arbiters of data ethics, we may find productive ways to interrogate the political, moral, and economic factors that make up these new ways of seeing and influencing through smart infrastructure.

DATAFICATION AS A TOOL FOR THE COMMERCIALIZATION OF PUBLIC SPACE

The visibility produced by the datafication of space has a particular politics. It is a byproduct of informational capitalism: people are seen, and become objects of policy and commercial intervention, through the data they emit by using particular spaces, services, and devices. This confers important components of the power to intervene on commercial entities, either in partnership with public authorities, or alone (Taylor and Broeders, 2015).

One example of this dynamic is the Flow system developed by Alphabet's Sidewalk Labs (Alphabet being the parent company of Google). Flow is a system for digitizing and centralizing urban transport data that is marketed to cities as a complete 'solution' for managing their transport systems (Harris, 2016). If a city adopts Flow's services, the provider will take charge of a number of key functions in the public transport system: it will coordinate subsidies for low-income residents, provide Google's mobile payment system for all transport payments, and optimize public parking by matching the location of vehicles to those of parking spaces, through a process of monitoring drivers' position via their mobile phones using Google Maps. Flow also, however, exacts a price from the city that adopts it. The system comes as a package which cities must adopt as a whole, and at a cost to the public sector monopoly on public transport provision. Flow demands that any passenger overflow in the transport system be diverted to ride-sharing companies such as Uber (with vehicles automatically called to overcrowded bus stops), and that the city share all public transport data with Uber in order to facilitate this. It also demands that the city share all parking and ridership information with Sidewalk in real-time, and that it commit passengers to exclusively using Sidewalk's payment infrastructure (Harris, 2016).

The public–private interface where systems such as Flow reside is problematic in that it normalizes using public resources to subsidize private-sector service provision.

Just as voucher programmes that fund students to attend private schools are criticized for undermining the public school system, Flow presents the risk that the data that allows the city to understand people's transport needs and identify shortfalls in service provision will instead become a tool to hone the business strategies of private transport services. This will inevitably undermine the city's prerogative to manage the public transport system so that the public can access it fairly and efficiently.

This example demonstrates how people's visibility changes when data is handled by both public and private actors. The city, as part of its administrative functioning, usually processes data on subsidies, travellers, and payments. It does so, arguably, as part of the social contract: we provide data about ourselves to the relevant public authorities so that they can fulfil their various functions. However, when Sidewalk needs to process the same data it must be provided separately to the private sector. It also requires more data: it wants to know where a driver is all the time, in case she needs a parking space. It wants to know where a subsidized rider is entering and exiting the bus, where she takes a ride-sharing service to if the bus is too full, and which bank account she uses to transfer money to the payment system. These visibilities, once commercial, have different implications. They transform citizens into customers, they make it possible to relate people's behaviour as consumers to their behaviour as travellers on public transit, and they tell a story about people's finances, work, and leisure that is valuable within the data market. A system such as Flow may optimize city transport, but to whose benefit? Public space becomes commercial space, public resources blend with commercial services, and a system that initially appears to create capacity and efficiency actually diverts public funds to private actors.

Many technologies of today's 'smart city' tend to approach service provision in ways that maximize people's visibility to private companies. Beacons used in retail areas connect with an app to push messages about special offers from retailers in the vicinity (Social Retail, 2017), but can also send notifications guiding people to local landmarks such as churches and official buildings, and provide public service announcements such as floods and evacuation warnings. 'Smart lampposts' used in cities around the world (Newman, 2015) are marketed as tools for energy efficiency and public safety (Humble Lamppost, 2016), but they are also arrayed with sensors that can monitor movement, behaviour, and mobile phone traffic. This sensing in public space is oriented towards risk assessment. It creates visibility that is then the basis for interventions by city authorities and law enforcement. The lampposts themselves can also be designed to intervene directly in people's behaviour by spraying scents or changing lighting when aggression is perceived by the array of sensors (de Graaf, 2015).

This public–private visibility is one example of the kind of problems that an ethics of digital geography must engage with. It emerges due to the particular political and market configurations that characterize big data analytics, and makes it hard to identify who should be the target of claims about ethics and moral choices. Who should we ask to be ethical towards whom? What kinds of data should we pay attention to and should we access them through city authorities or their private-sector partners? How do we know data is accurately representing the city if it is proprietary and protected? Unless we know who is acting through data technologies, and whom they are acting upon, it becomes hard to think clearly about these essential questions.

THE GROUP AND THE INDIVIDUAL

One reason for the currently high profile of data ethics is that big data presents new governance and rule-making problems. Kitchin (2014) has outlined how 'Big Data epistemologies' denote a shift in our strategies of knowledge creation: we are moving from targeting specific problems using honed data, to mining multiple datasets to detect patterns and generate hypotheses. This is the fundamental difference between big data and other forms of data, but it also results in real-world effects that we need to think about differently. As datasets become larger and our analytical strategies more inductive, and as new methods such as neural networks develop, which are at least partly opaque to both researchers and the populations we study, people are increasingly categorized and intervened upon in ways that target the group rather than the individual. This brings us back to Popke's (2009) call to think about the collective with regard to geographical research: our current approach to governing data is based on protecting individuals from individual, identifiable harms. It is not based on protecting the crowd from uncertain harms occurring through influence and manipulation, including those produced as a result of research. As the basis for claiming harm becomes foggier, so does our ability to understand what should and should not be done with data.

Yet this uncertainty about who is impacted, and how, is normality in the business of data analytics. As the manager of a living lab in the Dutch city of Eindhoven remarked, 'we are only Big Brother to the crowd' (de Graaf, 2015). The project that is using a smart lamppost does not need to identify the people walking below in order to target them for intervention and manipulation, just as policy-makers engaging in 'nudging' the public do not seek individual consent when they engage in experiments designed to induce behavioural change (Thaler and Sunstein, 2008).

These ways of making people visible are not subject to the legal framework for privacy since it derives from individual rights,[1] and those rights have been translated, in the European and US systems, into individual protections from data-related harms. This means that if data is de-identified, it is then considered fully safe and open for use. Such data is particularly important to researchers, who can use it to study the spatial dynamics of population, mobility, and development. Yet research demonstrates that even if data does not identify anyone directly, it can still impact them just as seriously as if they were identifiable (Raymond, 2016; Taylor, 2016b). In fact, data that is non-identifiable – although possibly, as Raymond (2016) puts it, 'demographically identifiable' – nevertheless tells a story. Big data is used to analyse group characteristics and dynamics as much as to identify individuals, for instance in terms of population and urban dynamics, risk estimation and predictive analytics, and network analysis of communications. Especially when analysed on the network level, it can tell us about the lives of groups, networks, villages, cities, even states, and is already being transformed into 'shadow maps' that allow for intervention on the collective level (Taylor and Broeders, 2015). Given these possibilities, researchers who go along with the assumption that 'anonymous' data is safe data may create real problems for the subjects of their research (see Raymond et al., 2013, for the case of satellite data).

THE TASK OF DATA ETHICS

The problems identified here represent just some of those raised by the new sources of data, and the new technologies becoming available for processing such data. There is an important disjuncture between the ethical parameters that are usual for researchers and the possibilities of the new digital data sources. Given this, we may do well to look beyond the standard set of rules regarding privacy and data collection – even though these, as Kitchin (2016b) points out, are a necessary precondition for preventing the abuse of citizens in the instrumented urban environment. Identifying impacts on society should logically be done by stakeholders within society more broadly, and foremost by citizen groups. Yet citizen participation is ill-defined in relation to the smart city: it is currently considered largely irrelevant in many high-profile urban digitization projects (Greenfield, 2013), and serious concerns are often sidelined until they become disruptive (Datta, 2015). Those promoting smart city projects genuflect to citizen participation initiatives (e.g., European Innovation Partnership on Smart Cities and Communities, 2016), but the smart city is primarily the technocratic city and the expert city (Shelton and Clark, 2016).

The rules we have are necessary but not sufficient. Even the rules developed to deal with digital data may not be right in every case: take, for example, the now common 'open research data' requirement that data collected by researchers must be placed in repositories to become accessible to the field. If we no longer know which data is risky, how can we decide which data to make open? Or if, for example, we target datafication's collective risks as well as individual ones, we cannot simply rely on the notion of an individual right to privacy and instead we end up with a different, more political and structural notion of what an ethics of digital geographies might need to accomplish. Such a structural approach would demand that we ask how data value chains and institutional controls might be configured to promote privacy, non-discrimination and autonomy, and that we critically historicize the problems of data as a way to identify what we are for and against (Dalton et al., 2016).

What approaches, then, provide ways to understand what is ethical with regard to digital geographic research? In order to assess what is fair and just in terms of the uses and impacts of data, it is necessary to include as diverse a set of stakeholders as possible. Several possibly overlapping frameworks are available. First, Purtova's (2015) notion of data as 'system resource', an ecosystem of people, platforms, and profiles, with distributed ownership, provides a way to argue against technocratic perspectives that may prioritize innovation over consensus. Alvarez León (2016) has made an economic analysis of such distributed data ownership with regard to geographic information, but a corresponding analysis from the ethical perspective, regarding who has rights over the data produced by instrumented and digitized urban space, would be a useful tool in thinking through how to respect different claims over data. As a starting point, the notion of overlapping stakeholders is clearly important: the most obvious groups to consider seem to be citizen associations; educators and research communities; local councillors and mayors; firms themselves; and national-level actors such as law-makers and regulators. These groups have entanglements that, if considered together, necessarily provide a multifaceted approach to determining what data should do, and how. One could be a member of an interest group or a town council at the same time as working for a corporation or as a teacher or researcher. Furthermore, the missing 'citizens' can be found in each type of group, since all these may be composed of individuals who live and work in urban space.

Another approach is to start from the point of view that data technologies should be used in ways that enhance human flourishing, dignity and integrity, and to test each new use of data against these benchmarks. These overarching perspectives can be found in the philosophy of information (Floridi, 2016), but also in international development (Heeks and Renken, 2018) and media and communications (Arora, 2016; Powell, 2016). By placing these perspectives in dialogue with each other (Taylor, 2017), we arrive at an argument that we need to build broad societal debates that can set the boundaries for experimentation with big data, and that can help think through what kind of rule-making process we want to adopt. What is clear is that our current tools for identifying and addressing the risks of our data economy are insufficient, and that the notion of 'data ethics' may be one of very few useful placeholders for the diverse set of discussions about rule-making and boundary-setting that are necessary. We need a new discussion about what shape ethical behaviour takes in relation to ubiquitous connectivity and the sensed environment: we must hope that data ethics can be the territory for that discussion.

Note

1. Notably in the Universal Declaration of Human Rights (Art. 12) and the European Convention on Human Rights (Art. 8).

REFERENCES

Alvarez León, L.F. (2016) 'Property regimes and the commodification of geographic information: An examination of Google Street View', *Big Data & Society*, 3(2). DOI: 10.1177/2053951716637885.

Arora, P. (2016) 'Bottom of the data pyramid: Big data and the Global South', *International Journal of Communication*, 10(19): 1681–1699.

Dalla Corte, L., van Loenen, B. and Cuijpers, C. (2017) 'Personal data protection as a nonfunctional requirement in the smart city's development', B. Anglès Juanpere and J. Balcells Padullés (eds), *Proceedings of the 13th International Conference on Internet, Law & Politics: Managing Risk in the Digital Society*. Barcelona: Huygens Editorial. pp. 76–92.

Dalton, C.M. and Thatcher, J. (2014) 'What does a critical data studies look like, and why do we care?', *Society and Space*, 12 May. Available at: http://societyandspace.org/2014/05/12/what-does-a-critical-data-studies-look-like-and-why-do-we-care-craig-dalton-and-jim-thatcher (accessed 17 July 2017).

Dalton, C.M., Taylor, L. and Thatcher, J. (2016) 'Critical data studies: A dialog on data and space', *Big Data & Society*, 3(1). DOI: 10.1177/2053951716648346.

Datta, A. (2015) 'New urban utopias of postcolonial India: "Entrepreneurial urbanization" in Dholera smart city, Gujarat', *Dialogues in Human Geography*, 5(1): 3–22.

De Graaf, P. (2015). 'Een biertje met Big Brother erbij op Stratumseind', *De Volkskrant*, 23 November. Available at: www.volkskrant.nl/binnenland/een-biertje-met-big-brother-erbij-op-stratumseind~a4192665 (accessed 23 November 2015).

Elwood, S. and Wilson, M. (2017) 'Critical GIS pedagogies beyond "Week 10: Ethics"', *International Journal of Geographical Information Science*, 31(10): 2098–2116.

European Innovation Partnership on Smart Cities and Communities (2016) 'Inclusive smart cities: A European manifesto on citizen engagement'. Available at: http://eu-smartcities.eu/sites/default/files/2017-09/EIP-SCC%20Manifesto%20on%20Citizen%20Engagement%20%26%20Inclusive%20Smart%20Cities_0.pdf (accessed 4 February 2018).

Floridi, L. (2013) *The Ethics of Information*. Oxford: Oxford University Press.

Floridi, L. (2016) 'On human dignity as a foundation for the right to privacy', *Philosophy & Technology*, 29(4): 307–312.

Floridi, L. and Taddeo, M. (2016) 'What is data ethics?', *Philosophical Transactions of the Royal Society A*, 374(2083): 1–5.

Georgiadou, Y., Verplanke, J., Lungo, J. and Mbise, M. (2016) 'Water point mapping in Tanzania: Making the voices of data collectors audible', paper presented at the 7th Rural Water Supply Network (RWSN) Forum: Water for Everyone, Abidjan, Côte d'Ivoire.

Greenfield, A. (2013) *Against the Smart City: A Pamphlet*. New York: Do Projects.

Harris, M. (2016) 'Secretive Alphabet division funded by Google aims to fix public transit in US', *The Guardian*, 27 June. Available at: www.theguardian.com/technology/2016/jun/27/google-flow-sidewalk-labs-columbus-ohio-parking-transit (accessed 4 February 2018).

Hatuka, T. and Toch, E. (2017) 'Being visible in public space: The normalisation of asymmetrical visibility', *Urban Studies*, 54(4): 984–998.

Heeks, R. and Renken, J. (2018) 'Data justice for development: What would it mean?', *Information Development*, 34(1): 90–102.

Humble Lamppost (2016) 'Humble Lamppost'. Available at: http://eu-smartcities.eu/initiatives/78/description (accessed 4 February 2018).

Kitchin, R. (2014) 'Big Data, new epistemologies and paradigm shifts', *Big Data & Society*, 1(1). DOI: 10.1177/2053951714528481.

Kitchin, R. (2016a) 'Getting smarter about smart cities: Improving data privacy and data security'. Dublin: Data Protection Unit, Department of the Taoiseach. Available at: www.taoiseach.gov.ie/eng/Publications/Publications_2016/Smart_Cities_Report_January_2016.pdf (accessed 4 February 2018).

Kitchin, R. (2016b) 'The ethics of smart cities and urban science', *Philosophical Transactions of the Royal Society A*, 374(2083): 1–15.

Kwan, M.-P. (2015) 'Critical visualization in landscape and urban planning: Making the invisible visible', *Landscape and Urban Planning*, 142: 243–244.

Lauriault, T.P. and Mooney, P. (2014) 'Crowdsourcing: A geographic approach to public engagement'. Programmable City Working Paper No. 6. Available at: https://papers.ssrn.com/sol3/papers.cfm?abstract_id=2518233 (accessed 4 February 2018).

Newman, L.H. (2015) 'Sheesh, even streetlights are getting cameras and internet connections', *Future Tense*, 2 October. Available at: www.slate.com/blogs/future_tense/2015/10/02/ge_intelligent_lamp_posts_have_cameras_sensors_may_come_to_new_york_city.html (accessed 13 July 2017).

Popke, J. (2009) 'Geography and ethics: Non-representational encounters, collective responsibility and economic difference', *Progress in Human Geography*, 33(1): 81–90.

Porter, J.R. and Purser, C.W. (2008) 'Measuring relative sub-national human development: An application of the United Nation's Human Development Index using geographic information systems', *Journal of Economic and Social Measurement*, 33(4): 253–269.

Powell, A. (2016) 'Hacking in the public interest: Authority, legitimacy, means, and ends', *New Media & Society*, 18(4): 600–616.

Purtova, N. (2015) 'The illusion of personal data as no one's property', *Law, Innovation and Technology*, 7(1): 83–111.

Raymond, N.A. (2016) 'Beyond "do no harm" and individual consent: Reckoning with the emerging ethical challenges of civil society's use of data', in L. Taylor, L. Floridi and B. van der Sloot (eds), *Group Privacy: New Challenges of Data Technologies*. Cham: Springer. pp. 67–82.

Raymond, N.A., Davies, B.I., Card, B.L., Al Achkar, Z. and Baker, I.L. (2013) 'While we watched: Assessing the impact of the Satellite Sentinel Project', *Georgetown Journal of International Affairs*, 14(2): 185–191.

Schuurman, N. (2009) 'Critical GIS', in R. Kitchin and N. Thrift (eds), *International Encyclopedia of Human Geography, Volume 2*. Amsterdam: Elsevier. pp. 363–368.

Sen, S.W., Ford, H., Musicant, D.R., Graham, M., Keyes, O.S.B. and Hecht, B. (2015) 'Barriers to the localness of volunteered geographic information', in *Proceedings of the 33rd Annual ACM Conference on Human Factors in Computing Systems – CHI '15*. New York: Association for Computing Machinery. pp. 197–206. Available at: https://doi.org/10.1145/2702123.2702170 (accessed 4 February 2018).

Shelton, T. and Clark, J. (2016). 'Technocratic values and uneven development in the "smart city"', *Metropolitics.eu*, 10 May. Available at: www.metropolitiques.eu/Technocratic-Values-and-Uneven.html (accessed 4 February 2018).

Smith, D.M. (1997) 'Geography and ethics: a moral turn?' *Progress in Human Geography*, 21(4): 583–590.

Social Retail (2017) 'Social Retail for smart cities'. Available at: www.digitalsocialretail.com/smart-city (accessed 12 July 2017).

Taylor, L. (2016a) 'No place to hide? The ethics and analytics of tracking mobility using mobile phone data', *Environment and Planning D: Society and Space*, 34(2): 319–336.

Taylor, L. (2016b) 'Safety in numbers? Group privacy and big data analytics in the developing world', in L. Taylor, L. Floridi and B. van der Sloot (eds), *Group Privacy: New Challenges of Data Technologies*. Cham: Springer. pp. 13–36.

Taylor, L. (2017) 'What is data justice? The case for connecting digital rights and freedoms on the global level'. Available at: https://papers.ssrn.com/sol3/papers.cfm?abstract_id=2918779 (accessed 4 February 2018).

Taylor, L. and Broeders, D. (2015) 'In the name of development: Power, profit and the datafication of the global South', *Geoforum*, 64(4): 229–237.

Thaler, R.H. and Sunstein, C.R. (2008) *Nudge: Improving Decisions about Health, Wealth, and Happiness*. New Haven, CT: Yale University Press.

United Nations (2014) 'A world that counts: Mobilising the data revolution for sustainable development'. Available at: www.undatarevolution.org/wp-content/uploads/2014/12/A-World-That-Counts2.pdf (accessed 4 February 2018).

24

KNOWLEDGE POLITICS

Jason C. Young

INTRODUCTION

The sociologist Manuel Castells (2004) argues that the world has been transformed through a process of fundamental structural change driven by the development of digital networks. These networks greatly augment the human capacity for the storage, analysis, and widespread communication of large amounts of information. Furthermore, the technologies that access them are cheaper and more ubiquitous than ever, meaning that more individuals have more opportunities to produce and consume digital information than ever before (Benkler, 2006). These digital networks also have a global reach, granting users the potential to connect with others across very large geographic distances. Digital networks thereby produce a small-world effect that allows ideas to travel quickly and widely to reach broad audiences (Bennett and Segerberg, 2013).

Given this deep connection between digital technologies and information, it is no surprise that digital knowledge politics has emerged as an important area of study. This is particularly the case given that the effects of digital technologies are not equal for all people or places. Digital technologies are not only composed of material bundles of hardware and software, but also constituted through the attendant social practices, logics, and methodologies. These have social histories that shape what types of knowledges they can effectively broadcast and to whom. This chapter identifies key research agendas emerging around digital knowledge politics. I begin by tracing geographic interest in knowledge politics to early debates around geographic information systems (GIS). I then discuss three areas of current research in digital knowledge politics: intersections of digital infrastructure and material inequalities; how digital spaces and practices shape the visibility and authority of knowledge claims; and the broader political effects of digital knowledge.

THE POLITICS OF GEOSPATIAL KNOWLEDGE

Digital knowledge politics is defined as the sets of practices that shape the degree to which different sets of knowledges are included (or excluded), made visible (or invisible), and given authority (or marginalized) within digital media (Elwood, 2010). Discussions of digital knowledge politics remain strikingly similar to earlier debates around GIS, due to their critical focus on interconnections between digital knowledge and power (Burns, 2015). In the 1990s, geographers extended critiques of cartography to emerging, digital forms of geospatial technology (Sheppard, 1995). They examined how GIS naturalizes specific ways of knowing the world, while simultaneously marginalizing others. Central to this research were questions about the co-productive nature of knowledge and power within GIS. Early GIS and society researchers asked questions about who had *access* to geospatial technologies, and what implications this had for the production and consumption of geospatial data. Participatory GIS (PGIS) research sought to expand GIS access and expertise to new communities. These projects fused geospatial technologies with local forms of knowledge, to increase the power of that local knowledge across a broad range of governance processes.

Moving beyond physical access, geographers also asked what types of *epistemological biases* are more subtly and digitally built into GIS, and how these biases shape the types of knowledge that are rendered *visible* and *authoritative* with the technology. Feminist geographers described how the prevalence of quantitative geospatial methods and reliance on secondary sources within the discipline lead GIS practitioners to privilege a scientific and objective epistemological stance that is undergirded by masculinist logics (e.g., McLafferty, 2005). Indigenous research similarly criticized how Western epistemological frameworks make it difficult to represent the holistic, perspectival, and experiential aspects of indigenous knowledge of place within GIS (Young, 2016).

These same geographers went beyond negative critique to engage in applied projects that opened geospatial practices to new ways of knowing. Feminist GIS practitioners applied GIS to increase its ability to represent contextualized, relational, and gendered forms of spatial knowledge. In a related vein, qualitative GIS research sought to design technologies better capable of storing qualitative data and performing qualitative analysis. Indigenous scholars, often working under the banner of PGIS, explored the tensions and possibilities of combining GIS with indigenous knowledge of place. Despite variations across these projects, they all emphasized the ways in which digital knowledge politics spills out to have *broader political and material effects*.

Geospatial technologies have transformed dramatically over the past decade, with the explosion of Web 2.0 technologies, user-centred technology design and collaboration, mobile devices, and big data. Geographers began a new round of research under banners including the geospatial web (geoweb), volunteered geographic information (VGI), neogeography, new spatial media, and crowdsourcing (Elwood et al., 2012). This research has expanded beyond explicitly geospatial technologies to examine the algorithmic control of space, augmented reality, geographical imaginations across broader digital spaces, and more. The quantity of available data has expanded dramatically; the nature of epistemological authority has shifted; and the tactics used to intervene in uneven knowledge hierarchies have changed (Burns, 2015; Elwood and Leszczynski, 2013). Despite these shifts, the fundamental questions first posed within GIS and society debates – about who controls digital representations of the world, what types of knowledge have differential access to and authority within digital spaces, and how digital spaces might become more epistemologically pluralistic – remain as relevant as ever.

The remainder of this chapter examines three key areas of research related to these questions, all of which I situate within a case study of the digital knowledge politics of Arctic environmentalism. More specifically, I examine how Canadian Inuit, an Arctic indigenous people, have used digital technologies to increase the visibility of Inuit Qaujimaningit (IQ), or Inuit knowledge, in discussions of Arctic environmental management in the face of climate change. This is an ideal case study because it highlights the potentials and limitations of digital technologies for overcoming epistemological gaps in the transmission of knowledge. IQ differs in important ways from the Western epistemologies that more often drive international policy and pervade many digital spaces. However, Inuit are increasingly looking for avenues through which to inject IQ into discussions, and digital media have emerged as one important space.

ISSUES OF ACCESS: DIGITAL INFRASTRUCTURE AND MATERIAL INEQUALITIES

A key area of research into digital knowledge politics centres around the material accessibility of information and communication technologies. How does the accessibility of digital technologies make it easier for marginalized groups to consume and produce information, thereby engendering new political possibilities? How do digital infrastructures intersect with pre-existing material inequalities to shape these possibilities? Some scholars heralded the web as a space that would cultivate epistemological pluralism, precisely because it gave more groups the ability to widely broadcast their views to dispersed audiences (e.g., Warf and Sui, 2010). In the Canadian Arctic, for instance, Inuit are using digital technologies to improve their communication with other communities and with the Southern politicians that control Arctic policy. Given the high cost of travel within the Arctic, the ability to cheaply broadcast one's perspective has opened new political possibilities (Young, 2017).

However, digital divides also reproduce inequalities that shape knowledge politics. Structural inequalities shape access to the infrastructure, from hardware and software to technical training, that is necessary for effective digital participation (Crutcher and Zook, 2009; Gilbert and Masucci, 2011; Graham and Zook, 2013). The effects are multiple – unequal access produces inequalities in *whose knowledge* comes to represent the world, *which epistemological systems* those users can draw upon, and *which parts of the world* those users choose to represent. The Arctic case study highlights the complexity of this knowledge politics. The historical context of the Canadian Arctic is one of settler colonialism, which has produced contemporary issues of poverty, high living costs, and lack of necessary infrastructure (Stevenson, 2014). These issues extend to the quality of Arctic communications infrastructure. Communities are most often connected to the internet via a series of satellites that are in geostationary orbit over the Equator, rather than more effective fibre-optic cables (Young, 2017). Outdated equipment within the communities then provides the 'last mile' connection between homes and satellites. This infrastructure produces internet service that is slow and unreliable, yet also incredibly expensive. These factors directly prevent Inuit from participating in online discussions, sometimes forcing them to choose between paying for the internet or food (Young, 2017).

These material inequalities also subtly shape *which* Inuit engage with the internet, and *what types of knowledge* those Inuit share. Internet access in the Canadian Arctic is centralized within larger communities, meaning that Inuit living within those communities use the internet the most. Inuit who live outside of the communities – often elders and hunters – have far less access to the internet. These are also the Inuit who tend to hold the most IQ, since they maintain the land-based lifestyles and practices foundational to the acquisition of this knowledge. This makes it less likely that IQ will be represented online (Young, 2017). The high costs and lows speeds of Arctic internet cause many Inuit to adopt file formats that are not effective at communicating Inuit knowledge. IQ is strongly rooted in experiential forms of learning and oral storytelling in the Inuktitut language, both of which are best supported through audiovisual media. Petersen (2012) argues that low-bandwidth networks commit epistemic violence against Inuit since they force them to engage in text-based and representational forms of knowledge transmission. The intersection of material inequalities with digital infrastructure thereby makes it less likely that IQ-holders will access the internet and more difficult to communicate IQ if they do gain access.

EPISTEMOLOGICAL BIASES: ACCESS, VISIBILITY, AND AUTHORITY

When users have full access to material infrastructures, the customizability of digital media makes it relatively simple to display one's own opinions, interests, and knowledges using a wide variety of strategies. Questions remain, however, as to whether anyone will ever see and believe the knowledge that has been shared. Issues of digital access are not magically solved once an individual has connected to the internet (Graham, 2011). Rather, digital spaces themselves reproduce inequalities that impact the relative power of different types of knowledge claims. This shift can expand the power of some forms of knowledge – with the widespread availability of crowdsourcing applications, for instance, some local, non-expert views have been granted authority that was once reserved for scientific authorities. However, even these applications are built around epistemological frameworks that dictate who can participate, what types of knowledge are permissible, and how that knowledge should be formatted and aggregated to gain authority (Sieber and Haklay, 2015).

A key area of research thus centres around the digital mechanisms and practices that shape how knowledge comes to count (Elwood and Leszczynski, 2013). One's relative ability to participate in digital knowledge politics is affected by governance practices such as censorship, the legal terms of use of websites and applications, cultural and linguistic norms, the opaque operation of algorithmic sorting processes, the representational practices of other digital users, and much more (Ballatore et al., 2017; Elwood and Leszczynski, 2011; Leszczynski, 2012). These factors determine what types of knowledge can be easily contributed, and shape the visibility and authority of that knowledge. The inverse is also true – these factors shape how easy it is to exclude, invisibilize, and delegitimize knowledge claims (Thatcher et al., 2016; Young and Gilmore, 2014). As Burns (2014: 53) points out, knowledge politics functions 'not simply through making knowledge visible, but also through the struggle for control of the *terms* of visibility'.

These processes are highlighted when comparing the relative access, visibility, and authority that IQ-based claims and Western scientific claims have across digital spaces. Young (2017) describes how digital norms and practices deter Inuit from contributing IQ-based environmental knowledge within highly visible digital platforms. Inuit feel uniquely constrained by the norms of antagonistic engagement built into these spaces. Antagonistic behaviour, like trolling, is rooted in partisan and masculinist forms of Western culture, runs counter to Inuit political norms of respectful consensus-building, and exacerbates ongoing mental health issues embedded within colonial histories (Phillips, 2016; Porter, 2017; Young, 2017). These norms dissuade Inuit from participating in sensitive environmental discussions, even when they believe they are being misrepresented. The prevalence of written English also makes the expression of IQ more difficult. Elders, shamans, and hunters are less likely to speak English, but also most likely to hold IQ. Furthermore, the translation of Inuktitut into English often strips Inuit environmental concepts of their holistic aspects, meaning that translations are likely to disadvantage attempts to express IQ (Cameron et al., 2015). These norms lead Inuit to participate more actively within sites that are oriented specifically towards Inuit, rather than within more globally visible sites. More globally visible sites tend to contain mostly knowledge claims based on Western scientific studies of the Arctic (Young, 2017). This balkanization decreases the likelihood of interepistemological discussions across knowledge systems, shields Western scientific studies from IQ-based critiques, and reinforces the hegemony of Western thinking.

Other practices ensure that IQ remains marginalized even when it is visible. The most visible digital representations of the Arctic erase Inuit and evacuate the environment of its social dimensions. By depicting the environment as a barren set of biological materialities, these representations undercut the need for a system, like IQ, that can engage with the normative and social aspects of environmental change. Many sites utilize citation practices that implicitly normalize Western scientific understandings of knowledge production. Wikipedia offers one of the most overt examples. The site requires users to draw only upon 'reliable' sources, defined as published and unbiased secondary sources. This functionally excludes the personal and experiential perspective built into IQ, particularly when IQ is passed along via oral tradition rather than in published publications (Young, 2016). When Inuit knowledge is included within digital discussions, it is most often framed as an individual and anecdotal observation of the material environment. These observations are thus severed from the broader and more holistic epistemological system from which they emerged. IQ-based knowledge can then be aggregated with other observations of the environment and interpreted through a Western scientific framework (Young, 2017). In this instance, the framing of IQ as a form of crowdsourced information undermines its epistemological foundations. When these representational techniques fail to co-opt IQ-based critiques of environmental management, Inuit are further delegitimized by being racialized and described as corrupt or primitive. Taken together, these techniques limit the visibility and authority of IQ, and ensure that it can be subordinated to Western knowledge frameworks.

THE BROADER POLITICAL AND MATERIAL EFFECTS OF DIGITAL KNOWLEDGE

A final area of research explores the effects that digital knowledge has on other political processes and material inequalities. Once knowledge has become digitized, represented, and communicated via digital media, what impact does it have upon the world? There is some debate around the degree to which the consumption of digital knowledge affects material action. Activist groups and politicians alike are increasingly adopting social media platforms to produce and consume information, network with others, manipulate public opinion, and mobilize political action. Some researchers, though, question whether these practices reliably produce more efficient forms of activism and governance, or simply a highly visible form of slacktivism that achieves little (e.g., Christensen, 2011). Researchers further ask whether digital media lead individuals to consider new political positions and perspectives, or simply act as balkanized echo chambers that reinforce already held beliefs and partisan behaviour (e.g., Bennett and Iyengar, 2008). At a micropolitical level, there is more consensus that the utilization of digital technologies for everyday tasks – from the use of Google Maps to the adoption of personal fitness trackers – has transformed how people understand and act within the world (e.g., Graham and Zook, 2013). Central to this analysis is an examination of how digital knowledge politics produces both empowering and marginalizing forms of material politics.

Early research was exuberantly optimistic about the empowering aspects of digital knowledge. Digital applications have proven capable of improving the political knowledge and efficacy of citizens, facilitating democratic deliberation, improving governance processes and the provision of basic services, and even allowing citizens to protest against inequality and oppose authoritarian regimes (e.g., Freelon et al., 2012; Livingston and Walter-Drop, 2012; Ruijgrok, 2017). On an economic front, the open production of digital knowledge can help to undermine certain proprietary business models, thereby opening new and more communally-oriented economic paradigms (Benkler, 2006). Returning to this chapter's Arctic case study, Inuit have used digital technologies to support inter-community solidarity-building and cultural regeneration, improve their capacity to consult over economic development projects, reach out to national and international government actors, and more (McMahon, 2013; Young, 2017).

Other research focuses on how the expansion of digital knowledge is generating marginalizing and disciplinary relationships. Digital technologies have expanded the scale and locations of surveillance, and proven effective at proliferating normalized representations of the world that affect how people behave (Graham et al., 2013). These processes often reinforce the spread of unjust and violent systems including racism, masculinity, and neoliberal governmentality (e.g., Leszczynski, 2014; Stephens, 2013). It is in this sense that digital technologies increase the unequal dominance of certain epistemes and subject-positions in the world (Graham et al., 2013). In the Arctic, these processes extend logics of colonialism by undermining Inuit culture and knowledge. Pasch (2008) argues that the prevalence of English on social media sites exerts assimilatory pressure on Inuit through the erosion of the Inuktitut language. Inuit are forced to express their thoughts using a colonial language and lose familiarity with their own language.

Young (2017) similarly finds that the spatialities and logics of digital technologies erode social practices and sites critical to the transmission of IQ. He finds that the centralization of internet within the home has led Inuit to spend less time socializing with one another in person, less time visiting elders outside of the community, and less time travelling out on the land or hunting. When Inuit are out on the land, their continued use of digital technologies is retraining Inuit bodies and eyes as they interact with the environment. Elders worry that the increased use of GPS technology is undermining Inuit abilities to safely navigate the ice (Young, 2017). They fear that the experiential and embodied forms of learning that underlie IQ are thereby being replaced by instrumental and representational forms of knowledge transmission. Others worry that Inuit youth are too often staring at their mobile devices rather than looking at the land, hearing the environment, listening to elders, or practising skills (Young, 2017). In each case, engagement with digital framings of the world is subtly injecting Western epistemologies into the everyday lives of Inuit.

CONCLUSION

Digital knowledge politics will continue to transform with the development of new technologies and technological practices. The expansion of augmented reality, wearable devices, the internet of things, and other technological forms will expand the availability of digital data and continue to blend digital and material worlds. As such, each of the areas discussed above will continue to offer new research possibilities. By way of conclusion, I identify newly emerging issues that will shape future research questions. First, the global ascendancy of post-truth politics has increased interest in how digital media are facilitating the erosion of the importance of truth in political debate, the popularization of new political movements, and increasing partisanship. This presents opportunities for digital researchers, both to analyse the role of digital technologies in transforming how truth matters in politics and to develop digital methodologies for exploring broader sets of knowledge politics. Second, the continued expansion of digital infrastructures to new global spaces provides opportunities for examining global sets of knowledge politics between very different epistemological systems. Geography research has focused primarily on the digital practices of a rather narrow group of elite users in the global North, which hinders rigorous understanding of digital encounters across very different cultural and epistemological systems. Expansion of the research agenda, to include more projects in the global South, and examinations of international dialogue between the global North and South, will overcome these research gaps. This will be particularly useful for understanding the role of digital knowledge politics related to partisan geopolitical issues, from climate change to globalization.

Finally, just as critical GIS researchers developed applied projects for expanding the accessibility and epistemological openness of GIS, there is room for geographers to engage in applied projects to intervene within digital knowledge politics. What types of digital mapping platforms or geolocational services might be developed to increase epistemologically pluralistic discussions, empower marginalized perspectives, overcome political partisanship through interepistemological dialogue, and reduce material inequalities? This research area will help geographers not only to better understand but also to shape digital knowledge politics.

REFERENCES

Ballatore, A., Graham, M. and Sen, S. (2017) 'Digital hegemonies: The localness of search engine results', *Annals of the American Association of Geographers*, 107(5): 1194–1215.

Benkler, Y. (2006) *The Wealth of Networks*. New Haven, CT: Yale University Press.

Bennett, W.L. and Iyengar, S. (2008) 'A new era of minimal effects? The changing foundations of political communication', *Journal of Communication*, 58(4): 707–731.

Bennett, W.L. and Segerberg, A. (2013) *The Logic of Connective Action*. Cambridge: Cambridge University Press.

Burns, R. (2014) 'Moments of closure in the knowledge politics of digital humanitarianism', *Geoforum*, 53: 51–62.

Burns, R. (2015) 'Rethinking big data in digital humanitarianism', *GeoJournal*, 80(4): 477–490.

Cameron, E., Mearns, R. and McGrath, J.T. (2015) 'Translating climate change: Adaptation, resilience, and climate politics in Nunavut, Canada', *Annals of the Association of American Geographers*, 105(2): 274–283.

Castells, M. (ed.) (2004) *The Network Society: A Cross-Cultural Perspective*. Cheltenham: Edward Elgar.

Christensen, H. (2011) 'Political activities on the Internet: Slacktivism or political participation by other means?', *First Monday*, 16(2). Available at: http://firstmonday.org/article/view/3336/2767 (accessed 4 February 2018).

Crutcher, M. and Zook, M. (2009) 'Placemarks and waterlines: Racialized cyberscapes in post-Katrina Google Earth', *GeoForum*, 40(4): 523–534.

Elwood, S. (2010) 'Geographic information science: Emerging research on the societal implications of the geospatial web', *Progress in Human Geography*, 34(3): 349–357.

Elwood, S. and Leszczynski, A. (2011) 'Privacy, reconsidered: New representations, data practices, and the geoweb', *Geoforum*, 42(1): 6–15.

Elwood, S. and Leszczynski, A. (2013) 'New spatial media, new knowledge politics', *Transactions of the Institute of British Geographers*, 38(4): 544–559.

Elwood, S., Goodchild, M. and Sui, D. (2012) 'Researching volunteered geographic information: Spatial data, geographic research, and new social practice', *Annals of the Association of American Geographers*, 102(3): 571–590.

Freelon, D., Kriplean, T., Morgan, J., Bennett, W.L. and Borning, A. (2012) 'Facilitating diverse political engagement with the Living Voters Guide', *Journal of Information Technology & Politics*, 9(3): 279–297.

Gilbert, M. and Masucci, M. (2011) *Information and Communication Technology Geographies: Strategies for Bridging the Digital Divide*. Kelowna, BC: Praxis (e)Press. Available at: www.praxis-epress.org/ICT/ictgeographies.pdf (accessed 4 February 2018).

Graham, M. (2011) 'Time machines and virtual portals: The spatialities of the digital divide', *Progress in Development Studies*, 11(3): 211–227.

Graham, M. and Zook, M. (2013) 'Augmented realities and uneven geographies: Exploring the geo-linguistic contours of the web', *Environment and Planning A*, 45(1): 77–99.

Graham, M., Zook, M. and Boulton, A. (2013) 'Augmented reality in urban places: Contested content and the duplicity of code', *Transactions of the Institute of British Geographers*, 38(3): 464–497.

Leszczynski, A. (2012) 'Situating the geoweb in political economy', *Progress in Human Geography*, 36(1): 72–89.

Leszczynski, A. (2014) 'On the neo in neogeography', *Annals of the Association of American Geographers*, 104(1): 60–79.

Livingston, S. and Walter-Drop, G. (2012) 'Information and communication technologies in areas of limited statehood', SFB-Governance Working Paper Series Volume 38. Berlin: Research Center (SFB) 700. Available at: www.files.ethz.ch/isn/154055/WP38.pdf (accessed 4 February 2018).

McLafferty, S. (2005) 'Women and GIS: Geospatial technologies and feminist geographies', *Cartographica*, 40(4): 37–45.

McMahon, R. (2013) 'Digital self-determination: Aboriginal peoples and the network society in Canada'. Doctoral dissertation, Simon Fraser University.

Pasch, T. (2008) 'Inuktitut online in Nunavik: Mixed-methods web-based strategies for preserving Aboriginal and minority languages'. Doctoral dissertation, University of Washington.

Petersen, R. (2012) 'Decolonizing the digital North', *Global Native Networks*, 10 October. Available at: https://globalnativenetworks.wordpress.com/2012/10/10/decolonizing-the-digital-north-why-inuit-need-better-broadband-now (accessed 4 August 2016).

Phillips, W. (2016) *This Is Why We Can't Have Nice Things: Mapping the Relationship Between Online Trolling and Mainstream Culture*. Cambridge, MA: MIT Press.

Porter, J. (2017) '"Go kill yourself": Social media messages encourage Indigenous youth to commit suicide', *CBC News*, 3 February. Available at: www.cbc.ca/news/canada/thunder-bay/social-media-suicide-1.3963322 (accessed 25 February 2017).

Ruijgrok, K. (2017) 'From the web to the streets', *Democratization*, 24(3): 498–520.

Sheppard, E. (1995) 'GIS and society: Towards a research agenda', *Cartography and Geographic Information Systems*, 22(1): 5–16.

Sieber, R. and Haklay, M. (2015) 'The epistemology(s) of volunteered geographic information: A critique', *Geo: Geography and Environment*, 2(2): 122–136.

Stephens, M. (2013) 'Gender and the geoweb: Divisions in the production of user-generated cartographic information', *GeoJournal*, 78(6): 981–996.

Stevenson, L. (2014) *Life Beside Itself: Imagining Care in the Canadian Arctic*. Berkeley: University of California Press.

Thatcher, J., O'Sullivan, D. and Mahmoudi, D. (2016) 'Data colonialism through accumulation by dispossession', *Environment and Planning D: Society and Space*, 34(6): 990–1006.

Warf, B. and Sui, D. (2010) 'From GIS to neogeography: Ontological implications and theories of truth,' *Annals of GIS*, 16(4): 197–209.

Young, J. (2016) 'Polar bear management in a digital Arctic', *The Canadian Geographer/Le Géographe canadien*, 60(4): 466–478.

Young, J. (2017) 'Encounters across difference: The digital geographies of Inuit, the Arctic, and environmental management'. Doctoral dissertation, University of Washington.

Young, J. and Gilmore, M. (2014) 'Subaltern empowerment in the geoweb', *Antipode*, 46(2): 574–591.

25

GEOPOLITICS

Jeremy W. Crampton

GEOPOLITICS AND DIGITAL GEOGRAPHIES

In this chapter I examine relationships between geopolitics and digital geographies. Geopolitics here consists of both state and corporate deployment of forms of governance, political policy, and international relations, particularly at the international (state-to-state) level. It is therefore often about power. However, it is not only about the centre exercising power over the periphery; tactics and procedures can boomerang back, or indeed be resisted and overcome. A signature aspect of digital geographies is also that they need not occur only at the state level – there are many ways in which they operate 'beyond the state'. For example, police departments may adopt technologies such as drones and spatial analytics which were originally developed by government. Commercial entities are as important as the state, if not in fact a form of neoliberal extension of the state. Finally, some 'everyday' digital geopolitics have attracted attention in videogames (Bos, 2016).

HISTORY

The relationship between geopolitics and digital geographies is not separable from the history of computing. Computers, and after World War II digital computing, arose to meet government requirements for encryption/decryption, calculation of missile trajectories, weather predictions during wartime, and analysis of data. Although computers came into their own during the second half of the twentieth century, a remarkable precursor was developed a century earlier: the Difference Engine developed by Charles Babbage and explained and promoted by the mathematician Ada Lovelace. Babbage began developing the Difference Engine in 1823 (and the Analytical Engine in 1833) to calculate mathematical tables for navigation and astronomy. A maritime economy, Britain relied on the production of timely and accurate tables, which had previously been calculated by hand – a tedious and slow process. Lovelace's notes on the Analytical Engine included an algorithm for the calculation of a certain class of numbers known as Bernoulli numbers, and this is considered the first published algorithm for a computer.

Although Babbage's Engines were not digital, they embodied 'almost all the functions of a modern digital computer' because they could be programmed (Campbell-Kelly et al., 2014: 42). Babbage was inspired by the Jacquard loom, a process for weaving textiles in any pattern using punch cards. This punch-card solution was later adopted by Hermann Hollerith who invented a scheme to tabulate census returns for the US Census of 1890 – a card for each citizen. Hollerith's company eventually became IBM, and the era of mass information processing was born.

But it was developments during World War II that properly launched the deep connection between the digital and geopolitics. Two in particular were critical: a theory of information (Shannon, 1948) and a theory of computing intelligence (Turing, 1950). This notion of intelligence is still with us today as geographical intelligence or GEOINT (the term was coined after 9/11 but has long historical antecedents). Turing's question 'can machines think?' lies at the heart of today's efforts towards machine learning, big data, and algorithms. Shannon's paper showed that information could be calculable, which meant it could be collected, measured, analysed, and communicated. Wartime computer developments in the USA (the Mark I computer at Harvard) and the UK (the work of Turing and colleagues at Bletchley Park to decrypt German Enigma ciphers) exemplified these developments, but it was the idea that was important, rather than the technology.

The idea – the dream – was governing via information and it was not new. The first rush to big data occurred in the nineteenth century; in 'the avalanche of printed numbers' (Hacking, 1982) and the rise of something called 'state-istics' (statistics) (Shaw and Miles, 1979). Today's urban dashboards (Mattern, 2015) have their roots in the same impulse (Medina, 2011). Dashboards (or big data) are never just a technical achievement but depend upon and exercise power (Kitchin et al., 2016).

Central to the success of both are data themselves. Data collection in quantity arguably began during the Cold War (Farish, 2010; Barney, 2014), first as analogue (film) and later digital. The US Corona programme, for example, was a top-secret effort to acquire imagery over the 'denied territory' of the Soviet Union (Cloud, 2001; Dalton, 2013). Acquired by reconnaissance satellites, the resulting data led to a reassessment of the 'missile gap' in the early 1960s, markedly changing America's foreign policy posture. A new classified agency was established in 1961 to manage these assets, the National Reconnaissance Office, with a budget today of more than $10 billion (Richelson, 2012; Gellman and Miller, 2013). This joined the geography intelligence agency, the National Geospatial-Intelligence Agency (NGA), with a budget of about $3 billion. Over the course of the Cold War, the USA developed ever-improving capabilities in remote sensing or intelligence, surveillance, and reconnaissance. Almost all of these data are digital and can be collected and analysed in real-time.

Over the past couple of decades, a number of corporate actors have become important in GEOINT. Satellites and rocket launchers are expensive, but with declining budgets after the Cold War several companies entered private–public agreements. One such is the United Launch Alliance, founded in 2006 by long-time military contractors Boeing and Lockheed Martin to provide space launch capabilities for the US government. In the meantime, products from commercial reconnaissance satellite companies such as DigitalGlobe which offer sub-metre resolution have been legally allowed to reach the market. Smaller satellites and reusable launchers have been developed by other companies, most notably SpaceX, which in 2016 launched its first GPS satellite. The wide-scale collection of digital spatial data is now entirely one of military–corporate agreements and contracts (Crampton et al., 2014).

A good example is Google Earth. Google did not originate this product, but bought it from a company called Keyhole in 2004 which had a 3D digital earth called EarthViewer (Crampton, 2008). Keyhole refers to the secret US reconnaissance satellite programme; codeword access to GEOINT intelligence is still designated TALENT-KEYHOLE. In the meantime, the CIA's venture capital investment arm In-Q-Tel provided funds in 2003 to Keyhole on behalf of the geospatial intelligence agency in order to support the US war in Iraq (In-Q-Tel, 2003).

A parallel development for the collection of geospatial data by government has been the proliferation of unmanned aerial vehicles (UAVs, or drones). Drones have a surprisingly long history. Undirected balloons were used in the American Civil War for aerial surveillance of enemy positions, while significant innovations in remotely controlled aircraft go back to World War I, such as the Dayton-Wright 'Kettering Bug'. During World War II, remotely piloted bomb delivery systems were developed. During the Vietnam War, drones were essential for performing bomb damage assessments (Ehrhard, 2010).

But it was the 1980s that saw the rise of the drone as a true weapon (rather than a retrofitted airplane), and the origins of drones like the Predator. Although Predator drones (officially designated the MQ-1) are now best known for their deployment in Afghanistan by the US military, and clandestinely in Pakistan and Yemen by the CIA, they were developed well before 9/11. After seeing deployments in Bosnia during the mid-1990s (Richelson, 2012), the Predator was first flown over Afghanistan in 2000 by the CIA. Immediately after 9/11 (October) the first armed drones were deployed, and were used to strike against a known associate of bin Laden (Schmitt, 2002). US spending on drones has ballooned from $284 million in fiscal year (FY) 2000 to $3.3 billion in FY2010 (Gertler, 2012).

Shaw (2016, 2017) argues that today's drones are socio-technical projections of empire, securing faraway spaces, reconnoitring and surveilling for purposes of force projection. During the Bush and Obama administrations, a new geopolitical policy of drone strikes was originated known as 'signature strikes' which did not require the identification of individuals. Rather, an analysis of behaviour, movements, and encounters would be performed based on multiple sources of intelligence, including drone reconnaissance in specific spatial locales occupied by militants. A related term is 'activity-based intelligence' (Phillips, 2014). According to Chamayou (2015), this strategy not only entails the projection of warfare into all spaces or what Gregory (2011) calls the 'everywhere war', but also erases the boundary between combatant and non-combatant, such that all are potentially dangerous and therefore in need of mass surveillance.

These technologies habitually boomerang back from the battlefield to the heartland (Stoler, 1995; McCoy et al., 2012). As Shaw (2017: 3) writes, 'the electronic battlefield, born in the mud and blood of Vietnam, has seeped into the bedrock of the modern smart city – which now seeks to sense and track our intimate mobilities'.

DEBATES

In this section I discuss three important debates: connections between military, commercial, and academic practices; trends towards loss of privacy and mass surveillance; and the power of automated and algorithmic regimes to manage and govern life.

Even before Eisenhower's famous 1961 warning about the burgeoning military–industrial complex, the ties between the US military and non-military contractors were often regarded with suspicion. In the American Civil War, for example, the US government contracted for military uniforms and the items sent were often made from 'shoddy' scraps of fabric that fell apart, giving rise to the modern meaning of the word as inferior (Nagle, 1999).

Between FY2000 and FY2012 the Pentagon spent more than $3.75 trillion on contracts with over 50,000 companies (Crampton et al., 2014). One of the key issues in this relationship is how geographical information/intelligence is acquired, accessed, and protected. As Stanger (2011) notes, when information is privatized, legal oversight is diminished, and may be further hidden through sub-contracts. In the USA, for example, the Freedom of Information Act does not cover information outside government (and within government only to executive branch agencies;

thus Congress is exempt). Such shifts from government to the corporate world of key government activities has been a focus of widespread debate, for example on the neoliberalization of democracy (Peck, 2014).

Where geographic data have been militarized or weaponized, authors have argued that this may problematically advance state interests at the expense of civilians (Bryan and Wood, 2015). But concerns also lie in the reverse direction, where portions of the massive amounts of corporately collected data on individuals become accessible to government. As was revealed in the Snowden documents and the media reporting on government warrantless wiretaps after 9/11 (Risen and Lichtblau, 2005; Risen, 2006), the US government collects metadata on all US phone calls, and is authorized to collect internet communications (under section 702 of the FISA Amendment Act of 2008, i.e., the PRISM programme). In response, privacy advocates have argued that strong encryption is necessary in the digital era, such that even telecommunications providers cannot decrypt messages – or, as in the case of the San Bernardino iPhone, unlock it at the government's request (the latter became moot when the FBI paid a third party to unlock the phone after Apple had refused to do so). History teaches us, however, that this is likely to be an ongoing debate. The 'clipper chip' controversy during the early 1990s resulted in a victory for digital privacy advocates when government plans for a 'back-door' into encryption were defeated. But in the wake of 9/11 and more recent terrorist attacks both in Europe and the USA, governments are re-examining digital rights to privacy, and may implement a similar decryption capability. Geolocational data are at the heart of this question, given its extremely revealing nature. The US Supreme Court decided in 2012 that a warrant was required to track a suspect with a GPS device (*US v. Jones*), and in another case will consider whether a warrant is needed to search locational data on a phone (*Carpenter v. US*).

Debates have also circulated around what are perceived to be increasing linkages between government (specifically the military) and academia. In terms of mapping and GIS, for instance, this has meant the proliferation of curricula that are designed around GEOINT, such as the USGIF GEOINT certificates. The USGIF is a non-profit that situates itself between academia, government, and industry with a board of directors drawing from the Department of Defense (DoD), NGA, academia, and corporate consultancies. Historically, academics have long contributed to the military, especially during wartime. Geography (especially GIS and mapping) has deep ties to national security, the military, and law enforcement and much of this draws on digital geographies. For example, predictive policing uses spatial analytics and digital mapping to identify future crime patterns. And according to a recent study, much of the $3 billion annually given to the top 100 most militarized universities is for research on 'intelligence technologies, cyber security, and big data analytics' (Arkin and O'Brien, 2015). The US GPS (known as Navstar), which is the basis of much geotagged data, was developed by the Pentagon. These linkages continue to be areas of debate around the influence on academia.

The third area of debate about digital geographies identified here is what has become known as algorithmic governance, or the increasing tendency to rely on machine learning, artificial intelligence, and algorithms for decision-making about aspects of human life (see Chapter 21). For Rouvroy and Berns (2013), algorithmic governance comprises three 'stages': the data double; the production of knowledge; and finally, action on behaviours (see also Amoore, 2017). Smart cities, big data, business intelligence and data governance all rely on and prioritize the digital. This topic is discussed in more depth elsewhere in this volume, but issues of debate include how representative are the data doubles (Leszczynski, 2017a), what is the nature of machine control (Deleuze, 1992; Sadowski and Pasquale, 2015), and how big a factor is machine bias (Angwin et al., 2016).

For digital geographies no issue is more important than surveillance and privacy (Leszczynski, 2017b). While some research has explored spatial masking for aggregate data (Kwan et al., 2004; Clarke, 2016), at the same time there are developments in facial-recognition technologies that unmask identities. In May 2016 the United States Government Accountability Office issued a report about the FBI's use of face recognition, which comprised more than 412 million images, mostly acquired through agreements with police departments and driving licences, but which suffered from numerous problems, including informed consent. Another government study of commercially available face-recognition algorithms noted that false positive identification (where an individual in a database is incorrectly identified) is just as concerning as false negatives (where an identification is missed), given that most police databases are racially unrepresentative (Grother et al., 2017). The report notes that false positives can be significantly reduced by the addition of location data. This suggests that real-time geolocational tracking of populations will become a desideratum of the state (via street cameras, police dash- and body-cams, or other mechanisms), and therefore this topic will likely remain of interest to digital geography studies.

FUTURE DEVELOPMENTS

In this section I conclude with a few indications of what are likely to be topics of concern in digital geographies. These are not prognostications – given the field's rapidly moving subject matter – but rather areas that already require attention. Following the concluding remarks of the previous section, we can identify *geosurveillance* as a likely continued topic for research. As the interoperable network of environmental sensors, analytics, and algorithms gets built out in smart cities and the internet of things (IoT), an issue for digital geographies will be the way that public space is increasingly privatized and surveilled. With reference to drones, for example, there are proposals to privatize the atmosphere (which is, above a certain height, the public domain) with 'drone lanes' by Amazon, although this has yet to develop. Facial-recognition technology is not only used to identify and track individuals. One study, for example, used algorithmic analyses of geotagged faces on Flickr to map the 'typical face' geographically (Islam et al., 2015). Such a study (which was funded by the DoD) could no doubt also be used to determine who is 'out of place'. In 2013, the intelligence community's IARPA announced its Janus Project to improve facial recognition by (in part) leveraging spatial information to create a 'face space', drawing on big datasets of faces 'in the wild' (not posed but captured from news media and other real-world sources).

A second area likely to interest digital geographers is the nature and prevalence of open or closed data. While a number of cities and governments provide open access to some geospatial data (e.g., OpenDataPhilly, the US Census), will it be the case, as the IoT becomes more corporatized, that databases will disappear into proprietary archives? Who has the right to these data? Indeed, are 'digital rights' (and digital rights management) the best way to frame this issue (Elwood and Leszczynski, 2011)? What are the tensions between public and private (Young and Gilmore, 2014; Zook et al., 2017)?

Finally, given the increasing reliance on digital technologies, a huge area of potential concern is cyber warfare, hacking, intrusion, and data breaches. As security expert Bruce Schneier (2017) framed it, with the IoT 'we're building a world-size robot'. Each device is networked to other devices, and security can only be as good as the weakest link in the chain. Reports of unpatched nanny cams, digital video recorders, modems, and even vehicles being captured into botnets are now routine. Cyber warfare is to some extent the issue of encryption (cyber vulnerabilities are in part encryption vulnerabilities). Cyber warfare is defined as offensive and defensive measures designed to achieve superiority of control of cyberspace (internet, networks, software, and hardware) or parts thereof. International political cooperation will be required to address these problems.

Although cyber warfare is often thought of as an activity practised by the state, attacks against corporations and the theft of credit card data can also be considered attacks against state sovereignty and symbols of statehood, and, hence, cyber warfare (Kaiser, 2015). Vulnerabilities to attack and their geographies include geostrategic chokepoints where the cables that carry the bulk of internet traffic come to shore (a modern digital equivalent perhaps of the Mackinder map!), the geographies of attacks and botnets that enable 'ransomware' such as the 'WannaCry' attack of early 2017, and the collateral damage from 0-day worms and viruses such as the US/Israeli-developed Stuxnet attack on Iran's nuclear reactors. As the British politician Tony Benn remarked, in the face of power, ask five questions: 'What power have you got? Where did you get it from? In whose interests do you exercise it? To whom are you accountable? And how can we get rid of you?' (Benn, 2001). All of these are critical for understanding today's geopolitics of digital geography.

REFERENCES

Amoore, L. (2017) 'What does it mean to govern with algorithms?', *AntipodeFoundation.org*, 19 May. Available at: https://radicalantipode.files.wordpress.com/2017/05/2-louise-amoore.pdf (accessed 5 February 2018).

Angwin, J., Larson, J., Mattu, S. and Kirchner, L. (2016) 'Machine bias', *ProPublica*, 23 May. Available at: www.propublica.org/article/machine-bias-risk-assessments-in-criminal-sentencing (accessed 5 February 2018).

Arkin, W.M. and O'Brien, A. (2015) 'The most militarized universities in America: A VICE News investigation', *Vice News*, 6 November. Available at: https://news.vice.com/article/the-most-militarized-universities-in-america-a-vice-news-investigation (accessed 5 February 2018).

Barney, T. (2014) *Mapping the Cold War*. Chapel Hill: University of North Carolina Press.

Benn, T. (2001) 'Address to Parliament', *Hansard*, 22 March. Available at: https://publications.parliament.uk/pa/cm200001/cmhansrd/vo010322/debtext/10322-13.htm (accessed 5 February 2018).

Bos, D. (2016) 'Critical methodologies for researching military-themed videogames', in A.J. Williams, N. Jenkings, R. Woodward and M.F. Rech (eds), *The Routledge Companion to Military Research Methods*. New York: Routledge. pp. 332–344.

Bryan, J. and Wood, D. (2015) *Weaponizing Maps*. New York: Guilford Press.

Campbell-Kelly, M., Aspray, W., Ensmenger, N. and Yost, J.R. (2014) *Computer: A History of the Information Machine*, 3rd edn. Boulder, CO: Westview Press.

Chamayou, G. (2015) *Theory of the Drone*. New York: New Press.

Clarke, K.C. (2016) 'A multiscale masking method for point geographic data', *International Journal of Geographical Information Science*, 30(2): 300–315.

Cloud, J. (2001) 'Essay review: Hidden in plain sight. The CORONA reconnaissance satellite programme and clandestine cold war science', *Annals of Science*, 58(2): 203.

Crampton, J.W. (2008) 'Keyhole, Google Earth, and 3D worlds: An interview with Avi Bar-Zeev', *Cartographica*, 43(2): 85–93.

Crampton, J.W., Roberts, S. and Poorthuis, A. (2014) 'The new political economy of geographic intelligence', *Annals of the Association of American Geographers*, 104(1): 196–214.

Dalton, C.M. (2013) 'Sovereigns, spooks, and hackers: An early history of Google geo services and map mashups', *Cartographica*, 48(4): 261–274.

Deleuze, G. (1992) 'Postscript on the societies of control', *October*, 59 (Winter): 3–7.

Ehrhard, T.P. (2010) *Air Force UAVs: The Secret History*. Arlington, VA: Mitchell Institute Press.

Elwood, S. and Leszczynski, A. (2011) 'Privacy, reconsidered: New representations, data practices, and the geoweb', *Geoforum*, 42(1): 6–15.

Farish, M. (2010) *The Contours of America's Cold War*. Minneapolis: University of Minnesota Press.

Gellman, B. and Miller, G. (2013) '"Black budget" summary details US spy network's successes, failures and objectives', *Washington Post*, 29 August. Available at: http://wapo.st/2K3oVyc (accessed 5 February 2018).

Gertler, J. (2012) *US Unmanned Aerial Systems*. Washington, DC: Congressional Research Service.

Gregory, D. (2011) 'The everywhere war', *Geographical Journal*, 177(3): 238–250.

Grother, P., Quinn, G. and Ngan, M. (2017) *Face in Video Evaluation (FIVE): Face Recognition of Non-Cooperative Subjects*. Washington, DC: NIST.

Hacking, I. (1982) 'Biopower and the avalanche of printed numbers', *Humanities in Society*, 5: 279–295.

In-Q-Tel (2003) 'In-Q-Tel announces strategic investment in Keyhole', *In-Q-Tel*, 25 June. Available at: www.iqt.org/in-q-tel-announces-strategic-investment-in-keyhole (accessed 5 February 2018).

Islam, M.T., Greenwell, C., Souvenir, R. and Jacobs, N. (2015) 'Large-scale geo-facial image analysis', *EURASIP Journal on Image and Video Processing*, 2015: 17.

Kaiser, R. (2015) 'The birth of cyberwar', *Political Geography*, 46: 11–20.

Kitchin, R., Maalsen, S. and McArdle, G. (2016) 'The praxis and politics of building urban dashboards', *Geoforum*, 77: 93–101.

Kwan, M.P., Casas, I. and Schmitz, B.C. (2004) 'Protection of geoprivacy and accuracy of spatial information: How effective are geographical masks?', *Cartographica*, 39(2): 15–28.

Leszczynski, A. (2017a) 'Digital methods I: Wicked tensions', *Progress in Human Geography*. DOI: 10.1177/0309132517711779.

Leszczynski, A. (2017b) 'Geoprivacy', in R. Kitchin, T. Lauriault and M. Wilson (eds), *Understanding Spatial Media*. London: Sage. pp. 235–244.

Mattern, S. (2015) 'Mission control: A history of the urban dashboard', *Places Journal* (March). Available at: https://placesjournal.org/article/mission-control-a-history-of-the-urban-dashboard (accessed 5 February 2018).

McCoy, A.W., Fradera, J.M. and Jacobson, S. (eds) (2012) *Endless Empire: Spain's Retreat, Europe's Eclipse, America's Decline*. Madison: University of Wisconsin Press.

Medina, E. (2011) *Cybernetic Revolutionaries: Technology and Politics in Allende's Chile*. Cambridge, MA: MIT Press.

Nagle, J.F. (1999) *A History of Government Contracting*, 2nd edn. Washington, DC: George Washington University Law School, Government Contracts Program.

Peck, J. (2014) *Constructions of Neoliberal Reason*. Oxford: Oxford University Press.

Phillips, M. (2014) 'A brief overview of activity based intelligence and human domain analytics', in D.G. Murdock, R.R. Tomes and C.K. Tucker (eds), *Human Geography: Socio-Cultural Dynamics and Challenges to Global Security*. Herndon, VA: United States Geospatial Intelligence Foundation. pp. 219–224.

Richelson, J.T. (2012) *The US Intelligence Community*, 6th edn. Boulder, CO: Westview Press.

Risen, J. (2006) *State of War: The Secret History of the CIA and the Bush Administration*. New York: Free Press.

Risen, J. and Lichtblau, E. (2005) 'Bush lets US spy on callers without courts', *New York Times*, 16 December. Available at: www.nytimes.com/2005/12/16/politics/bush-lets-us-spy-on-callers-without-courts.html (accessed 5 February 2018).

Rouvroy, A. and Berns, T. (2013) 'Algorithmic governmentality and prospects of emancipation: Disparateness as a precondition for individuation through relationships?' *Réseaux*, 177: 163–196.

Sadowski, J. and Pasquale, F. (2015) 'The spectrum of control: A social theory of the smart city', *First Monday*, 20(7). Available at: http://firstmonday.org/article/view/5903/4660 (accessed 5 February 2018).

Schmitt, E. (2002) 'Threats and responses: The battlefield; US would use drones to attack Iraqi targets', *New York Times*, 6 November. Available at: www.nytimes.com/2002/11/06/world/threats-responses-battlefield-us-would-use-drones-attack-iraqi-targets.html (accessed 5 February 2018).

Schneier, B. (2017) 'Click here to kill everyone', *New York Magazine*, 17 January. Available at: http://nymag.com/selectall/2017/01/the-internet-of-things-dangerous-future-bruce-schneier.html (accessed 5 February 2018).

Shannon, C. (1948) 'A mathematical theory of communication', *Bell System Technical Journal*, 27: 379–423, 623–656.

Shaw, I.G.R. (2016) *Predator Empire: Drone Warfare and Full Spectrum Dominance*. Minneapolis: University of Minnesota Press.

Shaw, I.G.R. (2017) 'Policing the future city: Robotic being-in-the-world', *AntipodeFoundation.org*, 19 May. Available at: https://radicalantipode.files.wordpress.com/2017/05/3-ian-shaw.pdf (accessed 5 February 2018).

Shaw, M. and Miles, I. (1979) 'The social roots of statistical knowledge', in J. Irvine, I. Miles and J. Evans (eds), *Demystifying Social Statistics*. London: Pluto Press.

Stanger, A. (2011) *One Nation under Contract: The Outsourcing of American Power and the Future of Foreign Policy*. New Haven, CT: Yale University Press.

Stoler, A.L. (1995) *Race and the Education of Desire: Foucault's 'History of Sexuality' and the Colonial Order of Things*. Durham, NC: Duke University Press.

Turing, A. (1950) 'Computing machinery and intelligence', *Mind*, 59(236): 433–460.

Young, J.C. and Gilmore, M.P. (2014) 'Subaltern empowerment in the geoweb: Tensions between publicity and privacy', *Antipode*, 46(2): 574–591.

Zook, M., Barocas, S. boyd, d., Crawford, K., Keller, E., Gangadharan, S.P., et al. (2017) 'Ten simple rules for responsible big data research', *PLoS Computational Biology*, 13(3): e1005399. Available at: https://doi.org/10.1371/journal.pcbi.1005399 (accessed 5 February 2018).

INDEX

4chan message board, 148–9

academia, link with government, 285–6
access
　and digital civics, 250
　and digital development, 229–30
　and digital industries, 193
　and knowledge politics, 271, 272–3
　to data, 88–9, 102–3
activism/protest, 253, 276
　see also resistance
activity-based intelligence, 284
actor network theory, 228
Acxiom, 244
Adey, P., 155
aesthetics, 3, 77
affect, 148–9, 168
affordability, and access, 229
agency
　of digital workers, 181–2, 183–4, 185
　and representation, 167–8
　see also resistance
agriculture
　arable production, 39–42
　dairy production, 44–6
　future of, 46–7
　livestock production, 42–4
　perceptions and changes in, 37–8
　and resistance, 196
air travel, 18, 63, 242–3
Airbnb, 200, 205, 212
algorithmic governance/governmentality, 156, 244–5, 246, 286
algorithms, 16, 31, 137
AlphaGo, 137
alt-right movement, 148–9
Alvarez León, L.F., 266
Amazon, 202, 211, 214
American Association of Geographers, 73, 96
Amoore, L., 155, 246
annotation for transparent inquiry (ATI), 102–3
anticipatory governance, 246

Anwar, M., 177
application programming interfaces (APIs), 89
arable production, 39–42
archives, 86–7
Arctic environmentalism, 272, 273, 274–5, 276–7
Arctic Spatial Data Infrastructure, 88
ARPANET, 190, 193
Arribas-Bel, D., 129, 133
Ash, J.
　on attention, 157
　chapters by, 1, 143
　on GIFs, 149
　on nature of digital technology, 20–1
Association of American Geographers, 73, 96
ATI (annotation for transparent inquiry), 102–3
atmospheres, 20–1
attention, 103, 157–8
audio recorders, 101
auditing, food traceability, 42–4
augmented realities, 17, 51, 182, 183–4
authority of knowledge claims, 274–5
automated vehicles (AVs), 4, 42, 66–7
　see also drones
automatic milking systems (AMS), 44–6
automation
　in agriculture, 41–2, 44–7
　and governmentality, 245
　of map production, 121
　and mobilities, 66–7
　and subjectivity, 159
availability, and access, 229

Babbage, C., 281–2
banking, 215–16
Barnett, C., 167
Barns, S., 30
Behrendt, F., 66
Belk, R., 203

INDEX

Benkler, Y., 201–2
Benn, T., 287
Berns, T., 156, 286
big data
  access to, 88–9
  characteristics of, 85
  and epistemology, 76, 77, 264
  and ethics, 264–5
  georeferenced, 85–6
  in historical context, 282
  quality of, 89
  see also datafication; dataveillance
Bingham, N., 166
bio-digital livestock, 42–4
Boy, J.D., 20
Boyer, C., 26
'brick and click' retailers, 202, 214
Brown, M., 76, 79, 114
Buhr, B.L., 42
Bunge, W., 107
business process outsourcing (BPO), 213

cameras, 101
capabilities approach, 228
capitalism
  and digital labour, 180–1, 183, 194–5
  and digital media platforms, 145
  and epistemology, 77–8
  and sharing economy, 203, 204, 205–6
car sharing, 66, 201
cars, 66–7
  see also Uber
Carto company, 133
cartographic model of world, 121–2
cartography
  histories of, 51–3, 119–20
  nature and evolution of, 118–19
  possible futures, 125–6
  relationship with GIS
    cartographic model, 121–2
    historical context, 119–21
    interactive process, 123
    internet as platform, 123–4
    salience of code, 124–5
  see also mapping
Cash, H., 103
Castells, M., 270
catalogues, 87
Catlin-Groves, C.L., 110

cellphones *see* mobile phones
Chamayou, G., 284
children, 63
  see also young people
Children's Urban Geographies project, 100–1
chord diagrams, 192
Chrisman, N.R., 120–1
cities
  computers and reconceptualising, 24–6
  concept of cybercity, 26–7
  concept of smart city, 27–30
  and digital governance, 239–40
  digital shadows of, 16–17
  future digital urbanism, 30–2
  see also smart cities
citizen science, 110–11, 114
citizens
  as consumers, 263
  in smart cities, 28–9, 263, 265, 266
citizenship, datafication of, 251–3
civic apps, 252, 253, 254
civics
  corporatization of, 254–6
  datafication of citizenship, 251–3
  emergence of, 250–1
  oppositional uses of, 256–7
  spatialization of, 253–4
Clark, G.L., 216
clearinghouses, 87
'click and collect' *see* 'brick and click' retailers
cloud work, 179
co-created projects, 111
Cockayne, D.G., 204
code, 27, 124–5, 195
Code for America, 255
code/space, 18, 46, 60, 195
coded spaces, 17–18
collaboration, of workers, 183, 184
collaborative projects, 111
colonialism, 14
combine harvesters, 39–41
commercial sector *see* public-private relations
competition, between workers, 180, 181
computational dispositifs, 64–6
computational social science (CSS), 132
computers, and urban planning, 25
computing, history of, 281–2
concentration of industries, 218
connectivity, 20–1, 26, 64

conspicuous mobility, 64
consumers, 243–4, 263
consumption sites, 183
content creation, 145–7
continuous connectivity, 64
contributory projects, 111
control, and governmentality, 245–6
Cooke, B., 113
Cope, M., 95
COR (Rio's Operations Centre), 28–9
Corona programme, 282
corporatization *see* public-private relations
counter-mapping, 256–7
Crampton, J.W., 281
Cresswell, T., 99
critical cartography, 120
critical data studies (CDS), 78, 89–92
critical GIS, 53, 75, 92, 97, 108–9, 119
critical turn, 96
crowdfunding, 145, 146–7
crowdsourcing, 111, 124, 194, 272, 274
Crowston, K., 111
CSS (computational social science), 132
cultural geography, 165, 167
cultural turn, 164
culture
   media and popular culture, 143–50
   representation and mediation, 164–70
   subject/ivities, 153–60
cyber warfare, 287
cyber-infrastructures, 87–8
cybercity, 26–7
cybermanufacturing, 217
cybernetics, 24, 239
cybersecurity, 232
cyberspace, 25, 165–6
cycling, 65, 66

dairy production, 44–6
Dalton, C., 91
data
   access to, 88–9, 102–3
   and critical data studies, 78, 89–92
   on digital industries, 191
   future impacts of, 136
   governance of, 264–5
   and 'internet of things', 217
   nature and evolution of, 83–6
   provided by Uber, 255

   as system resource, 266
   see also big data; open data
data analysis, digitization of, 96
data analytics, and governance, 243
data anxieties, 91
data collection, 96, 282–3
   see also methods
data determinism, 246
data ethics
   and commercialization of public space, 262–4
   concept and role of, 260–1, 265–6
   and digital development, 232
   group and individual, 264–5
data infrastructures, 86–9, 122
data monitoring, 65
   see also surveillance/monitoring
data quality, 89
data revolution, 129–30
data science (DS), 130, 131–5, 136
data sovereignty, 91
data spectacle, 77
data storage, 86–7, 88, 90, 122
data-based subjects, 154–8
data-brokerage, 244
data-driven cities, 30
   see also smart cities
data-driven science, 137
databases, 122
   see also data storage
datafication
   of citizenship, 251–3
   and commercialization of public space, 262–4
dataveillance, 241–4
Davies, A., 203
Davies, W., 246
de Souza e Silva, A., 15
DeLyser, D., 98
democratization, 193–5, 202
design, of development initiatives, 230–1
development
   and access, 229–30
   concept of, 225–6
   and data ethics, 232
   effects of, 229
   and environmental unsustainability, 231
   future developments, 232–4

historical context of, 226–8
   project design, 230–1
   theoretical approaches to, 228
difference *see* social differences/categories
Difference Engine, 281–2
diffractive technospaces, 19
digital, defining, 3–4
digital convergence, 213
digital devices, 64, 101
   see also mobile phones
digital divides, 112, 193, 225, 230, 273
   see also inequalities
digital geographies
   introducing, 1–6
   themes *see* culture; economies; methods; politics; space(s)
digital humanities, 98, 114
digital industries *see* industries (digital)
digital infrastructure, 272–3
   see also data infrastructures
digital platforms
   and affect, 148–9
   and content creation, 145–7
   and micro-cultures, 147–9
   and popular culture, 143–4, 150
   rise of, 144–5
   role in sharing economy, 204–6
digital rights, 234, 285, 287
digital shadows, 16–17
digital space
   as augmented, 17, 51, 182, 183–4
   as distinct, 182, 183
   see also space(s)
digital technologies, impact of, 1–2
digital turn, 5–6, 73, 108, 130, 131
digitization, 225
   of analogue media, 143–4
   of data, 86
   of methods, 96
   of traditional sectors, 210–12, 214–18
   see also development
directories, 87
disciplinary governmentality, 245
discourses, 3
disruption, and impact of digital, 212, 218
distribution, 183, 206–7
   see also logistics
Dodge, M., 17–18, 36, 195
drones, 283–4, 286–7

DS (data science), 130, 131–5, 136
Dual Independent Map Encoded (DIME) file, 120

e-commerce, 202, 214–15
e-governance, 240
e-government, 240
e-waste, 231
economies
   digital industries, 188–97
   labour, 177–86
   sharing economy, 200–8
   traditional industries, 210–19
Egypt, 14
Elman, C., 102–3
Elwood, S., 109
emergency, and smart cities, 28–9
empiricism, 75
employment *see* industries (digital); industries (traditional); labour (digital)
employment status, 206–7
encryption, 285, 287
entrepreneurship, 30, 233
environmental unsustainability, 231
epistemological bias, 271, 274–5
epistemological pluralism, 273
epistemologies, 73–9, 272
ethics
   automation, subjectivity and, 159
   and commercialization of public space, 262–4
   concept and role of, 260–1, 265–6
   group and individual, 264–5
   and mapping, 125
exploratory data analysis, 137
Extreme Citizen Science (ExCiteS), 111

facial recognition, 286, 287
FairPhone, 231
family life, 62
farming *see* agriculture
feminist perspectives, 75, 271
finance sector, 215–16, 227
First Nations/indigenous groups, 14, 91
   see also indigenous knowledge
Fischer, C.S., 190
flashing, in phone use, 229
Flickr, 166
Flow system, 262–3
food traceability, 42–4

Forlano, L., 26
Foucault, M., 64, 238, 245
4chan message board, 148–9
French, S., 195

Gabrys, J., 64, 251–2
gender, 110, 230
General Electric, 217
general purpose technologies (GPTs), 212
generation, of movement, 61
geo-humanities, 99–100
geocomputation, 130–1, 136
Geoghegan, H., 106
geographic information systems *see* GIS
geographical intelligence (GEOINT), 282–4, 285
geopolitics
    algorithmic governance, 286
    future developments, 286–7
    historical context of, 281–4
    military–commercial–academic links, 284–6
    nature of, 281
    privacy and surveillance, 285, 286
georeferenced big data, 85–6
geoweb, 110, 124, 254, 272
Germany, 217–18
Gerster, R., 229
Gieseking, J., 76
GIF animations, 149
Gillespie, T., 204
GIS (geographic information systems)
    critical GIS, 53, 75, 92, 97, 108–9, 119
    critiques and debates, 14, 53, 75–6, 77, 99, 108–9, 271–2
    and governance, 240
    and government–academic links, 285
    interaction with data science, 132–3
    nature and evolution of, 118–21
    ontology and epistemology of, 75
    participatory, 14, 109, 271
    and power, 120
    qualitative and quantitative data in, 97, 101, 112–13, 271
    relationship with digital cartography
        cartographic model, 121–2
        historical context, 119–21
        interactive process, 123
        internet as platform, 123–4
        salience of code, 124–5
    relationship with mapping, 50

GIScience, 109, 119, 130–1
global context, knowledge politics in, 277–8
Global Positioning System (GPS), 101, 120
globalization, of value chains, 213
Google bombing, 183
Google Earth, 101, 166, 283
Google governance, 194
Google Maps, 16, 17, 194
governance
    algorithmic, 156, 244–5, 246, 286
    aspects of, 238
    contemporary forms of, 241–4
    of data, 264–5
    effects of digital knowledge on, 276
    historical context of, 239–40
    and internet freedom, 233–4
    and smart cities, 28–9
    and surveillance in cities, 27
    transforming governmentality, 244–6
governmentality, 156, 238, 244–6
GPS (Global Positioning System), 101, 120
GPTs (general purpose technologies), 212
Graham, M., 16, 17, 177, 180, 184, 194
Graham, S., 27, 195, 196
Gregg, M., 77
grounded visualization, 101
groups, data ethics relating to, 264–5

hackathons, 252, 253
Haiti, 63
Haklay, M., 194, 254
Hall, S., 167
handheld devices, 64
    see also mobile phones
Harada, T., 62
Harley, J.B., 120
Harvard Computer Graphics Laboratory, 120–1
Harvey, D., 180
health risks, 42–3
healthcare, 232
Herod, A., 181–2
Hill, D., 251
Hochman, N., 19
Hollerith, H., 282
housing, 256–7
Hudson Yards, 246
Human Development Index, 260
hybrid spaces, 15–16, 26

INDEX

IBM, 28, 282
ICT4D (information and communication technologies for development), 226
  see also development
ICTs, and movement, 61–2
IETF (Internet Engineering Task Force), 193
immanent development, 225, 229
inclusiveness, 110, 113–14, 261
indigenous knowledge, 272, 273, 274–5, 276–7
indigenous people, 14, 91
indigenous research, 271–2
individuals, data ethics relating to, 264–5
industrial internet, 216–17
industrialized agriculture, 38
'Industrie 4.0' initiative, 217–18
industries (digital)
  centrality of, 188
  democratizing, 193–5
  and development, 233
  future developments, 196–7
  historical origins of, 189–91
  locating, 191–3
  role in producing space, 195–6
industries (traditional)
  blurred boundaries between, 211–12
  digitization of, 210–12, 214–18
  finance, 215–16
  impact of digital on, 211–18
  manufacturing, 216–18
  retail, 214–15
  see also agriculture
inequalities
  in access, 193, 229–30, 250, 272–3
  and citizenship, 253
  and development, 225
  and digital industries, 193
  and digital shadows, 16–17
  gender, 230
  and knowledge claims, 274–5
  and participatory methods, 112
  see also social differences/categories
information technology (IT)
  spending on, 211
  see also ICTs
Instagram, 19–20
institutional theory, 228
intelligence *see* geographical intelligence
intentional development, 225, 229
interactive processes, mapping, 123

interconnected technologies, and mobilities, 64–6
internet
  access to, 229, 273
  and governance, 233–4, 240
  history of, 190–1
  as mapping platform, 123–4
internet addiction, 103
Internet Engineering Task Force (IETF), 193
internet freedom, 233–4
Internet Mapping Project, 192
'internet of things' (IoT), 217
Inuit Qaujimaningit (IQ), 272, 273, 274–5, 276–7

Kapiszewski, D., 102–3
Kar, B., 113
Kent, J., 66
Keyhole, 283
Kickstarter, 146–7
Kinsley, S., 153, 166
Kitchin, R.
  on big data, 85, 129, 264
  chapters by, 1, 83, 238
  on code and space, 17–18, 195
  on smart cities, 29, 262
Kleine, D., 225
Kneale, J., 166
Knopp, L., 76, 79
knowledge politics
  access issues, 272–3
  broader effects of digital knowledge, 275–7
  definition of, 271
  epistemological biases, 274–5
  future research, 277–8
  origins of, 270
Knowles, A., 99
Kothari, U., 113

labour (digital)
  in capitalist context, 180–1, 183, 194–5
  concentrations of, 184
  defining, 178
  and development, 233
  employment status, 206–7
  historical context, 178–9
  oversupply of labour, 180
  and place–work link, 177, 178–9
  and political economy, 206

reconceptualising spaces of, 182–5
regulation of, 184–5
and reorganization of work, 194–5
and subject positions, 158–9
workers as active agents, 181–2, 183–4, 185
see also industries (digital); industries (traditional)
labour geographies, 181
Langley, P., 145, 204–5
language, 17, 133–5, 229, 276
Lauriault, T., 83
Leszczynski, A.
   chapters by, 1, 13
   on data and governance, 252
   on data and subject, 156
   on mediation, 18, 168–9
   on methods, 98, 108
   on ontology, 74
Leyshon, A., 145, 202, 204–5
light detection and ranging (LIDAR) sensor, 4
livestock production, 42–4
location-aware mobile devices, 15
location-based services (LBSs), 64, 123
locational information, 156
Lodato, T., 253
logics, 3
logistics, 63, 213, 214–15
   see also supply chains
Longhurst, R., 166, 169
Luque-Ayala, A., 24, 29

M-Pesa, 227
McArdle, G., 85
MacEachren, A.M., 123, 124
McHaffie, P., 120
Malmgren, E., 148–9
Manovich, L., 19
manufacturing sector, 216–18
map-territory relations, 13–15
mapmaking
   and epistemological critiques, 75–6
   histories of, 51–3
   relationship with mapping, 50–1
mapping
   counter-mapping, 256–7
   debates, 53–5
   and digital civics, 254
   of digital industries, 192–3

futures of, 55–6
interactive process of, 123
nature of, 50
neighbourhood and MAUP, 133–5
origins of digital mapping, 51–3
relationship with GIS, 50
relationship with map making, 50–1
and spatial humanities, 99
see also cartography
mapping industry, 255
mapping platforms, 123–4
Mark, D.M., 74
Martin, C.J., 203
Marvin, S., 29
MAUP (modifiable areal unit problem), 133–5
meaning, and representation, 167, 168, 169
meat, traceability of, 42–4
media, 143–4, 150
   attention, subjectivities and, 157–8
   digital platforms and affect, 148–9
   digital platforms and content creation, 145–7
   digital platforms and micro-cultures, 147–9
   rise of digital platforms, 144–5
mediation, 18–20, 167–9
memes, 148–9
methods
   cartography and GIS, 118–26
   data and data infrastructures, 83–92
   epistemologies, 73–9
   participatory, 106–14
   qualitative, 95–103
   statistics, modelling and data science, 129–38
metropolization, 218
micro-cultures, 147–9
military, 120, 285–6
Mitchell, P., 100
mobile lives, 63
mobile phones, 101–2, 227, 229, 230, 231
   smartphones, 20–1, 123, 213, 251
mobilities
   and automation, 66–7
   concept of mobility, 60
   and interconnected technologies, 64–6
   qualitative research on, 101–2
   and subject/ivities, 155–6
   and technology with specific functions, 61–3
   see also traffic management; transport data
mobility-as-a-service (MaaS), 65
modelling *see* spatial modelling

modifiable areal unit problem (MAUP), 133–5
modification, of movement, 61
monitoring *see* surveillance/monitoring
Monmonier, M., 52
Moriset, B., 210
movement, 60, 61–2
movies, 144
music, 202

National Geospatial-Intelligence Agency, 283
National Reconnaissance Office, 282–3
neighbourhood, 133–5
Neistat, C., 146
neogeography, 110, 194, 254, 272
net localities, 15
network capital, 63
network connectivity, 20–1
networked cities, 26
neutrality, ICTs, movement and, 61
new spatial media, 272
New York City (NYC), 30

Offenhuber, D., 252
offshoring, 213
One Laptop per Child (OLPC) initiative, 227
Ong, A., 246
online exchange markets, 145
online shopping, 202, 214–15
ontics, 3
ontogenesis of space, 17
ontology, 74, 75
open data, 30, 88, 111, 257, 287
    see also ATI
open production, 276
open research data, 265
open science, 88
open source software, 111
open source technologies, 194
OpenStreetMap, 124
opposition *see* activism/protest; resistance
O'Sullivan, D., 118
outsourcing, 179, 213

panopticism, 26–7
participation
    of citizens in smart cities, 28–9, 265, 266
    nature and meaning of, 113
    political *see* civics
    of users in digital industries, 193–4
    see also access

participatory GIS (PGIS), 14, 109, 271
participatory historical geography, 114
participatory methods
    citizen science, 110–11, 114
    crowdsourcing, 111, 124, 194, 272, 274
    future developments, 113–14
    GIS and P/PGIS, 108–9, 271
    key challenges, 112–13
    nature of, 107–8
    neogeography, 110, 194, 254, 272
    VGI, 110, 124, 194, 254, 272
    Web 2.0, 110, 254
participatory turn, 107–8
Pedwell, C., 148
peer-to-peer networks, 202
Pepe the Frog, 148–9
perturbations, 20–1
PGIS (participatory GIS), 14, 109, 271
picket lines, 183
Pickles, J., 14, 53, 77
place, link with work, 177, 178–9
platform capitalism, 205
platform cooperativism, 206
policing, 243, 246, 285
politics
    civics, 250–7
    of data, 89–92
    development, 225–34
    of distribution, 206–7
    ethics, 260–6
    geopolitics, 281–7
    governance, 238–47
    knowledge politics, 270–8
    and participatory methods, 107, 110
Popke, J., 260, 264
popular culture, 143–4, 150
    definition of, 144
    digital platforms and affect, 148–9
    digital platforms and content creation, 145–7
    digital platforms and micro-cultures, 147–9
    rise of digital platforms, 144–5
portals, 87
positionality, 261
positivism, 75
post-truth politics, 277
power
    and cartography, 119–20
    and digital industries, 196
    and GIS, 120
    and governmentality, 245–6

and representation, 167
power/knowledge
  in critical data studies, 90–1
  and smart cities, 29
PPGIS (public participation GIS), 14, 109, 271
practice, and mobilities, 62
precision agriculture, 39–42
Predator drones, 283–4
predictive policing, 243, 246, 285
predictive profiling, 242
predictive systems, 245, 246
Predix, 217
privacy, 264, 285, 286
private sector *see* public–private relations
problem-oriented approach to cities, 25, 27–8
processual epistemologies, 76
profiling, 155, 242
programming *see* code
protests *see* activism/protest
pseudo-sharing, 203
public administration, 243
public participation GIS (PPGIS), 14, 109, 271
public–private relations
  commercialization of public space, 262–4
  corporatization of civics, 254–6
  corporatization of governance, 29
  in geopolitics, 283, 284–5
Purdam, K., 111
'pure play' e-tailers, 202
Purtova, N., 266
push notifications, 21
Pykett, J., 157

qualitative GIS research, 97, 271
qualitative methods, 95
  digital/spatial/geo-humanities, 98–100
  future developments, 102–3
  historical context and debates, 96–8
  shifting practice, 100–2
quantitative approach, 129–30
  epistemologies of, 75
  futures, 136–8
  and GIS, 97, 112–13
  historical context of, 130–2
  interaction of perspectives, 132–5, 136
queer theory, 76

radical cartography, 54
radio frequency identification (RFID), 63, 232
Raisz, E., 52–3

Rankin, W., 120
raster data model, 122
Ravanelle, A., 206–7
reflexivity, 113
regionalization, 134
regulation, 184–5, 233–4, 240
relational databases, 122
repositories, 87, 88, 90
representation
  and bias, 110, 135
  challenges to dominant, 167
  concept of, 164–5
  of cyberspace, 165–6
  of digital industries, 192–3
  in epistemological critiques, 75, 76, 77
  and GIS, 75, 76, 77, 99
  and mediation, 167–9
  and mobilities, 62
  role of digital technology in, 166–7
reputational economies, 205
Requests for Comments (RFC) system, 193
resistance, 14, 196, 256–7
  see also activism/protest
responsibility, of citizens, 252
retail sector, 202, 214–15
Reynaud, M., 149
RFID (radio frequency identification), 63, 232
Richardson, L., 200, 204
rights (digital), 234, 285, 287
Rio de Janeiro, 28–9
risk assessment, 263
Robinson, A., 51
robotic milking, 44–6
Rolls-Royce Plc, 217
Rose, G., 31, 32, 98, 164, 169
Rouvroy, A., 156, 286
Royal Geographical Society, 73
rural spaces
  limited technology in, 36–7
  scholarly neglect of technology in, 37
  technology and agriculture, 37–8
    arable production, 39–42
    dairy production, 44–6
    future, 46–7
    livestock production, 42–4

Salomon, I., 61–2
Schor, J.B., 207
Schuurman, N., 53, 74
Schwanen, T., 60

scopic regimes, 77
SDIs (spatial data infrastructures), 87–8
Second Life, 15
security, 63, 242–3, 287
  see also policing
self-employment, 206–7
self-monitoring apps, 64–5
self-regulation, 65, 245
self-selection bias, 135
semiconductors, 212–13
sensors, 4, 263
service work, 178–9
servitization of manufacturing, 217
Shannon, C., 282
sharable goods, 201
shared mobility, 66, 201
sharing economy
  discourse of sharing, 203–4
  and distribution, 206–7
  future developments, 207–8
  historical context of, 201–3
  nature of, 200
  role of digital platforms, 204–6
Shaw, I.G.R., 284
Sheller, M., 63
Shelton, T., 250, 253
Shenmue 3, 146–7
Sheppard, E., 196
Sidewalk Labs, 262–3
Silk Road, 178
skills, and access, 229
slippy map, 123–4
smart agriculture, 46–7
smart cities
  and citizen participation, 28–9, 265, 266
  commercialization of public space, 262–4
  concept of, 27–8
  and data ethics, 261–4
  and digital shadows, 16
  examples of, 28–30
  and technical expertise, 253
smart lampposts, 263
smart mobility, 65–6
smartphones, 20–1, 123, 213, 251
Smith, B., 74
Smith, D.M., 260
Smith, N., 120, 121
social contract, 263
social differences/categories
  and digital cities, 31

and digital civics, 254
digital divide and gender, 230
and digital labour, 233
and mobilities, 62–3, 66
and participation, 110, 114, 194
and subject/ivities, 158
  see also inequalities
social media, 145, 146, 148–9, 166, 276
social problems, 25, 252
social sharing, 201
software (code), 124–5, 195
software-sorting, 27, 195
space(s)
  mapping, 49–56
  mobilities, 60–7
  produced by digital industries, 195–6
  rural spaces, 36–47
  spatialities, 13–21
  urban spaces, 24–32
  see also digital space
spatial data infrastructures (SDIs), 87–8
spatial humanities, 99
spatial modelling
  future developments, 136–8
  historical context of, 130–1
  interaction with data science, 132–5, 136
spatial science, 75
spatial turn, 98, 99
spatialities, 13–21
spatialization of digital civics, 253–4
spatio-temporal fixes, 180–1
stakeholders, and data ethics, 266
Stanger, A., 284
statistical doubles, 156
statistics
  future developments, 136–8
  historical context of, 130–1
  interaction with data science, 132–5, 136
Stephens, M., 194
Stevens, M., 112
Strain, W., 55
structuration theory, 228
subject positions, 153–9
subject/ivities
  conceptualising, 153–4
  digital generation of, 154–8
  discerning digital subjects, 158–9
subjectification, 154–5
substitution, of movement by ICT, 61–2
Sui, D., 98

INDEX

supply chains, 42–4, 213, 232
    see also logistics
surveillance/monitoring
    in cities, 26–7, 29
    drones, 283–4, 286–7
    future research, 286–7
    and geopolitics, 283–4, 285, 286–7
    and governance, 234, 240, 241–4
    of mobilities, 63, 65
    and subject/ivities, 154–8
surveillant assemblage, 156
Suzuki, Y., 146–7
system resource, data as, 266

TaskRabbit, 207
Taylor, L., 260
technical expertise, 253, 255–6
technicity, 76
technocratic governance, 244–5
telecentres, 227, 230
telecommunications, and urban spaces, 25–6
telephones
    history of, 190
    see also mobile phones
territory–map relations, 13–15
Tesco, 202
text review, 102
Thatcher, J., 73, 74, 91
Thrift, N., 32, 195
time displacement hypothesis, 62
Timeto, F., 19
Tomlinson, R.F., 121
Townsend, A., 251
traceability, 42–4, 232
traditional industries *see* industries (traditional)
traffic management, 85, 240, 243
transport
    automated, 4, 42, 66–7
    see also Uber
transport data, 85, 262–3
truth, post-truth politics, 277
Tucker, K., 114
Turing, A., 282
Twitter, 89, 133–5

Uber, 200, 206, 255, 262
uberization, 212
Uitermark, J., 20
UN World Summit on the Information
    Society, 226

unmanned aerial vehicles (UAVs), 283–4, 286–7
urban planning, 24–5
urban spaces
    computers and reconceptualising, 24–6
    concept of cybercity, 26–7
    concept of smart city, 27–30
    and digital governance, 239–40
    and digital shadows, 16–17
    future digital urbanism, 30–2
    see also smart cities
Urry, J., 63
user participation in digital industries, 193–4
user-generated content, 145
user-operators, of ARPANET, 193
USGIF (United States Geospatial Intelligence
    Foundation), 285

value chains, globalization of, 213
VGI *see* volunteered geographic information
video games, 146–7
video-conferencing, 62
visibility
    and datafication of public spaces, 262–4
    of knowledge claims, 274–5
visual, in epistemological critiques, 77
vlogging, 146
volunteered geographic information (VGI),
    110, 124, 194, 254, 272

Waitt, G., 62
Wakeford, N., 26
Walmart, 214
water pumps, 227–8
Web 2.0, 110, 254
Wiggins, A., 111
Wikipedia, 166
Wilson, M.W., 49, 64, 103, 157, 252
Wood, D., 27, 50–1, 120
work
    impact of digital communication on, 191
    link with place, 177, 178–9
    and subject positions, 158–9
    see also industries (digital); industries
        (traditional); labour (digital)

Young, J., 270, 277
young people, 100, 101–2, 103
YouTube, 145, 146, 166

Zimmermann, S., 229
Zook, M., 16, 17, 188, 194